PRAISE FOR *THE YEAR BABE RUTH HIT 104 HOME RUNS*

"Comparisons of athletes from different eras are always fraught with difficulty—different rules, equipment, nutrition, and training, to name a few. Since baseball is very much a game of statistics, this is particularly true of its players. Nonetheless, Bill Jenkinson's impeccably researched book effectively makes these comparisons, leaving little doubt as to whom was the best of the best. We consider *The Year Babe Ruth Hit 104 Home Runs* a must read for any fan of the Babe or baseball."

> —Julia Ruth Stevens and Tom Stevens, daughter and
> grandson of Babe Ruth

"Amidst all the turmoil of banned substances and our national pastime, especially regarding the home run, comes this persuasive, landmark work by historian Bill Jenkinson. After years of painstaking, innovative research, the author puts to rest once and for all any question as to who is baseball's ultimate slugger. By analyzing Ruth's every at-bat, and comparing him to the game's all-time power roster, Jenkinson proves conclusively that Babe Ruth truly is the 'Sultan of Swat.' Now, when someone challenges the Babe's preeminent ranking, a retort is waiting to be gleaned in Bill's credible masterpiece. A must read for every baseball purist!"

> —Michael Gibbons, Director of the Babe Ruth Museum

"All baseball fans know that Ruth was one of the greatest and most beloved ballplayers of all time, and this work of incredible research explains in great detail his dominance of the game."

> –Cal Ripken Jr.

D0860823

THE YEAR

Babe Ruth

HIT

104

HOME RUNS

Recrowning Baseball's
Greatest Slugger

THE YEAR
Babe Ruth
HIT
104
HOME RUNS

Bill Jenkinson

CARROLL & GRAF PUBLISHERS
NEW YORK

THE YEAR BABE RUTH HIT 104 HOME RUNS
Recrowning Baseball's Greatest Slugger

Carroll & Graf Publishers
An Imprint of Avalon Publishing Group, Inc.
245 West 17th Street, 11th Floor
New York, NY 10011

AVALON
publishing group incorporated

Copyright © 2007 by Bill Jenkinson

First Carroll & Graf edition 2007

Frontispiece photograph courtesy of the National Baseball Hall of Fame and Museum, Cooperstown, New York

Library of Congress Cataloging-in-Publication Data is available.

ISBN-13: 978-0-78671-906-8
ISBN-10: 0-7867-1906-0

9 8 7 6 5 4 3 2 1

Interior Design by *Ivelisse Robles Marrero*

Printed in the United States of America
Distributed by Publishers Group West

For Marie

Contents

Introduction

I NEVER INTENDED to write a book about Babe Ruth. When I started my research many years ago, I was on a quest for a kind of Holy Grail of baseball. Inevitably, it brought me to the career of the Bambino. It started in 1979, when I did some reading on one of my favorite baseball topics: "tape measure home runs." More descriptively, it is the subject of great batting power or distance hitting. Even more to the point, I wanted to know who hit the ball harder and farther than anyone who has played the game. This is not simply a matter of who hit the most homers. We already know that answer. The great Henry Aaron walloped 755 home runs in Major League games, and the *Baseball Encyclopedia* will give us the rest of the list, whenever we choose to look at it.

But I was asking a different question. Who is the Paul Bunyan of baseball? Of the millions of guys who have swung a bat, who among them is the strongest of the strong? Granted, a 330-foot solo home run has the same box-score result as a 500-foot solo home run, but in a world fascinated with both quantification and power, it seemed like a reasonable question. Our culture is replete with such queries. Where is the longest river? What is the tallest building? Who is the fastest runner? But when I went in search for the answer, there was none.

There were no definitive works on this subject. The more I looked, the more frustrating the situation became. I found legions of folks just like me; baseball fans are naturally drawn to that basic question about the identity of the most powerful batsman. I found several sports-writers who considered writing a book on the topic. In each case, they had been dissuaded by the enormity and seemingly impossible nature of the requisite research. Although disappointed, I understood the commonsense aspect of the issue. In order to definitively judge and compare the power of every slugger who ever played, it would be nec-essary to study the distance of all their home runs. That data simply wasn't available. Or was it?

When I began my inquiries, I had no plans to do comprehensive research. I envisioned a few trips to the Philadelphia Public Library to look up some of the great homers that I remembered. I was mostly interested in former Phillie Dick Allen, who was a personal favorite. He hit some balls over the left field grandstand at old Connie Mack Sta-dium that made me dizzy just watching them. I recall thinking: *There's no way that anybody ever hit a ball farther than that.* That sentiment came up at the dinner table when I was a teenager, whereupon my dad smiled benignly, and invoked the names of Babe Ruth and Jimmie Foxx. At a family picnic a short time later, my uncles responded in much the same way with stirring accounts of the deeds of those long-dead legends.

Sure enough, when I dug into the microfilm newspaper accounts of Allen's great homers, I encountered repeated references to Ruth and

Foxx. Every writer knew someone who had seen those guys play, and, in a few instances, the older scribes had firsthand memories. I read rousing and poignant stories from bygone days about balls flying out of Connie Mack Stadium, which was Shibe Park back then. I was hooked.

Without knowing what I was doing or where I was going, I jumped into an exhaustive study of the great sluggers. It was a genuine labor of love, and it led me directly to George Herman Ruth. The Babe. I knew that my father was a reliable source of information, and I expected Ruth to have left a legacy of genuinely long home runs. But I was also a grounded individual who knew the difference between fact and fiction. I expected Ruth or Foxx to be the strongest hitter of his time. That, in itself, would be impressive, and validate the hindsight of my family. But guys of those old eras couldn't possibly compete on purely physical terms with modern athletes. Right? Once again, we're not talking about the number of home runs that Babe Ruth hit. We're talking about *how far* he hit them.

In any athletic function that can be measured, there are no known examples of competitors from the distant past comparing to a present-day athlete. How high do they jump? How much weight can they lift? How fast can they swim? But what about "how far can they hit a baseball?" If you could determine how many feet Babe Ruth or Jimmie Foxx hit a baseball, you could be sure that it wasn't as far as Reggie Jackson or Mike Schmidt. It was just a matter of digging out the information about the hitters from each generation. A big task to be sure, but one that needed doing. I was reasonably confident about the conclusions before I even did the work.

Men like Ruth and Foxx were the best of their era, but they predated the wonders of modern weight lifting and sophisticated strength training. Science and common sense compelled the presumption that they would fall short of the newer bionic types. But something odd happened along the way. The more I learned about Ruth and Foxx, the better they looked . . . especially Ruth. In my initial studies, Babe seemed to have belted them farther than any of the modern guys. Something must have been wrong with my research, so I dug deeper.

I read all his biographers, and I salute each one of them. But I still wanted more. So I followed him by way of contemporary accounts, wherever he went. Fortunately, Ruth was in his prime during the peak of America's newspaper culture. Everywhere he went, writers followed him, and they left thousands of highly descriptive articles about almost everything he did. From Florida to Maine, from Virginia to California, I rode along in his wake, and enjoyed the ride at every turn. I consistently found myself in a strange world, where the unlikely became commonplace, where the seemingly impossible actually happened. It was the bizarre but entrancing world of Babe Ruth.

It was a journey that challenged me, amazed me, and, ultimately, forced me to accept the limitations of my own intellectual inclinations. I discovered a man who was larger in life than most fictional heroes are in their make-believe worlds. In just reading about the man, I felt the magnetism of his astounding life force. As I write this, it is now twenty-seven years later, and I have lived with Babe Ruth almost every day since then. It has been all joy and wonder. I entered a world created by an individual man that is so consistently full of surprise, laughter, and astonishment that I never get tired of it.

I thought time and again of that old proverb: "If something seems too good to be true, then it is too good to be true." Well, the everyday deeds of Ruth certainly seemed, at the very least, too grandiose to be true, but facts are facts. I was pleased to learn that the writers from Ruth's day were highly reliable. They certainly were stylistically different from today's reporters, but it took only a short time to adjust to those superficial differences. When it came to factual content, they were almost always right on the mark. That observation is based upon the experience of reading multiple newspaper stories of every game that Babe Ruth played. One writer might enliven his prose by referring to Ruth as "The Caliph of Clout," while another might call him "The Blasting Behemoth." However, when it came to the objective accounts of actual game events, there was a clear pattern of consistency.

Eventually, a thought began to emerge. Despite all that had already been written, the whole story had still not been told. There were still aspects of Ruth's career that needed elaboration. Not his biography, since the essence of his life had been well represented. Another biography wasn't necessary, but a specific treatise was. And so I decided to write a book about Babe Ruth.

Specifically, I intend to focus on the three aspects of his career that have yet to be properly addressed. First and foremost, Ruth's historic batting power will be discussed and analyzed. Second, Babe's so-called hidden career of about 800 exhibition and barnstorming games will be examined. Students of baseball should know about the pageantry and cultural significance of these special events. Third, the comparative degree of difficulty experienced by Ruth during his career will be carefully explored. It is natural to assume that Babe Ruth enjoyed relatively benign conditions (especially offensively) during his era. However, a comprehensive overview will demonstrate that the opposite was true for Ruth as an individual player.

Occasionally, it is difficult to listen to pundits discuss the career of Babe Ruth. They usually mean well, and some really do know their subject. But, sadly, many are way off track, and speak in terms of obsolete clichés and inaccurate images. No individual, including myself, can ever capture the entire essence of Babe Ruth . . . he was too big for that. But I have tried my best to enhance the body of knowledge on this singular man and clarify the facts of his career.

The book is divided into three parts. The first serves as a journey through Ruth's career using his tape measure home runs as landmarks. Part Two follows with individual chapters on the three aforementioned issues (power, hidden career, and comparative difficulty). In the final chapter, which will summarize Ruth's place in baseball history, an effort will also be made to project what would have happened if Babe had played in modern times. Part Three will be empirical in nature, containing original photos, diagrams, charts, and lists. And at various intervals throughout this treatise, references will be made to Ruth's miraculous 1921 season. Piece by piece, that story will unfold, and the reason for this book's title will be made clear. A recrowning of sorts will take place by the final chapter: an explanation of why this man who hit 104 "home runs" in one season is the greatest slugger in baseball history.

And when it seems appropriate, I will write in the first person. I want others to know Babe Ruth as I do. It is my hope to engage in a kind of personal conversation between writer and reader. The ultimate purpose is to familiarize modern fans with Babe Ruth as he really was . . . gifted beyond rational expectation . . . intensely human and flawed . . . literally unique and unforgettable.

Part One
The Career

"He was one of a kind and there can never be another one. The man was a combination of ballplaying talent, personality, magnetism, show business, drama, and innocence that had to have been hand-crafted by some celestial artisan that was probably too pleased to want to top himself and too wise to try."

—Donald Honig, *The New York Yankees: An Illustrated History*

1

Fact Transcends Myth

BABE RUTH IS the most legendary athlete in the history of American sports. Normally, over time, this kind of reverence creates hyperbole regarding the actual deeds of the subject. But not in the case of Babe Ruth. Although still largely revered in the hearts and minds of most Americans, his true level of greatness has been somewhat misplaced. He was *better* than his legend suggests. His real-life accomplishments transcend his myth. Of course, knowledgeable fans will expect proof. This book will provide that proof.

The story began the moment young George Herman Ruth stepped onto a ball field. He was the original natural. Whatever position he played, whatever he tried to do, he did it better than anyone else. And so it was when he turned professional just after his nineteenth birthday with little or no expert coaching. He immediately established himself as a world-class pitcher. There was no "development" for Ruth, just instantaneous success against every level of competition, including the Major Leagues. And that virtuosity never left him. Long after switching to the outfield in order to bat every day, Ruth demonstrated that he remained a great pitcher. As a fading thirty-eight-year-old slugger on the last day of the 1933 season, Babe pitched an official complete game victory against the Boston Red Sox, his first Big League mound appearance in three seasons, and only his second in twelve years. Make no mistake. Babe Ruth was one of the best pitchers in the history of his sport.

He was also a superior base-runner, and he became a highly proficient outfielder and first baseman. Most important, he remains the greatest hitter who ever picked up a bat. Some folks make a wishful argument for Ted Williams, but the facts say otherwise. Teddy Ballgame did have the second-highest career slugging percentage at .634, but Ruth finished first at .690. That's a 56-point difference in a very important statistical criterion in measuring a player's offensive production. After Ruth switched from pitcher to outfielder in 1919, his career percentage was .705! If you combine on-base-percentage, where Williams is first to Ruth's historical second (.483 to .474), the gap closes slightly. The combination is referred to as OPS (on-base plus slugging), but Babe still leads by 48 points. It's really no contest. By any rational method, it always comes back to Babe Ruth as baseball's best batsman. And why is that? To me the answer is simple. Babe hit the ball harder than anyone else. Sure, he had great coordination, reflexes, and eyesight, but the key is his historically superior power. And that is a story for the ages.

Nobody born in the nineteenth century should be able to compete in purely physical terms with the best athletes playing in the twenty-first century. Science has seen to that. Medicine, nutrition, equipment, and exercise technology have evolved dramatically in the last several decades to the point where old athletes often seem like ineffectual caricatures. In the individual sports that objectively measure performance, like track and field, swimming, and weight lifting, the results speak for themselves. All the world records from fifty years ago have been broken over and over again. Look back to 1954, when Roger Bannister rocked the sports world by becoming the first man to run a mile in less than four minutes. Now, fifty-three years later, several high school kids attain that performance level each year. In the popular team sports like basketball and football, just watch old game films to recognize the difference. It is immediately apparent that today's athletes are bigger, stronger, and faster. That does not mean that Wilt Chamberlain and Jim Brown couldn't play in today's NBA and NFL. They were rare athletic prodigies who could play in any era. But if they somehow magically reappeared now in the same bodies in which they originally played, they would not be as dominant. Their physical superiority would be somewhat negated. The key would be to allow them the opportunity to train for a year under modern conditions. Then turn them loose, and they would be terrific.

The nature of baseball is somewhat different, since specialized skills are emphasized more than general athleticism. But speed and strength are still very important. That is obvious. Look at the amazing success of Barry Bonds in his career after he added about thirty pounds of muscle mass. He started hitting the ball harder than he ever had as a younger man, mainly due to training options that didn't exist in the past. It would be natural, therefore, to assume that Bonds and his muscular contemporaries hit the ball harder than their predecessors. And, for the most part, that would be true. That conclusion would seem even more relevant in a comparison with Babe Ruth, the best of his era, who played his last game seventy-two years ago. In purely physical terms, Ruth couldn't possibly measure up to the modern players. Could he? Well, actually, he could.

To my astonishment, twenty-eight years of intense research has revealed that Babe Ruth hit baseballs harder and farther than any man who ever played. If he somehow reappeared today in his old body, he wouldn't need a year of modern training to succeed. It would help him, of course, but it wouldn't be necessary. He would arrive with demonstrable physical superiority, and that makes him unique in the annals of sports. It is a story that should be evaluated by biologists, anthropologists, and scientists from other relevant fields. It's certainly a tale that stretches credibility, but the data is irrefutable. Accordingly, the entire narrative of this book will focus on Babe's unnatural but intoxicating power, how far he launched baseballs. But, along the way, we will also talk about Babe Ruth the pitcher, Babe Ruth the all-around player and, of course, Babe Ruth the consummate showman and personality extraordinaire.

For twenty-two years, from 1914 to 1935, this man awoke each morning, and lived a life so full of rich and unusual experiences that each of his days surpassed a year in the life of the average person. By the 1920s, when Ruth was at the peak of his popularity, he seemed to live each minute like the world was about to end. A typical day would include a ballgame in which he would astonish competitors, teammates, and fans, but it would also include so much more. He would likely have risen in mid-morning, and consumed an enormous breakfast of a dozen eggs, a pound of bacon, and a loaf of bread. Then he would take off in a stylish roadster automobile and drive at breakneck speed to a personal appearance somewhere, anywhere, in the New York City area. Upon arriving, he would greet the hundreds of people waiting for him as if each were his favorite person on the planet. Babe would then participate in some ridiculous promotion that only he would consider doing. He might wear some outrageous costume or ride a wild animal, and everyone in attendance would remember it until the day he died. Of course, along the way, he would have signed countless autographs, shaken innumerable hands, and posed for endless photographs.

While driving to the ballpark for the late-afternoon game, he might see something flashy in a store window and jam on his brakes. Parking on the sidewalk, he would burst into the store and point to the object of his affection. He wouldn't ask the price, but simply say he had to have it, and pay for it from a thick roll of large bills. Off he would go to Yankee Stadium, honking his horn and waving to strangers in the certain knowledge that they were thrilled at the mere sight of him. Entering the clubhouse like a tidal wave of pure animal energy, he gave each teammate a wink and a nod, but rarely called them by name. He would ask a clubhouse boy to fetch him half a dozen hot dogs and wolf them down as he was dressing.

As Ruth entered the field, the other players would stop and gaze in his direction, hoping that he would take batting practice. When he did, all eyes were on him as he generated sights and sounds that never ceased to amaze his fellow professional athletes. This was an undying ritual. As long as he played, opponents and teammates alike would stop their preparations, and look and listen in awe of what was happening in the batting cage. The resounding crack of Ruth's bat against ball was like no sound produced by any other man. The sight of the ball soaring into oblivion was unlike any other vision seen on the field. If fellow pros never got tired of those events, imagine the reaction of a fan who saw Ruth just once in a lifetime.

Often, before games, Babe would be called to home plate or the grandstand to participate in a ceremony. Either some organization had to honor him, usually with gifts, or some visiting dignitary had to meet him, usually with childlike enthusiasm. Once the game started, anything might happen, and, over the course of twenty-two seasons, just about everything did. Mostly, Babe Ruth played extraordinary baseball, but he was not immune to incessant personal demands even with the game in progress. Admirers ran onto the field to shake his hand, bands marched across the playing surface to celebrate his deeds, and games were interrupted to acknowledge his records. Babe talked regularly with bleacher fans while playing the outfield, and often sat with them when the Yankees batted and he was not due to hit. When the game ended, Ruth had to deal with a New York media that included as many as eighteen daily newspapers. After answering copious questions, he then faced the omnipresent gauntlet of kids seeking his signature on anything from a program to the palms of their hands.

Then, off he would go for dinner, perhaps to the home of Lou Gehrig's parents in New Rochelle, where Babe would start with a jar of pickled eel. He followed that with two or three plates of sauerbraten along with anything else Mama Gehrig was serving that night. Ruth might then take in a show or attend a boxing match, but keep in mind that he craved all the pleasures of the flesh. Accordingly, Babe would often spend a few hours of intimate time with a willing female partner. After Ruth's second marriage in 1929, those adventures were significantly curtailed, but his marital bed certainly got a lot of use. A game of cards might be in order about 2:00 A.M., as Babe was winding down with some sandwiches. Sometime around 4:00 A.M., he would finally retire for a few hours' sleep, whereupon he would wake up, and start the whole process over. And those were his easy days! When the Yankees were on the road or especially when they were playing exhibition games, things really got hectic. And this went on day after day, year after year.

In sorting through all the daily chaos, Ruth's incredible physical stature and superhuman energy rose to the top. That amazing physicality was primarily manifested on the ball field, where he consistently played like no other man. But it also carried over to everything he did. Babe had a zest for living that was unparalleled. He loved life so intensely that he pulled everyone along with him. His aura of boundless joy was infectious, and almost everybody he met was changed by the encounter. After meeting Ruth, people smiled more often and laughed more readily; he was a joy giver.

Ruth wasn't perfect; no human being ever is. He was crude and vulgar, especially as a young man. Although reasonably intelligent, he was not educated, and remained uninterested in many important matters about which he should have cared. But he somehow overcame his liabilities and became the best in his field of endeavor. Along the way, he enriched the lives of millions of people by entertaining them and infusing them with optimism and hope. And that is an extraordinary legacy.

On the matter of Ruth's Homeric batting power, a few preliminary words are in order. There will be repetitive linear references regarding how far he hit his home runs. Without some standards or guidelines, those references will lose their impact. Any baseball hit farther than 400 feet is noteworthy. Anything hit farther than 450 feet reflects great power at the Major League level, since most Big Leaguers never hit a ball that far. Anything approaching 500 feet is legitimately historic.

As already discussed, today's players are bigger and stronger than ever. But despite that fact, in the last decade, only Mark McGwire, Adam Dunn, Jim Thome, and Sammy Sosa have recorded confirmed 500-foot home runs in Major League games. Andres Galarraga, J. D. Drew, Joe Borchard, Wily Mo Pena, and Richie Sexson may have done it, but we can't be sure. Their best shots were interrupted high in mid-flight, and none of those drives have certain 500-foot credentials. McGwire did it several times, but even Big Mac had to wait until late in his career. He needed years of intense weight training and nutritional supplements before he could reach that rarified distance plateau. As great as he is, Barry Bonds has never hit a confirmed 500-footer in game conditions. Bonds is physically capable of launching such a blow (I have seen him take batting practice), but he hasn't done it yet.

Anyone who follows baseball has heard stories about 500-foot or even 600-foot home runs. As a general rule, they should be ignored. Does that mean that everyone telling a story about such a long home run is a liar? No. It simply means that they probably do not understand the physics of a batted ball. Once a ball reaches its apex or highest point, it has spent most of its speed and energy, and will fall back to earth in a rapidly declining trajectory. Witnesses to great home runs will often see them fly 400 feet, and then get knocked down in mid-flight by the upper deck of an enclosed stadium. Such balls may still be 60 feet high at that moment, and observers sincerely believe that they would have flown 100 feet farther. In truth, the ball was on its way down, and probably would have traveled only another 50 or 60 feet.

When modern sluggers have been asked to hit official Major League

balls as far as possible, they've rarely been able to produce authenticated 500-foot drives. In the All-Star home run derbies, a few drives
have traveled that distance, but they were accomplished with special
"rabbit balls" made for the occasion. And most of those were hit inside
enclosed stadiums. Almost every time modern-day Big Leaguers have
hit a ball that has returned to ground level or even near ground level,
they have fallen short of 500 feet. It is not a coincidence.

Even Mark McGwire, the longest hitter of the modern era, was
unable to reach 500 feet at the home run derby in Boston in 1998. His
best shots were landing in a parking lot or on a low roof that was elevated just a little above home plate. He wasn't getting the benefit of any
artificially added distance as is the case in the enclosed stadiums. Does
that mean that Big Mac couldn't hit 500-footers? No. He just couldn't
do it any time he wanted to, even under optimum conditions. In a real
ballgame, the degree of difficulty rises drastically. The truth is that
most Major League players never even see a 500-foot home run. It's just
too far. So, if some poorly trained guy born in the nineteenth century
did it, you've got quite a story.

Let's now travel through the career of George Herman Ruth and
slow down as we pass his incomparable tape-measure drives. They
will serve as signposts in a journey that no one has taken until now.
Ruth was born on February 6, 1895, in a rough waterfront section of
Baltimore, Maryland, to ethnic German parents. His mother was often
too sickly to watch after him, and his father was too busy tending his
saloon to care. George grew up wild and out of control. He was placed
in a school for juvenile delinquents at age seven, and was there, off and
on, until he left in 1914 to play ball for the Baltimore Orioles.

Much of what happened to Ruth as a child influenced his personality as an adult. His was a tough early life, but he learned lessons that
served him well in later years. He certainly didn't get enough attention,
and that might account for his love of the spotlight. And, of course, little
George was encouraged to play baseball, and we can thank our lucky
stars for that.

2
The Flamboyant Prodigy:
1914–1925

ON FEBRUARY 27, 1914, nineteen-year-old, six-foot-two-inch, 185-pound George Ruth walked out of Saint Mary's Industrial School, which had been his primary home for twelve years. An athletic force of almost unimaginable scale had just been introduced to the world of sports. A few days later, Ruth left Baltimore for Fayetteville, North Carolina, where he began training for the first time as a professional athlete. By the time he returned to his hometown less than one month later, young George had already done things on a baseball field that no one could have envisioned.

Ruth had agreed to a $600 contract on Valentine's Day to play for the independent Baltimore Orioles of the International League, which was only one notch below the Big Leagues. His only experience before that time had been as a schoolboy playing for Saint Mary's and a few other teams of similar caliber. On March 7, he took the field for his first intra-squad game in Fayetteville, and proceeded to astonish local onlookers as well as his veteran teammates. Until then, the longest hit ever made at the Fair Grounds had been struck by the legendary Jim Thorpe of Olympic fame. On this day, Ruth drove the ball far into a corn crop beyond right field for a memorable home run. According to hometown witnesses, this blow of about 435 feet outdistanced Thorpe's drive by a wide margin. George had been signed as a pitcher, and this display of prodigious bat-ting power, by a teenager no less, left everyone incredulous.

In his first spring training game against Major League competition on March 18 versus the Philadelphia Phillies, George pitched effec-tively for three innings. The next day he threw the final three and two-thirds innings and was credited with the win. The Phillies were impressed with the fire-balling youngster, but it was thought that things would be different a week later when Ruth faced Connie Mack's World Champion Philadelphia Athletics. The game was played in Wilmington, North Carolina, and George was not at peak form. The A's put seventeen men on base and assumed that they would eventually vanquish the upstart. As the innings rolled by, the kid kept on fighting and somehow survived. When the game ended, the mighty Athletics had scored only two runs, and Ruth had pitched a nine-inning victory.

Back in Baltimore on April 5, Ruth pitched and won a spring exhi-bition game against the Brooklyn Dodgers, but again made his primary impression as a hitter. Casey Stengel played right field that day for the Dodgers and got in trouble early in the game when Ruth's long drive nearly sailed over his head. Stengel caught the ball on the run, but manager Wilbert Robinson gave him hell for the near embarrassment. No Major League team wanted a rookie Minor League pitcher knocking extra-base hits against them. When Ruth batted again, the comical Casey retreated so far in right field that he was sure no batted ball could reach him. The game was played at Back River Park, where there was no right field fence. For the rest of his life, Stengel talked about what happened next. The entire Brooklyn team went into collective shock when Ruth still managed to drive the ball far over Stengel's head for a stupendous triple.

Unfortunately for the Orioles, 1914 was the first of two years that a third Major League was in existence. The Terrapins played across the street in the newly formed Federal League, and Oriole attendance suffered. Ruth was an immediate sensation, winning fourteen League games by early July. But, in order to survive financially, owner Jack Dunn was forced to sell Ruth's contract to the Boston Red Sox. Before he left, however, Ruth acquired the nickname that he kept for the rest of his life. He was referred to as Dunn's "new babe," which soon simply morphed into "Babe."

Arriving in Boston on July 11, Ruth was inserted as the starting pitcher and won his first official Major League game 4–3 against the Cleveland Indians. Actually, the Red Sox already had a great pitching staff and didn't need Babe that season. They had obtained him for his great potential. After playing sparingly during the next month, Ruth returned to the International League as a member of the Providence Grays, who served as the Red Sox top affiliate. In his first game on August 22, Babe delivered one of his signature performances. He pitched a complete game win versus Rochester and blasted two triples. The one in the ninth inning helped win the game and landed beside the flagpole on a hill in center field. The record crowd of 12,000 hailed it as the longest drive they had ever seen, and many threw their straw hats onto the field in tribute.

Entering September, the Grays were battling Rochester and Buffalo in a close three-team pennant race. At Toronto on the fifth, the remarkable teenager remained impervious to the pressure and pitched a one-hit shutout. This was also the day that Ruth hit his first official professional home run. According to the *Providence Journal,* it was a "tremendous drive" far over the right field fence.

Two days later, Ruth threw another complete game victory, and he did it again two days after that. He was allowed to wait until the third day for his next start on the twelfth, when he pitched yet another nine-inning win. The Grays traveled to Newark two days later for a double-header, and Ruth pitched brilliantly for the entire first game, but lost 2–0. In the tense second game, he relieved in the seventh inning, but lost again. After personally losing two games in one day, Ruth and the Grays trailed Buffalo by a half-game. It was natural to think that the boy wonder had finally run out of gas.

However, beginning on September 18, Ruth started and won his next three outings during a six-day stretch that resulted in the International League Pennant for Providence. In those three games, Babe struck out more than a batter per inning. That alone was an amazing accomplishment in an era of significantly fewer strikeouts. When one considers the fatigue factor due to Ruth's recent workload, as well as the enormous pressure on a kid fresh out of reform school, it is difficult to believe.

Since the Red Sox season was not over, Babe returned to Boston and pitched two final games, including a complete game win over the New York Yankees. The Sox finished second behind the Athletics, and both the team and their young southpaw stud looked forward to the 1915 season. Including spring training, exhibitions, and both International and Major League contests, Babe Ruth won thirty-one games in 1914. And consider that he had been basically inactive on the Red Sox bench for about a month. As a sidebar, he set distance-hitting records in three different cities.

1915   Ruth began the 1915 season as a Major Leaguer, but there were legitimate questions about how much he would play. The Red Sox pitching staff was one of the best in history. Among the Red Sox starters were Dutch Leonard, Rube Foster, Ernie Shore, Smoky Joe Wood, and fellow rookie Carl Mays. Babe was sure to succeed, but would he get a chance that year?

Ruth arrived for spring training on March 6 in Hot Springs, Arkansas. Finally eating as much as he wanted, Babe had added about

15 pounds to his lean frame over the winter. Ruth weighed in at a muscular 199 pounds and was ready to go.

Babe performed well enough during spring play to earn a spot in the starting rotation over Carl Mays. He was slightly wild, but, over time, control would not be a problem. Ruth used an excellent moving fastball with a sharp-breaking curveball, a difficult combination to hit. Of course, he was also an exceptional hitter. On March 23, Babe slugged a homer to right field at Majestic Park in Hot Springs during an intra-squad game. It was his only spring homer in competition, but he hit plenty during batting practice. A few weeks into the regular season, he still had not distinguished himself with the bat, but, at the Polo Grounds in New York on May 6, he did something that changed baseball forever. In the third inning against Jack Warhop, Ruth blasted a ball into the right field upper deck for his first Major League home run.

On a return visit to New York on June 2, Babe smashed his second homer. This one also landed in the right field upper deck, but it was still rising as it crashed into a vacant seat. It was an eye-opener for Yankee fans, who rarely saw that kind of power. Unhappily, Ruth also broke his foot while sliding in the same game. He missed the next few weeks, but he returned in top form. At Fenway Park on the 25th, he defeated the Yankees, and set a Boston-area distance record with his third home run. Ruth walloped the ball deep into the right center field bleachers. This was a local record that Babe would reset about a dozen times during the course of his career. By the end of June, the Red Sox were playing well, but they trailed the Chicago White Sox by seven and a half games.

July was a good month for Ruth and his team. He shut out the Washington Senators on the 5th, while bashing a triple off the right field fence. The Bosox then successfully toured the "western cities" of Cleveland, Detroit, Chicago, and finally St. Louis. It was there at Sportsman's Park against the Browns on July 21 that Babe had his best day of the season. He pitched into the ninth inning, and won 4–2.

Those four runs were primarily the result of four rockets hit by Ruth in as many at-bats. He finished with one single, two doubles, and his fourth and final homer of the year. One of those doubles landed beside the center field flagpole and would have been the stadium's longest drive if not for Babe's home run. That monumental blow was the first of countless Ruthian clouts that remains noteworthy even today with our ever-increasing standards for true "tape measure" status. The right field bleachers were located only 315 feet away, but Babe's belt soared so far over them that the ball landed on the opposite side of adjoining Grand Avenue (aka Grand Boulevard). That roadway was one of the widest in the country and measured 120 feet across. When the battered sphere finally alighted on the far side of the street, it had flown about 475 feet. Not bad for a pitcher in the dead ball era.

By the end of July, Boston had overtaken Chicago for first place. Ruth and his buddies took on the incomparable Walter Johnson and the Washington Senators at Fenway Park on August 14. This was the first in a series of man-to-man match-ups between Ruth and the "Big Train" during the next few years. Babe won this one 4–3 and collected two singles. Boston now found itself contending with Detroit rather than the fading Chicagoans. Ruth and Dutch Leonard combined to beat the Tigers at Navin Field in a 2–1 thirteen-inning classic on the 25th. The race stayed close until the Tigers came to Boston for a crucial four-game series in mid-September during a brutal heat wave. In the first game, which was won 6–1 by Detroit, Cobb and Sox pitcher Carl Mays had a disagreement. Ty actually threw his bat at Mays and was attacked by a group of hostile Boston fans. By then, the heat had killed fourteen New Englanders and was obviously affecting people's behavior. The police managed to prevent any further on-field violence, and both clubs vowed not to repeat the incident.

The Red Sox then won the next two games, which resulted in a must-win situation for Detroit in the fourth and final game. On Monday, September 20, Babe Ruth took the mound for Boston and led the Sox to a 3–2 victory. Even the feisty Tigers couldn't overcome a four-game deficit with so little time to play. Boston finished two and a half games ahead of them and faced the Philadelphia Phillies in the World Series. Ruth had to defer to his more experienced teammates and only got to pinch-hit during the Series. Boston won four games to one, but it was an extremely close and competitive series. Babe was disappointed that he didn't play more, but he understood the reasons. Plus, he knew that it had been a remarkable season for a twenty-year-old rookie, and that he would be back.

On October 17, 1915, Ruth played in his first unofficial post-season game. It was just a local affair at Mount St. Joseph College near Babe's home in Baltimore, but it was also a new chapter in Ruth's life. He pitched three innings for Irvington versus Catonsville and hit a double. In years to come, Babe would use the post-season forum to create some of the greatest spectacles in the history of his sport.

In an era dominated by pitching, Ruth already stood out. The American League ERA was 2.94 in 1915, but Babe bettered that by a half run per game at 2.44. He finished with an 18 and 8 record, and pitched 218 innings. The league batting average was a puny .248 and slugging an anemic .326. Ruth managed .315 and .576 respectively, and his slugging percentage was 85 points higher than the official league leader. As a pitcher, Babe did not bat often enough to qualify for the top spot. Ruth's four home runs led the Red Sox and were only three off the best mark. He was still not old enough to vote, but he was a World Champion with his best yet to come.

1916   The Red Sox trained once more in Hot Springs. As part of their conditioning each day, they hiked over the mountains from the Majestic Hotel to their practice field. At a time when cardiovascular training was largely ignored, this activity was much needed. In the first squad game on March 17, Babe launched a long drive to right center field that looked like a sure home run. To everyone's astonishment, outfielder Olaf "Swede" Henriksen literally ran through the wooden fence, and made the catch! As always, Ruth clubbed plenty of batting practice homers, but wasn't able to connect in any of the spring games. The Sox still had basically the same staff of great pitchers, but there would be one big difference. On opening day at Fenway Park on April 12, Babe Ruth was their starter, and he would remain their ace for the entire season. He won that first game against the Philadelphia Athletics 2–1, and followed with a 5–1 win over Walter Johnson on the 17th.

After slowing down a little in May, Babe again tangled head-to-head with Walter Johnson on June 1 at Fenway. Both were in top form, and neither team recorded an extra-base hit. When the dust settled, the Sox won 1–0. During Ruth's approximately four-year pitching career, he and Johnson faced each other many times with Babe emerging with a 6 and 3 record. Several of their match-ups were classics. Walter Johnson was probably the best pitcher who ever lived, but Babe Ruth was just a shade behind him. The two men were vastly different in temperament and personality, but both were gifted with nearly unbelievable athletic ability. Ruth is regarded as baseball's greatest slugger, but was a great pitcher. Johnson is known as his sport's best pitcher, but was an outstanding hitter. Both men could also field and run the bases with admirable skill. The Big Train was quiet and shy, while the Big Bam was loud and aggressive, but the two men became good friends. They also left us a legacy of amicable personal rivalry that ranks among the most admirable in the annals of sports.

In Detroit on June 9, Ruth hit his first home run of the season and it was a beauty. The ball landed deep in the bleachers just right of center field about 460 feet from home plate. It was hailed as the longest ever in Navin Field (later known as Tiger Stadium). Babe hit just three homers in 1916, and, oddly, they were bunched into a four-day span. At his next stop in St. Louis, he added the other two in consecutive games.

The following month, the Browns came to Boston. Ruth didn't knock any balls out of the park, but he did manage to knock out St. Louis's catcher. During his start on July 18, Babe ripped a triple and later tried to score. In a close play at the plate, he collided violently with catcher Hank Severeid and knocked him unconscious. There are no statistics for collisions on the baseball field, but, if there were, Ruth might be the all-time leader. While running the bases, he ran into fielders. When chasing fly balls, he ran into teammates and fences. Often, he was injured as a result, but that never dissuaded him from playing ball and living life full speed ahead.

When Ruth shut out the Tigers on July 31, the Red Sox moved into first place by a half game. By the end of August, they had increased their lead over Detroit to three games. During that month, Babe's personal highlight was yet another masterpiece at the expense of Walter Johnson. He threw a thirteen-inning complete game shutout on August 15 with the final score reading 1–0.

The race tightened once more, and, upon taking the field on September 17 in Chicago, the Red Sox trailed the Tigers by a game and the White Sox by a half game. No problem. Ruth took the mound in front of a record crowd of hostile fans and won 6–2. Four days later in Detroit, Babe took his next turn, and whipped the Tigers 10–2, while contributing a single and a triple. In his next outing in Cleveland, he shut out the Indians, and followed that with another shutout of the Yankees. With the American League Pennant on the line, Babe Ruth, at age twenty-one, pitched four complete game victories over his toughest opponents in just twelve days. End of pennant race.

In the 1916 World Series, the Red Sox played the Brooklyn Dodgers. Ruth only pitched in one game, but he made it count. Playing in Boston on October 9, Babe gave up a first-inning run on an inside-the-park homer, when two outfielders collided. But that was it for the Dodgers. For the next thirteen innings, Ruth held them scoreless, and the Bosox won 2–1 in fourteen innings. Boston went on to win their second straight Series four games to one.

Two days after the Series ended, Ruth and a few of his teammates played an exhibition game in New Haven, Connecticut. Babe pitched all nine innings in a 3–3 tie against a local club that was bolstered by Ty Cobb just for this occasion. American League president Ban Johnson heard about the game, and sent word to the players reminding them of the rule barring post-season appearances by World Series participants. They ignored him and went to New Hampshire under the pretext of sightseeing. Once there, they just happened to play another game in the town of Laconia. Ruth again went all the way on the mound against a local team and also asserted himself on offense. Babe smacked a single, double, and home run that sailed far over the right field fence in a winning effort. After those two games, the group disbanded and went home for the winter. For punishment, Johnson withheld their World Series emblems and required payment of small fines, a slap on the wrist that may have caused Ruth to disdain that particular rule. The full consequences would not be known for another five years.

Ruth didn't hit as well in 1916 as he had the year before, but he was still a factor with a bat in his hands. He batted .272 and slugged at a .419 average with eleven extra-base blows. Offensively, the American League was dominated by the threesome of Tris Speaker, Ty Cobb, and Joe Jackson. That trio may have been great, but, on the whole, scoring was low. The league batting average was just .248, and slugging was .324. So even then, Babe was a superior hitter. However, his pitching numbers were absolutely awesome. He went 23 and 12 with one save and a league-leading ERA of 1.75. He was third in strikeouts with 170, but first in shutouts with nine. Babe also amassed 324 innings pitched and compiled twenty-three complete games. He was truly great, but he still wasn't playing the position where he could make the greatest impact.

1917   Babe Ruth reported to spring training in Hot Springs on March 5, lean and fit and ready to anchor the Bosox pitching staff again. Upon breaking camp three weeks later, Boston played a far-ranging series of exhibition games that would become a staple in Babe's career. All teams of that era played in more places than teams of today, but, as two-time World Champions, the Sox were particularly marketable. As time passed and Ruth's fame grew, it was his personal magnetism that prompted his teams to schedule extra games wherever and whenever they could. On their way to opening day in New York on April 11, the Red Sox played eleven games from Memphis to Kansas City to Toledo and other towns along the way.

Boston had expectations of another championship and started the season well with Ruth's opening day victory over the Yankees. But in Chicago, the White Sox were assembling their own juggernaut. Chicago ace Eddie Cicotte pitched a no-hitter on April 14 and went on to have his best season. And they had slugging Joe Jackson in the outfield, who had been acquired from Cleveland in 1915. Meanwhile, back in Boston, Babe was up to his usual tricks. He won a complete game against New York at Fenway Park on the 21st, while banging balls all over the lot. All three of his extra-base hits struck the outfield walls in different directions: left field, deep left center, and right field.

On May 7 at Griffith Stadium in Washington, Ruth again defeated Walter Johnson and the Senators by a 1–0 score. Babe threw a two-hitter and drove in the only run with a 400-foot sacrifice fly. Four days later in Detroit, he tormented another baseball immortal by beating Ty Cobb and the Tigers 2–1. Early on, Ruth struck out Cobb, who took it personally and wanted revenge. While on base later in the game, Ty found Babe covering third, and made his customary hard slide with spikes flying. Apparently, Ruth anticipated the move and avoided Cobb's spikes. At the same moment, Babe decided to turn the tables and use this rare opportunity to dish out some corporal punishment to the master.

Instead of merely tagging Cobb, Ruth walloped him on the head with the ball. Ty was not only ruled out, he was knocked out. When Cobb tried to stand up two minutes later, he was still groggy. While Babe and Walter Johnson got along famously, Ruth and Cobb didn't like each other. Then again, Ty Cobb didn't like anybody. When Ruth dethroned Cobb as the game's greatest player, Ty resented him bitterly. The two men had fistfights on and off the field, and they both gave as good as they got. In later years, there was a type of reconciliation, but on the field they were oil and water.

June was an unusual month for Babe Ruth. He faced Eddie Cicotte and the White Sox in Boston on the 16th, and found himself losing in the top of the fifth inning. It was raining at the time, so the home fans swarmed onto the field in an effort to cancel the game before it became official. The ploy failed and the Chisox won 7–2. A week later, Ruth took the mound against Washington and started arguing balls and strikes after the first batter. Umpire Brick Owen ejected Ruth, who promptly went goofy. Charging from the mound, the enraged Ruth took a swing at Owen, and then he was really in trouble. Baseball may have been wilder in those days, but it was never okay to punch an umpire. Babe was suspended for a week and fined $100. Despite Ruth's temper and lack of self-control, most umpires genuinely liked him. He would often argue calls and occasionally get tossed. But he would never again physically assault any of the men in blue.

Things returned to normal in July as Ruth pitched a one-hitter in Detroit on the 11th to win 1–0. The only hit never left the infield, but Babe personally smashed three bullets including a long triple. Moving on to St. Louis, he beat the Browns 4–2 in ten innings and collected three more hits along the way. As of July 30, Chicago led the Red Sox by two games, but the teams then began a four-game series in Boston amidst a World Series atmosphere. Ruth held the Chisox to four hits in the opener and won 3–1. However, the teams split the series, and the White Sox were in front with two months to go.

On August 10 at Fenway Park against Detroit, Babe pitched and won. As was often the case, however, fans left the park talking more about his hitting than his pitching. In the fifth inning off Big Bill James, Ruth launched one to center field that soared over a bread sign and landed in the eighth row of the bleachers. Those seats were 430 feet away, so this drive had a total flight distance of about 465 feet. Babe had broken his own Boston distance record. Later in the month, the Bosox traveled to Comiskey Park for another showdown with Chicago. Ruth saved a win for Carl Mays in the first game with brilliant ninth-inning relief. But despite pitching well again the next day, he lost his start by a score of 2–0. The White Sox then began to pull away.

At the Polo Grounds on September 15, Babe smashed a line drive home run high into the right field upper deck. It was the longest drive of the year in New York except for a foul ball hit earlier that day by Ruth. That one sailed far over the grandstand roof, and would have been judged fair under today's rules. Back then, it was just a loud strike. Unfortunately for Ruth and other sluggers of that era, potential home runs were not judged fair or foul according to where they passed over the outfield fences. The ruling was based upon where the ball landed or was last seen. After 1930, the rule was changed to the modern format. Ruth was actually victimized by his great power in this regard. Many of his home runs flew so far beyond the fence that they had a greater tendency to drift into foul territory before leaving the umpire's line of sight. The impact of this rule on Babe's career production will be analyzed in depth in the chapter pertaining to comparative difficulty.

As usual, Babe went all nine innings, and defeated the Yankees by a score of 6 to 3. But by the end of September, the race was essentially over. When the Red Sox played a charity game on the 7th, Ruth pitched, and also won the pregame fungo contest with a drive of 402 feet. Baseball types even then had a fascination with distance as evidenced by their effort to stage this type of unofficial event. When it was all over, the Red Sox finished in second place, nine games behind the champion White Sox. In the World Series, Chicago defeated the New York Giants four games to two in a tough, well-pitched six-game struggle.

Babe Ruth had been individually great again. He went 24 and 13 and recorded a 2.01 ERA. He increased his innings pitched to an amazing total of 326 and completed an astonishing thirty-five games. At the plate, he batted .325, and slugged .472 in a year that the league averages were .248 and .320 in those respective categories. Babe also blasted two home runs that flew farther than any others recorded that season. Ruth's star was still rising, but his world was about to change. The United States had entered World War I earlier in the year, but the conflict had not yet significantly impacted Major League Baseball. The 1918 season would be different.

1918   When the Red Sox reported to spring training at Hot Springs again in March, no one knew how the war effort would affect the upcoming season. It was already apparent that some players would be leaving, but how many? It was a question that would not be completely answered until halfway through the season. Ultimately, it was decided that the season would end on Labor Day, but there were players who left on an individual basis throughout the year. Either way, the Sox knew that they would have a manpower shortage by the time they reached camp. As a result, they went ahead with an experiment to play Ruth in the field on certain days that he was not pitching.

In the first exhibition game on March 17 against Brooklyn, Babe played first base and hit two home runs. The second one went so far to right field that even the Dodger bench stood and cheered. It was the longest hit ever made at the local ballpark in Hot Springs known as Whittingham Park, but was overshadowed by Ruth's next homer a week later. Babe was back on the mound this time against the Dodgers. In the third inning, he blasted the ball so high over the right field fence that it cleared the street and trolley tracks before landing in a pond beside an alligator farm. The exact distance of this drive is unclear, but the evidence indicates a flight of about 500 feet. Ruth added two more homers on March 30 in Little Rock, although the second in the ninth inning was officially limited to a single when the winning run crossed the plate. The Red Sox then left on a lengthy preseason tour that took them through Texas, Louisiana, Alabama, and Tennessee.

Ruth pounded the ball all spring, batting .429, but started the season again as a pitcher. In the opener against Philadelphia in Boston on April 15, Babe threw a four-hitter and won 7–1. For the month, Ruth won 3 and lost 1, while the Red Sox went 11 and 2 to assume first place. Babe belted his first home run on May 4 at the Polo Grounds, but was the losing pitcher. He probably rattled manager Ed Barrow's sense of baseball tradition with his power that day. Not only did Ruth homer that afternoon, he also smacked a long double and two other balls with home run distance that were barely foul. Barrow relented and put his ace pitcher in the lineup as a fielder the following game.

On May 6, 1918, Babe played a position other than pitcher in a Major League game for the first time, when he started at first base against the Yankees. Naturally, he blasted a homer. Boston then traveled to Washington, where Ruth again played first base in the first two games of the series. His home run off Walter Johnson on May 7 was the first hit by anyone that season over the distant fences at Griffith Stadium. For his effort, Babe won a suit of clothes from a local tailor. Two days later, he renewed his mound rivalry with Johnson. The Big Train won this episode 4–3 in ten innings, but Ruth had his share of fun. He went 5 for 5 in the maelstrom of Johnson's legendary 100 mph fastballs. Babe's performance included three doubles and a triple that flew about 430 feet into center field.

When the Bosox returned to Fenway Park, Babe Ruth began his outfield career by starting in left field against the St. Louis Browns. He certainly wasn't a polished fly-chaser yet, but, as always, he sure was eager. On May 16, Babe tried so hard to catch a foul fly ball that he ran full speed into the box seats. From the plate on the 18th against Detroit, he hit a double so far over Ty Cobb's head in center field that it flew past the remote flagpole in the old Fenway configuration. Standing on second base, Babe taunted Ty. But should Ruth have been laughing, when Cobb limited him to two bases on a drive of 460 feet? Perhaps not, but Babe Ruth found humor easily.

It wasn't funny, however, when Babe took his wife Helen on a picnic the next day and got so sick that he was out of action for ten days. The problem began as a sore throat, but some dubious medical treatment aggravated the situation. The relatively primitive status of medicine in those days will be discussed later. In June, Ruth pitched and played first base, left field, and center field. By then, he enjoyed hitting more than hurling and rather defiantly told manager Ed Barrow that he didn't want to pitch anymore. The two argued heatedly over the matter, but eventually arrived at a compromise. The die was cast. Babe Ruth was on his way to being an outfielder as well as the greatest slugger of all time.

Back in Washington on June 30, Babe reversed a Walter Johnson fastball and defeated him with a tremendous tenth-inning homer far over the high right field wall. Then on July 8 in Boston, Ruth won the first game of the doubleheader against Cleveland with a tenth-inning shot about thirty rows into the distant right field bleachers. It was a line drive of about 490 feet and the longest ever witnessed in The Hub. But it wasn't a home run. According to the rules of the day, the game ended when the runner from first base crossed home plate. Babe had missed out on a spring training homer the same way earlier that year, but this was the only time he lost an official Major League home run due to that old rule. It was soon changed to its current form.

This photograph taken in 1917 shows the old configuration of Fenway Park prior to 1934. The arrow shows where Babe Ruth's mighty double landed beyond Ty Cobb on May 18, 1918. *(The Brearley Collection, Boston, Massachusetts)*

By the following day, first baseman Stuffy McInnis was ill, and Ruth volunteered to fill in for him. Something interesting happened soon afterward. Babe Ruth became a fielding force on the baseball diamond. Considering his remarkable athletic ability, it could not have been a surprise. Until then, Babe had made occasional great plays from the pitcher's mound, but, early on, he was somewhat raw as either a first-sacker or outfielder. However, two days after temporarily taking over for McInnis, Ruth recorded twenty putouts at first base, and made a spectacular unassisted double play. By the time McInnis returned for a July 17 doubleheader, Babe looked like an old pro in the infield. That was the day that Ruth played left field in game one, and pitched a rain-shortened shutout in game two. By the end of the month, Boston writers were raving about Babe's prowess as an outfielder as well as his virtuosity as a hitter. No one knew what he would do next.

It was about then that Secretary of War Newton Baker issued his so-called Work or Fight proclamation. Every able-bodied male American would be required to contribute to the war effort in some way. It meant that Ruth, as well as the other players who hadn't enlisted, would soon have to decide on their immediate futures. During his recent rift with manager Barrow over the pitching issue, Babe had almost joined a team sponsored by the Bethlehem Steel Shipyards in Chester, Pennsylvania. Nominally, Ruth would have been working in a war-related industry, and would qualify for a military deferment. In actuality, he would still be a professional ballplayer, just not in the Major Leagues. Many Big Leaguers had already made similar moves. But, at this point, Babe still had a little time to make up his mind.

Essentially, Ruth spent the rest of the 1918 season dividing his time between pitcher and left field. The Red Sox played well, while the White Sox were just plain bad. Cleveland and Washington were Boston's main competition, but the Red Sox had just enough to prevail. During the crucial month of August, Babe started eight games on the mound and completed seven of them. He threw an amazing total of seventy-three innings, while going 6 and 2. On the 24th, Ruth stole home in the second inning and injured his leg. Despite limping badly the rest of the day, he pitched a complete 3–1 victory. Later that night, Babe's father was killed in a bizarre brawl outside his bar in Baltimore, and Ruth missed a few games while attending the funeral. But on August 31 at Fenway Park, Babe pitched the whole way against Philadelphia, winning 6–1, thereby clinching the American League title. In that game, he also hit a 445-foot double to center field. That two-base hit illustrates a point about baseball history that is highly relevant in evaluating Ruth's lifetime production. It is also essential in selecting the title for this book.

During most of Babe's subsequent career in New York, he played in ballparks that had short right field boundaries. There is a natural tendency, therefore, to assume that he benefited from the stadium dimensions that were common in that era. Actually, a few other towns also had relatively close right field fences, but, as a whole, Ruth had it much tougher than modern players. In Ruth's time, every American League team played on a field with a center field boundary of 450 feet or more. Today there are no fields with such dimensions (the closest is Fenway Park's 420-foot angle in right center field).When Babe played for Boston, the center field corner was over 500 feet away. In his later years at Yankee Stadium, the center field fence was at least 490 feet from home plate. For every home run he gained to right field, Ruth lost at least three in center field and the adjoining power alleys.

Returning to 1918, it was decided that Babe would focus on pitching during the World Series against the Chicago Cubs. He completed the first game with a masterful 1–0 shutout. In his previous World Series appearance as a pitcher in 1916, Ruth finished with thirteen consecutive scoreless innings. So, entering the fourth game of this Series, Babe had a scoreless streak of twenty-two innings. It was September 9, and Ruth again pitched spectacularly despite an injured middle finger on his pitching hand. Babe's mighty triple accounted for the first two runs, and he did not allow a run until the eighth inning. Boston won 3–2, as Ruth set a World Series record of twenty-nine straight scoreless innings. The old record belonged to Christy Mathewson, and the new mark would last forty-two years. The Red Sox won the Series in six games and were World Champions for the third time in four years.

Babe then played in a few post-season exhibition games, including one in Lebanon, Pennsylvania. That is where Bethlehem Steel Company had another of its largest plants, and Ruth considered moving there to obtain his military deferment. But World War I was winding down, and Babe returned to Boston. During the 126-game 1918 schedule, Ruth compiled a 13 and 7 pitching record, while also playing 59 games in the outfield and 13 at first base. His ERA was 2.22 over 166 innings. At the plate, Babe batted .300 and amassed a .410 on-base percentage, which was second highest in the American League. His .555 slugging average was tops. Ruth tied for the league lead with eleven home runs and added twenty-six doubles and eleven triples. Babe also stole the first six bases of his career and certainly would have been American League MVP if that award had existed at the time. Babe Ruth was still in his ascendancy, but the Red Sox would have to wait eighty-six years to fly so high again.

1919   When the Red Sox arrived at their new spring training home in Tampa, Florida, World War I was over. However, many Americans were still in uniform, and Major League Baseball wasn't quite ready to return to complete normalcy. They decided to use a 140-game format instead of the standard 154-game schedule. Even spring training started late; the players didn't work out until March 22. Babe Ruth actually began two days later due to a brief salary dispute. Once in camp, Ruth made it clear that he did not want to pitch. His permanent move to the outfield was now inevitable, but one final chapter of the saga had still to be written.

Babe immediately fell in love with Florida and spent the rest of his baseball life cherishing his visits there. The Sox used Plant Field for all of their training, including both practices and exhibition games. It was a fairground in the shape of an oval with a racetrack (for horses) around the perimeter. In an intra-squad game there on April 1, Ruth hit a tremendous home run that began one of the most eventful months in an extraordinarily eventful life.

Three days later on April 4, the Red Sox played the New York Giants in the first exhibition game of that spring. The Giants started right-hander Columbia George Smith, and he did just fine in the first inning. Leading off the second inning for the Red Sox was a brawny fellow named Ruth who violently connected with a 3 and 1 fastball. The ball rocketed toward right center field, where right fielder Ross Youngs sprinted to catch up with it. Youngs was an excellent outfielder, and he had oceans of open space with which to work. But the ball kept going and going as if gravity had somehow been suspended. Youngs looked like a speck on the horizon when he finally gave up near the inside track railing. The soaring sphere finally came back to earth near the outside railing as onlookers gaped in astonishment. The landing point was marked and then measured the next day.

Unfortunately, that measurement was not formally recorded at the time, and there is some disagreement about the precise linear distance. Subsequent accounts ranged from 540 feet to an absurd 612 feet. Based on a thorough review of all the facts, the likely distance was 552 feet. Considering that the final stage of the so-called live ball evolution did not occur until the next year, such a drive should have been impossible. Some measure of specificity may be missing from the analysis, but there is sufficient data to confirm this drive as one of the few greatest feats of strength in the history of sports.

On the way north to open the official season, Ruth kept blasting. He set another local distance record in Richmond on April 15, and then arrived in Baltimore for a two-game series on the 18th. His return home must have imbued him with special powers, because he performed at an unnatural level. Even for Babe Ruth, what happened next was beyond anticipation.

Playing at Oriole Park, which had been Terrapin Park in the days of the now-defunct Federal League, Ruth hit a home run in the third inning. It sailed over the right field fence as well as a telegraph wire across the street. He walked in his next at-bat, but followed that with a monstrous blast between two houses in deep right center field. The *Boston Herald* likened the length of this drive to his recent effort in Tampa. In the seventh inning, Ruth belted one into the pine trees across Greenmount Avenue near where his first homer had landed. He now had three home runs in his last three official at-bats, and the pressing question was would he bat again? He did. In the ninth inning in his final appearance, Babe clubbed the ball over the fence near the right field foul line for his fourth straight home run. Everyone was stupefied; nothing like this had ever happened in professional base-ball. Bobby Lowe had hit four homers at Boston's Congress Street Grounds in 1894, but the left field fence was only 250 feet distant. Similarly, Big Ed Delahanty hit four in a game in 1896, but two of his drives remained inside the playing field at Chicago's West Side Park. One of Ruth's homers flew about 350 feet, two others over 400 feet, and the best (number two) traveled about 500 feet. Babe didn't hit his against a Major League team, but he was facing very determined oppo-sition against his former team in the highly competitive International League.

This old newspaper photo shows the landing places of Ruth's four homers at Baltimore's old Oriole Park in 1919. *(Baltimore News American Photograph Collection, Special Collections, University of Maryland Libraries)*

The next day Babe Ruth was the starting pitcher versus the Orioles. Everybody was still buzzing about the events of the day before, and Jack Dunn was adamant about stopping his one-time protégé. In his first at-bat, Ruth faced right-hander Rube Parhham, who threw him a fastball. The *Baltimore Sun* described the pitch as "fully 3 inches outside." The result was "fully" amazing. The ball wound up on the roof of a three-story house beyond the right center field fence, and may have traveled farther than all the other homers. When Babe batted again, Dunn called upon Lefty Kneisch for the specific purpose of stopping Ruth and ending the carnage. Moments later, Kneisch's specially selected half-speed curveball landed at the base of yet another house beyond the right field fence. Six home runs in six at-bats! Those lucky fans in attendance weren't sure how to react. Some stood and cheered wildly, while others were so incredulous that they just stared in disbelief.

When the streak finally ended in his next appearance, Ruth took three vicious swings and missed with all three. However, that strikeout is a reminder of another extraordinary aspect of Babe's accomplishment. He may actually have hit those six straight homers on six straight swings. There isn't sufficient description in the newspapers to know for sure, but there is enough to know that it is possible. It doesn't seem credible that any human being could hit six prodigious home runs in six swings against that level of pitching, but this was Babe Ruth. He did things on the baseball field for twenty-two years that nobody will ever do again.

When the Red Sox opened the 1919 season at the Polo Grounds on April 23, Ruth was in left field. Of course, he hit a home run, and all appeared well. But a few days later, he broke a training rule and clashed again with manager Ed Barrow. In truth, there was still a lot of friction over the pitching issue. Ruth didn't want to pitch, but Barrow wanted the option of using him at his discretion. The two almost came to blows, but they finally reached a permanent understanding. Ruth did pitch off and on for the rest of that season according to Barrow's choice. But it was the last year that Babe pitched on a serious basis.

It turned out to be a banner year for Ruth, but not so good for the

Red Sox. Owner Harry Frazee's first love was the Broadway stage, and he produced shows on a regular basis. He had sustained some recent losses, and it affected the operating budget of his ball club. Basically, he couldn't afford both, and it was the Red Sox who suffered. Frazee began losing players, which resulted in a downward spiral that damaged the Bosox for years.

On May 30 in a Memorial Day doubleheader in Philadelphia, Ruth pitched the first game, winning 10–6. In the second game, he played left field and bombed a home run so far over the fence in right center field that it cleared Twentieth Street, landing on top of a two-story row house. Not only was it hailed as the longest ever at Shibe Park, but Connie Mack called it the longest he ever saw (up to that time). When May came to an end, Boston was in sixth place with a 12 and 16 record.

As the season proceeded, Ruth hit home runs at a startling pace. By July 18, he had eleven, which put him slightly off pace for the record of twenty-seven set back in the 1880s. That day in Cleveland he added two more. The second occurred in the ninth inning with the bases loaded, two out and Boston trailing 7–4. Cleveland pitcher Fritz Coumbe refused an order from his manager and challenged Ruth. The result was both dramatic and predictable. Coumbe was soon watching Ruth's drive sail over the right field wall, cross Lexington Avenue, and crash onto the roof of a house. He lost the game as well, perhaps, as his pride.

Also in July, a couple of events took place that point out an often-overlooked aspect of Babe's total game. On the seventh in Boston, he hit a left field double and then scored from second base on a bunt. A few weeks later at Fenway Park, he went from first to third on an infield hit. It is often forgotten that Babe was a very good base runner until late in his career. He also became a top defensive outfielder. He demonstrated that on July 3 with a running, leaping catch in Philadelphia. Four days later in Boston, he continued to plague the Athletics with his defense by making another spectacular catch followed by a great throw.

By September, the Red Sox were out of contention, but Ruth still had a lot to do. He wanted the home run record and was closing in. On September 20 in Boston, Babe pitched the first game of a doubleheader against the White Sox that was touted as "Babe Ruth Day." In the ninth inning, he won the game with an awesome opposite field drive over the scoreboard clock in left center field. The ball broke a window across Lansdowne Street and gave Ruth twenty-seven homers for the year. Four days later at the Polo Grounds, Babe hit the record breaker by smashing one far over the right field grandstand roof. He added his twenty-ninth and final four-bagger versus old friend Walter Johnson on September 27.

The Red Sox finished in fifth place with a 66 and 71 record. The White Sox won the American League pennant, but disgraced themselves and their sport by throwing the World Series to the Cincinnati Reds. For the year, Ruth batted .322 and compiled an imposing .657 slugging percentage. He also drove in 114 runs and scored 103 times. On the mound, he had a 9 and 5 record with a 2.97 ERA.

At the conclusion of the season, Ruth played an exhibition series in New England and upstate New York. He then traveled cross-country to California. There he participated in several more games and lingered in Hollywood to film a movie. This was an important step in Babe's career. These post-season games (commonly referred to as "barnstorming") became a means for him to play in cities and small towns that otherwise would never have seen him. If you include all non-league games in the final total, at the end of Ruth's playing days, he performed in about two hundred locations outside the Major League circuit. On this trip, he visited Los Angeles, San Francisco, Oakland, and Sacramento, where he hit at least one home run at every stop. The homer at Recreation Park in San Francisco reportedly landed almost 200 feet beyond the right field fence. It is difficult for us to understand the significance of these events. We now have ESPN and other television networks showing us the highlights of every game. In those days, folks had newspapers and nothing else (radio coverage was still a few years away). To actually see Babe Ruth hit a baseball was an experience that no one ever forgot.

This also appears to be the time that Babe Ruth began to fully understand the potential of his personal showmanship. When functioning as a ballplayer, Ruth was all business. He had too much pride in his reputation to act any other way. But he was learning that baseball was a series of brief athletic movements interspersed with long moments of inactivity. He found that he could fill those lulls with crowd interaction without losing his concentration. Between innings, and sometimes even between batters, Babe could talk to fans or even pantomime messages to them. On this trip to California in 1919, Babe Ruth discovered that he was more than a magnificent athlete. He was a virtuoso performer who could amaze people in one moment with his tremendous power and make them laugh in the next instant with natural comedic instincts.

Back home in Boston, owner Harry Frazee decided that he could no longer afford to pay Ruth's escalating salary. On January 5, 1920, in a deal that stunned the sports world, he sold Ruth to the New York Yankees for the then-amazing sum of $100,000 plus a substantial loan. Babe loved Boston, but he soon learned the benefits of playing in the Big Apple. It was there that the media spotlight shone brighter than anywhere else. Ruth had finished the 1918 season as a superstar. By the end of 1919, he had replaced Ty Cobb as baseball's single biggest megastar. Now he was moving to New York, where he became a legend.

1920 Ruth got an early start in his first year as a Yankee by reporting to spring training on February 29 in Jacksonville, Florida. As of March 4, he hadn't done anything heroic on the ball field, but had made his mark nonetheless. After devouring three pounds of steak along with a bottle of chili sauce, he was declared the team's new eating champion. Before long, he impressed his new mates in more conventional ways. He looked fast patrolling center field in practice, and his power during batting practice was devastating.

In a game against Brooklyn on April 1, he hit his first Ruthian home run as a Yankee. Still playing in Jacksonville, he powered one over the center field fence that created a local sensation. That fence was 429 feet from home plate, and the ball touched earth about 75 feet past that point. Naturally, it was recognized as the city's longest. After breaking camp, the Yanks headed north, and, among other places, stopped in Winston-Salem, North Carolina. Again, the Dodgers were the opponent. In order to accommodate the overflow crowd, organizers roped off a cozy right field boundary. As a result, any ball hit into that area was designated a ground-rule double. Ruth hit three such balls that day, and was officially credited with two doubles and a foul. Unofficially, he probably clubbed three home runs with the longest-ever combined distance. Obviously, that distinction is hard to judge. Babe himself hit three long homers in a game several times, as did other great sluggers. However, this threesome appears to be the most awesome.

The field was inside a half-mile track, which was common in that era. The first blow was directed just right of center field and landed near the outside of the track before rolling into a gully. It also cleared the ring of outfield spectators by a substantial distance, as would all three. This drive of about 500 feet was limited to a double because of the aforementioned local rule. Ruth's next blast went in the same general direction, but flew much farther. It cleared the track and bounded out of sight. Damon Runyon, who was reporting for the *New York American* at the time, estimated that the ball would have cleared the center field bleachers at the Polo Grounds. The third and final drive struck by Ruth hugged the right field foul line and landed about 200 feet past the crowd. Since the umpire couldn't see where the ball landed, he made a guess and ruled it foul. In fact, the ball had returned to ground about ten feet fair as was later confirmed by those watching the game from right field.

We do not know the exact total distance of those three legitimate home runs on April 8, 1920. However, there is compelling evidence that it is somewhere close to 1,600 feet. Those balls were hit in a competitive game against Big League pitching, which suggests that this accomplishment may be the most underrated of Babe Ruth's career. If anyone else ever hit three such homers in a game, it has somehow escaped the gaze of history.

The Yankees and their new star opened the 1920 season in Philadelphia on April 14. Ruth played center field and hit two singles, but he dropped an eighth-inning fly ball that led to two Athletic runs and a 3–1 loss. Babe was so fired up for his Polo Grounds premiere eight days later that he hurt himself before the first pitch. He swung so hard in batting practice that he actually strained his right rib muscles and twisted his left knee. He left the game after striking out and then missed the next several contests. It was not the debut that he had envisioned. As of April 30, Ruth had no home runs, and the Yanks were in sixth place. But the following day, things got better in the Big Apple.

In the sixth inning of the May 1 ballgame against his former teammates, Babe Ruth connected with a Herb Pennock offering as only he could do. The ball rocketed skyward and cleared the imposing right field double-decker grandstand by thirty feet. Those stands were scandalously close, at 257 feet directly down the right field foul line, but they angled out severely (135 degrees). This drive by Ruth passed over the roof between the third and fourth flagstaffs from the foul pole, which meant that it left the premises at a distance of nearly 400 feet from home plate. Babe benefited from a few "cheap" homers down the line, but he lost many more in the cavernous areas in the distant power alleys. By the time Ruth left the Polo Grounds three seasons later, only three other players had reached the far-off right center field bleachers in their twelve-year history. No one knows the length of Babe's first official Yankee homer, but it landed far out in adjoining Manhattan Field somewhere around 500 feet away. It was the latest of many that would be categorized as New York's longest.

Playing right field now, Ruth had an up-and-down May. Despite an illness and another injury, he struck twelve homers and made a series of spectacular catches in the outfield. His most entertaining performance was on the 11th in New York against the White Sox. Ruth went 3 for 3 with two home runs and a triple. The three-bagger was hit so hard that it split a wooden plank in half in the right center field fence. After his second round-tripper, Chicago Hall of Fame second baseman Eddie Collins was so disgusted that he threw his glove at Ruth as he circled the bases. By Memorial Day, the Yanks were in third place at 38 and 23, while Cleveland was in first.

During mid-June, the Yanks went on a four-city, sixteen-game road trip. In Chicago, Ruth overcame a strong crosswind and became the first man to clear the right field bleachers.

He almost did it again in the ninth inning, but the wind blew this one just foul. Windy City fans appreciated Babe as an athlete and showman, and enjoyed his visits. They also tended to be demonstrative. When popular Sox pitcher Dick Kerr walked Ruth in the ninth inning the next day, they booed him lustily. Hundreds also promptly walked out.

On June 25 in New York against the Red Sox, Ruth hit two more tremendous home runs. In those days, the Polo Grounds' two-tier grandstand did not extend all the way to center field. It wrapped around the right field foul pole, but stopped about halfway to center. From there the bleachers continued around the entire outfield. Ruth's first home run on this occasion landed near the top of those bleachers just right of center field and left writers looking for new ways to say "longest ever." In the later years of his career, they basically gave up. By then, they had used every superlative in the English language so often that they would simply use "Ruthian" when Babe hit one of his best shots.

Since the American League was founded in 1901, there had been no pennants in New York. With the arrival of Ruth, as well as new ownership, the Yankees ultimately became synonymous with success. But it took a little time. By the end of June 1920, they trailed Cleveland by one game, and the Yanks were learning how to win. Babe and his buddies continued to play well in July as Ruth shattered his year-old home run record. He needed only until July 19 to hit Number 30, which turned baseball upside down. No one knew what to expect. Could a man really hit fifty home runs in a single season? Babe Ruth thought so. The opposition tried to stop him in every possible way, which included a steady diet of pitches outside the strike zone. It may have been at this time that Ruth made a decision that he carried with him for the rest of his baseball life. If he wanted to swing the bat on a regular basis, he would have to chase pitches that other players could ignore. His career is replete with instances of home runs and other key base hits made off pitches well outside the strike zone. Conditions improved later, when Lou Gehrig batted behind Ruth, but they were never normal.

On August 9, the Yankees arrived in Cleveland for a crucial four-game series. In the first game, Babe walked three times, and struck out swinging twice. But, as usual, he helped his team by making a great catch and two assists. The next contest saw Ruth carried off the field with a wrenched knee, but he was back in the lineup the following day. Babe limped badly and didn't hit much that series, but he continued to shine in the outfield. New York swept all four games and remained in the pennant chase. By month's end, they still trailed by only one game, but now it was a three-team race. Chicago was back in contention, as Shoeless Joe Jackson was enjoying one of his greatest seasons (and definitely his last). Before the next year, Jackson and several of his teammates would be banished for life due to their roles in allegedly throwing the 1919 World Series.

The Yankees returned to Cleveland on September 9 for three final games against the Indians. Ruth hit a homer onto a house porch across Lexington Avenue in game one, but the Yanks lost 10–4. In the next game, he added a second home run and barely missed out on a third. The greatest defensive outfielder of that era thwarted him. Tris Speaker, the wondrous Gray Eagle, roamed to Dunn Field's (later called League Park) center field scoreboard to work his magic. He caught Babe's mighty blast 460 feet away, but New York won anyway. Ruth collected two doubles and two intentional walks in the series finale, which resulted in a 6–2 victory. The Yankees were still in it, but a week later their bubble burst in Chicago. Babe managed only three singles in three games, and New York lost them all. The Yankees fought on, but their season was over. They finished in third place: three games behind Cleveland and one behind Chicago.

Babe Ruth had shattered the home run record by blasting a then-unimaginable total of 54. His slugging percentage was a mind-numbing .847. To put that in perspective, it was 215 points ahead of runner-up George Sisler. For the year, Sisler led the league in batting average (.407), total bases (399), and base hits (257). He also finished second in doubles, triples, and home runs. How could a player with a year like that finish more than 200 points behind in slugging percentage? The only explanation came in the form of a 215-pound freak of nature named Ruth. Babe also batted a robust .376, drove in 137 runs, and scored another 158. American League pitchers walked Ruth 148 times in his 142 games, which was 51 more than anyone else.

Babe made several barnstorming appearances on the East Coast at the conclusion of the season, but broke a small bone in his wrist in Oneonta, New York, on October 15. He went ahead with plans to play a series of games in Cuba, sailing on October 27. During that tour with John McGraw and other members of the New York Giants, Ruth made a pile of money. Babe's wrist had not completely recovered, but he still played reasonably well. And fortunately for the Cuban fans, he was able to hit one of his signature drives. Playing against the Almendares Blues in Havana on November 8, Babe smashed a monumental home run to deep left center field. The English-language *Havana Post* described it as the "longest and deepest line drive ever seen here." The ball landed between the "Sol" sign and the center field corner more than 500 feet from home plate. Returning home, Ruth vowed to have an even better season in 1921. Nobody thought that was possible, but Babe proved everyone wrong.

Babe Ruth early in his career as a New York Yankee *(Philadelphia Athletics Historical Society)*

1921 Babe Ruth reached the peak of his athletic prowess in 1921. And, yes, that includes his more celebrated year in 1927. Accordingly, we are going to bypass this season in this space and continue with Babe's career narrative. Chapter Four will be devoted to the adventures of the 1921 Bambino, and the full impact of this season will be fully addressed at the conclusion of this book. We will simply note here that Babe hit fifty-nine homers in 1921 and led the Yankees to their first American League pennant. They then lost in the World Series to the New York Giants. Ruth soon went ahead with his barnstorming tour, even though Commissioner Landis had decided to enforce the rule prohibiting World Series participants from such customary activity. Babe called off the trip after a few games, but it was too late to avoid serious discipline. So, despite the power and glory of that amazing season, Ruth ended 1921 under a cloud.

1922   As was his custom, Ruth stopped at Hot Springs on his way to spring training. He had been told the extent of his forthcoming punishment during a vaudeville tour in December. Babe would forfeit his World Series share, and be suspended for six weeks. Ruth thought that Landis would relent, so he paid little heed. Babe played golf, hiked in the mountains, and prepared for the 1922 campaign. The Yankees trained in New Orleans, their third site in three years. That was fine with their star outfielder, since the Crescent City was a great place to be Babe Ruth. He arrived there on March 10 weighing a fit 217 pounds, and he appeared ready for another monster season.

The Yanks did all their New Orleans training (practices and games) at a minor league field named Heinemann Park. In his first batting practice there, Ruth cleared the 486-foot sign in center field. Three days later, he took BP wearing his golf clothes. He seemed oblivious to adversity. Then the hammer fell again, this time with finality. The haughty commissioner was anxious to establish his supreme authority and was intent on making an example of the game's top player. The suspension would stand. Babe could play in spring training events and exhibition games, but he could not play in league games until late May.

It was a real misfortune for baseball and for Ruth. He played superlatively all over the South and Southwest in March and early April, including two of his typical "longest ever" pokes in Galveston and San Antonio. The one in Galveston flew 100 feet over a cigar sign in right field. In Richmond, he belted a homer off Burleigh Grimes that landed in the James River. But, when the season opened at Griffith Stadium in Washington on April 12, Ruth was sitting in a box seat. The loss of his life's primary passion was even harder than he had anticipated. Taking baseball from Babe Ruth was like taking drugs from an addict. There was bound to be a strong reaction, and, when Ruth finally played his first game on May 20 at the Polo Grounds, there was. The anticipation for his return was tremendous, but Babe wasn't himself. He had tried to use his time off positively, even having his tonsils removed on May 4. He may not have completely recovered from the operation, but more than any physical malady, Ruth was in a poor state of mind.

In his first at-bat of the 1922 season, Babe Ruth struck out. Using an improbable bright-green bat, he went hitless for the day as the Yanks lost to the Browns before an overflow crowd of 38,000. The next few games weren't much better as Babe began to press. He even switched to a yellow bat, but the magic had been temporarily misplaced. Against the Senators on May 25, Ruth singled to center field, where Sam Rice momentarily juggled the ball. Seeing an opportunity to atone for his recent failures, Babe headed for second base. He was called out on a close play, whereupon all the frustrations of the past few months seemed to culminate. Ruth jumped up and threw a handful of dirt at umpire George Hildebrand, who immediately ejected him. As Babe left the field, one fan became particularly abusive, causing Babe to leap onto the dugout roof to challenge him to fight. The man ran away, leaving Ruth bellowing with rage. As he walked to the clubhouse, Babe heard a mixture of cheers and boos, and Babe saw that he gone too far. He was lucky to receive only a one-game suspension.

Ruth promised to behave better, and he did for a while. He also began playing first-rate all-around baseball. He patrolled left field artfully and ran the bases with a perfect balance of prudence and aggression. Arriving at Comiskey Park for the first time on June 6, Ruth received a welcoming ovation from the Chicago fans. Responding to the positive energy, he enjoyed his best series to date. On the seventh, he ripped a long double and just missed a home run as his huge drive drifted foul after clearing the right field bleachers in fair ground. The next day Babe adjusted his aim and knocked one over the seats that stayed fair. On the last day in the Windy City, Ruth walloped the ball on a line over the center field fence, which had never previously been accomplished. It was a blow of about 480 feet. Babe seemed back on track, but the euphoria didn't last long.

On June 19 in Cleveland, Ruth again argued an umpire's decision and was ejected from the game. This time he received a three-game suspension, but petulantly insisted on taking batting practice the next day, which added two more games to the sentence. Finally, on June 26, Babe had a meeting with Commissioner Landis before his game at Fenway Park. Landis acted reasonably and admitted the unfairness of the rule banning World Series participants from barnstorming. He even promised to make an early decision to change the rule. Those words were a tonic for Ruth. He was never a deep thinker, but he was reasonably intelligent and highly emotional. Apparently, his sense of fairness had been challenged, and he had spent months in inner turmoil. Now he was free of the demons that had haunted him. Babe was suspended one last game for arguing a third strike later in the year, but witnesses agreed that the umpire overreacted. On the whole, he was a model citizen and played baseball as only he could.

Ruth began July by hitting five home runs in an odd five-game series against the Athletics. At least it was odd by today's standards. The first two games were played at Shibe Park in Philadelphia, but the third day was a Sunday. The blue laws were still in effect, and Sabbath games were prohibited in Philadelphia and a few other places. This played hell with the schedule and the travel patterns for the players. The Yanks and A's played their third game in New York and then returned to Philly for the final two. Babe's fifth homer left Connie Mack shaking his head. The venerable Mack always liked Ruth, but he didn't like losing to him. As was the case with every manager, he had strict rules about how his pitchers should handle Babe. In this instance, Mack had no quarrel with Buzz Eckert, who served up the home run on a pitch that was about eight inches low and outside.

Later that month, New York ventured to St. Louis to play the league-leading Browns, whose first baseman George Sisler was having another great season. This time he was complemented by slugging outfielder Ken Williams, who was having a career year. And mixed in with that dynamic duo was someone who mattered only to the Yankees. His name was Hub Pruett, a little junk-balling lefthander pitching in the Majors for one reason: he could get Babe Ruth out. Whereas star teammate

Urban Shocker and the legendary Walter Johnson had nightmares about pitching to Ruth, "Shucks" Pruett vexed the mighty Bambino. He threw a tricky screwball that usually left Ruth swinging at air and twisting like a pretzel. This was Pruett's rookie year, and he would fan Babe ten of the first thirteen times he faced him. Luckily for Ruth, he mostly avoided Pruett in this series, and the Yankees won four straight vital games. Despite that triumphant effort, New York finished July a few days later trailing St. Louis by one and a half games.

Meanwhile, back in the Big Apple, something was happening that would profoundly affect the life of Babe Ruth. Yankee Stadium was under construction directly across the Harlem River from the Polo Grounds. Ruth's new playpen would be built in less than a year and cost (including the land) a modest $3 million. It would become an enduring shrine to the man and his sport. It would also be ready by opening day of the next season.

On August 2, the Yankees began a series in Cleveland, where Ruth made an array of great defensive plays. He also totaled eight hits in four games, helping the New Yorkers sweep another set. When they arrived in Detroit on Sunday August 6, they played in front of a record crowd. Babe hit a single and a home run, but his bid for another homer was thwarted by the overflow throng. His center field smash landed beyond the flagpole 470 feet away, but some of the fans were standing there in a roped-off area. It was ruled a double according to a prearranged agreement. Bad fortune plagued Ruth during the entire visit. He launched a towering drive the next day that appeared headed into Canada, but a powerful incoming wind knocked it down into Ty Cobb's glove at the bleacher wall in right center field. In the following game, Cobb raced into deepest center and leaped at the fence to take away another potential home run. The *Detroit Free Press* rated this catch as the greatest of Ty's exceptional career. Ruth finally overcame fate and the elements, recording his second homer in the last game. He pounded the ball into the center field seats as Cobb and the wind conceded defeat.

After leaving Detroit, the Yankees played an exhibition game in

Syracuse. During the 1922 season, they also competed similarly in Rochester, Cincinnati, Akron, Buffalo, and three times in Baltimore. During those games, Ruth clouted five home runs, smiled for hundreds of cameras, shook hands with thousands of kids, and signed countless autographs. No one ever felt cheated. Babe had the uncanny ability to make everyone feel that he was there just for him.

Playing back in the Polo Grounds on August 16, Ruth hit a double and a homer about 430 feet. The next afternoon, with fielders cringing, he got a single on a ten-foot bunt as his fans roared with appreciation. Three days later, he bunted safely again while his second long homer of that same contest overcame a ninth-inning deficit to win the game. The jubilant sellout throng carried their hero across the field to the clubhouse in tribute. By the end of the month, the Yankees had surged into first place, but the Browns were right on their heels.

When the Yankees began an epic road trip on September 11, the pennant was still in doubt. They played their final eighteen games during the next three weeks with at least one appearance in all seven rival American League cities. Ruth started the long trek in grand style by going 4 for 5 in Philadelphia. He hit two doubles and two home runs, and his only out occurred when center fielder Frank McGowan robbed him at the fence. On the 17th, New York came to St. Louis holding a half-game lead. They won the first game 2–1 before a packed house of 30,000 howling Browns fans. Babe batted in the sixth inning of the next game with another sellout mob yelling for his blood. Why not? On the mound was none other than Hub Pruett. Ruth was not accustomed to failure, but, in his brief history against Pruett, he had been pitiful. However, he was still Babe Ruth, and finally demon-strated that reality to the little southpaw. His timely drive sailed high over the right field pavilion and out onto Grand Avenue as the Yanks won again. Babe went hitless in the final game, but he contributed a great running catch and an assist to yet another sweep. The Browns never quit, but those losses proved too much to overcome. The Yankees would ultimately prevail by one game.

By his personal standards, Ruth had a sub-par season. He finished with thirty-five home runs, but Ken Williams led with thirty-nine. Williams also topped the league in RBIs and total bases, while teammate George Sisler led in batting average, stolen bases, hits, and runs scored. Babe did manage to win the slugging title at a rate of .672. More importantly, he hoped for better things in his return bout with the Giants in the World Series. Unfortunately, it didn't happen. With Babe batting an anemic .118, the Yankees lost four games to none. Ruth made no excuses, but, in fairness to him, he was a little unlucky. He hit a few balls very hard that went directly at Giant fielders, including a 450-foot shot to center field in the third game. In a short series, there isn't always time to change bad karma. Either way, Babe accepted this reversal, and, in later years, he set numerous records that would ensure his World Series legacy.

True to his word, Judge Landis overturned the barnstorming ban that had caused all the trouble the previous fall. Soon after the Series ended, Ruth and teammate Bob Meusel left on a seventeen-game tour through America's heartland. When he returned to New York in November, Babe attended an Elks Club dinner. State senator and future mayor Jimmy Walker reminded Ruth that his various behavioral indiscretions had not been a good role model for children that year. Babe wept openly at the thought of failing the kids who adored him and made a sacred vow to make amends. When he returned the following spring, Babe Ruth was on a mission.

1923   Ruth arrived for spring training in New Orleans on March 8, 1923, weighing a lean 205 pounds, which confirmed his discipline and hard work during the winter months. A case of the flu slowed him at first, but he was a workaholic that spring. Babe blasted four spring homers, but his longest blow was a 500-foot double on the 31st off the top of the scoreboard at Heinemann Park. When camp ended, the Yankees and Dodgers embarked on an arduous tour that took them through Louisiana, Mississippi, Texas, Oklahoma, and Missouri. Ruth played very well, and, as he headed for home, his thoughts centered on opening day at brand-new Yankee Stadium.

April 18, 1923, was a day to remember. The opening of a sports arena had not been so passionately anticipated since the Roman Colosseum in the first century. First of all, it was gigantic. When built, Yankee Stadium was twice the size of any existing ballpark in Major League baseball. Attending a game there in 1923 was like experiencing a waking dream. The morning of the first game Babe Ruth said that he would give a year off his life to hit the first home run. After all, the place was already being called "The House That Ruth Built."

On that beautiful spring day, everything went right. A staggering total of nearly 70,000 fans were allowed to enter, and another 30,000 were turned away. All of them were seen gaping upward at the towering three-level grandstand, which might have come directly from an H. G. Wells novel. Once inside, they saw the greenest grass they would ever see, the result of 116,000 square feet of specially grown sod from Long Island. The place was packed with dignitaries, and John Philip Sousa provided the music. Asking for only one thing more, their prayers were answered in the third inning. On a 2 and 2 count off a slow-breaking ball from Boston's Howard Ehmke, Babe Ruth pounded a savage line drive to right field. The ball rose slightly and then crashed into the crowd about twenty rows into the open bleachers. What followed was perhaps the loudest sound that had ever been heard on a baseball field. Seventy thousand supercharged New Yorkers screamed with one voice as a grinning Ruth circled the bases. At home plate, he stopped momentarily and raised his hat amidst the deafening crescendo. The Yankees won the game 4–1, and were now playing in the finest arena in the world. And Babe Ruth was again center stage in the baseball universe.

During the next two games something happened that was profoundly important to understanding Ruth's career. Babe bombed a 475-foot drive to deep left center field on April 19. Despite the Homeric length of this drive, it was only a triple. In game three of the series, the same thing happened again . . . twice. Ruth's triple landed past the running track in remote left center near where the one fell the day before. Then he drilled a double in the ninth inning onto the track in straightaway center to win the game. Babe hit three balls over 450 feet in those two days and had no home runs. In 1923, it was 500 feet to deepest center field in Yankee Stadium. The plate was moved out ten feet for the next season, but the center field fence was still 490 feet away, where it would remain for the rest of Babe's career. The power alley in left center was never closer than 470 feet on the field that Ruth called home for the next twelve years. For the record, no man, right or left handed, ever hit a game ball over that fence until after it was relocated much closer in 1936. The foul lines measured only about 300 feet during Babe's tenure in the great Bronx ballpark, but most of the other dimensions were prohibitively difficult to overcome. Modern players use the term "Death Valley" to describe the left center field gap marked by the 399-foot sign in today's Yankee Stadium. If they only knew!

This view of Yankee Stadium shows where three long Ruthian drives landed during the first three games ever played there. Each would easily result in a home run in any Major League ballpark today. (Baltimore News American *Photograph Collection, Special Collections, University of Maryland Libraries)*

On April 29, the Yankees were in Paterson, New Jersey, to play the first of many in-season exhibition games. Late in the contest Ruth hit the longest drive that any of the 12,000 attendees had ever seen. According to the *New York World,* the ball "cleared [the right field] bleachers, a 60 foot street, a barn and two fences." From a compilation of all firsthand accounts, it is believed that this drive flew about 515 feet. As usual, hundreds of kids swarmed onto the field. They engulfed Babe in front of the dugout and tried to carry him around the field. Instead, they only managed to drop him on the ground, where he was nearly trampled. When this perilous fiasco was repeated, Ruth's teammates came to his rescue by cordoning him from the crowd with their wooden bats. The police then intervened, escorting the smiling Bambino from the premises. As he left, Babe continued shaking hands and signing autographs. Ruth was always straightforward on this matter. He enjoyed those exhibitions thoroughly, but he regarded them as significantly more taxing than the regular season games.

During May, Babe belted nine home runs; a few of them had his special long-distance stamp. But another aspect of Ruth's game was getting even more attention. He was leaner and faster than he had been in years and was flying around the bases and outfield. Until he was old and fat, Babe always played a good all-around game. But this was different. He seemed obsessed. He was running the bases like Ty Cobb and playing the outfield like Tris Speaker. On May 1 in Washington, Ruth stole home to tie a game in the seventh inning. Then on a return visit a few weeks later he faked the same play and caused the pitcher to balk. Also in D.C. on May 3, Babe ended a 3–2 win with a perfect throw from deep right field to third base. In Detroit on the 14th, he robbed Cobb of extra bases and executed a perfect double play throw to second base the next day. On the 24th in Philadelphia, Ruth made another great running catch and recorded another assist. And so on and so on. Game accounts for the entire season are filled with glittering descriptions of Ruth in the field and on the bases. It may not have been Babe's best power year, but it was his best as a finesse player.

Entering June, the Yankees were in first place, where they intended to stay. They were playing well, but the most important event of the month did not occur on the field. On June 11, 1923, New York signed Lou Gehrig to a contract. He was a local boy who had played baseball and football at nearby Columbia University. The Yanks were well aware of his considerable athletic ability. It would be two years before he became a fixture in the Yankee lineup, but he would prove well worth the wait. Until Gehrig arrived, Ruth was not followed by anyone in the batting order that opposing pitchers really feared. As a result, he walked continuously, and, perhaps even worse, had to swing at bad pitches on a regular basis. During the 1923 season, Babe walked a then-record 170 times, and some of those bases-on-balls were pretty peculiar. On June 16 at the Stadium, against Hub Pruett of all people, Ruth was purposely passed in the third inning with the bases already filled. St. Louis won the game 3–1, so the oddball strategy worked. After Gehrig arrived, teams still pitched around Ruth, but not to such a ridiculous level.

July was Babe's best power month when he connected for ten homers. The first one was hit against the Senators and landed halfway up the right field bleachers at Yankee Stadium. The triple-deck right field grandstand did not extend into fair territory in Ruth's day; that was added years later. Babe aimed at a vast tier of open bleachers that rose about seventy rows from field level. No human being, not even Babe himself, ever cleared that target in a game. It wasn't far to those seats along the right field foul line, but the back of those bleachers was about 500 feet away. They were also about 50 feet high. As a result, every home run that Ruth pulled to the right side in his twelve years at Yankee Stadium landed somewhere in those bleachers.

Babe's next homer occurred in the following game, providing the climax to an eventful day. In the eleventh inning, the game was tied 1–1. The Yanks had trouble scoring, largely due to three intentional passes to Ruth. The Senators' Goose Goslin sent a long drive to right field, where Babe gave chase. At the last moment, he threw himself into the air and made a spectacular rolling catch. The problem was that he landed headfirst and was knocked unconscious. After about two minutes, Ruth revived, and the fans could breath again. The game remained tied until the fifteenth inning, when Babe came to bat against lefthander George Mogridge, a crafty control pitcher who was regarded as unusually effective against the great Bambino. He had relieved Walter Johnson in the ninth inning earlier that year just to face Ruth. On this occasion, Babe prevailed, lining the ball into the right field bleachers to win the game. As he crossed home plate, Ruth was greeted by about a thousand back-slapping fans who had rushed past the helpless security guards.

Also in July, Babe demonstrated his peak power for the year. In batting practice in St. Louis on the 7th, he broke a window at the Igou Motor Company office across Grand Avenue. It was nearly 500 feet to the far side of that roadway, but Ruth then cleared it twice in actual games. In the middle of a visit to Detroit later that month, the Yanks used an "off day" to play in Grand Rapids. Babe hit two long home runs, and the second blow was a memory maker. It cleared the scoreboard in right center field by fifty feet and came down in a distant tree. In an interview fifty-nine years later, teammate George Pipgras chose to talk about this drive, and his awe was evident. This was a man who served in World War I, played in three World Series, and later umpired in the Major Leagues for nine seasons. And yet at age eighty-three, he was still gushing about an exhibition game event that occurred nearly sixty years earlier. If Babe Ruth's power affected a man like that, consider the impact on the average fan.

The year 1923 was exceptional for exhibition games, even by Ruthian standards. During the American League season alone, the Yankees played fourteen unofficial games. Babe added individual appearances at the Polo Grounds as well as at a financially troubled Catholic parish in Philadelphia. Ruth hit twelve unofficial home runs in those contests. It was all for the best, since New York made a mockery of the American League pennant race. By midsummer, the result was a foregone conclusion, and the Pinstripes went on to win their third straight flag by a whopping sixteen games.

Ruth, of course, had been sensational. It's a toss-up as to whether he was better as a showman or as a player. On August 20 in Chicago, Babe found himself in left field in the ninth inning of a lopsided Yankee victory. When a dog ventured into Ruth's territory, he cavorted around the outfield with his new canine playmate. Just as Earl Sheely came to bat, Babe tossed his glove at the playful pup, who promptly sped off with Ruth's mitt in his mouth. Sheely then whacked the ball into left field. No problem. Babe nonchalantly glided over to the ball, and caught it barehanded. Then, in his exhibition appearance at Toronto the following week, Ruth had the brass to tell his pregame audience that he could hit the center field clock with a batted ball. As the fans laughed, Babe turned around, and smacked it fungo-style directly off the clock.

Along with his league-leading 41 homers, Ruth added 45 doubles and 13 triples for a slugging percentage of .764. Unfortunately, Detroit's Harry Heilmann had a career year and batted .403, thereby denying a batting title to Babe, who hit a lifetime best .393. Ruth also drove in 130 runs and scored 151. Combining his batting average with his 170 walks, Babe amassed a .545 on-base percentage. Just as important, he finished third in outfield putouts with 378. That was an amazing total for a guy who played primarily in left or right field. Only two center fielders finished ahead of him. He also threw out twenty base runners from the outfield and added seventeen stolen bases. It was extraordinary stuff, but the Giants were waiting again in the World Series, and Ruth would not be satisfied with just individual accomplishments.

On October 10, the Giants won the first game 5–4 on Casey Stengel's home run. Babe came up huge in game two, pacing a 4–2 victory with two homers, two walks, and a 440-foot fly out. The first home run flew majestically over the right field grandstand roof at the Polo Grounds and alighted in Manhattan Field. In his *New York World* column the next day, Heywood Broun wrote what may be the most memorable line ever recorded in baseball chronicles. He summarized the events of the game by declaring: "The Ruth is mighty and shall prevail." Stengel, reaching the apex of his playing career, won the third game 1–0 with another four-bagger. But that was the end of the line for John McGraw and his Giants as the Yankees and Ruth swept the final three games to become World Champions. For the six games, Babe hit .368, struck three home runs and slugged 1.000. Each Yankee received a winner's share of $6,160.46, which was big money in those days. It was the sweetest possible vindication for the man who had been so embarrassed the preceding autumn. This time he was able to completely enjoy his barnstorming tour, which stayed surprisingly close to home. Ruth played a series of games in western New York and northern Pennsylvania, where he also hunted and fished. Babe was at peace with himself that winter, but the rest of the American League was not standing still.

1924   The Yankees held spring training in New Orleans again in 1924. Babe Ruth arrived on March 10, after his annual stopover in Hot Springs as well as his usual bout with the flu. He was heavier this year at about 230 pounds, and he started rather slowly. Babe struck only one competitive homer during camp, but he still made his mark. He hit two 470-foot fly outs near "the ditch" in center field and two 490-foot doubles off the fence just beyond that point. And as soon as the Yanks headed north, Ruth heated up. After breaking camp, the first tour game was played at Monroe Park in Mobile, Alabama. The center field fence was nearly as far away (485 feet) as it was at Yankee Stadium (490 feet). Nonetheless, Babe's fifth inning drive sailed cleanly over the barrier as the local populace gawked in wonderment. Then on April 8 at Caswell Park in Knoxville, Ruth thundered one over the center field scoreboard at a distance of 450 feet. So much for Babe starting slowly; he was ready to go.

The Yanks opened the season on April 15 with a 2–1 win in Boston and next went to Washington. Babe collected a triple and home run off thirty-six-year-old Walter Johnson, but old "Barney" won anyway. Johnson had now been in the American League since 1907 without ever winning a pennant or appearing in the World Series. He was running out of time, and his chances were not good. The Senators were a perennial second division team. As one pundit said: "Washington is first in peace, first in war, but last in the American League." As April ended, New York was tied for first place with Detroit.

Ruth spent almost the entire month of May playing at home in Yankee
Stadium. The scoreboard had been placed atop the low bleachers in
deep right center field, too far for even Ruth to reach. But he came close
a few times that month. His homer on May 13 landed two-thirds up the
bleacher slope just right of the scoreboard. Two days later, Babe clubbed
the ball almost as far, but even closer to center field. He was getting the
range. Ruth paused a couple weeks to recover from a case of bronchitis,
but resumed the bombardment on May 30. This time, his colossal drive
was measured; it was interrupted in mid-flight near the top of the right
center field bleachers 476 feet from home plate. In the last game of the
month, Babe was knocked unconscious in a collision with a teammate
chasing a fly ball. Typical of Ruth, he refused to leave the game, but his
long ball streak appeared over. Not so. In the ninth inning, he summoned all his formidable strength and pounded the ball heavenward in
the general direction of Yonkers. On and on it carried until it thumped
against a bleacher bench just below the scoreboard a little right of dead
center. The estimated flight path was 525 feet. Babe never did hit that
scoreboard in a game, but he came much closer than anyone else.

Yankee Stadium, New York: Babe Ruth's longest center field home run at
Yankee Stadium: hit on May 31, 1924. (Baltimore News American *Photograph
Collection, Special Collections, University of Maryland Libraries*)

Since most of May was spent at home, the Yanks were obliged to undertake a long road trip. On the way to Chicago, they stopped in Louisville, where Babe affected the town like the Kentucky Derby. Before the game at Parkway Field, he posed for photographs with a rather eclectic mix that included children, dwarfs, and Confederate Civil War veterans. He was then presented with a loving cup from an organization that claimed some kinship to him. In batting practice, he blasted balls to places never thought possible and then walloped a couple even farther in the game against the Colonels. One went foul in right field, and, according to *The Times* of Louisville, collided with a grain elevator "100 yards" beyond the fence. The other passed high over a sign in deep right center that had never previously been approached. After the game, Ruth hurried to the Sutcliffe Company, where he handed out miniature bats as part of a local promotion. Following dinner, he visited the newspaper office and assisted the editor in setting the type for the day's story. Climbing aboard the train that night, he rubbed liniment on his right wrist, which he had sprained shaking so many hands. He remarked in his typically candid fashion: "Kentuckians are the hand-shakingest people I ever saw."

By the next morning in Chicago, Ruth's wrist felt better, but his stomach hurt. When questioned, he acknowledged eating a midnight snack of twelve hot dogs. How else does a ballplayer recover from a wrist injury? Three days later, he was well enough to spend the morning hitting autographed balls to kids at Lake Michigan. He then proceeded to Comiskey Park, where he contributed a home run and a sensational catch to a winning effort, and then to St. Louis. On June 10, Babe participated in pregame activities for George Sisler Day when an army blimp flew overhead at an altitude of 350 feet. It dropped base-balls, with Ruth catching one and coming close to hitting the dirigible with his return throw. Playing next in Detroit against Ty Cobb, Ruth was nearly beaned by the Tigers on June 13 in the ninth inning with a 10–6 lead. Bob Meusel batted next and was hit hard by a pitched ball. All hell broke loose, with Cobb and Ruth in the middle of what was described as a "riot." The Detroit police could not clear the field, whereupon the game was forfeited to the Yankees. As the Tiger manager, Cobb was seen as the instigator, and Babe escaped with a $50 fine. When June came to an end, the Yankees were in second place behind the surprising Washington Senators.

Ruth and the Yankees took charge in July. Babe blasted fourteen home runs, and his team started blasting the Senators. Over the Fourth of July weekend in Washington, the two teams played five games in three action-packed days. New York won both ends of an A.M.–P.M. doubleheader on Independence Day by scores of 4–2 and 2–0 as Ruth collected a single in each game. Another twin bill followed, and, in the first game, Herb Pennock out-dueled Walter Johnson 2–0 as Babe ripped a single and two savage doubles. Ruth also picked off a runner from right field who had strayed too far from first base. In the nightcap, Babe went 0 for 3 with a sacrifice bunt as Washington won 7–2. The fifth and final contest was played on Sunday, July 6, and the Senators wanted it badly. But Babe Ruth stood in their way. He hit two doubles, including one bomb off the bleacher wall in deep left center field. That was followed by a home run in the same direction that landed in the tenth row. He added a stolen base, and, when the Yankees scored four ninth-inning runs, they prevailed by a 7–4 count. New York had won four of five on the Senators' home turf and had sent a message to their new rivals.

Back at Yankee Stadium later that month, Ruth reprised the essence of his 1923 season. He made one spectacular defensive play after another. His bat was busy, too. On July 20 versus Cleveland, he smashed a line drive so hard that it is frightening to even consider. Facing Dewey Metivier in the second inning of the second game, Babe unleashed a screaming liner right past the pitcher's head. The *New York Times* said the ball: "grazed pitcher Metivier's glove," while the *Herald-Tribune* observed: "it nearly tore Metivier's ears off." They all agreed that the ball continued rising until it flew over the center fielder's head and landed beyond the flagpole. It then bounded into the fence almost 500 feet away with so much force that it ricocheted twenty feet back to the flagpole. There are legions of stories (some true and some apocryphal) about the fear that pitchers felt facing Ruth from only sixty feet away. This is the only one you need to hear to understand that, if a pitcher wasn't afraid, he wasn't rational. The force of this blow was more than sufficient to kill someone.

As July ended, New York was on top, but Washington and Detroit were right behind. Meanwhile, Babe was on a torrid hitting streak. From July 5 through August 9, he went 73 for 143, which is a very long time to maintain a .500 average. For a man who swung as hard as Ruth, it was an amazing feat. Historian David Stephan has determined that Ty Cobb went 85 for 169 in 1912 for the longest-ever .500 streak, but Ty hit only seven home runs during that year. Ruth hit seventeen homers during his .500 streak alone.

Cobb was still going strong, and now that he and Ruth were competing in a pennant race, their rivalry was as intense as ever. The Yankees and Tigers played seven times in August with New York winning four. Each game was all-out war with no quarter given or sought. Huge crowds attended in both cities, and both teams played well. But while they were pounding each other, the Yanks and Bengals were overtaken by the surprising Senators. Everybody kept expecting them to fade, but, as August closed, they had regained first place.

The Yankees kept battling. Ruth was fighting off arm and ankle injuries when the team arrived in Boston on September 8 for four games. In that time, Babe clouted two 500-footers halfway up the center field bleachers, and New York won all four. Traveling to Chicago, they were only one game behind Washington. And yet they still stopped in Buffalo for an exhibition game. Naturally, Ruth was expected to wow everybody, and he did so by hitting two mighty homers and agreeing to all requests for autographs and special appearances. But at what price? By today's standards, it would be unthinkable to schedule extra games at such a time. But the Twenties were a different era, with exhibition baseball woven into the fabric of the sport.

On their prior trip to Chicago, the Yankees had actually forfeited a league game in order to keep an exhibition appearance. Trailing the Tigers by only one run going into the ninth inning, they called off the contest at Yankee Stadium in order to make a six o'clock train. The reason? They had a game set for the next day in Indianapolis, while they were en route to Chicago. That was on July 24, when they were neck and neck with Detroit in the pennant chase.

The Senators finished in a blaze of glory. Walter Johnson's team finally won their first pennant. They finished $1^{1}/_{2}$ games ahead of New York and 6 ahead of Detroit. Nobody blamed Babe Ruth; he had another great season. Once again, he led the league in home runs (46) and slugging percentage (.739), this time by 206 points. And for the only time in his career, Babe won the batting championship with a .378 average. He walked 142 times and scored his usual imposing number of runs (143). But his RBIs were somewhat low at 121, which should have been a signal to the Yankee brass that some of their key players were aging. Ruth's offensive support was slipping, and the lineup needed an overhaul.

Meanwhile, the 1924 World Series was getting underway at Griffith Stadium in Washington. The Senators were matched against the New York Giants, who seemed to have a stranglehold on the National League pennant. Walter Johnson pitched the first game, performing heroically, but losing 4–3 in twelve innings. He lost his next start as well, but came back to pitch four brilliant relief innings in winning game six, which also lasted twelve innings. The Washington Senators were World Champions, and everyone in baseball rejoiced for the Big Train. During the Series, Ruth and Cobb sat together at the Polo Grounds and finally made peace. They continued to compete fiercely against each other, on the diamond and on the golf course, but they never again behaved like enemies. When the World Series ended, Ruth departed on his most ambitious barnstorming tour to date.

It started in Kansas City on October 13 and finished in Anaheim on October 31. In between, Babe went places and did things that seem fictional in retrospect. After blasting two homers in Minneapolis, he traveled west by train across North Dakota, Montana, and Idaho, while feasting on buffalo steaks, duck, and wild rice. At almost every water stop, there was an impromptu party. Ruth would come out on deck and get to know the local folk there waiting for him. Arriving in Spokane, he went 5 for 6 including a monumental center field homer. Then, in Seattle between hospital visits, banquets, and the neverending speeches, Babe walloped three home runs in one game. The first flew over a gas station across the street and was hailed as the longest ever hit in the Pacific Northwest. The third went even farther. After playing the saxophone for conjoined twins, he departed for Portland. There he led a parade and played golf with a baseball bat. Naturally, in the game, Ruth hit a home run over a nearby foundry. And so it continued through San Francisco, Oakland, Los Angeles, and San Diego.

It all came to a fitting climax in Anaheim, when Babe pitched one last time head-to-head against Walter Johnson, who hailed from those parts. A detailed description of this extraordinary game is included in Chapter Five, "Hidden Career." When Ruth returned to New York, he began looking forward to the 1925 season. Everyone assumed that Babe Ruth and the Yankees would be back as strong as ever. They would be dead wrong on both counts.

1925   The Yankees finally found their permanent spring training home when they settled in St. Petersburg, Florida, in 1925. After engaging in his customary preparatory activities at Hot Springs, Babe Ruth arrived amidst great excitement on March 1. He participated in grueling workouts the next two days and announced his weight at 225 pounds. But he looked much heavier. Estimates ranged up to 250 pounds, but no one complained, since he played so well.

After a minor setback (a chip fracture in his left hand), Babe was back at full speed by the second exhibition game. That contest was played at Waterfront Park, a first-rate facility. However, a hotel stood directly across the street in right field, and it was decided to keep that building out of play. Accordingly, any ball bounding onto the property was a ground rule double. When Babe's tremendous sixth inning blast on March 18 sailed completely over the expansive width of First Street, it landed on the porch. Even he laughed when he had to stop at second base. The Yanks broke camp on March 25 and faced the Dodgers on March 29 in Montgomery, Alabama, on another field with no fences. It occasioned one more "double for the ages" as Babe pummeled one onto the cinder track in faraway right center. This drive was measured at 497 feet. Starting the month of April, Ruth was playing great and living large.

Games rolled by in Birmingham, Nashville, and Atlanta. Babe seemed unstoppable. Then a warning light went on after the second Atlanta game, when Ruth became ill during the night with chills and fever. A doctor was called in, but he incorrectly diagnosed a recurrence of Babe's annual flu bug. Ruth then hit two homers in Chattanooga on April 5, including one that was immensely long. His next stop was Knoxville, where he continued his bizarre exploits with still another titanic blow into a tree across the street at Caswell Field. Was this guy even human? Sadly, the world would receive a resounding *yes* to that question within twenty-four hours.

The great Ruthian façade crumbled the next morning at the train station in Asheville, North Carolina. Allegedly, Babe had eaten one of his customary huge midnight meals the night before and developed an intense stomachache. The pain worsened throughout the night as he was jostled on the rough train ride over the Smoky Mountains. Arriving in Asheville in the morning, he collapsed. No one thought that the illness was serious, but Ruth was sent ahead to New York as a precaution. After two weeks of tests, it was announced that Babe had a stomach abscess that would require surgery. The operation was performed on April 17 at St. Vincent's Hospital and termed a success. Babe, known as a quick healer, was expected back in the lineup within three weeks, but it didn't happen this time. After two weeks, he could barely sit up in bed. Throughout May, he progressed slowly as the Yankees struggled in the second division. It was ultimately decided that Babe would return to action on June 1 at Yankee Stadium against Washington. It was a bad decision. Ruth simply wasn't ready to compete. When he did return, he played badly. He also behaved recklessly and irresponsibly.

June 1, 1925, was a fateful day in baseball history. Not only did Babe Ruth return to action, but young Lou Gehrig pinch-hit in the eighth inning. The next day Lou started at first base for ailing veteran Wally Pipp and stayed in the Yankee lineup continuously for the next thirteen years. It was the birth of the "Iron Horse." Ruth, however, was more like paper than iron. Over the course of the following three days, he connected solidly four times, but generated no home runs. His best shots were falling short of the fence. Little by little, Babe got stronger, but it was a very slow process. On June 30, Ruth had a total of three homers, and the Yanks were in sixth place with a 29 and 38 record. Even worse, the Babe wasn't himself. The illness had affected his attitude; he wasn't enjoying the game of baseball. He had never been fond of manager Miller Huggins, but now he often snapped at the little fellow for no apparent reason.

On July 1 at Fenway Park in Boston, Ruth hit a pair of four-baggers, and everyone hoped that the worst was over. At Sportsman's Park in St. Louis on July 8, Babe blasted an opposite field shot that topped the left field bleachers and hit the scoreboard. It was the only time that a left-handed batter accomplished this deed in a stadium that remained in use until 1966. Ruth clubbed eight homers in July, but he also missed three games in Cleveland. Publicly, it was said that he was resting, but, in truth, Huggins had benched him after an argument. Understandably, the Yankees wanted Ruth to curb his wild lifestyle and concentrate on baseball. He wouldn't listen to anyone, and bigger problems were on the horizon. New York finished July still in seventh place, and it was obvious that 1925 was a lost season.

Babe made a great diving catch on the Yankee Stadium turf against Detroit on August 7, but wrenched his back in the process. Again, he was slow to heal. More importantly, he didn't try very hard to rehabilitate the injury. He was partying all night and showing up late at the ballpark. When he belatedly breezed into the clubhouse in St. Louis on August 29, Huggins was waiting for him. In fact, the Yankee skipper had already discussed the situation with owner Jacob Ruppert. As a result, Huggins knew in advance that he would have club support if he disciplined their wayward superstar. To his utter amazement, Ruth was suspended indefinitely and fined $5,000 for general misconduct. He went to Chicago to appeal to Commissioner Landis, but the judge had already departed for a vacation. Ruth then returned to New York to plead his case to Ruppert. But the matter had been previously decided, and Babe was told that his fate was in the hands of Miller Huggins. Ruth maintained that he was being made a scapegoat for the team's poor play.

On that point he was probably right. However, he had acted destructively ever since he left the hospital, and a little firmness was overdue. In the end, Huggins got his way, and Babe stayed benched until he apologized. When he returned to the lineup in Boston on September 7, he was the first man on the field. Almost predictably, Ruth celebrated his return with a monstrous home run. In game two of a doubleheader, he connected off Buster Ross, sending a towering drive some thirty-five rows into the bleachers in right center. It was his longest batted ball of the year and the 300th of his career. In the subsequent series in Philadelphia, Babe hit three more homers. He really was playing much better this time, but it was too late to have any real value. The Yankees ended the season in seventh place. Washington won the pennant again, outdistancing New York by an appalling twenty-seven games. Ruth's statistics were a personal nightmare as he batted only .290. He was limited to twenty-five home runs and a .543 slugging average, which were good numbers for other men, but not Babe Ruth. He failed to lead the league in a single offensive category.

In truth, most observers believed that Babe Ruth was over the hill. Who could fault their thinking? The man was thirty years old, and just had his worst season in twelve years as a professional. It's true that he had not been at his physical best, but that was due to illness, not injury. Everyone knew that Ruth burned the candle at both ends, and the prevailing thought was that he was fading prematurely. It was assumed that his glory days were in the past. The Yankees were viewed pretty much the same way. Until a few years before, they had not been a successful franchise. Ruth came along, and meteoric performance led them to three straight pennants. Now that Babe was in decline and other key players were aging, they would likely return to second-rate status. Ruth and the New York Yankees didn't frighten the rest of the American League as they looked ahead to 1926.

Babe decided not to barnstorm that fall, but he did agree to make a few local appearances. He competed at Ahrco Field on Long Island on October 4, where he picked up three base hits, but no homers. However, he smacked one so far in batting practice that the organizers decided to measure it. The final math confirmed a flight of 538 feet. Ruth had not hit a ball that far since his fateful collapse in April. It meant that his strength had returned in full. In addition, his confidence and mental toughness were being reforged. When he became ill, Babe hadn't known how to handle it. But the painful experiences of that year had finally put him in touch with the man he needed to be. He was no intellectual, but he realized that he needed to change. Ruth had always worked hard on the field, but he knew nothing about proper training. Babe needed help, and, in December, he got it in the form of Arthur McGovern. Artie was a former boxer who managed a gymnasium for serious fitness buffs in New York. McGovern had helped Ruth prior to the 1923 season and would now supervise him on an annual basis. Essentially, Babe Ruth had ended the first half of his baseball life and was now starting the second.

The unknown reality was that neither Ruth nor the Yankees had hit their prime yet. Starting in 1926, Babe Ruth would sustain a period of greatness that has never been rivaled in baseball history. Until overtaken by age eight years later, Babe ruled his sport like no one before or since. And his team soared right along with him. The New York Yankees became the single most successful franchise in the annals of team sports. No one knew it in 1925, but they were just learning how to be champions. Lou Gehrig and Earle Combs were on the team, but their quality was still unknown. Guys like Tony Lazzeri, Bill Dickey, and Lefty Gomez were on their way, and they would all learn to be Yankees. They'd put those pinstripes on, and dare other teams to beat them.

The player was now a man, and the team was now a force. They just needed a rival to create sports mythology. Fortunately, that piece of the puzzle was taking shape in Philadelphia. Connie Mack had already built two dynasties, but, due to financial constraints, he could never keep them for long. But Mack was then in the process of creating his last and greatest powerhouse. Al Simmons, Mickey Cochrane, and Lefty Grove were already in place. Jimmie Foxx, George Earnshaw, and others would soon take the field beside them. Over the next seven years, either the Yankees or the Athletics would win the American League pennant every season. When the Yankees didn't win, they were still great. Decades later, *Sports Illustrated* named the Athletics of that era as the best team ever; other experts have identified the Yankees as the greatest. They battled in a crucible of fierce competition and unrivaled pageantry that baseball will not likely see again. In the middle of that whirling landscape strode Babe Ruth.

3

The Wondrous Veteran:

1926–1935

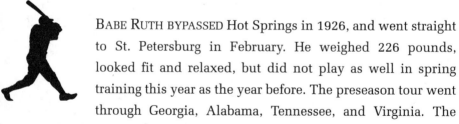BABE RUTH BYPASSED Hot Springs in 1926, and went straight to St. Petersburg in February. He weighed 226 pounds, looked fit and relaxed, but did not play as well in spring training this year as the year before. The preseason tour went through Georgia, Alabama, Tennessee, and Virginia. The Yanks then opened at Fenway Park in Boston with a 12–11 victory as Babe went 3 for 6 with two doubles. In Washington, Walter Johnson pitched an amazing fifteen-inning 1–0 shutout versus the A's, but it was a bittersweet experience. At age forty, that workload in cold temperatures was too much, and the Big Train would never be the same again. Only one week later, Ruth went 5 for 6 against him in D.C. with a home run that flew 100 feet beyond the right field wall. New York won 18–5

as Johnson lasted just three innings. That magnificent warrior retired at
the end of the 1927 season.

Meanwhile, another great fire-baller was emerging to replace
Johnson as Ruth's chief pitching adversary. It was Robert "Lefty" Grove
of the Athletics. Whereas Johnson was gentle and kind, Grove was
explosively short-tempered and confrontational. As his nickname
stated, Grove also pitched from the left side, which gave him an advantage against Ruth. When they met on April 28, 1926, the Yanks won
3–0, but Babe struck out twice. Leading up to his matchup against
Grove, Babe had bashed two tremendous homers near the top of the
right center field bleachers against Boston at Yankee Stadium. New
York finished the month in first place with a 12 and 3 record.

The Yankees stayed close to home in May and enjoyed a good
month. They played three games in Philadelphia, four games in
Boston, and the other twenty-one in New York. Of those twenty-eight
contests, they won nineteen. Ruth slugged twelve home runs and conclusively proved that his power was undiminished. He launched a
number of balls into the upper rows of the vast right field bleachers;
the second of two hit on May 19 landed sixty rows high. But his
longest came in Boston and still reigns as the mightiest ever in Beantown. The bleachers there were 100 feet farther from home plate than
those in New York. Ruth's monumental clout on the 25th came down
five rows from the top or forty-five rows from the bottom. That meant
that it traveled 512 feet horizontally, when it met a wooden bench 28
feet above field level. It was a blow of biblical proportions. Even the
people in Boston, who knew Babe well, were dumbfounded.

In June, the Yankees played in all eight American League cities along
with a few other towns during exhibition appearances. Ruth suffered a
series of nagging leg injuries, but performed heroically. His ten homers
were divided among seven different parks with his longest liftoff on
June 8 in Detroit. That one, off Ulysses S. Grant Stoner, sailed completely

Fenway Park Boston: Babe Ruth hit a ball in 1926 to a place in Fenway Park that no one else has ever approached. *(Philadelphia Athletics Historical Society)*

across Trumbull Avenue in right field, crashing onto the roof of a taxi on Plum Street. That blow has been consistently reported as flying 600 feet, but the facts simply do not support such a claim. After hitting the taxi, the ball bounced several times and then rolled to the end of the block. Perhaps the flight distance and total distance (including the roll) blurred together and became indistinguishable. It is a fact of baseball history that once a home run is reported in a certain way, even grossly overstated, the original report is often accepted as true. If a writer from a major newspaper described a great home run as a "600-footer," the account, regardless of its authenticity, would be told and retold. Over time, it would develop the aura of fact. Baseball lure is replete with such fish stories. This particular drive by Ruth was terrific, flying about 520 feet, but it certainly didn't come close to the traditionally reported length of 600 feet. Babe Ruth needs no hyperbole to reign as the king of all sluggers.

By July, the Yanks had an eight-game cushion, and 1925 seemed like a bad dream. Rookie second baseman Tony Lazzeri was having a fine season, while providing New York with unusual power for his position. In his first full year as a starter, Lou Gehrig was a revelation. He hit sixteen homers along with forty-seven doubles and twenty triples. Just as importantly, he batted behind Ruth and made opposing pitchers think hard before walking the Bambino. Those frequent bases on balls were a recurring frustration for a man of such unbridled spontaneity. During one of his many intentional walks on July 10, Babe couldn't restrain himself; he stepped across the plate to take a cut. He was ruled out for leaving the batter's box. The problem was never completely alleviated, but Gehrig's presence in the lineup helped greatly.

Of Ruth's seven July homers, the last one on the 31st was the best. Confronting a strong incoming Lake Michigan wind at Chicago's Comiskey Park, Babe pounded the ball directly over second base. Center fielder Johnny Mostil had often retreated deep into Comiskey's wide-open center field to rob Ruth of extra bases. As he sped backward, Mostil assumed he would do it again. Against that howling wind, nobody could clear the fence at a distance of 450 feet. And Johnny Mostil could catch anything that stayed inside the park. But to everyone's amazement the ball kept boring through the breeze and passed over the 12-foot fence. Mostil simply shrugged his shoulders.

Ruth and his playmates had not reached their potential in 1926, but neither had the Athletics. Philadelphia was a solid first division club that year, but they were about two years behind New York in their development. The Yankees and Ruth maintained a solid lead over second-place Cleveland throughout August, and the A's followed in the third spot. Entering September, New York and Philly squared off in seven straight games that previewed the next six years. They took turns beating each other as the Yanks won four and lost three. But it was the emerging individual matchups that were the most fun.

A particularly intense level of personal combat was fast developing between Ruth and Lefty Grove. Grove had a blazing fastball and a temper to match; he refused to give Babe any measure of deference or respect. As the years passed and Grove's stature grew, Ruth bristled at comparisons between Lefty and Walter Johnson. According to Babe, there were no comparisons: Johnson was faster and better. Ruth and the Big Train had competed fiercely for years, but there was always mutual admiration between them. When Grove competed against Ruth with hostility, Babe accepted his ground rules. The two battled for years in the way that Ruth and Ty Cobb had waged war. For most of 1926, Babe had little success against Grove; a few base hits, but no home runs. Finally, on September 3 at Shibe Park, that changed. Ruth's fourth-inning towering blast soared so high that it passed almost out of sight. It gave the appearance of being the highest pop-up that anyone had ever seen, except that it came down on an awning on the far side of Twentieth Street. This round went to the Bambino.

When the Yankees arrived in Cleveland for a six-game series on September 15, they led the Indians by five and a half games. With Ruth walking eight times, New York lost four of the first five. Suddenly, the lead was only two and a half games, and that's when Lou Gehrig became a Major League force in a pressure situation. He rapped three doubles and a homer. Lou caused enough damage by the seventh inning that, when Ruth batted, he actually got a sweet pitch to hit. Babe bashed it into deep center field for a home run of his own, and the Yankees won 8–3. They kept plugging away until September 25, when they swept a doubleheader in St. Louis to clinch the pennant. In those two games, Ruth hit a single, double, and three home runs, while walking three times. After what happened in 1925, it was splendid vindication for the man and his team.

Babe had a great comeback season. He led the league in home runs (47), slugging average (.737), total bases (365), walks (144), RBIs (145), and runs (139). He also finished second in batting with a .372 average. Not bad for a guy who was supposedly washed up one year before. The Yankees ended with a record of 91 and 63, which was three games better than Cleveland and eight ahead of Philadelphia. Now they had to face a tough St. Louis Cardinals team in the World Series, a team led by legendary player-manager Rogers Hornsby as well as the resurgent pitching icon Grover Cleveland Alexander. The teams split the first two games at Yankee Stadium, where 63,000 attended both contests. In the second game, thirty-nine-year-old Alexander retired the final twenty-one Yanks in going the distance. The Cardinals won game three, but New York stormed back to win the next game behind Ruth's three titanic home runs. Game five went to the Yanks, and, moving back to New York, St. Louis won again behind the masterful complete game pitching of "Pete" Alexander.

That resulted in a decisive seventh game at The Stadium, where Babe's third-inning homer opened the scoring. Entering the bottom of the seventh, the Cardinals led 3–2. According to legend, Alexander celebrated his second victory the night before and was decidedly hungover. He assumed he wouldn't have to pitch, but he was wrong. When the Yankees loaded the bases, Hornsby called for Alexander, who staggered in from the bullpen. He struck out Tony Lazzeri and held the 3–2 lead until two out in the ninth inning. That's when Babe Ruth came to bat. He had already hit his fourth Series homer and walked three times. The Cardinals decided to walk him again, and take their chances with Bob Meusel, who was not hitting well. Babe took matters into his own hands and tried to steal second base. He was thrown out, and St. Louis won the game and World Series.

Over the decades since 1926, Babe Ruth has received a lot of criticism for his base-running gamble that unsuccessfully ended that World Series. Some even suggest that it was a low point in Babe's career. An understanding of Ruth and the game of baseball suggests otherwise. The man tried to steal second base because his team had to score a run right then. Meusel wasn't likely to get an extra-base hit against Grover Cleveland Alexander. Babe was out on a close play with a perfect throw from the catcher. Even that fact is sometimes misrepresented. It has occasionally been said that Ruth "was out by a mile," which is just plain false. That play was one of the first recorded on film, and modern stop-action conclusively demonstrates the closeness of the play. Either way, that's not the point. The heart of the matter is that Ruth had the guts to try to win, regardless of the risk of criticism.

Along with extraordinary natural ability, athletic courage was the essence of Ruth's greatness. With two strikes, he disdained choking up and still swung for the fences. He understood that the minimal benefit of putting a weak ball into play was not worth reducing his power output on about every third swing. He struck out more than anyone of his era, but produced a higher slugging percentage than anyone in history. He pitched, played the outfield, and ran the bases the same way. Babe relentlessly pursued victory and greatness, and never let fear of failure or ridicule deter him. No one else has tried to steal a base with two outs in the ninth inning of the final game of the World Series. If Ruth hadn't tried to steal that base, the Yankees' chances of winning would have been reduced. If he hadn't possessed the guts to take that chance, Babe Ruth would not have become the game's greatest player.

On the rare occasions that Babe Ruth failed, he showed another of his signature qualities, resilience. The day after losing in the World Series, he started his barnstorming tour by blasting a pair of balls into the street against the Brooklyn Royal Colored Giants in New Jersey. He went on to Wilkes-Barre and hit a demonstration drive so far that it literally cleared two fields located side by side. Games rolled by in Perth Amboy, Scranton, Lima, Kingston, and Montreal, where Ruth struck two home runs. In that same game, he played pitcher, first base, and shortstop, and also umpired an inning. From there, Babe visited Portland, Atlantic Highlands (New Jersey), South Bend, and Des Moines, where he hit three gigantic homers. He ventured to Michigan's Upper Peninsula to play his last game of the year in Iron Mountain on October 28. He somehow summoned the energy to then travel to Minneapolis, where he began twelve weeks on the vaudeville tour. It had been an amazing year. The next year would be better.

1927   After making another movie in Hollywood during February (Ruth made several during his career), Babe returned home to New

York just long enough to sign what was at the time the most lucrative contract in sports history. It was for three years at $70,000 per year, which was more money than most Americans would ever see in their lifetimes. When he arrived in St. Petersburg on March 7 for spring training, Babe weighed 223 pounds and claimed to be in the best shape of his life. Ruth was now thirty-two years old, but he still appeared to be in his athletic prime. In a game against Cincinnati on the 23rd, Babe busted two long homers at Waterfront Park to enhance that image. When the Yanks broke camp a few days later, their spring tour competitors were the same St. Louis Cardinals that had defeated them in the World Series. As expected, the crowds were unusually large. Ruth's all-around play stayed at a high level everywhere he went. When New York hosted Philadelphia on April 12 to open the regular season, there were 72,000 rabid fans expecting a memorable year. They got it.

Yet, Babe fared poorly in that first game facing Lefty Grove. He struck out in his first at-bat, and went 0 for 3 until leaving with dizziness in the sixth inning. New York won anyway, 3–0 behind Waite Hoyt, and they were off and running. Ruth played well the rest of the series as the Yanks won three with one game ending in a tie due to darkness. In game four, Babe hit his first home run and threw out Al Simmons at home from deep right field. When April ended, the Yankees were 9 and 5, and Ruth had four homers.

The itinerary in May was brutal. The Yankees had no scheduled days off. Including exhibition games, there were no breaks until June 6. One of those extra contests was on May 6 in Fort Wayne, Indiana. The Yanks, designated the home team against the Lincoln Lifes, were tied 3–3 in the bottom of the tenth inning. Not only were they in danger of losing to a semipro team, they were worried about missing their train connection to Chicago. No problem. As Ruth walked to the plate amidst a group of adoring children, he matter-of-factly announced to the crowd of 3,500 that he was about to end the game. A moment later, the ball was flying high over the right field fence to the far side of Clinton Street, and the Yankees were heading for the train.

Babe enjoyed a good month of May by cracking twelve home runs and keeping the Yanks in first place. In Washington on the 23rd, Ruth bombed one into the center field bleachers, which were 441 feet from home plate. That was almost as long as the ball he hit into the center field seats in St. Louis on May 11. By the time he arrived at Shibe Park in Philadelphia for a Memorial Day doubleheader, Babe was officially hot. He went 2 for 5 in the morning 9–8 loss, but Connie Mack reverted to form in game two, intentionally passing him in a tight spot. During the walk, Ruth offered to hit one-handed. Maybe the silly gambit actually worked, because Babe got a good pitch to hit in the eleventh inning. He smashed it into the upper deck in left center field to win 6–5. Ruth's four hits and two homers paced New York to a sweep of another twin bill versus Philly the following day. In game two, his tremendous home run onto the housetops across Twentieth Street in the fifth inning turned the contest into a rout. When Babe batted again in the seventh inning, he took one swing right-handed and then turned around to hit a double left-handed. The Yankees were winning, and Ruth was having fun.

In the middle of his pregame batting practice at Yankee Stadium on June 11, Babe stepped away, saying that he "felt a homer coming on" and didn't want to waste it. He walked in his first at-bat, not getting a chance to swing. In the third inning, however, Ruth saw one he liked and bombed it almost to the scoreboard atop the right center field seats. Still facing Cleveland's Garland Buckeye in the fifth, he walloped a pitch to the top of the towering right field bleachers and almost out of The Stadium. As Ruth rounded the bases, Indians catcher Luke Sewell made an impromptu inspection of Babe's bat. He discovered nothing except that he had a harder time lifting it than he did his own bat. During his career, Ruth used bats ranging from 54 ounces, when he was young, to 38 ounces at the time he retired. The one Sewell examined was about 44 ounces and was the heaviest in play at that time. Babe called it "Black Betsy."

In the first of two games at Fenway Park on June 22, Ruth slugged a pair of enormous homers. The first hit a building across the street near the flagpole just left of center, and the second went through the opening in the old right center field bleachers before colliding with a garage on one bounce. The next day Lou Gehrig hit three home runs, prompting folks to start taking notice of his long ball proficiency. Lou had struck the ball hard all through 1926, but finished with the unspectacular total of seventeen four-baggers. It was different this year. Some of last season's doubles and triples were carrying into the seats for home runs.

When the Yankees stopped in Springfield, Massachusetts, for another exhibition game, Babe walloped two dingers and smacked a right-handed double. It was cute stuff except that Ruth wrenched his right knee and missed four straight regular season games. He returned on June 29, going 4 for 5 in New York. All four hits were smoked, and his only out was driven so hard that it ripped the first baseman's glove. Babe concluded the month with a home run to give him twenty-five for the season. The Yanks were ten games ahead at 49 and 20, and that guy named Gehrig also had twenty-five home runs.

On the Fourth of July at Yankee Stadium, a record throng of 72,641 attended the doubleheader with the Senators. Ruth collected five hits, but none were home runs. That is not to say that he didn't unleash his great power. His triple in game two flew over Tris Speaker's head by about forty feet and bounced against the bleacher wall beyond the center field flagpole. It was a blow of some 475 feet. The Yankees then left on a western road trip with exhibition stops in Buffalo, Toronto, St. Paul, and Johnstown, Pennsylvania. Playing left field in Detroit on July 9, Ruth felt that a Tiger fan had interfered with him while he was trying to make a play. He argued the no-call for five minutes with his cap turned sideways. The next time up the crowd booed him mercilessly. Babe calmly plastered the ball to the top of the bleachers just right of center field for his third homer in two days. Those same fans then cheered him lustily as he circled the bases.

Returning home on July 26, Ruth went 7 for 9 including two long homers in a doubleheader against the Browns. His overall play was beautiful to behold. On the 30th, he threw out a runner at home plate from the right field embankment that was described by the *New York Times* as a "perfect strike." As the month ended, there was no pennant drama as the Yanks had already made a shambles of the race. But there was a duel that was generating tremendous interest all around the country. Who would be the home run king in 1927? At that point, Ruth had thirty-four, but upstart teammate Lou Gehrig had thirty-five.

On August 5 in the Bronx, Babe hit what the *New York World* called "the longest two-bagger ever." This ball hit the fence in dead center on the first hop, having flown about 480 feet. Hitting Herculean drives that did not result in home runs was getting to be an annoying habit. Just six days prior, Ruth struck two balls in the same game that were caught near the flagpole. There was nothing he could do but keep pounding the ball like nobody else, letting others worry about the details. Leaving on their next trip, the then-called "Bronx Bombers" stopped at Association Park in Indianapolis. Ruth's breathtaking homer on this day soared high over the right field boundary, and landed half a block away beside a coal car. One such epic homer in a lifetime would be a thrill to most athletes, but Babe bettered it the following day in Chicago on August 16.

A new double-deck outfield grandstand had been erected at Comiskey Park earlier that year. The architect had predicted that no one would ever hit a ball onto the roof of that 75-foot-high structure. It was symmetrical, and located 365 feet away along both foul lines. Ruth started the day by squelching a first inning Sox rally with a perfect throw home from deep left field. He also doubled and walked twice. Not bad, but just a tease for his fifth-inning exploit. Facing Tommy Thomas, he launched a missile to right field that easily surpassed the grandstand roof. The ball traveled with unabated speed, and landed in an adjoining parking lot. Incredibly, the *New York Herald Tribune* stated that this superhuman drive was hit against the wind. Four days later at League Park in Cleveland, Babe blasted another homer almost as far. For the month, Ruth hit nine four-baggers, and led Gehrig 43 to 41.

This aerial view of Comiskey Park shows the landing point of Babe Ruth's epic home run on August 16, 1927. It was the first drive to clear the two-tier outfield grandstand. *(National Baseball Hall of Fame Library, Cooperstown, New York)*

On September 2 in Philadelphia, Ruth lined his forty-fourth homer over the center field fence, but Lou added his forty-second and forty-third. The next day Babe had two singles and a 425-foot fly out to center as Lefty Grove blanked the Yankees 1–0 for their only shutout that year. Then, in a Labor Day doubleheader in Boston, Ruth was limited to just one double as Gehrig caught up with his forty-fourth home run. Yet another twin bill followed on September 6, and "Buster" Gehrig did the unthinkable by passing Babe Ruth with homer number forty-five. One inning after Gehrig passed him, the mighty Bambino came roaring back with all the power and majesty of the king he truly was.

Babe stepped up to bat in game one's sixth inning with a strong wind blowing from left to right field. Ruth timed an offering from Tony Welzer and savagely smashed it through the breeze just left of straight-away center field. The ball raced on and on, easily clearing the high wall over 400 feet away. It touched down after a ride of at least 500 feet.

The writers in the press box gulped hard and tried to figure out if they had just witnessed yet another "longest ever" Ruthian drive. Some said yes, others invoked the recent memory of the two that Babe had blasted on June 22, while still others opted for Babe's homer of May 25, 1926. Ultimately, their only consensus was that they had never seen any human being hit a baseball nearly as hard as Babe Ruth. Before the Yanks left Boston the following day, Babe had left Lou completely in the dust by clubbing four more impressive homers. Gehrig would add only two more circuits to his season's log, but Ruth was now taking aim on his 1921 record of fifty-nine.

Babe's fiftieth home run was hit on September 11 at Yankee Stadium, where New York was scheduled to play the rest of their games. It resulted in a fusillade of straw hats thrown onto the field that necessitated a three-minute cleanup. For the first time, Ruth acknowledged that he had a chance at the record. But he cautioned that it would only be possible if opposing pitchers gave him some decent balls to hit. Probably due to the lack of a pennant race, he got his wish. In the remaining seventeen games, Babe walked only nine times. He was locked in, bashing seven more out of the park in the next fourteen games. With the nation watching, Ruth needed three home runs in his three final games. Would he do it? If anyone needs an example of rising to the occasion, look no further than September 29, 1927 at Yankee Stadium. Under great pressure and scrutiny, Babe Ruth hit the baseball as if he were a character out of fiction. He officially went 3 for 5 with two home runs, but that doesn't tell the whole story. Babe also flied out to the right center field fence, blasted two balls just foul into the right field bleachers, and tripled off the fence in right center field. In all, the man hit six balls for home run distance in this single contest. When Ruth connected for Number Sixty the next day, it had already been assumed.

It was also anticipated that the Yankees would demolish the Pittsburgh Pirates in the World Series. And that's pretty much what happened. They won four straight games with Babe batting .400 and whacking two homers. It was the only way this magical season could have ended. For the year, Ruth batted .356 and slugged .772. Along with his sixty homers, Babe drove in 164 runs and scored 158 more. As a team, the New York Yankees won 110 games, which is an astounding total for a 154-game schedule. Lou Gehrig became the game's newest superstar with his forty-seven home runs and 175 RBIs. After such an amazing year, only an extraordinary barnstorming tour would suffice. And that's what Babe and Buster accomplished. The two were now almost inseparable. Their season of long competition had drawn them closer together instead of apart. Ruth played the role of the world-wise older brother, and Gehrig the dutiful protégé. They toured across the country, playing twenty-one games in nineteen cities, ending in southern California. Along the way, Babe Ruth walloped twenty home runs and earned $70,000. It was a year out of a sportswriter's imagination, but it really happened. Could anything top it? No. Not really. But 1928 wouldn't be bad either.

1928   Arriving in St. Petersburg on February 26, 1928, Babe Ruth announced that he wanted to hit sixty-one home runs and win the World Series again. After playing multiple rounds of golf waiting for the official opening of spring training, he eventually picked up his bat on March 6 at newly renovated Crescent Lake Park. Ruth promptly knocked six balls into the lake. He weighed 224 pounds and looked fit. Babe stayed healthy all spring, but hit few long balls until leaving Florida. Playing in Montgomery on April 1, he became the first player ever to reach the center field fence atop the embankment with his mighty triple. Three days later in Charlotte, Ruth performed another first by actually blasting one of his two center field homers over the flagpole. Everything was ready for opening day on April 11 at Shibe Park.

In that first game, Babe hit a long center field triple as the Yanks defeated the A's and Lefty Grove in uncomfortably cold weather. However, Grove and his mates retaliated by beating New York 2–1 in their home opener on Friday, April 20, before 55,000 disappointed fans.

With better weather and a weekend date, the attendance would have been much higher. In the off-season, the Yanks had increased The Stadium's capacity by more than 10,000 seats. The construction of a three-tiered grandstand in left field came just in time to support the team's emerging rivalry with Philadelphia. Babe had a decent month with four home runs, and the Yankees assumed first place with a 10 and 3 record. Ruth also managed to squeeze in one of his many return trips to Baltimore, where he always seemed to play his best. Playing an exhibition game on the 15th, he struck a homer that sailed over the clock near center field and collided with a telephone pole.

Babe began the month of May in grand fashion by going 4 for 5 at Griffith Stadium in Washington, D.C. His homer landed high in the bleachers in dead center, generating the usual debate about which of Ruth's many such blows was his longest. Back at Yankee Stadium three days later, Babe went 4 for 4 with a bunt single and home run deep into the seats in right center. On the 10th, Ruth's three-run sixth inning homer beat Cleveland 4–2, and this drive was historic. Depending on how one defines "opposite field," Babe may have hit the longest-ever opposite field home run on this occasion. He definitely hit some to left center field that went farther, but this ball went to dead left field. Actually, we can still envision this drive, since it was hit to a part of Yankee Stadium that hasn't changed much in the intervening years. Look out to the center field end of the left field grandstand, and picture a line drive crashing into the seats just under the mezzanine. It's about 460 feet to that point, and the ball still had a little flight left in it. It was definitely "opposite field" by any definition. Very few modern right-handed power hitters have reached that spot, which adds perspective. Cleveland general manager and former Hall of Fame umpire Billy Evans added further color to the event by describing the pitch that Ruth hit as "high and a foot outside."

For the month, Babe clubbed fifteen homers, but his triple on the final day may have been more fun than any of them. Facing the Senators in the fifth inning with Leo Durocher on first base, Ruth blasted a tremendous drive to the cavernous left center field at The Stadium. Left fielder Goose Goslin got a good jump, as he started off in pursuit, causing Durocher to hold between first and second base. The ball finally landed just out of Goslin's reach on the embankment about 460 feet away. By that time, Ruth was standing next to Durocher, and they both took off like a pair of bank robbers. Goslin retrieved the ball and threw it to his first relay man, *center* fielder Red Barnes. He threw it to shortstop Bobby Reeves, who tossed it to first baseman Joe Judge. That was three relays, and they still weren't finished. Judge finally threw the ball to catcher Muddy Ruel, who missed Durocher, but tagged out the sliding Ruth on a close play. It's extremely unlikely that any of us will ever see such a play in a professional ballgame, since we don't have any ballparks with 470-foot power alleys. Of course, even if we did, would anybody other than Babe Ruth find a way into such an implausible scenario?

Playing at Comiskey Park in Chicago on June 10, Ruth continued his uniquely high level of opposite field power (along with his flair for entertainment). He hit two home runs, including one into the left center field upper deck. Once again, that was a difficult task for a strong batsman from the right side. During the game, fans approached Ruth four times in left field to shake his hand. That was not encouraged in those days, but it wasn't cause for automatic fan ejection as it is now. In Babe's case, it happened on a regular basis. Folks approached him for handshakes, backslaps, autographs, or whatever else they fancied in a momentary meeting. Since he didn't seem to mind, officials never made any serious effort to prevent it. Two days later, Ruth drove another ball into the left center field upper deck, but Lou Gehrig stole the show with two triples and two home runs.

After playing exhibition games in Johnstown and Harrisburg, Pennsylvania, the Yankees went to Philadelphia on June 27 for three games. Babe Ruth never hit four home runs in a Major League game, but he came close a number of times, including game two of this series. He smashed two homers over the scoreboard in right center field, but two other drives in the same direction missed by inches. Ty Cobb, who would retire at the end of this season, was in right field that day, and he retrieved one of Babe's drives that had been lined off the top of the right center field fence. In probably his final act of competitive defiance toward Ruth, Cobb then leaped high at the fence to snare another near homer off Babe's bat. Ruth closed out the month with eleven more circuit clouts, which put him on pace to break the record again. He would eventually slow down, but not for a while. New York was in first place with an eleven-game advantage over Philadelphia, and no other team was anywhere near contention.

Throughout July, Babe battled an intense heat wave as well as lingering back and shoulder injuries. He still accumulated forty-four base hits and eleven home runs. Two of those four-baggers were noteworthy: one for drama and the other for brute force. The dramatic homer was hit in New York on July 18 with the White Sox ahead in the ninth inning. The score was 8–6, and two were on with two out. Ruth victimized future Hall of Famer Ted Lyons, lining one of his fastballs into the right field bleachers. As he circled the bases, a mob of spectators rushed onto the field to run alongside their hero.

The especially forceful home run was launched at Fenway Park on the 23rd. It came in the sixth inning against Deacon Danny MacFayden, and finally ended the debate that had started the previous September 6. Onlookers concluded that they had just seen Ruth's longest-ever center field homer in Boston. The ball flew over the old 30-foot-high wooden wall just left of straightaway center field on almost the exact same line as the one in 1927. It then carried across Lansdowne Street and landed on top of the two-story garage. Babe had reached that building before, but not quite so far to center field. This astonishing drive flew well over 500 feet. When July ended, the Yankees' lead over the Athletics had shrunk to five and a half games.

The two teams did not meet in August, but Philly kept up the pressure. Ruth played well, although his home run production decreased. He belted six for the month with his mightiest coming on the 15th in

New York. That ball flew heavenward in a towering parabola, appearing momentarily to have disappeared out of Yankee Stadium. Then the high-flying horsehide came to rest in the uppermost rows of the right field bleachers. When August concluded, the Yankees' lead was down to only two games. Much of the problem centered on crippling arm injuries to star pitcher Herb Pennock and slugging second baseman Tony Lazzeri. In any case, the Yankees were definitely concerned, and they started looking ahead to the A's impending visit to the Bronx.

New York continued to slide in the first week of September until Babe won their September 8 battle against Washington with a late homer. But on that same day, Philadelphia won two games, taking over first place on the eve of their four-game set in New York. The town was in an absolute frenzy for the Sunday doubleheader showdown the following afternoon. All tickets were long since sold, and, counting standing-room admissions, an immense throng of 85,265 packed into Yankee Stadium to watch baseball history. The New York City police department estimated that 100,000 others had been turned away. In batting practice, Ruth and Gehrig put on an awesome show that even impressed the Athletics. The Yankee lineup was something to behold, but the A's were pretty potent themselves. Entering the series, Connie Mack warned almost all his pitchers not to challenge Babe with any fastball strikes. With that strategy, they pretty much held him in check that day. Ruth went 1 for 6 with a double off the right field fence and two intentional walks. But the other Yanks contributed enough to win both games by scores of 5–0 and 7–3. New York had edged back into first place, and would now face Lefty Grove in game three.

This would be the critical game in the series. Lefty had won fourteen straight decisions and would not back down to anyone. Mack placed no restrictions on his flame-throwing ace, smiling at the thought of a man-to-man confrontation between Grove and Ruth. Another 51,400 fans from both cities attended the next meeting, and it was a beauty. Going into the bottom of the eighth inning, the Athletics led 3–1, and Grove had been masterful. Ruth had struck out, walked, and grounded out. But then Lefty allowed a few bloop hits. Suddenly he found himself facing Babe in a tie game with a man on second. This was the scene that everyone wanted to see. Ruth versus Grove. Power against power. With the count at one ball and one strike, Lefty reached back and unfurled a blistering fastball that could barely be seen. Babe swung from his heels, and the next sound was like two speeding locomotives in a head-on collision. The ball sped away from Ruth's massive bat straight to the fortieth row of the bleachers in right field. The crowd was delirious. They threw everything they could get their hands on and raised the noise level to a din that could be heard back at Shibe Park. The Yanks won 5–3, and, even though Philadelphia won the last game, it had been a life-saving series for New York. They were back on track.

Philadelphia Athletics 1928: arguably the most impressive roster in Major League history. *(Philadelphia Athletics Historical Society)*

Both teams then left on road trips to the four western towns in the American League. They stayed in place in the standings for two weeks with New York traveling to Detroit on September 27 for their final season series. In those four games, Ruth uncorked four prodigious home runs, and the Yankees finally clinched the pennant. New York won 101 games, and Philadelphia won 98. These A's were a genuinely great team and would prove that time and again during the next few years. Now it was back to the World Series for New York, where they would get a chance to avenge their 1926 defeat to the St. Louis Cardinals.

The first two games were played at Yankee Stadium in front of huge crowds. Despite limping from a late-season knee injury, Ruth was splendid. In those games, he went 5 for 7 with three long doubles as New York won by scores of 4–1 and 9–3. Moving on to St. Louis on October 7 for the third contest, Babe's limp appeared worse. He ripped a powerful drive to the base of the center field fence, but was held to a single. However, when the Cardinals turned a double play with Ruth on second base, they were reminded never to underestimate this man. He saw a split-second opportunity and headed for home. The ball arrived just before he did, but Babe bowled over catcher Jimmie Wilson and scored. The Yanks won 7–3 with Lou Gehrig hitting two home runs. In game four, Ruth was overpowering. Batting in the seventh inning against twenty-one-game winner Bill Sherdel, he had already hit a homer. "Wee Willie" Sherdel was known for "quick pitching" unwary batters, but he had been warned by league officials not to try it during the Series. He snuck a quick one past Ruth for an apparent strikeout, but the umpire ruled the play as an illegal pitch. The Cards and their fans were furious, but Sherdel had to pitch again to Babe. This time Babe was ready for the ball, which was soon sailing far over the right field pavilion for home run number two.

When Ruth returned to left field in the bottom half of the inning, the hometown faithful were still in a rage about the Sherdel ruling. Babe Ruth was at the epicenter of those seething emotions, and, predictably, the fans vented their feelings at his expense. As Babe took his position, he was booed mercilessly. Worse than that, soda bottles were thrown at him. What to do? Ruth was no dummy, and certainly understood the danger of his situation. The natural inclination would be to call time out and run off the field until authorities controlled the vengeful throng. How did Babe Ruth handle the threat? He walked over to one of the bottles, and, picking it up, pretended that he was taking a refreshing drink. He then laughed, and waved gratefully to the watchful crowd. The next move was up to them.

Surprised at Babe's reaction, the fans did nothing at first. Then slowly, little by little, they began laughing themselves. By the end of the inning, the problem had been completely defused, and the crowd actually clapped for Ruth as he returned to the dugout. As if on cue, Babe then blasted his third home run before resuming his defensive duties. St. Louis baseball fans have long been regarded as among the most knowledgeable in baseball circles. And so it was on October 9, 1928. They knew they were witnessing a performance for the ages. When Ruth ran back to left field, where he had been attacked and vilified fifteen minutes earlier, he was now passionately and lovingly cheered. Ruth soon closed out the Series with a great running catch in foul ground in the ninth inning. The Yankees had won consecutive World Series in four game sweeps, and no team has yet to duplicate that accomplishment.

In the Series, Babe batted .625 and slugged 1.375! Who could blame him for instigating a wild and raucous celebration party on the train ride back to New York? For the season, Ruth totaled 54 home runs, while attaining a batting average of .323. Based upon his 380 total bases in 536 at-bats, Babe's slugging percentage was .709. He knocked in 142 runs and personally scored 163 times. Those numbers explained why at age thirty-three Babe Ruth was still the best baseball player on the planet.

Once again, Babe and Lou Gehrig capitalized on their World Series success with an ambitious barnstorming tour. It started in Brooklyn two days after the Series ended and worked its way north into Canada. Back in Watertown, New York, on October 22, Ruth had his best day of the post-season. He clubbed three home runs over the racetrack in right center and then campaigned for Democratic presidential candidate Al

Smith. The trip then headed west through Louisville and Dayton before wrapping up in Denver. By November 5, Babe was home in New York applying for a resident hunting and fishing license. It was time to relax. Fortune had again smiled on Babe Ruth and the Yankees in 1928, but the Philadelphia Athletics were already waiting for the next season to start.

1929   When Babe Ruth worked out for the first time of the '29 season on March 4 at Crescent Lake Park, he was atop the sporting world. At a reasonably fit 230 pounds, he seemed invincible. But something was troubling Ruth that set off a disturbing chain of events. Babe was Catholic, and he and his wife Helen had never divorced despite years of separation. When she died unexpectedly in a fire in suburban Boston on January 11, 1929, Ruth was racked with guilt and sadness. He had lived in New York for years and had established a permanent romantic relationship with another woman. As Babe practiced and played through spring training, he was carrying a heavy emotional burden.

The Yankees chose that particular year to schedule an unusually grueling series of preseason games that took them 4,500 miles by way of Alabama, Texas, Oklahoma, Arkansas, Georgia, and North Carolina. On April 4, in Waco, Texas, 11,000 fans showed up at Katy Field, which had a seating capacity of 4,000. In order to accommodate everyone, a section of right field was roped off for standing room. That's where Babe's double struck a boy on the head, whereupon the contest was delayed as the child was escorted to Ruth for amends. Thankfully, the child was not seriously injured, and he made out just fine. He got to meet The Babe, and had the ball autographed. When the Yankees finally arrived back in New York, they still had two more practice games. The Bombers squared off against the Brooklyn Dodgers at Ebbets Field, where Ruth belted two homers. The second flew so far over the right field wall and Bedford Avenue that it was labeled the longest drive ever launched in Flatbush.

Babe Ruth's great preseason home run at Brooklyn's Ebbets Field in 1929. *(Philadelphia Athletics Historical Society)*

Babe's return to Gotham also reunited him with Claire Hodgson, who had been his "significant other" since he separated with Helen. The two decided it was time to marry. That was on April 17, and the Yankees opened the 1929 season the next afternoon at Yankee Stadium. On his first at-bat, Ruth hit a line drive over the 402-foot sign in front of the left field grandstand for an auspicious home run. As he crossed home plate, Babe blew a kiss to Claire, who was watching from a nearby box seat. After the 7–3 victory, Ruth was mobbed by hundreds of children, who made it difficult to leave the field. In a newspaper article the next day, Babe acknowledged his love for the kids, but added presciently: "They're hard on a fellow's health."

After playing in Philadelphia on Saturday, April 27, the Yanks appeared the next day in Washington before returning to Philly on Monday. The prohibition against Sunday baseball in the Quaker City created absolute havoc in scheduling. From there, they went to New York and then swung through the west. They returned home for seven games, and then visited Boston and Washington. During that time, there were no days off. As usual, there were breaks in the official American League calendar, but the Yankees filled every open date with an exhibition game. In fact, there were no real respites until June 24. In May alone, the Yankees played exhibitions in Pittsburgh, Binghamton, New Haven, Hartford, and Chambersburg. At each of those stops, Babe Ruth was the focal point of a celebration that invariably was the highlight of the year for that community.

After the game in Chambersburg on May 31, Ruth complained of illness and back pain. He stayed in the lineup two more days, but then finally succumbed to a physical and nervous breakdown. When questioned about the cause, Babe made specific reference to the rigors of the exhibition appearances. He endured demands beyond anything imposed on any other player, but the events of that spring conspired to push him beyond his seemingly inexhaustible limits. Babe Ruth was human, too. At the time, no one knew just how sick he really was. His nerves were shot, and he was experiencing heart murmurs. Ruth should have rested for three months, but, after resting for three weeks, he returned to serious action against the rampaging Philadelphia Athletics on June 21 at Yankee Stadium.

Without Ruth, New York had no chance against Philadelphia. For that reason, he resumed play in a pressure-packed doubleheader before a Friday crowd of 66,145 against Lefty Grove. While Grove prevailed in game one 11–1, Babe stormed back with two homers and seven RBI for an 8–3 win in the nightcap. With Ruth playing, New York salvaged two games out of five against their current archrival, and then headed for D.C. There on June 26, Babe went 4 for 5 featuring a gigantic center field home run and a spectacular diving catch. Concluding that series, New York traveled to Philadelphia for a three-game set on A's turf. Game one went to Philly. Game two was rained out. Game three again brought the Yankees and Ruth face-to-face with Lefty Grove, who had a nine-game winning streak. Shibe Park was stuffed to overflowing with 40,000 rabid fans. Another three or four thousand viewed the proceedings from the rooftops across Twentieth Street beyond right field. The Athletics smelled the blood of the wounded champions. But Babe Ruth wasn't dead; he was merely tired. And that was not enough to stop him from blasting two home runs against an incredulous Grove. New York won on the shoulders of the Bambino, but even he couldn't carry them all the way to another pennant.

In truth, the Philadelphia Athletics were just too good for the Yanks that year. The biggest difference between 1928 and 1929 was the emerging stardom of starting pitcher George Earnshaw and first baseman Jimmie Foxx. During Ruth's career, there was only one man who could rival him for pure power. That man was Double X from the farmlands of Maryland's Eastern Shore. Just as the Athletics of that time may be the most underrated team in history, Foxx is probably the least-heralded of the game's true superstars. That year he batted .354 and hit thirty-three home runs, some of which approached Ruthian proportions. He could play any position and run like a young stallion. And Jimmie was only twenty-one years old.

Another interesting development in the 1929 season was the use of numbers on players' uniforms for the first time. The Yankees were the organization to initially employ this system of identification. They assigned numbers according to a player's position in the batting order. Since Babe Ruth batted third, he was given number three with Lou Gehrig wearing number four, designating his clean-up role. Accordingly, if anyone looks at old film and sees Ruth with a number on his back, it should be understood that Babe was at least thirty-four years of age.

In early July, Babe played outstanding baseball, but he pulled a leg muscle on the 17th that caused him to miss five more games. After returning on July 24, he remained healthy for the duration of the season. Ruth belted a twelfth-inning home run about fifty rows into the right field bleachers in New York on the 28th, and again found himself engulfed in backslapping fans as he circled the bases. Three days later, Babe participated in another of the seemingly endless ways of exhibiting him to the public. Back in 1912, a pitcher by the name Big Ed Walsh set the fungo-hitting distance record at 418 feet. Walsh was a premier hurler for the Chicago White Sox in his day and had once won forty games in a season. On this occasion, his son was the starting pitcher for the visiting White Sox, and Yankee management could not resist the chance to sell a few extra tickets. From near home plate, Ruth fungoed several balls toward the center field bleachers. The result was predictable. His best shot sailed 447 feet, thereby smashing the seventeen-year-old standard by a 29-foot differential. Such diversions were probably a good idea, since, by the end of July, the Yankees trailed the Athletics by ten games.

If the Yankee organization ever feared for Ruth's well-being as a result of his May illness, they got over it rather quickly. By August, everything was back to normal. Babe played awesome baseball and took center stage in exhibition games. On August 2, he swatted a 460-foot triple to left center at the Stadium. That was fine, but twice in recent days Ruth hit comparable balls that had been caught for outs. No Yankee slugger before the Stadium's renovation in the 1970s escaped the specter of those daunting dimensions. On the 9th, Babe fully returned to form by playing an exhibition game in Albany. There was a sellout gathering of 10,000 at Chadwick Park, who saw Ruth blast the first-ever homer over the center field fence near the flagpole. When the game ended, Babe was seen leading a troop of Boy Scouts from the field.

The following day in Cleveland, Ruth pounded a mammoth drive to right field. That blow soared far over the high wall and was last seen clearing a house on the far side of Lexington Avenue. Of all American League stadiums, this was the hardest place to evaluate Ruth's drives for great distance. It was about 370 feet to the houses outside the park, but there was no way to follow the ball beyond those structures. Everyone agreed that this hit traveled a considerable distance past the houses, but we can never know just how far. The next day Babe poked his 500th career home run over the same high right field wall, but this one didn't fly so far. It was recovered by a passerby, who traded it to Ruth for $20 and an autographed ball. When the month ended, Babe had the satisfaction of hitting fourteen home runs, but his proud Yankees were eleven games behind the high-flying A's.

September 1, 1929, was a Sunday, and the Yankees played the Red Sox at Braves Field instead of Fenway Park. There were still some residual restrictions on Sabbath baseball, and Fenway was too close to a church for such competition. Babe smoked a first-inning line drive that day that carried to the top of the seats in dead center field. Until just the year before, it had been 550 feet to the deepest center field angle. The Braves prudently erected bleachers in that vast wasteland, shortening the boundary to about 400 feet. Accordingly, it was 450 feet away and 30 feet up at the spot where Ruth's blow landed beneath some ad signs. It was quite a poke. As was often the case, the burning question was whether this homer or Babe's almost identical shot on June 30 had been the mightiest ever in those grounds.

There was no such debate four days later when Ruth and the Yankees played the inmates at Sing Sing Prison on the Hudson River. Babe smacked three homers that afternoon, but it was his first that is still being discussed today. It roared over the forty-foot outer wall and past a machine-gun tower in the center. The ball then crossed the New York Central railroad tracks and landed high on an overlooking hill. Since that ball field has since been removed, there is some debate about the exact distance, but it was at least 520 feet. Babe recorded countless "longest ever" distance records, but this one authored inside a prison ranks among the most unusual.

The Yankees were just playing out the schedule when manager Miller Huggins died prematurely of erysipelas at age fifty on September 25. He and Ruth had never been friends, but Babe had grown to respect Huggins. There was some talk about Ruth succeeding Huggins as manager, but nothing ever came of it. Former Yankee pitcher Bob Shawkey was named to the post in the following month, and Babe never did get a chance to lead a Major League team. He finished that season with remarkable statistics considering all the time he lost due to illness and injury. Ruth played in 135 games, hitting forty-six home runs. He also batted .345 and slugged .697. Along the way, Babe drove in 154 runs and scored 121 times. The Yankees won a respectable eighty-eight games, but the Athletics blew away the field with 104 victories.

In view of the stressful nature of the past several months, Ruth decided not to barnstorm in 1929. He first attended the World Series between the Athletics and Chicago Cubs, which the A's won in five games. Babe then went home to his new bride. He did play in a select few games in the New York area, but mostly enjoyed the domestic life that had eluded him in the past. By all accounts, Ruth's marriage to Claire was very successful, and afforded him much-needed stability. Babe would be thirty-five when he next took the field, and it was crucial that he take care of his personal resources. With Claire's help, he did. He had already accomplished more than any other ballplayer, but Ruth cherished his role as America's top sports hero. He intended to prove all over again in 1930 that he was the greatest baseball player in the world.

1930   By February, most of the stress and strain of the year before had faded in the life of Babe Ruth. He and Claire arrived early in Florida, and Babe had a good time fishing and playing golf. When Ruth worked out for the first time on March 3 in St. Pete's, he looked hale and hearty. For some reason, there was no official announcement about his weight, but veteran Ruth watchers estimated it at 230 pounds. His early batting practice showed the usual great power, but, more important, he looked faster than he had been in the past few seasons. A week later, Babe signed the best contract of his career. It was for two years at $80,000 per annum, which was a king's ransom in those hard economic times. The agreement also stipulated that Ruth would receive 50 percent of the gate receipts from all exhibition games. It was a long-overdue concession by the Yankees. Babe's crucial service in that aspect of the club's operation had gone mostly unrewarded for a decade.

Once again, the Yankees embarked on a demanding spring tour at the close of camp. They scheduled eighteen games in eighteen days across seven states, including seven different cities in Texas. In one of the two Houston games, a fan in a box seat pleaded with Babe to smack a homer, which Ruth proceeded to do. When Babe touched home plate, the man was standing there looking over at him as if he had descended from heaven. Two days later in San Antonio, Babe hit a distance-record home run, and, three days after that, did the same thing in Wichita Falls. When Babe tore a calf muscle in Dallas on April 6, he was ordered to rest for a week. He hated the thought of disappointing fans, especially those who rarely had a chance to see him play.

So, two days later in Memphis, Ruth limped up to bat in the first inning and smashed the ball so hard that it broke the wooden right field fence. He managed to hobble to first base, where he was replaced by a pinch runner. Babe then ambled to a side gate, where a taxi returned him to his hotel room. As he left, Ruth smiled and waved to the crowd, who were overjoyed at the memories that this amazing man had just created. He had performed for about thirty seconds, but no one felt cheated. In order to play the next day in Nashville, Babe spent most of his time in left field sitting in a rocking chair and signing autographs. Ruth then played a few innings in Chattanooga after a morning appearance at Lookout Mountain of Civil War fame. Hitting a fungo off Umbrella Rock, Ruth launched one high into the air that landed at the bottom of the slope. It was officially recorded as a drive of 2,656 feet. Babe took hitting seriously, but laughed hilariously at the thought of folks hearing about that one.

By opening day in Philadelphia on April 15, it seemed as though the Yanks had already played a season of baseball. But they were now facing the champion Athletics and Lefty Grove, which rudely reminded them that this was the real thing. In front of the usual Yanks–A's sellout at Shibe Park, Ruth flied out to deep center in his first at-bat of the year. Batting again in the third inning, Babe turned around a Grove fastball, lining it deep to right center field. As it soared over the scoreboard, Ruth settled into a trot to enjoy his first home run. Suddenly, there was a crashing metallic sound, and the ball mysteriously appeared back on the field. Standing on second base, the confused Bambino was advised that the ball had struck a loudspeaker on top of a pole above the scoreboard. That object was located about 400 feet away and 20 feet high. Babe clearly deserved his homer, but there was no ground rule covering this eventuality, and the umpires had no choice but to rule the ball in play. Ruth argued the unfairness of the situation, but, at that moment, he had no idea just how unfair it was. For that he would have to wait until the end of the season. The Yankees wound up losing the ballgame 6–3.

A week later, the Athletics came to Yankee Stadium for the Bombers' home opener in front of 66,000 New Yorkers. As Babe batted in the bottom of the ninth inning, there were two out with one man on and the Yankees trailing 7–6. Ruth belted one high and deep to right center field, another smash that appeared to be a sure home run. And this one would be a game winner. But for the second time in a week, fate intervened; this time in the form of a sudden incoming breeze. As he neared second base, Babe realized that center fielder Mule Haas had caught his drive against the fence. The Yanks lost again, and Ruth was angry. The Athletics would find out just how angry the next time the two rivals met. For the month, Ruth finished with only two homers, while New York was 3 and 8.

April may have frustrated Babe Ruth, but the month of May would make amends. On the 4th, he blasted the first of thirteen homers, a shot that almost reached the top of the right field seats. Ruth played well through the rest of the long home stand, but was looking forward to returning to Philadelphia. He had to stop in Boston first, and passed the time by powering one of the longest line drives ever seen. It was hit in a Sunday game at Braves Field and carried to the top of the right field bleachers known as the "jury box." That was 435 feet away, but the ball was still screaming at a height of about 40 feet. Most observers judged that if left unimpeded, the ball would have struck the armory

across the street. It was a great way to get ready for back-to-back dou-
bleheaders at Shibe Park three days later.

In his first at-bat in game one against George Earnshaw, Babe
knocked the ball over the right field fence into Twentieth Street. Earnshaw bore down in their next encounter in the third inning, garnering
very different results. Instead of giving up a 365-foot homer, he
allowed a 500-foot monstrosity that cleared the right field fence and
landed on the second row of houses past Twentieth Street. Those two
blows were worth five runs, but the Athletics were scoring at a faster
pace. By the time Ruth batted in the eighth inning, the Yanks were losing,
and Connie Mack had put Lefty Grove on the mound to ensure the victory. Babe still had a score to settle from opening day, and he settled
it. He bombed one that seemed to touch the clouds before descending
into the fans watching from the rooftops across the street. Ruth had
three home runs, but the Yankees lost 15–7. The A's won the nightcap
as well.

Up to this time in 1930, no matter what Babe did against Philadelphia, it wasn't enough. So he showed up on Thursday May 22 determined to set things straight. Facing Howard Ehmke in the third
inning, Ruth detonated the baseball equivalent of a nuclear explosion.
This one somehow surpassed the one off Earnshaw the day before. It
bypassed the right field fence, Twentieth Street, a row of houses, an
alley with backyards, another row of houses, and ultimately returned
to earth in Opal Street. It's hard to believe that a mortal being could
hit a ball that far, but there is undeniable proof that it happened.
During this research process, three different individuals provided
confirmation. That list included Allen Lewis, who was a boy at the
time and later became a respected writer for the *Philadelphia
Inquirer.* The following day in 1930, there was also confirmation in
three newspapers: the *Philadelphia Record,* the *Philadelphia Public
Ledger,* and the *New York World*. Opal Street was a minimum distance
of 505 feet from home plate, so this beastly thing flew somewhere in
excess of that length.

Babe Ruth's monumental home run onto Opal Street at Shibe Park on May 22, 1930. *(Philadelphia Athletics Historical Society)*

Before the day was over, Ruth added two more long homers to give him six in two days as New York crushed Philadelphia 10–1 and 20–13. But the fun wasn't over. In another two days, the same teams met in yet another twin bill, this time in Yankee Stadium. Babe was still going bananas. In the first game, he hit a homer high into the right field bleachers and made several fine plays in the outfield as the Yanks won 10–6. In game two, the 66,000 attendees watched him drop a bunt single, hit a sacrifice fly, and wallop one of the great home runs in Stadium history. Contemporary newspaper accounts agreed that the ball landed near the top of the bleachers in right center field. They did not give any further details. However, Yankee pitcher Waite Hoyt and Athletics catcher Cy Perkins both later swore that the ball landed in a barrel of water kept in the top row in case of fire. If true, this drive came as close to leaving Yankee Stadium as any that has ever been struck. Either way, it was power on a grand scale, and Ruth was pleased. The Yankees won again 11–1, and, for just a little while, the

A's monkey was off Babe's back. New York finished the month in third place with a 22 and 17 record.

June was another outstanding individual month for Babe Ruth. But, by the time it ended, it was obvious that Philadelphia would win the pennant again. They were just too good, and Babe could do only so much as one player. He cracked fifteen homers and made a series of wonderful defensive plays. But Philly kept pulling away. On the 13th in Detroit, Ruth made a perfect throw home to record the final out in a one-run victory. Two days later, in a wild game at League Park in Cleveland, Babe walked in his first four at-bats and then powdered the first pitch he swung at into the center field bleachers. According to the *New York Telegram,* Indians fans "gasped in awe." And, three days after that, in an Albany exhibition contest, Ruth broke the distance record in Hawkins Stadium with another potent shot to center.

Babe couldn't keep up that homer pace all year, but he never stopped playing great baseball. He missed some time after tearing a fingernail from his left ring finger trying to prevent a home run. With the hand injury limiting his power, Ruth was held to six homers in July. The Yanks were ten games behind the Athletics and now trailed the Senators as well. But as the season swung into August, Babe was still going full throttle. He made another run of outstanding defensive plays early in the month and kept colliding with catchers at home plate. With all this, he wrenched his back, but still wouldn't quit. Ruth recorded eight homers in August, and showed up for work on September 1 with a fire still burning in his belly.

Babe was battered and sore from his season-long exertions, but the Yanks were playing the Athletics in front of 72,000 ardent supporters. Team trainer Doc Painter told Ruth not to play in the doubleheader, but he wouldn't hear of it. It would make a great story if Babe won the day with amazing deeds, but it didn't happen this time. This is a good tale anyway. How many modern athletes would drag themselves out on display under these circumstances? The man was in severe back pain in a situation where New York trailed Philadelphia by thirteen games with only one month left. Why was he playing? Entering the ninth inning of the first game, Ruth had gone 2 for 4 with two singles. Batting this time with a 3–2 deficit, Ruth watched as Connie Mack specifically called in Lefty Grove to pitch to him. As the two ultimate warriors eyed one another, Babe dug in at the plate. This would be another classic confrontation of primal force against brute strength.

Facing some of the fastest fastballs ever thrown, Ruth went down swinging. Players in the infield and dugouts declared that they could actually hear the sound of both ball and bat speeding through the air. Babe Ruth had struck out, and the Yankees lost. Some might regard this as a defeat for Ruth, but not those who know best. They see the similarities between these events and those of the last game of the 1926 World Series. Why was he playing? He was playing for pride and because he was not afraid to fail. It was his sense of self, recognizing his role as America's greatest ballplayer. It drove him this day and every other day. No negative thoughts ever deterred him. He never took a backward step on the baseball field. Yes, he was a great natural athlete, but he was a whole lot more than that. He was Babe Ruth.

By the end of September, Ruth was feeling much better. He was back at Shibe Park against the same Athletics, where the season had started seemingly ages ago. Babe pounded a hard drive into right center field, and nobody thought much about it. Another home run for Ruth? Who cares? The season is over; the A's have already clinched the pennant. Then bang! The ball hit the same exact loudspeaker that had been hit on opening day. The odds of this occurrence are off the charts. It had never happened before, and the Athletics, who thought it would never happen again, hadn't bothered to change the ground rules. Ruth was held to another double that should have been a home run. He wound up the year with forty-nine homers. With either a little luck or a little responsibility on the part of the A's, he would have reached fifty for the fifth time.

Undaunted, Babe took the mound two days later on September 28 in Boston to pitch the last game of the season. He hadn't pitched in a Big League game in nine years, and this was a rare opportunity to relive his athletic youth. The chances of defeat and embarrassment were extremely high. But Ruth took the ball and marched onto the mound in front of the same people who remembered him as one of the best left-handed pitchers of that era. And he pitched wonderfully. Entering the eighth inning, he had been practically unhittable. Ruth tired in the ninth, but still managed to hurl a complete game 9–3 victory.

The Yankees finished in third place with eighty-six wins. The Athletics won 102, and the Senators came in second with ninety-four victories. Along with Ruth's forty-nine dingers, he batted .359 and slugged .732. He scored 150 runs and knocked in 153. Babe even stole ten bases. He then served as a guest writer for the Christy Walsh Syndicate at the World Series, where the Athletics defeated the Cardinals to repeat as World Champions. Ruth played a few barnstorming games in the New York area, but didn't wander too far from home after the season. He would be thirty-six years old in 1931 and wondered if he would ever win another pennant.

1931   When the Yankees took their first batting practice on March 3, they had a new manager in Joe McCarthy. He came from the Chicago Cubs, replacing Bob Shawkey, who had been regarded as too soft on his players. Apparently, Marse Joe hadn't seen much of Babe Ruth, because he almost swallowed one of his cigars at the sight of his legendary outfielder taking BP. Several prolific drives wound up in the water at Crescent Lake Park, a place no National Leaguer could reach. McCarthy had not been a gifted player himself; he never made it to the Big Leagues, and he had to work hard for the respect of his players, especially Ruth. But by the end of his career in 1950, Joe McCarthy was regarded as one of the best managers to ever turn in a lineup card. He and Babe were never close, but they won a lot of ballgames together. Could they win enough in 1931 to overcome the A's, who appeared better than ever?

Ruth reported to camp weighing 228 pounds, which was ideal for that stage of his career. Babe did well and made no complaints, but most players reported that the baseball was not as lively as the year before. And they were right. In that era, the National and American Leagues had different manufacturers for their "official" balls. And there were no standard specifications. Until Ruth came along, both leagues used balls that were essentially alike in performance characteristics. But with Babe leading the charge, the AL pulled away from the NL in the financially profitable matter of power. By 1929, the gap had widened into a chasm. The NL had no one to match Ruth, Gehrig, and Foxx, and tried to remedy the problem through artificial means. However, they overdid it, and got caught with their hands in the cookie jar.

Offensive production went right off the charts with Hack Wilson's fifty-six home runs and 190 RBI as the most embarrassing proof of the collusion. The American League ball was probably altered a little from time to time, but never as suddenly and dramatically as its NL counterpart. Predictably, both leagues slowed down the sphere in 1931, and the players recognized it immediately. The seams felt higher, which would reduce offensive production in two ways. First, pitchers could grip the ball better and get more rotation on their breaking pitches. Second, the higher stitches would increase the drag coefficient of the ball, thereby reducing the flight distance. Over the decades, there seems to have been a gradual, but inevitable, increase in the flight capacity of Major League baseballs. But it sometimes took one step backward before taking two steps forward, and that seems to be what happened in 1931. Before the 1934 season, the two leagues finally agreed to use the same manufacturing specifications. It remains today the only time that the baseball hierarchy has publicly addressed this compellingly important issue.

Meanwhile, back in St. Petersburg, Babe Ruth was having a typical spring. On March 26, the Yanks played against the House of David, which was a bearded Jewish team. Ruth picked up a couple of base hits, and played the outfield wearing long whiskers. On April 2 in Chattanooga, he batted against a seventeen-year-old female pitcher, and took three mighty swings, while pantomiming a dramatic strikeout.

Three days later in Nashville, he was back in his real-life persona, smashing a home run so far over the right field fence that it also cleared an adjoining livery stable. As usual, Babe was full of optimism, predicting a pennant for the Yankees. He based his hopes on the further development of young players like outfielder Ben Chapman and the acquisition of third baseman Joe Sewell. He also believed that the Athletics would be weaker, since he heard reports that some of their players were overconfident and undertrained. Ruth was right about Chapman and Sewell; they both had fine years. But he was wrong about the Athletics, who were still fabulous.

Babe and the Yankees opened the season in New York on Tuesday, April 14, versus Boston before 70,000 true believers. He went 2 for 3 with a homer and stolen base as the Bombers won 6–3. The following Sunday, the Athletics came to town, and 80,403 attended the latest confrontation between the two magnificent rivals. Ruth played spectacular defense, but went hitless in a 3–2 loss. However, the next afternoon, he walloped two gargantuan home runs off George Earnshaw to pace a 5–4 victory. That first homer nearly cleared the right field bleachers. When New York won again the next day 12–1 to take the series, the Yanks felt pretty good. But in Boston on the 22nd, Babe tried to bowl over former All-American football player Charlie Berry at home plate and got much the worse in the collision. He wound up in a Boston hospital for four days with nerve damage in his left leg, and did not fully recover for two more weeks. New York finished April in third place with an 8 and 6 record.

On May 1, the Empire State Building officially opened in New York. The Great Depression was crippling the U.S. economy, but there was optimism in the nation's largest city. Babe Ruth and Lou Gehrig still played for the Yankees, and, to New Yorkers, they were unconquerable. The previous two years had been an aberration, and those upstart A's would be put in their place. There was just one problem with that rose-colored view. Philadelphia was awesome. The 1931 Yankees were a damn good baseball team, but those Athletics were as good as any team that ever put on spikes. When the Yanks went to the Quaker City for a five-game set on May 25, the A's were on a fifteen-game winning streak.

Lefty Grove won the first game 4–2, while striking out Ruth in the seventh and ninth innings. Philly won game two as well, but Babe finally halted the streak at seventeen games with a single, double, and homer in game three. Ruth collected two hits in the fourth contest, but the Yanks lost a heartbreaker 6–5. In the fifth and final game, New York led at one point as Babe bombed another homer. If they could just win this final battle, they would only lose one game on enemy soil. But Connie Mack brought in Grove to relieve in the eighth inning, and he shut the door. In the bottom of the ninth, Grove hit a double and then tallied the winning run himself. It was a crushing blow. Neither Babe Ruth nor any of his teammates would quit, but observers knew that nobody could beat the A's over a 154-game schedule. For the year, Robert Moses Grove finished with a 31 and 4 record with an E.R.A. of 2.06. In his 289 innings, he pitched 27 complete games and saved five others. The Yankees had no one to match him.

Entering June, Ruth had only nine home runs, but he maintained a high batting average. Plus, his overall play was excellent. For the first time, he was actually adjusting his hitting style to his advancing years. Babe admitted that he was using a shorter grip on the bat and that he was spreading his feet wider. So far, the results included more opposite field hits but fewer homers. In June, however, the power resurfaced. He didn't hit the ball quite as far as in 1921, but he still hit it farther than anyone else. On the 19th, the Yanks departed on their standard four-city western road trip that included St. Louis, Chicago, Cleveland, and Detroit. It started with a grueling twenty-four-hour train ride in suffocating heat to St. Louis. Those trains were not air conditioned, and neither were the hotels or clubhouses of that time. During that trip, the Yankees played eighteen games, and every one of them took place in temperatures exceeding 90 degrees. The players had no real relief the entire time. It was not an easy time to be a Major League ballplayer.

Along with the Babe, Lou Gehrig was also enjoying a banner year. Lou was hitting homers regularly, and driving in runs at a record pace. In July, Gehrig hit eleven home runs and Ruth added ten, as the Yankees went 23 and 10. In the first inning at home against Boston on July 8, Ruth smacked one into the right field bleachers for a rather routine four-bagger. Later in that game, he really connected, but aimed his shot in the wrong direction. Center fielder Tom Oliver raced over the cinder track, up the incline, and caught the ball two steps from the deepest corner. It was a drive of about 480 feet for an out. It's impossible to know how many times this happened to Ruth, but twenty-two fly outs of 450 feet or more have been confirmed during Babe's play in Yankee Stadium alone. During the course of his long career, Ruth recorded outs at least fifty times on balls that would be tape measure home runs for modern players.

In an exhibition game in Albany on July 30, Babe blasted two homers over the right field fence and a single that almost broke it (there are authenticated accounts of Ruthian drives breaking wooden fences in ballparks around the country). After the game the next day in Boston, Babe came out onto his hotel balcony, when he heard a commotion. An awning two floors below him was ablaze, but rather than wait for the fire department, Ruth rushed inside and filled a pitcher with water. He then extinguished the flames with a carefully aimed pour and bowed to the cheering crowd that had gathered at street level. It seems that Babe Ruth was destined to be the center of attention wherever he went or whatever he did.

Heading into August, the Yankees were eighteen games over .500, but they trailed the Athletics by fifteen. Babe was having another great year, and all he could do was to continue being Babe Ruth. In Detroit on August 15, he pounded a sixteenth-inning homer to pace a Yankee victory. Afterward, teammates confirmed that Ruth had announced the blow before he hit it. Six days later in St. Louis, Babe recorded his 600th career home run by smashing the ball far over the pavilion in right center field. Then in Chicago, Ruth had a sensational five-game series with ten hits including three doubles, a triple, and two thunderous home runs. Not content with those efforts, Babe also signed autographs before each inning in left field for delighted Windy City children.

Along with his many other records, Ruth almost certainly signed more autographs than any player in history. Upon leaving Chicago, the Yanks stopped in Scranton for a ballgame, and local writers were more impressed with Babe writing his signature than with his batting power. He clubbed a 450-foot center field double, but also signed every single autograph request. That included pleas from a bunch of kids who had watched from a nearby coal dump until the contest was rained out in the seventh inning. The game had been a sellout, and Ruth just couldn't bear to disappoint anyone. He waited for those youngsters while his teammates were getting dressed, and then signed his name until every eager child went home happy. The only modern player with a comparable history of fan accommodation is Cal Ripken Jr.

The Yankees went on to finish the season in second place as Babe ripped nine September homers to finish with forty-six for the year. For the first time, Gehrig matched his total. Lou also set an American League record with 184 RBIs. Ruth personally knocked in 163 and scored 149 times. Despite walking 128 times, Babe collected 199 hits, while batting .373 (second only to Al Simmons at .390). Ruth also led the Major Leagues in slugging one more time with a mark of .700. New York won 94 games that year, but Philadelphia won the extraordinary total of 107. Could anyone ever beat them again? The answer was yes. The St. Louis Cardinals managed to dethrone the Athletics as World Champions in a tough seven-game series, which was more prophetic than anyone realized at the time.

After the World Series, Babe left on a particularly ambitious barnstorming tour that began in Kansas City on October 13 and concluded in Los Angeles on October 31. Something happened along the way that was truly historic. In San Diego on October 19, 1931, Babe Ruth played in his first night game. Appearing under the lights at Navy Field, he bombed numerous batting practice homers along with one home run in the game. Afterward, Ruth commented that he didn't like the artificial light, but played again the next night at Wrigley Field in Los Angeles. He couldn't have minded it too much, since he ripped two doubles and the longest home run ever in the City of Angels. That ball flew out of the park past the flagpole in dead center and was found in a garage near Avalon Boulevard. Ruth also played a morning game in Oakland and an afternoon game in San Francisco on the 23rd, where he hit a combined total of twenty-one balls out of the two ballparks. Two were official competitive home runs, while the others came either in BP or demonstration at-bats. All the while, Babe was proclaiming the end of the A's dynasty, citing overuse of Lefty Grove and George Earnshaw. This time, Ruth was on the right track. Grove wasn't about to fall apart, but the A's were ready to slip. Plus, the Yanks were about to get a little better. Ruth would be thirty-seven years old in 1932, but he couldn't wait to get started.

1932   The New York Yankees started spring training earlier than ever in '32. After playing tournament golf and hunting alligators since his arrival in St. Petersburg on February 4, Ruth took his first batting practice on the 29th. Babe blasted a series of tremendous drives in every direction, showing that his power was intact. But, when he went to the outfield, he appeared a step slower. There was no announcement about Babe's weight, but it was apparent that he had added some pounds. A few weeks later, he signed a one-year contract for $75,000, but it would be the last time that negotiations would be amicable. In truth, Ruth was slipping as a ballplayer. He was still a formidable offensive force, but, this season, he would be less than average defensively. He was also slowing down on the bases, whereas his speed and aggressiveness had once been a constant threat. In short, Babe was still a good ballplayer, but he was no longer the best. But one thing would never change; he remained the most popular athlete in America.

Ruth's top spring performance occurred on March 26 against the

Phillies in St. Petersburg. Babe went 3 for 3 with two homers and five RBIs. Both home runs were lined wickedly to right field, and he launched three others that went just foul. The Yankees completed camp a few days later and began their annual two-week expedition to wherever they could make some money. This trip included games in Birmingham, Memphis, Louisville, Cincinnati, Indianapolis, and Columbus. Ruth was particularly memorable in Memphis on April 2, where he thumped a monstrous center field homer and sat in the left field seats with local children while the Yankees batted. All in all, the Yanks looked very good, and they showed up at Shibe Park in Philadelphia for the season opener bristling with confidence.

It was April 12, 1932, and the weather was cold and damp. It was a terrible day for a baseball game, but the 16,000 fans who braved the unpleasant conditions were treated to a historic performance. The Athletics started George Earnshaw, and the Yanks countered with Lefty Gomez. He was no Lefty Grove, but a fine pitcher nonetheless. In his first at-bat, Ruth hammered the ball over the fence in right center and onto a rooftop across Twentieth Street. It was a drive of about 480 feet, giving New York a quick 3–0 lead. Lou Gehrig added a solo shot in the third inning, and then Babe matched his earlier deed in the fourth. Earnshaw was still on the mound as Ruth blasted one over a roof in right field. The Yankees went on to win 12–6 as "Moose" Earnshaw surrendered ten runs in just four innings. Sadly, he was never again the same dominant pitcher as in the past few seasons. But all was not utter darkness that afternoon for the A's. In the seventh inning off Gomez, young first baseman Jimmie Foxx belted a gigantic home run to straightaway center that traveled even farther than either of the mammoth shots Ruth had hit. The Yankees were stunned. They knew that Double X had great power, but they had no idea how much. Much of their season would be spent learning about the awesome ability of the muscular farm boy from Maryland's Eastern Shore.

Babe paid a price for his Philadelphia heroics by developing a nasty cold and fever that kept him in bed for days. But when the Bombers opened at Yankee Stadium against Lefty Grove, he was in right field. It was April 20, and 58,322 hopeful fans came to see how their Yankees measured up to the three-time champions. They liked what they saw. Ruth homered into the right field bleachers and led New York to an 8–3 win. They also enjoyed the sight of Babe scampering all the way from first to third base on a passed ball. Ruth was slowing down, but this was a reminder never to take him lightly. The A's came back to take game two by a score of 8–6 with five ninth-inning runs. In the final game of the series, Ruth smacked a homer and long triple to left center to win 16–5 before 41,208 satisfied customers. It was a bittersweet victory, however, because he broke his favorite bat in the process. That wouldn't mean much to a current player, since bats are broken often in today's game. But things were different then, especially for Ruth. The wood of his bats was so heavy that he rarely broke one. He often kept the same bat for months at a time, and they became friends and allies doing battle together.

Lou Gehrig also hurt his ankle that day, and Babe replaced him at first base during the last two innings. Of course, Gehrig was back in the lineup the next day. He was well on his way to playing in over 2,000 consecutive games and becoming the legendary "Iron Horse." Unfortunately, it was about this time that the great friendship between Ruth and Gehrig was severely damaged. Until then, they did almost everything together, but a petty dispute between the two families grew into a long-term feud. The two men didn't argue in public, but they ignored each other for the last few years that they were teammates. Ultimately, when it was determined that Gehrig had a fatal illness in 1939, a devastated Ruth visited his former friend and the two reconciled. Before Lou's tragic and premature death in 1941, they spent time together remembering those wondrous days of their halcyon primes.

Babe hit six home runs in April, and the Yanks closed out the month in first place with a 10 and 3 record. Ruth was happy. He may not have been the same overpowering performer he once was, but he felt less pressure this way. He enjoyed the realization that the Yankees could win even if he didn't do something extraordinary. Babe badly wanted to play in his tenth World Series, and he sensed that this could be the year. The New York pitching staff appeared stronger than it had been in a long time. Red Ruffing had been acquired from the Red Sox in 1930, and this was the year that he began to fulfill his Hall of Fame expectations. Rookie Johnny Allen would capitalize on his fastball and fiery temperament to make a huge contribution. Lefty Gomez would enjoy his second straight star-level season, and veteran George Pipgras would finish his Yankee career with his best work in four years. New York finally had a pitching staff that could compete with Philadelphia.

Ruth and the Yanks had a solid month of May with the man belting eight homers and the team winning eighteen of twenty-six games. They led the Athletics by six games despite thirteen May home runs by Jimmie Foxx. The two old adversaries then started June with a six-game series at Shibe Park. New York got a dose of reality by losing both ends of a doubleheader on the first day. In the early game, Lefty Grove relieved in the ninth inning and held the fort until the A's won in the 16th by an 8–7 count. The Yankees won game three, and the series moved to game four on June 3. It was on this day that longtime Giants manager John McGraw announced his resignation, which became the leading sports story around the country. That was unfortunate for Lou Gehrig, because, on that same day, he hit four home runs against the Philadelphia Athletics. And he almost added a fifth when his ninth-inning blast was caught in deep center. It was typical of Gehrig's entire career. As great as Lou was, he was always in someone's shadow, mostly Ruth's. When Babe finally retired and Gehrig began to assume the role of number one Yankee, Joe DiMaggio came along. Fans always loved Lou Gehrig, but there were never the right circumstances to idolize him. And so it was on this day.

The Yankees won this slugfest 20–13, and Babe contributed a double and long home run. The teams then split another twin bill to halve the series. On that final day, Grove came in to face Ruth again in a ninth-inning relief appearance, which was a common practice when the Yanks and A's played. Relief pitching had not advanced to today's level of sophistication, but Babe Ruth wouldn't have noticed. He was the one man who almost always had to confront the opposition's best. Babe dealt with special defenses, special pitching patterns, and anything else that could be conceived to stop him.

When New York started its western swing on June 7 in Detroit, something else happened to note another difference between then and now. Ruth hit a run-scoring fly ball, but was credited with an out instead of a sacrifice. That scorebook rule had been changed before the 1931 season, and had not yet been changed back. It cost Babe some points on his career batting average. On June 12 in Cleveland, he knocked in six runs with a double and two dingers, one of which landed on a house across Lexington Avenue. The next day, he ripped another homer and turned a slick double play with a shoestring catch and quick throw to second base. Things went well the entire month as Babe posted nine homers, and the Yankees increased their lead to eight and a half games. The only cloud in the sky was the play of Jimmie Foxx. On June 25 at Yankee Stadium, he struck a titanic home run into the left field upper deck. It was his twelfth homer of the month, and folks were seriously considering his chances of breaking Ruth's record of sixty.

On July 3, the Yankees played the first Sunday game ever at Fenway Park. It was a breakthrough for both the ballplayers and schedule makers. The next day in D.C., catcher Bill Dickey got involved in an altercation and broke the jaw of Senator catcher Carl Reynolds. Dickey was suspended for a month, but the Yanks marched on without him. On the 12th in New York, Ruth walked all four times he batted against the St. Louis Browns, but turned the tables by advancing to third base after one of those passes. He then took off to steal home and forced the startled pitcher into a balk. Babe's maneuver should not have come as a surprise, since he stole home ten times during his remarkable career. But Ruth then tore a hamstring muscle six days later. He missed the following nine games, and, according to team doctors, he was still disabled on July 28 when the Yanks visited Cleveland. But Babe demanded to play. Manager Joe McCarthy acquiesced, whereupon the supposedly crippled old man smashed a mighty double and two lengthy home runs to drive in seven runs. When July ended, the Bombers still maintained an eight-game lead, and Ruth had eight more homers.

The Yanks were now the best team in the League, and the pennant race had little drama. New York and Philadelphia did not play each other in August, while the Yankees stretched their lead to an insurmountable eleven games. Babe smacked nine additional home runs to give him thirty-nine with a month to play. Was another fifty-homer season possible? No, it wasn't. During a Labor Day doubleheader against the beleaguered A's at Yankee Stadium, Ruth delighted 70,772 onlookers with a stupefying line drive that carried well past the 429-foot sign in deep right center. The Yanks drove the final nail into the Athletics' coffin by winning both games. Babe should have been jubilant. However, he was experiencing pain in his right side, which worsened as the team headed to Detroit. Ruth was sent back to New York, where physicians diagnosed appendicitis. They advised against surgery, telling Babe to stay home to rest. But he became so weak that he couldn't reach the bleachers even once when he resumed batting practice on September 17. There were concerns that he would be unable to play in the World Series against the Chicago Cubs.

The inactivity must have been torturous for Ruth, particularly in view of Foxx's challenge to his home run record. That noble effort fell a little short as Jimmie finished with fifty-eight homers, but Babe had inalterably been replaced as the game's premier slugger. Ruth did recover sufficiently to play in the final five games, strong enough by then to reach Fenway Park's distant right field bleachers for his forty-first and final home run of the season. The Yankees won 107 games to Philadelphia's 94, which was the exact inverse of the preceding year. Despite playing in only 133 games, Babe's statistics were impressive. He finished second to Foxx in homers and slugging (.661 to .749), and wound up fifth in batting at .341. Ruth knocked in 137 runs, scored 120, and still led the league with 130 bases-on-balls. Despite his recognizable decline, when all was said and done, Babe Ruth led the Major Leagues in on-base percentage by 20 points (.489 to .469) over runner-up Foxx. He would certainly be a factor in his tenth World Series.

The Yankees won the first game in New York as Red Ruffing went the distance. Ruth contributed a single and two walks. The Bombers prevailed again in game two with Lefty Gomez pitching a masterful complete game 5–2 victory. Babe managed a line drive single off the right field fence and another base on balls. The teams then traveled to Wrigley Field in Chicago for the third game. It was October 1, 1932, and 51,000 fans saw history unfold in front of them. Even before the game started, Ruth's power was a factor. The Cubs had erected a four-story temporary stand outside the right field wall to accommodate the special demand for tickets. Babe's batting practice included nine balls high into those seats with one landing in the top row. In later years, the Cubs admitted to being awed. In the first inning of the actual game, Ruth revisited those same seats off Charlie Root for an early lead. By the fifth inning, the contest was tied 4–4, when Babe came up to bat under a barrage of verbal abuse from the Chicago bench. This, of course, was the occasion of Ruth's famous "called shot."

There is still legitimate disagreement about whether or not Babe actually predicted what followed. Either he pointed to the center field bleachers to announce his intention to hit the ball there, or he defiantly gestured that he only needed one pitch. It really doesn't matter. Either course of action is extraordinary in the context of that moment. With two strikes and two balls under immense pressure, Babe Ruth proclaimed his invincibility in front of the world and then acted on it. His monumental clout sailed over the center field wall, landing near the flagpole almost 500 feet away. It was an incomparable moment by the only truly incomparable athlete this nation has yet produced. Renowned writer Westbrook Pegler stated that everyone present "came away from the baseball plant with a spiritual memento of the most gorgeous display of humor, athletic art and championship class any performer in any of the games has ever presented." Lou Gehrig followed with his second homer of the day, and the Yanks won 7–5. Not surprising, the dazed Cubs succumbed 13–6 the next day, and New York swept the Series.

Babe Ruth welcomed home by Lou Gehrig after his "called shot" home run in the 1932 World Series. *(Philadelphia Athletics Historical Society)*

Ruth returned to New York, where he took a well-earned rest. That winter he played golf, hunted, and reflected on the realization of his dream to play in ten World Series. He didn't know it, but 1932 was the last year that baseball would be joy and laughter for him. He still had some good times in front of him, but he had ascended to the top of the mountain for the final view from the summit. Babe would play for three more seasons, but age and the unavoidable attrition of his punishing schedule had finally caught up to him.

1933   Babe Ruth always enjoyed coming to Florida, but 1933 was not as much fun as other years. The Yankees had offered him a one-year contract at $50,000, a 33 percent cut. He was insulted and angry. Ruth freely acknowledged the financial realities of the worsening Depression as well as his advancing age. He was willing to accept a reduction, but one-third was a slap in his face. For the first time as a Yankee, his salary discussions were confrontational. Babe, weighing in at 232 pounds, did not participate in the first squad game on March 11, but kept in shape by taking batting practice. As always, he wowed observers with a stream of tremendous drives into the lake.

When Babe started missing exhibition games starting on the 14th, everyone knew that the dispute was for real. Eventually, a rather resigned Ruth agreed to a $52,000 one-year deal on March 22. He played his first spring game two days later against the Boston Braves and smacked a home run. But that would be Babe's only preseason homer as he soon developed a bad cold. Then, the season opener against the Red Sox on April 12 was rained out in New York.

Babe Ruth's karma never stayed negative for long, and his life improved in the second half of April. He belted five homers, and the Yankees entered May in first place with a mark of 11 and 4. They played Philadelphia four times, winning each contest. The A's weren't their chief concern this year. Connie Mack had hit another monetary wall and sent Al Simmons to the Chicago White Sox. More of his top players were soon to leave town, and the Athletics' best and last dynasty was over. It was the Washington Senators who appeared to be the Yankees' fiercest rival this time around. They had won only one fewer game than the A's in 1932, and were better this year. That was the team that Bill Dickey had fought the season before, and, sure enough, the two teams got into a huge brawl at Griffith Stadium on April 25. These were not the nice-guy Senators of Walter Johnson, but the pugnacious battlers of player-manager Joe Cronin.

Ruth and New York went west in early May and played for the first time in Cleveland's new Municipal Stadium. It was a gigantic place with the worst home run dimensions of any twentieth-century Major League ballpark. The foul poles were reasonably positioned at 320 feet from home plate, but the fences quickly angled out to 435-foot power alleys. The bleachers extended from that point at a uniform distance of 470 feet across center field and back to the other power alley. It was a graveyard for sluggers, and Babe hated it. In that first game, Ruth blasted one 450 feet to right center, where Earl Averill made an easy catch. Babe never hit a homer in Municipal, and no one ever reached the bleachers in the stadium's subsequent sixty-year history.

Before returning home, the Yanks played exhibition games in Indianapolis and Wheeling. In both places, Ruth bombed prodigious center field drives that wound up as doubles. They both hit fences beside the respective flagpoles close to 500 feet from home plate. It was the usual Ruthian exhibition fare in other ways as well. At Perry Stadium in Indy, Babe pitched the first two innings and was hit above the right kneecap with a line drive. In retrospect, the risk seems appalling, but, luckily, the injury wasn't serious. That became apparent a few days later in Wheeling, when the irrepressible man-child was seen doing a somersault at first base.

Back at Yankee Stadium on May 17, Ruth legged out a base hit on a bunt. That naturally raises the question as to how often he employed this unlikely strategy. It may be surprising, but Babe Ruth was a superb bunter who often reached base that way. There are forty-two confirmed instances of bunt singles in Ruth's career. And it is likely that there were more that were not mentioned in newspaper accounts. But power was the essence of Ruth's game, and he still possessed plenty of that. In a doubleheader against the White Sox on the 28th, he belted three out of the park, including one missile over the 429-foot sign in right center.

The Bombers then returned to D.C. for a much-anticipated Memorial Day showdown with the second-place Senators. Three games were played over two days, and the Yanks won two as Babe collected two singles, a double, and a triple. Washington was tough, however, and New York felt a sense of relief when they played Philly eight times in June. Ruth did well, and had an especially good time on the 10th, when he twice took Lefty Grove downtown. Babe hit eight homers that month, and the last one was a throwback to his glory days. It came on the 28th in Detroit, and flew well past the 455-foot marker in dead center field. As June ended, Ruth had seventeen home runs, more than fine for a thirty-eight-year-old outfielder. But the Yankees had slipped one game behind the determined Senators.

On the Fourth of July at Yankee Stadium, those Senators came for an important twin bill, and the fans responded with a turnout of 77,365. It was baseball as it was meant to be. Both teams played inspired ball, but Washington prevailed in two close games. Ruth recorded three hits including a home run, but all doubts about the Senators' legitimacy were dismissed. Thoughts then temporarily shifted to the so-called Game of the Century, which was the name given to the first All-Star Game, scheduled for July 6, 1933, at Chicago's Comiskey Park. Of course, Babe Ruth was there, as were all the great stars of the sport. The game was played for charity, and, at the time, no one knew that it would evolve into an annual event. It could have been a once-in-a-lifetime happening, and was regarded as a very big deal. Predictably, Ruth hit the first-ever All-Star homer by smashing a third-inning line drive into the right field grandstand. It was the difference in the game, which was won 4–2 by the American League.

Against the Browns on July 14, Ruth dove into a box seat at Yankee Stadium to make a miraculous catch. In so doing, he injured his right arm and left big toe, which caused him to miss the rest of the game. The next day, fans were just hoping that Ruth would play, but they got a lot more than that. He banged out two long home runs, just missing two more on drives of comparable length. One was caught in deep left center field beyond the running track, and the other was snagged against the 429-foot sign in right center. Once again, providence prevented Babe from attaining the magical four-home-run mark. Soon after, the Yankees returned to Washington for a four-game must-win series against the Senators.

The first round on July 27 proceeded into extra innings. Batting in the tenth frame with a man on third base and one out, Ruth was walked intentionally. Ordinarily, that would not be noteworthy, but Lou Gehrig hit directly behind Babe. At this relative stage of their careers, it would seem that Lou would have been the more feared batsman. But that's not the way opposing managers plotted their strategy. Time after time, they walked Ruth in crucial situations to face Gehrig. Once again in 1933, Babe was passed more often than Lou (114 to 109) even though their positions in the batting order would indicate the opposite. It worked on this occasion, as Washington won 3–2 later in the tenth inning. The Senators won again in game two despite Ruth's wicked line-drive homer, but the Yanks prevailed in the third match. The final game was played on July 31 and was critical to New York's hopes. In the first three games, Babe had been issued a total of six bases on balls, but Joe Cronin inexplicably changed plans on this day. Ruth rose to the opportunity, going 4 for 5 with two doubles and a triple. That three-base hit arrived with the bases loaded. It clanged off the top of the wall in center field at the 441-foot mark. The Yankees won 13–9, and stayed within one game of the Senators.

Up until August, things had gone reasonably well for Babe Ruth and the New York Yankees. But that was the month when advancing age finally compromised the Babe. His team wilted along with him. It was uncommonly hot, even for that time of year, and Ruth was clearly tired. When New York began a road trip to St. Louis on August 15, Babe had only one homer for the month, and the Yanks were losing ground. Something happened then that had never happened before. Without illness or injury, Ruth volunteered not to play. He was just too worn out. It was a sobering realization that not even the mighty Bambino would last forever. Babe stayed out of the starting lineup for two days, and then missed four more games before August 31. By that time, New York had fallen eight and a half games out, and the pennant was pretty much a lost cause. In truth, Ruth wasn't able to bounce back until the weather cooled off in the second half of September. It took twenty years to find out, but Babe Ruth had limits.

Once Babe was thoroughly rested, he played well again for the remainder of the season. In hindsight, the Yankee management was incomprehensibly dense not to have treated him with more care and restraint. He was thirty-eight years old and a physically large man. Whenever Ruth was on the field, he played all out, and was always burdened with enormous public relations duties. If given just an occasional day off before hitting that wall of total fatigue, he almost certainly would have remained productive. And who knows what the team might have accomplished? When rested and uninjured, Babe Ruth could still play good solid baseball.

On September 17, he banged homers in both games of a double-header. In the early game, he scored the winning run by romping home from second base on an infield error. During the latter contest, he narrowly missed powering a ball out of Yankee Stadium when his great drive curved foul into the top of the stands. Six days later in Boston, Ruth walloped a homer halfway up the center field bleachers at Fenway Park. Back in New York on September 28 against Washington, Babe thumped his next home run about fifty rows into the right field bleachers. By that time, the Senators had clinched the pennant, and members of the New York Giants were on hand to scout them for the forthcoming World Series. According to the *Washington Evening Star,* those National Leaguers were "awed" at the sight of Ruth's ageless power. Babe then finished the season as he had in 1930 by pitching a complete game victory and clubbing a homer. Just to start things off that day, he also won a pregame fungo-hitting contest.

Despite winding up eight games behind Washington, the Yanks had a respectable year with 91 wins. Ruth was also respectable. His 34 homers were again second to Jimmie Foxx, who had 48. He was third in slugging at .582 and fourth in on-base percentage at .442. Babe batted .301, scored 97 runs and drove in 103. His biggest problems occurred on defense, where in 137 games, his putouts were down to 222. But, all in all, it wasn't bad; it just wasn't Ruthian. Actually, the team's downfall was the same as it had been a few years ago: pitching.

In 1933, the Yankees outscored the Senators 927–850, and led both leagues in scoring. But New York's team ERA was 4.36 compared to Washington's 3.82. Regardless of Ruth's predictable decline, the Yankees needed to improve their pitching if they expected to succeed in 1934.

After watching the World Series, which was won by the Giants, Babe took his family on a working vacation to Hawaii. Arriving on October 19, he was treated like royalty. Along with a lot of golf, sightseeing, parades, and banquets, Ruth played three baseball games. In the first two in Honolulu, he recorded three singles and a homer, but he didn't do anything sensational. Nobody was complaining. On the contrary, everyone thought his visit was a complete success. But Babe still loved the spotlight, and he had not performed in Hawaii in the past. So he agreed to one last game in Hilo on October 29, and this time he was satisfied. Ruth went 3 for 5 with two homers and six RBIs. The home runs flew 450 feet and 475 feet, and Babe sailed away savoring the knowledge that the islanders would never forget him. He had no illusions about his future, and he was finally allowing himself to revel in his past.

1934   Spring training '34 was a much better experience than '33 for Babe Ruth. He was prepared for another significant pay cut and stoically accepted a one-year contract for $37,500. He was well rested, although slightly overweight at 235 pounds. Babe just played surprisingly good baseball. As always, Ruth was also extremely considerate to his fans. On March 13, he delayed the start of his workout for twenty minutes until everyone seeking either a photograph or autograph was satisfied. His first competitive home run came on the 17th in St. Petersburg, when he slugged one far over the right field fence against the Boston Braves. The following week, he took advantage of the cozy ballpark in Clearwater, smacking four homers in two games versus the Newark Bears. After breaking camp on April 1, the Yanks went to Atlanta for a pair of games, where Babe also squeezed in a round of golf with Bobby Jones. When he batted for the first time in Chattanooga on April 9, a band marched onto the field, and the game was halted until

Ruth signed each of the instruments. Babe batted an impressive .415 in the process. He was ready for opening day in Philadelphia.

When the Yankees took the field at Shibe Park on April 17, 1934, the Athletics were a shadow of their recently great squad. The fire sale had continued, and Hall of Fame catcher Mickey Cochrane had left for Detroit as player-manager. In the second game, Ruth sparked a win by knocking the ball through a window across Twentieth Street. He recorded his second homer three days later in Fenway Park, which had been significantly renovated in the off-season. Babe then blasted two homers in the Yankees' annual exhibition game in Albany, but he complained about a lingering "cold" in his chest. This also was an annual event for Ruth. Each March or April, he got sick playing in the cold weather, and, as he got older, these maladies got worse. When April ended, Babe still felt poorly. However, New York was 7 and 4 and in first place.

On May 1 in Griffith Stadium, the Yanks defeated the Senators for the second straight day, and noticed an apparent decrease in Washington's competitive fire. They were right. The Senators never really got it going that year and were not a factor in the pennant race. Something else happened that day that was particularly relevant to the Babe Ruth situation. After reaching base late in the game, Babe gave way to pinch runner Sammy Byrd, who went on to score. Byrd had been replacing Ruth in the field and on the base paths late in games for a few years. Along the way, he had earned the nickname "Babe Ruth's Legs." There are no official statistics for how often Byrd or Myril Hoag (who did similar mop-up work) scored after Babe reached base safely. However, it occurred on a rather regular basis in Ruth's later seasons and was a mixed blessing. Babe got some much-needed rest, but he also lost credit for numerous runs that were largely due to his ability to get on base.

Against the Tigers on May 4 and 5, Ruth launched three long line drive home runs into Yankee Stadium's right field bleachers. You would think that Babe would have left well enough alone, but, the next afternoon, he was seen hitting fungos for ten minutes before the game. When asked about his activity, Ruth explained that he was trying to achieve "more lift" on his batted balls. Today's hitting instructors would probably cringe at that practice, but Babe Ruth was always recognized as a keen student of the game. He certainly wasn't intellectually well rounded, but he rarely made mistakes on the field. It's unlikely that Babe ever got much help with technique. We know that he essentially taught himself how to hit by watching classic batsmen like Joe Jackson. And who can argue with the results? But was his batting brilliance the product of uncanny natural ability or the effect of his self-tutoring? Almost certainly, it was a combination of both, with the accent on the innate ability factor. Ruth might not have listened even if someone had tried to help, but the record indicates that no one dared to try.

The Cleveland Indians resumed playing some of their games at League Park in 1934, and Babe smashed a 460-foot center field triple there on May 21. That was one of the times that Myril Hoag scored in his place. The Tribe looked good, having moved ahead of the Yanks into first place by the end of the month. Ruth was functioning reasonably well until he was hit on his right wrist by the first Major League pitch thrown by a young A's lefthander named Mort Flohr. That happened on June 8, and, although no bones were broken, it sent Babe into a prolonged slump. Before the game at Yankee Stadium on the 24th, Ruth met famed dancer Bill "Bojangles" Robinson, who sprinkled some "goofer dust" on him for luck. The alleged elixir was merely table salt, but Babe responded with a second-inning grand slam. After the contest, Ruth got together with Robinson in the clubhouse and asked him for more of the magic dust.

A few days later, the Yankees were in D.C. for a series, but Friday was an open date. The Bombers took the opportunity to travel to Norfolk by boat for an exhibition game. Babe went 4 for 4 with a pair of doubles, but the most noteworthy event was the errant pitch that struck Lou Gehrig in the head. He was knocked unconscious for five minutes and was diagnosed with a concussion. The next afternoon, Lou was back in the starting lineup at Griffith Stadium. His consecutive game streak was a marvel of courage and determination, but it came at a heavy price. Any study of Babe Ruth includes insights into the adversity that was overcome by the Iron Horse in setting that standard. For the record, even though that game was eventually postponed in the fifth inning, Gehrig smacked three triples before the rains came. As June came to a close, New York was back in first place with a one-game advantage over Detroit.

The 1934 All-Star Game at the Polo Grounds was not as much fun for Ruth as the first one had been. Babe went 0 for 2 with two walks and one of the five straight strikeouts recorded by Carl Hubbell, for which the game is usually remembered. Ruth had no time to dwell on those events, because the Yanks then went to Navin Field in the Motor City for a big four-game series. The Tigers won three of the four, but Babe salvaged some pleasure by blasting his 700th career home run on July 13. It was a magnificent blow that flew completely across Trumbull Avenue, and landed about 505 feet from where it started. Ruth was exultant and, as he reached home plate, bellowed: "Seven-hundred! Let's see some sonovabitch top that!" Well, two "sonovabitches" named Henry Aaron and Barry Bonds did top that mark, but it took a long time and vastly different circumstances.

Navin Field Detroit: Babe Ruth's 700th home run at Navin Field in Detroit; it flew about 505 feet. *(Burton Historical Collection, Detroit Public Library)*

A few days afterward, Babe reached another milestone by walking for the 2,000th time. But in the next game, Gehrig blistered a liner off Ruth's right shin as Babe ran from first to second. He went down in a heap, and doctors predicted that he wouldn't play for at least two weeks. As usual, Ruth returned sooner than expected, but he never fully recovered during the regular season. On July 31, the Yanks were still in first place, but the dogged Tigers were just percentage points behind.

Just as in the year before, August was a bad month for Babe and his team. On Tuesday the 14th, the Tigers came to town for five games beginning with a doubleheader. The Bengals were now blessed with a slugger of their own in the person of young Hank Greenberg, who had grown up near Yankee Stadium. The place rocked to a sellout throng of 79,000, but Ruth was a nonfactor as Detroit swept the twin bill. The Yankees did salvage two of the games in the series, but Ruth's biggest contribution was a great diving catch in right field during game four. There was less sunshine in right field than in left at Yankee Stadium, which is why Babe played that position in New York. In some ballparks, the opposite was the case, and Ruth would defend left field. That was one of the few perks that the Yankees ever extended to Babe as a ballplayer. As the month rolled on, Ruth did win a few games with timely drives over or against the outfield fences, but it wasn't enough. By the end of August, the Tigers had a commanding four-and-a-half-game bulge over the Yanks.

Nothing happened to stem the Detroit tide, and September was mostly occupied with speculation over Ruth's limited future. The Tigers clinched the pennant on September 24. Meanwhile, Babe made a series of ceremonial farewell appearances around the American League. No formal decision had been reached about his status in 1935, but everyone realized that the end was near. The Yankees had another good year by winning ninety-four games, but second place wasn't good enough in the Bronx. Ruth hit only twenty-two homers and batted .288 that season. He drove in eighty-four runs and scored seventy-eight, but his defense was now a liability. His slugging average was still good at .537 as was his on-base percentage at .447. Babe Ruth was still dangerous with a bat in his hands, but he was slow in the field and rarely healthy. The truth was that the Yankees didn't know what to do with him. Fortunately for everyone, a grand All-Star tour of Japan was scheduled after the World Series, and Babe was invited. He would be gone for months, which created some breathing room.

Soon after attending the Series, which was won in seven games by St. Louis, Ruth prepared for his epic journey. He sailed from Vancouver for Hawaii on October 20 amid rumors that he would replace either Connie Mack of the Athletics or Joe Cronin of the Senators as manager. That was fine with Babe, who acknowledged his readiness to take on a new role. For a variety of reasons, neither job was ever offered to him, nor was any other Major League managerial position. Until the day he died, that missed opportunity was the greatest sadness in Ruth's life. For the present, Babe was excited about playing on foreign soil and anxious to meet new fans. There was a brief stop in Honolulu, where one game was played to keep the team in some semblance of baseball shape. The Americans then arrived in Tokyo on November 2 and were treated to a motorcade along the Ginza (Tokyo's equivalent to Broadway) before a half-million cheering fans. Everything was ready for the first game two days later at Meiji Shrine Stadium, where all 65,000 seats had already been sold.

In that first game, Babe got little to hit, going 1 for 3 with a single and three walks. But over the course of the entire eighteen-game series, he was absolutely sensational. Ruth's teammates included such stars in their primes as Jimmie Foxx, Lou Gehrig, Earl Averill, and Charlie Gehringer. It didn't matter. Somehow, he rolled back the clock, and clearly outshone them all. He bombed thirteen home runs and batted .408, which were both significantly better than anyone else. Babe also led the American contingent in every form of fan interaction, and the Japanese seemed to worship the ground he walked on. More details of the tour will be provided in Chapter Five.

The group then traveled to Shanghai, China, for a single game on December 5. After playing three final games in the Philippines, most of the team returned home across the Pacific. However, Ruth and three others continued west, circumnavigating the globe with stops in Java, India, France, and England. Babe and Claire arrived back in New York on the S.S. *Manhattan* on February 20, 1935. Reporters asked him what he would do next. Ruth had no clear answer. He didn't have a contract with the Yankees, but he wasn't quite ready to retire. He heard that the Boston Braves were interested in him, and he would check into that. After Japan, Babe felt reinvigorated and ready to lick the world.

1935   After considering his options, Babe accepted an offer from the Boston Braves. It included the triple role of player, assistant manager, and team vice president, and, ostensibly, would lead to the club's managerial position. The Yankees were also pleased, since they could look magnanimous in granting Babe his unconditional release. They did that on February 26, saying they didn't want to hinder Ruth in advancing his career. On March 1, Babe was back in Boston to sign his one-year contract for $25,000 and a percentage of any profits. The city was overjoyed at his return and treated him as a messiah. Bostonians had never accepted Ruth as a New Yorker. To them he remained a local institution, and it seemed natural that he was back where he belonged. By a coincidence, the Braves also trained in St. Petersburg, where Ruth was also regarded as a local icon. When he arrived on March 4, Babe received his second tumultuous welcome in a week. Unfortunately, the Braves' owner, Emil Fuchs, wasn't the benign patriarch that he had portrayed to Ruth, and Babe's golden carriage would soon turn into a pumpkin.

On March 5, 1935, Babe Ruth stepped up to the plate at Waterfront Park to take his first practice swings as a National Leaguer. It was a place that he knew well, and he knocked the fifth pitch far over the right field fence onto the hotel porch. Much of the scene looked familiar, but Ruth was wearing a uniform with bright red trim instead of the gray Yankee pinstripes. Plus, he would compete against the New York Yankees instead of leading them. Since the Braves and Yanks trained in the same town, they scheduled several games against one another. The two teams played before unusually large crowds until they broke camp in early April. Babe was somewhat heavy at 235 pounds, and he hit no official home runs in Florida. But he clubbed a lot of long fly outs, including a 460-footer into a stiff breeze off Dizzy Dean. The aging Bambino was still lethal at bat. The biggest question was where to play him on defense.

Ruth, of course, was known as an outfielder and had once been a great pitcher. But he was also a highly experienced first baseman, since that was his usual position during exhibition games. As he got older, the Yankees would have shifted him to first, but for the presence of Lou Gehrig. When Babe joined the Braves, regular first sacker Baxter Jordan was involved in a contract dispute, so Ruth played most spring games at that position. Jordan finally signed, but Ruth wanted to stay at first base. At age forty, Babe wasn't a good defensive performer at any position, but he was best suited to stay where he had practiced. Plus, he was Babe Ruth. Who was Buck Jordan? He was a solid pro, but, in ten Major League seasons, Jordan hit a total of seventeen home runs. Yet when the season opened, Jordan was at first base, and Ruth was in left field. It didn't make any sense. Playing first base instead of the outfield would have helped to keep Babe in the lineup, and wasn't that what the Braves wanted? As Ruth soon discovered, nothing about the Boston Braves organization made much sense.

As the Braves headed north toward Boston and opening day, Babe started to assert himself. In Savannah on April 4, he pounded a 500-foot shot into the remote right field bleachers, a hit that was longer by far than any other drive in city history. In BP, he had hit one even farther that cleared the bleachers. Three days later in Newark, Ruth smashed two homers, the second one being the longest ever at Ruppert Stadium. It cleared the fence in deep right center field by some 50 feet and landed outside the park about 500 feet from where it began. Babe's overall spring production hadn't been impressive, but he was peaking at the right moment. It was almost time for the season opener on April 16 at Braves Field in Boston. Gala festivities had been arranged, and a large crowd was expected. It was the kind of scene that always inspired the best in Babe Ruth.

When the big day came, the weather was a disappointment. The temperature hovered around 40 degrees in windy conditions, and there were snow flurries off and on all day. Nonetheless, 23,000 vocal fans came to the ballpark including the mayor, various dignitaries, and five New England governors. They all came to welcome the Bambino back to Beantown. The opposition was the New York Giants and pitching legend Carl Hubbell. In his first at-bat, Ruth smashed an RBI single past Hall of Fame first baseman Bill Terry into right field. An amazed Terry admitted afterward that he hadn't even seen Babe's bullet until it passed him. Ruth then scored later in the first inning for a 2–0 lead. By the time Babe batted for the third time in the fifth inning, he had also made a sensational diving catch.

The day was already a success, but Ruth wasn't finished. He nailed a Hubbell offering high into the gray clouds that sailed far over the head of right fielder Mel Ott. The ball carried well past the fence between the "Jury Box" bleachers and the grandstand, landing 430 feet away. Hubbell groaned, Ruth grinned, and the fans went bananas. The Braves had hired Sitting Bull's grandson, Crazy Bull, as a kind of mascot, and he lived up to his name by wrapping himself around Babe as he crossed the plate. It was yet another seemingly fictional moment in the real life of Babe Ruth. The Braves won the game 4–2, and Ruth was involved in all four runs.

Along with the joy and triumph of opening day came an unwanted but predictable side effect. Babe got sick. As usual, the malady was labeled a "chest cold," but it was almost certainly bronchitis or even pneumonia. It would be a month before he fully recovered. It made it even tougher than normal for an aging athlete to perform. Another problem was that Babe's situation with the Braves wasn't what had been promised. First, on the matter of money, sharing profits meant nothing if there were no profits. The financial status of the organization was much worse than Ruth had realized. Second, manager Bill McKechnie had no intention of stepping aside and moving into the front office. There would be no opportunity to manage the Braves any time in the foreseeable future. Third, the team was just plain bad. They had a fine young slugger in outfielder Wally Berger, but not much else. Babe soon understood that he had been duped by Fuchs, but tried to make the most of the circumstances.

Ruth hit his second homer on April 21, but used the occasion to complain about the wind patterns at Braves Field. Babe wasn't making this up. It was a fact that strong breezes blew in from the Charles River, and made it difficult to hit the ball for any distance, especially in April and early May. According to Ruth, he had already lost four legitimate home runs due to the wind, and contemporary newspaper accounts support his position. But Babe marched on and did the best he could. The next day, the Braves played an exhibition game in Albany, where Ruth socked a pair of 400-foot doubles. He also collided with Hack Wilson, who had a physique like a fireplug. The result was a sprained left knee that lingered for weeks.

A part of Ruth's new job was taking batting practice before games. He still did that better than anyone, and the alluring spectacle helped sell tickets. During BP at Ebbets Field on the 26th, he knocked the ball across the street and through a second-story window. The Dodgers had the damage repaired that night, but Ruth came back the next day and broke the same window. As April turned into May, Babe kept pounding the ball in practice, but wasn't doing much in the games. His batting average remained below .200, and he still didn't feel well.

On May 20, Ruth returned to Wrigley Field for the first time since the 1932 World Series. The next day he bombed his third homer of the season against a house across Sheffield Avenue in right field. Flying about 440 feet, it was the hardest ball he had hit since opening day. More important, Babe acknowledged that he was finally over his "cold," and expected to hit well with the onset of warmer weather. The Braves moved on to Pittsburgh, where Ruth went 0 for 3 in the first game. But in the process, Babe whacked two fly outs to Paul Waner in right center that traveled more than 400 feet. In the next game, Waner again roamed to the wall near right center to catch Ruth's towering fly. Babe's statistics were terrible, but he was hitting the ball hard. He was due to break out. Then came May 25, 1935, and Babe didn't just break out, he exploded!

Batting in the first inning at spacious Forbes Field, Ruth lifted a high drive that carried into the lower deck of the huge right field grandstand. It was an imposing poke of close to 400 feet. When Babe hit again in the third frame, he faced Guy Bush, a former nemesis from the '32 Cubs. Ruth nearly broke the ball in half by blasting it on a rising line into the upper deck in right center field. That blow might have traveled 500 feet if not impeded in mid-flight. The only thing that stopped witnesses from talking about it for weeks was Babe's next at-bat.

Opposing Bush again, this time in the fifth inning, Ruth reached back to 1921 and pummeled the ball with such ungodly force that Pirate players were seemingly dumbstruck. Fifty years later, Bush readily admitted that he was still incredulous about what he saw. The ball rocketed upward toward right field, surmounting the 86-foot-high grandstand by another twenty feet. It disappeared from sight, giving indications that it might never return to earth. But eventually it did. The occupants of 318 Boquet Street confirmed that the ball landed smack on the roof of their home with a resounding crash. The flight distance exceeded well beyond 500 feet. Babe slowly pigeon-toed around the bases as players, umpires, and fans stared in bewildered awe. It was a moment of utter magic and the last home run that Babe Ruth ever hit in a Major League game.

This view of Forbes Field in Pittsburgh shows the landing point of Babe Ruth's final three (Numbers 712–714) official home runs on May 25, 1935. *(Transcendental Graphics)*

Ever since 1933, Ruth's career had been a continuous stream of ups and downs. He was magnificent one day, giving hope of eternal youth, and seemingly an old man the next. And so it was at the end. After banging the ball hard for four straight days, culminating with his improbable three-homer performance, Babe appeared invulnerable to age. However, only one day later at Crosley Field in Cincinnati, those images abruptly halted . . . this time permanently. It had been declared Babe Ruth Day in the Queen City, and, in batting practice, Ruth drove ball after ball out of the park. Then the game started, and Babe pulled a leg muscle. He could barely walk, and he would never get another base hit. The end came at Philadelphia's Baker Bowl on Memorial Day, May 30, when he grounded out weakly to first base. Ruth knew he couldn't play for a while anyway and requested permission to attend a reception in New York City. When Fuchs peevishly refused, Babe made up his mind to retire. Being warned of Ruth's intentions, Fuchs decided on a preemptive strike and announced that Babe had been fired. It was an ignominious end to the greatest athletic career in sports history.

And it didn't have to happen. A cursory look at Ruth's 1935 numbers indicates that he was ready for the scrap heap. He batted a measly .181 and hit only six home runs. But some of the extenuating circumstances have already been discussed. When you examine Babe Ruth's last years closely, it becomes apparent that, when healthy, he still played excellent offensive baseball. Ultimately, Ruth was forced out of the game by two factors. He kept getting "chest colds," and his legs were weak. How those conditions might have been avoided will be discussed in a later chapter. Now take a longer look at those 1935 statistics in the total context of everything that happened.

Ruth played in twenty-eight of the Braves' thirty-five games until his retirement, but he was either sick or injured for about twenty-five of them. In that time, he lost five home runs to unusually adverse winds, and five other times was retired on long drives that would have been homers under ordinary circumstances. Specifically, those three 400-footers in Pittsburgh would have been certain homers in any other National League Park except possibly the Polo Grounds. Other examples include two long drives to the Cubs' Chuck Klein at the base of the Jury Box in Boston on May 9 and 11. He also hit a series of line drives and hard smash groundouts that went for outs. Cardinal Hall of Fame second baseman Frankie Frisch got in the way of a few of those and testified to their brute force.

Over the course of a whole season, those things would have evened out. And when Ruth was finally healthy for the first time since opening day, he genuinely pounded the ball. If just half of those lost homers had gone out, he would have hit eleven by the time he quit. Even allowing for continued lost time at his earlier rate, Babe would have been on pace to hit forty-eight home runs for the season. His batting average would also likely have risen to the level of respectability. Eventually, Ruth would have lost his ability to play at the Major League level, but it hadn't happened yet. If he had had the benefit of modern health care and athletic training, he almost certainly would have been productive for another two or three years.

Either way, it remains today as the greatest career in baseball history. Babe's lifetime batting average was .342, which is nearly incredible considering how hard he swung. His slugging percentage is higher than anyone else by 56 points at .690, and exceeded .700 when he wasn't pitching. Ruth's on-base percentage is second all-time to Ted Williams at .474, resulting largely from his 2,056 base-on-balls. He scored 2,174 runs (tied for third) and drove in 2,209 (second all-time). Of course, he also blasted 714 home runs, whose combined distance is laughably longer than anyone else's. Any way you work those statistics, Babe Ruth emerges as the game's greatest offensive force. And he accrued those numbers while pitching for about four full seasons! On the mound, he won ninety-four games, while compiling a .671 winning percentage and 2.28 ERA. For the record, those are the sixth and tenth best ratings ever in those respective pitching categories. During his prime years, Ruth was also a top defensive outfielder and a feared base runner. And the man played in ten World Series (winning seven), where his numbers were somehow even better. Don't bother to quantify the total thrills and pure joy that Babe provided, because those factors are beyond estimation.

4

The Ultimate Season:

1921

 IT IS NOW TIME to revisit Babe Ruth's 1921 season, which was so stupendous that it deserves its own chapter. Most fans know that Babe enjoyed his most celebrated season in 1927, but few realize that he was at his best in '21. In fact, when he reported to the Yankees' new spring-training headquarters in Shreveport, Louisiana, in early March, Ruth was about to embark on the greatest individual season in baseball history. There have been many superb seasonal performances over time, including Ty Cobb's ten years before and Barry Bonds's eighty years later. But considering all factors, Ruth in 1921 was transcendent. He set performance standards throughout the entire season that no other baseball player has ever approached, accomplishments that seem unbelievable in retrospect.

Oddly, this was the first year that Babe's weight became an issue. After a two-year absence, Ruth returned to Hot Springs, Arkansas, for the alleged purpose of shedding some winter poundage before reporting to spring training. Apparently, Babe spent as much time at the racetrack and nightspots as at the bath house and mountain trails because, when he arrived in Shreveport on March 6, he looked over-weight. But Ruth claimed that he had hiked, golfed, and played basket-ball throughout the winter, concluding that he was fit and ready for a monster season. He was right.

In his first batting practice, Ruth smacked nine balls over the fences at Gasser Park, including a tape measure shot to center field. The fol-lowing day, in his first intrasquad game, he belted another one in the same direction. That competitive homer flew past the flagpole, which was 424 feet distant, and was instantly labeled as the longest in the city's history. Then on March 13 against the minor league Shreveport Gassers, Babe went 6 for 6 with three titanic homers. He got an extra chance in one of those at-bats by lifting a foul pop so high that it actu-ally knocked down the Gasser first baseman as he tried to catch it. Sim-ilar scenarios occurred many times in Major League games. Whether he was launching towering pop flies or ripping torrid ground balls, no fielder enjoyed catching Babe Ruth's batted balls. The incidence of offi-cial errors on Ruthian drives was much higher than normal, but there are no statistics to tell the exact frequency.

After breaking camp on April 1, the Yankees scheduled one of their typical spring tours, working their way north for opening day. They played games in New Orleans, Birmingham, Atlanta, Winston-Salem, Richmond, Baltimore, and finally at Ebbets Field in Brooklyn. Ruth's play was adequate. During his long years as a player, Babe tended to fall into the habit of sliding on one side only for extended periods of time. First, he would slide right for a while, then to the left, and so on. In the spring of 1921, Ruth was continuously flopping onto his right side while sliding into bases. As a result, his right wrist had become sore and swollen, and he started the season wearing a bandage.

There was some concern, of course, but, then the official season opened. It was April 13, 1921, and 39,000 New Yorkers packed the Polo Grounds to see the Yankees take on the Philadelphia Athletics. In his first at-bat, Babe lined a single off the right field wall and scored the Yanks' first run of the season. Ruth went 5 for 5, including two doubles (one flying 455 feet) as New York won 11–1 behind staff ace Carl Mays. Three days later, Babe hit his first home run. It aptly demonstrated the difference between hitting homers in Ruth's time and the present. His circuit was a high fly ball that landed in the nearby right field upper deck. If Ruth were playing today with a typical 330-foot foul line, it might have been caught. But, in that same game, Babe hit two long fly outs (to center and right center) that would have easily cleared any modern fences. He also hit two long fouls, one of which would certainly have been ruled fair under today's conditions. Ruth never hit four home runs in a Major League game. But, if he had played with current rules and stadium dimensions on April 16, 1921, he might have done so. Instead, he wound up with one four-bagger.

Something interesting then happened on April 27 versus the Senators in New York. Babe had strained his right knee sliding into first base ten days earlier, rendering him nonthreatening on the base paths. He went 0 for 2 that day, but, typically, walked twice. That's when he reminded the Senators who Babe Ruth really was. First, he scored from second base on a sacrifice fly to center field. Later, he advanced from first to third base on an infield hit. Although a little pudgy at this stage of his career, Ruth could run very well. Over the years, he would gain weight, lose it, and then gain it back. But for most of his time on the baseball diamond, Babe Ruth was a fast runner regardless of his girth. In 1921, he stole seventeen bases and ran the bases with skill, daring, and aggressiveness.

On May 6 at Griffith Stadium in Washington, D.C., Babe hit that park's longest home run by thumping one over the 40-foot scoreboard in deep right center field. When the ball landed near a house across a street and backyard, it had been airborne for about 490 feet. He then left with his mentor from his teen years, Brother Mathias, on an overnight visit to Mount Saint Mary's School near Baltimore. That evening he gave a speech to the students. The following morning he engaged in a hitting exhibition that lasted over an hour until all the balls were lost. Ruth then drove back to D.C., where he had to face Walter Johnson. Unfazed and undaunted, he broke his one-day-old local distance record by about 30 feet. This drive sailed majestically over the 30-foot center field wall at a point 450 feet from home plate. It was astonishing.

Four days later in his *New York American* column, Babe said that he had never hit a ball harder. According to Ruth, much of the unnatural force came from Johnson's blinding fastball. He anticipated it and made perfect contact with perfect timing. Babe wrote this about the pitch from his honored adversary: "It was the swiftest pitched ball I ever faced—and, I feel, the swiftest, truest ever flung by an arm that has no equal for pitching." Ruth felt that this drive would have cleared the center field bleachers at the Polo Grounds. And he predicted that he would eventually do just that if other pitchers had the nerve to challenge him with fastballs over the plate.

Griffith Stadium, Washington, D.C.: Babe Ruth's tremendous center field home run off Walter Johnson at Griffith Stadium on May 7, 1921. *(Philadelphia Athletics Historical Society)*

The Yankees then left on another long road trip with Ruth making his mark at every stop. In a four-game series in Detroit, Babe seemed to be everywhere. His tremendous center field home run won the first game 2–1, but the next day he was out (barely) trying to steal home, thereby losing by the same score. His homer and long ninth-inning triple won the third game. Going into the ninth inning of the final contest, Ruth had walked three times. The Tigers led 4–3 when Ruth batted again, but now the bases were loaded. Detroit had no choice. In came the pitch and out went the pitch (against a strong wind) to the center field wall, driving in three runs for the victory. Moving to Cleveland, Babe belted one 480 feet to the top of the wooden bleachers just left of dead center field for yet another local distance record. That happened on May 14, and three days later he blasted a comparable drive just right of center. Then in St. Louis, Ruth hit his longest home run of the month and possibly his longest yet in a Major League game.

Starting that fourth game against the St. Louis Browns on May 25, Ruth was in a foul mood. He didn't have a hit in the series. The Browns simply wouldn't throw him any decent pitches. They had walked him six times, including twice intentionally with runners on first and second base. Entering the seventh inning, Babe's frustration had mounted even more. He had managed to get a hit in the fourth inning, but he also had been hit by a pitch and struck out. Worst of all, he hit a 460-foot shot to the center field wall just the inning before that was caught by Bill "Baby Doll" Jacobson. Veteran spitballer Urban Shocker was still on the mound when Ruth batted again with two out and two men on. The Browns led 5–3 at that point, and manager Lee Fohl wanted to pass Babe once more. Shocker was a proud man as well as an intense competitor, and he talked Fohl into challenging Ruth. As usual, it was a bad idea.

Babe bombed this one so far to center field that Jacobson could only stand and watch. Sportsman's Park had not been renovated yet, and the bleachers were a minimum of 460 feet away. Despite that imposing distance, the ball landed high in the seats, and Babe had one more "longest ever" on his resume. The *St. Louis Globe-Democrat* reported the distance as: "500 feet at a rough minimum estimate." The *New York Times* said; "200 yards" (the equivalent of 600 feet), but the most likely distance was about 535 feet. If this sounds like a pattern, it was. Before the 1921 season ended, Ruth hit at least one genuinely historic tape measure home run in all eight American League cities. At this point, he wasn't even half finished.

Sportsman's Park, St. Louis: Babe Ruth recorded one of many historic 1921 home runs in St. Louis on May 25. *(Philadelphia Athletics Historical Society)*

Of course, Babe wasn't just hitting them far; he was also hitting them often. He clouted ten in May, and increased the pace with thirteen in June for a season total of twenty-eight. Suddenly, his "unbreakable" home run record (fifty-four in 1920) seemed breakable. At home on June 11, Babe reached for an outside pitch and lined it into the right field lower deck. The Yanks' opponents were the Detroit Tigers, who then employed the irascible Ty Cobb as their player-manager. Ruth knew that Cobb had a standing order not to give him hittable pitches, so he mocked the Georgia Peach as he rounded the bases.

When Ruth drilled another homer in the next game, Cobb went ballistic. He sprinted in from center field and publicly berated pitcher Harvey "Suds" Sutherland. The Sunday crowd watched with relish as Sutherland gestured that his 3 and 0 offering had been a foot outside. Meanwhile, Babe was ecstatic knowing that he had put his nemesis into such a rage. Before the game even started, Ruth had refused to have his photo taken with Cobb. In response, Ty pantomimed a gorilla as he pointed at Babe. The two men argued all day and nearly engaged in fisticuffs three times. Sadly for Cobb, his ordeal was just beginning.

The Yankees had played nineteen games in seventeen days, and had a pitching shortage. So, Manager Miller Huggins asked Ruth to pitch against Detroit on June 13. Babe complied, and, although he didn't pitch great, he did well enough to win. In the process, Ruth struck out Cobb and held him hitless during five innings of mound work. Ty rarely fanned (only nineteen times all year), so this event was particularly mortifying. Cobb lost the psychological battle as well. His pride had been challenged, so he told his pitchers to go after Ruth. Babe started seeing fastballs over the plate, and, as usual, they went out faster than they came in. One came to rest in the upper deck in right, while another became the first ever to reach the distant center field bleachers. On the last day of the series, Ruth added the final insult by walloping two more epic home runs. The first almost cleared the left field bleachers (one of the longest-ever opposite field blows), and the second landed even higher in the center field seats than the record breaker of the previous day.

In those days in the Polo Grounds, there was an exit gate at an angle between two sections of bleachers in deep right center field. It was through this gate that the players walked to and from the clubhouses situated under the bleachers. That spot was 433 feet from home plate, and from there the fence angled out again to its most distant point. At that farthest angle (just right of dead center), the distance was about 475 feet. No one had ever come close to reaching that section of the bleachers until Ruth did it in consecutive days. The first landed in an exit stairway near the green backdrop curtain and bounced against a clubhouse door. That curtain extended from the aforementioned deepest corner to yet another angle in deep left center field.

When Babe did it the second time, he reached the seventh row even closer to the green curtain. Veteran groundskeeper Henry Fabian confirmed the outfield dimensions, and the two blows were estimated at 480 and 490 feet, respectively. It's no wonder that Cobb hated Ruth. Before Babe, Ty had been the game's preeminent player. Not only was Ruth now the top dog, but his power made Cobb's one-base-at-a-time style seem weak and obsolete. During this confrontation, Ruth hit six home runs, and the Yankees won all four games.

Polo Grounds, New York: Babe Ruth's memorable home runs into the center field bleachers at the Polo Grounds on consecutive days in 1921. *(Associated Press)*

It wasn't just Babe's competitive play that was in top form. His showmanship was also shining very brightly. On June 19 before the contest at the Polo Grounds with the White Sox, Ruth engaged in one of his most crowd-pleasing activities. Babe not only hit pitched balls better than anyone else, he was arguably the preeminent fungo hitter of his generation. He would often put on pregame displays that would leave the crowd gasping. Ruth could hit the ball so high in the air that some fielders, even Major Leaguers, would get dizzy waiting for them to come back to earth. Needless to say, they were very hard to catch. On this occasion, Babe decided to go it alone. He lofted a pop-up so high that it almost went out of sight. But, when it finally did descend from the heavens, there was Ruth catching it barehanded. It was an astonishing display of athleticism, but almost routine business for George Herman Ruth.

After their home stand, the Yankees visited the Red Sox at Fenway Park. On June 20, Babe drove one far over the old wooden wall just left of dead center that landed on the garage across the street. Three days later, he pummeled the ball two-thirds of the way up the right field bleachers. In this case, we have a rare opportunity to judge the distance of these drives with current landmarks. Fenway was restructured in 1934, but not all the changes were drastic. The outfield bleachers were converted from wood to concrete, but the location and dimensions remained basically the same. And they're still there, as is the garage across the street. The left center field homer touched down on the two-story garage about 470 feet away, while the right field homer struck a bench 20 feet above field level at a linear distance of about 490 feet.

But Babe Ruth was not just a human howitzer, he was also a very good-natured fellow. Between games of the second consecutive double-header on June 23, Babe didn't even bother to go into the locker room. Instead, he sat in the Fenway stands with a Catholic priest, who had escorted a group of schoolboys to the ballpark. While his teammates and opponents rested inside, Ruth signed autographs and laughed away the minutes. The newspapers didn't mention it, but Babe almost certainly wolfed down a few hot dogs while hanging out with his adoring young buddies.

In that same series, Ruth made a spectacular running catch in right center field. It was only one of many for the year. Returning home to the Polo Grounds on June 24, Babe went flying into foul ground in left field to make yet another sensational grab. Admittedly, the description of outstanding defensive plays can be subjective, but numbers speak for themselves. While playing left field for most of the season (he made the Boston catch in one of his few center field assignments), Babe accrued 348 putouts. That was fourth-best among all American League outfielders, including the eight center fielders. That total irrefutably confirms the speed and dexterity displayed by Ruth as a defensive performer.

When the Yankees-Senators game on June 28 was rained out at the Polo Grounds, Ruth had some unexpected time on his hands. Never one to sit still, Babe drove out to Long Island to visit the training camp of heavyweight challenger Georges Carpentier. Ruth was a friend of champion Jack Dempsey, and had already spent time with him. Babe loved to watch boxing; he was a fixture at almost every important ring event in the New York circuit. So, as a sort of unofficial sports ambassador, he felt obligated to meet Carpentier, who had come to the United States from France. Babe and Georges got along fine, even going for a ride in Ruth's new roadster. Afterward, Babe acknowledged that he liked Carpentier, but predicted a Dempsey victory.

When the fight took place before 90,000 attendees in Jersey City on July 2, Ruth was not among them. He was occupied in a doubleheader at the Polo Grounds, where he blasted two mammoth home runs and thumped the ball all day long. Collectively, Babe went 3 for 5 with three walks, a stolen base, and two homers ruled foul after flying over the grandstand roof. Although he fought valiantly, Carpentier got thumped as well. Babe was heartbroken about missing the fight, but he got together with Dempsey that night to celebrate. Observers of the two powerhouses agreed that it was pretty much a toss-up as to who had hit the hardest earlier in the day.

Entering the month of July, New York was in second place just behind Cleveland. Before leaving for an extended western swing that would include four crucial games with the Indians, the Yanks played three more at home versus the Athletics. In game two of the Fourth of July twin bill, Ruth launched a pop-up near second base that almost left the earth's atmosphere. It was so high that Babe himself said that it was his highest ever. Jimmy Dykes had the loathsome duty of trying to catch it, but really had no chance. After nearly breaking Dykes's hand, the ball dropped loose and was ruled an error. Jimmy was a pretty tough fellow, but he admitted that he had been overmatched.

That was the same day that Ruth wagered $3,000 that he would break his own home run record. Since he was betting on himself to perform in a positive way and, since there were no rules against such activity, he was not punished. What a character! The gambling man and the Yankees then left for Chicago, but stopped in Rochester and Pittsburgh for exhibition games along the way. Those appearances were two of the ten that New York scheduled during the official season.

In the third Chicago game, Babe Ruth went 1 for 4 with a single. Pretty routine, right? Not really. His third-inning single was lined up the middle, but he almost ruined center fielder Johnny Mostil with two other drives in the same direction. In the first inning, Babe had hoisted a towering fly to deepest center field, where Mostil finally staggered under it at the fence. Johnny got a reprieve in the fifth inning, when Ruth hit a foul home run to right field and then tormented left fielder Bibb Falk with a lofty fly out to that sector. Then, in his final at-bat in the eighth inning, Babe decided to pick on Mostil one more time. Johnny was regarded as one of the best fly chasers of the 1920s, but nothing was easy when the Bambino hit the ball.

Ruth powered another one heavenward over second base, and Mostil had nowhere to hide. He drifted back, and waited . . . and waited . . . and waited some more. Eventually, gravity won out, and the ball collided with Mostil's glove before bounding out onto the grass for a two-base error. Writer I. E. Sanborn of the *Chicago Daily Tribune* had this to say: "It was a shame to give John an error, although he was camping right under the fly. It was just like trying to catch a ball dropped off three Washington Monuments piled on each other." Hello Mr. Mostil, meet Mr. Dykes; you two might have something in common.

In a return series in Detroit, starting on the 16th, Ty Cobb got some much-needed redemption by ranging deep into center field to rob Ruth of two extra-base hits. Two days later, he resorted to his old tactics, walking Babe in his first four at-bats. When Ruth came up in the eighth inning with an 8–1 lead, Cobb relented and allowed Bert Cole to pitch to him. Babe connected with all his immense power and smashed the ball nearly lopsided. It roared outward in a straight line over second base and went directly toward the extreme end of the stadium in dead center field. The ball cleared the fifteen-foot wall at the corner of Trumbull Avenue and Cherry Street, and splattered down in the intersection. Of all Ruth's mighty home runs in 1921, this was probably his mightiest and will be discussed further in a later chapter.

The Yankees then concluded their western tour with the much-anticipated four-game clash in Cleveland. Babe's only hit in game one was a line drive single off the 45-foot right field wall. That boundary was only 290 feet down the foul line, and Ruth benefited from some occasional cheap home runs in that direction. But not on this trip. In game two, he hit the wall again in right center for another long single. Then, in the third battle, Babe smashed one so hard off the top of the right field barrier that it bounced all the way back to first baseman Doc Johnston, who threw him out going for a double. Ruth finally changed directions in the last game, but had little to show for it. He did manage one lengthy triple over Tris Speaker's head in distant center field, but the Gray Eagle caught another one near the same spot. The two teams split the series, and Ruth was happy to leave League Park.

Back at the Polo Grounds on July 30, Babe finally got his long-awaited next homer against the visiting Indians. But the Yankees were creamed 16–1, and Ruth had to wait one more day to have some real fun. The game was delayed by rain, but the Bambino entertained the eager crowd by putting on one of his patented fungo-hitting exhibitions. When play finally started, everyone was sloshing around in a mud bath. Most of the players were displeased, but Ruth had a ball during the 12–2 victory. He went 3 for 4 with a single, long triple, and even longer home run, as well as a walk, stolen base, and foul homer. At one point, he tried to score from first base on a right field single, but was thrown out on a close play. Predictably, he barreled into catcher Steve O'Neill and knocked him woozy. The man was irrepressible.

By the way, Babe's four-bagger might have been his best of the year on home turf. He rocketed the ball far over the center field end of the right field grandstand roof. It came down somewhere in Manhattan Field near Eighth Avenue, but we can't be sure exactly where. The horsehide flew well over 500 feet and was favorably compared to the recent Detroit poke. Ruth bombed many monumental shots over that eighty-foot-high roof, but they were soon lost from sight. It is a shame that the Yankees didn't look for witnesses who might have confirmed at least some of the landing points. History would have been well served if they had. Whether home or away, there are no reports of Yankee officials ever leaving the ballpark to investigate the length of their star employee's longest drives. When the game and month ended, the Yanks still trailed the Tribe by two games.

August brought more of the same. New York played well, and Babe Ruth played great. After hitting ten homers in July, Babe added ten more. Ruth lined his thirty-ninth savagely into the upper deck at the Polo Grounds on August 6. He then added his fortieth and forty-first two days later in the same place. They were also struck with wicked velocity: the first banged into the roof façade in right, and the second screamed into the bleachers in right center. All three were hit so hard that the New York press had a hard time thinking up the right adjectives. They used terms like: "screamer," "terrific," "ferocious," "sizzling," "tremendous," and "shattering," as well as many others. Regardless of how they were described, the total was rising quickly. And Babe kept track; he wanted to break that record.

But another element of Ruth's all-around game now surprisingly resurfaced. Despite his intense desire to surpass his prior home run standard, Babe started bunting more and more. Why? It is simple, really. Ruth was in the middle of a pennant race, and he would do anything within the rules to win. He bunted safely on August 8, August 10, August 13, August 31, September 8, September 15, and sacrificed on August 30. Power, speed, and guts are a combination that is hard to beat.

When the Yankees departed on their final extended road trip on August 10, it was a whopper. They were scheduled to play in six of the seven other American League towns and not return home until September 1. Babe kept belting homers, and, of course, at least one of them had to be beyond belief. It was on August 17 in Chicago's Comiskey Park that sheer incredulity was next inspired. Ruth scorched a rising line drive that kept climbing long after it should have been falling. It flew high over the single-deck bleachers in right center field, landed in a soccer field, and rolled toward an armory. This was another blow of genuinely historic proportions.

Comiskey Park was one of the few symmetrical baseball stadiums in the country. It was 365 feet down both foul lines and about 455 feet to center field. The power alleys were in the 400-foot range, and, as anyone can guess, it was regarded as a death trap for power hitters. There was no double-deck grandstand; that wasn't built until 1927. But the single-deck bleachers were about 50 feet deep and rose about 30 feet above field level. There was also a tall scoreboard directly beyond the center field fence. It was difficult to hit a ball into the first row of those bleachers, but the idea of clearing them near center field was totally absurd. Then along came Babe Ruth with his 54-ounce bludgeon.

Newspaper accounts estimated the flight of the ball from 475 feet to a ridiculous 650 feet. As usual, the actual descriptions were more helpful in the quantification process. The *New York World* said that the drive went: "clear over the right center bleachers higher than the big scoreboard in center field." The *Chicago Daily Tribune* used this language in part: "direct line for dead right center . . . sailed clear over the bleachers out near the scoreboard . . . 15 or 20 feet over."

And the *New York Tribune* had this to say: "over the right field bleachers . . . still traveling at high speed when progress halted by an armory." On the fun side, the *New York Sun* reported that: "the out-fielders didn't move and the infielders just laughed." The best estimate is 550 feet, which is farther than any human being should be able to hit a baseball.

It is understood that these references to 500-foot distances are repetitive. But the reader is encouraged to remain cognizant of the extraordinary nature of such recurring greatness. This season is still the only time in baseball history that so many drives of historic distance were struck by one man. By way of example, when Barry Bonds hit seventy-three home runs in 2001, his longest (excepting altitude-enhanced Denver) was 462 feet. In Ruth's day, any drive of that length to center field wasn't good enough for a homer. And 462 feet was the approximate distance of Babe's belt in St. Louis on August 20, just three days after his drive in Chicago The ball merely bounced off the bleacher wall in center, and Ruth was limited to a triple.

On August 21, Ruth clubbed yet another ball about the same distance that flew over the right field pavilion at Sportsman's Park. Sadly for Babe, the umpire was able to follow its flight as it passed to the far side of Grand Avenue. Even though this drive went out of the park in fair territory, it was ruled foul according to the rules of that time. It was one of at least twelve foul homers that Ruth hit during that tumultuous season. How many of those would be judged fair by modern rules? We just don't know. August ended with the Yanks out of first place by a half game, and Ruth six short of his own home run record.

It was about this time that the Babe finally relented to the pressure building from within the scientific community. He was a freak of nature, and everyone wanted to know how he produced such batting power. Throughout the season, Ruth had articles appear under his byline in the *New York American* and had already addressed this issue on several occasions. He had been visited by biologists, psychologists, doctors of all types, and even hypnotists: all wanted to know how he could hit baseballs so inconceivably far. Once in Chicago, two scientists (exact discipline unknown) turned up at his hotel room and actually stuck pins in him. After he threw them out, he vowed to have nothing more to do with any of them.

But finally, sportswriter Hugh Fullerton, whom Babe knew and trusted, convinced him of the importance of such tests. After a grueling game at the Polo Grounds, Ruth and Fullerton hurried over to Columbia University, where two psychologists analyzed their famous subject. The results were published in the October edition of *Popular Science Monthly,* and will also be addressed in a subsequent chapter. Ruth's explanation was somewhat less sophisticated than the scientists': "When I see the ball coming, I swing my head off."

When the Yankees played a Labor Day doubleheader in Boston, Babe went 3 for 9 with a single, long triple, and impressive home run. The sellout crowd at Fenway Park lapped it up, but they may have been more impressed with their beloved Bambino's defense. He raced in from left field early in game two and snagged a foul fly just behind third base. His momentum actually carried him to the edge of the visitors' dugout, where he yanked out a support post attempting to avoid injury. Ruth made a catch of comparable quality the next day. During this stage of his career, Babe Ruth could really throw the leather.

Babe then finished some important personal business on September 9 at Shibe Park in Philadelphia. That was the only place in the AL where he had not hit a monstrously long home run during the 1921 campaign. When his fourth-inning drive passed high over the bleachers just left of center field, the mini-quest was over. The ball was last seen passing through a tree on the far side of Somerset Street. According to the Athletics' groundskeeper, who took measurements after the game, that greenery was situated 500 feet from home plate. It was also Ruth's fifty-fourth home run, thereby virtually assuring himself a new record.

Shibe Park Philadelphia: Babe Ruth's 510-foot home run into a tree in deep left center field at Shibe Park in 1921. *(Philadelphia Athletics Historical Society)*

The official record breaker was delivered on September 15, 1921, at the Polo Grounds. It was another beauty. Babe smoked a line drive into the upper deck all the way to the center field end of the grandstand. The *New York Post* wrote: "It traveled straight on a line into the extreme end of the upper right field tier." And the *New York World* added these comments: "in the extreme corner of the upper right field stands, so fast that the eye could scarcely follow." For good measure, Ruth launched number fifty-six the next day so far over that right field grandstand that the *New York American* suggested that the ball may have landed on Eighth Avenue. They also opined that it was Ruth's longest of the year in New York City. Any way the ball was judged, it was monstrous.

Now it was stretch time, and New York and Cleveland were neck and neck. The Yankees had never won a pennant since their creation in 1901, and they felt the pressure as the Indians came to town for a four-game showdown on September 23. When the two teams took the field at the Polo Grounds, they were deadlocked in a tie. They split the first two games, and New York won big in game three. They had a one-game lead, but the fourth and final tilt would be huge. Up to that point, Ruth was 5 for 8 with four walks and no home runs. Cleveland came out breathing fire and scored three runs in the first inning. Babe cooled them off by countering with an immense homer in the bottom of the frame off Cleveland ace Stan Coveleskie. The Bambino then cleared the right field roof in the fifth inning and added a 450-foot opposite field double along the way. When the smoke cleared, Ruth had five RBI in an 8–7 victory.

But it wasn't over yet. There was still a week left and a few more ballgames to win. After being shut out by the Browns, the Yankees traveled back to Philly for two more games. But, to everyone's horror, Babe Ruth did not accompany his team. He stayed home as rumors circulated that he had suffered a nervous breakdown. With Ruth, everything was big: his home runs, his appetites and, yes, even rumors concerning anything to do with him. Actually, he just had a cold and was in uniform the next day at Shibe Park. When that game was rained out, the two teams arranged a doubleheader the following afternoon in New York. The Yankees won the first game and finally had their pennant.

During that stretch run, Babe had some further intimate encounters with the peculiar outfield dimensions at the Polo Grounds. His fly out to Chicago's Amos Strunk on September 14 came down near the Eddie Grant Memorial in deepest center field. Ruth then slammed a triple the next day that short-hopped the center field screen. His next triple, on the 18th, landed between the Grant Memorial and that screen. It was on September 26 that Babe blasted the aforementioned opposite field shot against the fence in deepest left center. All four drives flew a minimum of 450 feet, but none resulted in home runs. If you hit the ball down the lines, you made some easy homers; if you didn't, you were in big trouble.

If the Yanks thought that the pressure was off, they were very much mistaken. They then had to play their hometown rival New York

Giants in a best-of-nine World Series. It was the ultimate matchup, featuring John McGraw's strategic brilliance versus Babe Ruth's animal power. Both teams played in the Polo Grounds, but the Giants owned that park and had already ordered the upstart Yanks to leave. The Series would not be a lovefest. New York was in an absolute frenzy, as the Giants were installed as 6 to 5 favorites.

In game one on October 5, Ruth drove in the first run of the Series with a line drive into center field. Nothing more was needed. Yankee ace Carl Mays shut out the National League champions on five hits, breezing his way to a 3–0 victory. The Yanks took the field the next day amidst a circus-like atmosphere. During batting practice, Ruth's wife Helen flew over the ballpark at an altitude of 2,000 feet and dropped three inscribed baseballs by way of parachute. Never one to ignore a good time, Babe celebrated the moment by pounding a stupendous BP drive high into the center field bleachers. It was easily the longest drive that anyone had ever seen at the Polo Grounds; the fans went nuts.

When the game started, Ruth reached base on all four at-bats, including three walks and a fielders' choice. He stole second and third base on successive pitches in the fifth inning and later scored a key run. Waite Hoyt did even better than Carl Mays, whitewashing the Giants 2–0 on a masterful two-hitter. It looked like a Yankee stampede, but a seemingly minor incident would soon change baseball history. Remember when Babe kept sliding on his right side earlier in the year? Well, he had stopped doing that. Instead, he was now hitting the dirt on his left side. When he stole third base during the game, he had scraped his left elbow, and, during the night, the wound became infected.

It already looked bad when Ruth did the same thing the following day. He fired a line drive single into right center in the third inning to drive in two runs. Miller Huggins then signaled for a hit and run, but Bob Meusel swung through the ball. Babe slid hard into second base, and, as he was tagged out, he really ripped his arm open. At day's end, the Yanks had been humbled 13–5. As the fourth game on October 8 was rained out, the Yankees received word that Babe's condition had worsened to the point that he would miss the rest of the Series. Suddenly, the Yankee circus was over.

Against his doctors' advice, Ruth made a surprise start the next day, somehow contributing a line drive single and tremendous home run. It seemed like a miracle, but the Giants won anyway, 4–2. By the time Babe took his position the next day in left field, he could barely stand up. The infection had spread through his body, and he was a very sick man. He played anyway. Swinging weakly, Ruth struck out three times. But he reached base on a fourth-inning bunt and then streaked all the way home on Meusel's double. That exertion caused Babe to collapse in the dugout, but it had also given his team a 2–1 lead. Hoyt was great again, and he beat the Giants by a 3–1 score. The Yanks were one game up, and a glimmer of hope returned.

But, later that night, a team of physicians examined Ruth and put their foot down. Fearing permanent injury, they demanded that Babe not play. That was it. Without their leader and siege-gun, the Yankees lost three in a row. In the ninth inning of the final game, the Yanks trailed only 1–0, and Ruth was permitted to pinch-hit. He feebly grounded out to first base, and the 1921 World Series was over. It was a bitter pill. But when the injury healed quickly, Ruth decided to go through with a prearranged barnstorming tour. It was all that critics needed to claim that the injury had never been that serious. Babe got upset, but soon bounced back and departed for Buffalo to start his post-season itinerary.

The new commissioner, Judge Kenesaw Mountain Landis, had other ideas. He decided to enforce a previously marginal league rule that World Series participants were barred from post-season games. It was a stupid rule that was soon repealed, but it was in the books. Ruth didn't take Landis seriously at first and played the first few games in western New York and upstate Pennsylvania. Of course, Babe's injury had been very serious indeed, but it was an infection, not a broken bone. By the time Ruth arrived in Buffalo, it had been ten days since the original trauma.

Once the problem was brought under control, Ruth returned to full vigor. In five games, he smacked four long home runs and batted over .500. But Yankee co-owner T. L. Huston caught up with Babe in Scranton and convinced him that Landis was on a mission. Realizing his mistake, Ruth canceled the rest of the tour. Of course, Huston was right about the Judge, who wanted to prove himself at the expense of the game's greatest player. Everyone soon knew that Babe would start the 1922 season with a suspension. Since this extraordinary season came to an unhappy ending, it has tended to be underrated. For sure, Ruth's 1927 season was more felicitous, and Babe probably enjoyed it more than 1921. The Bambino finally reached the magic plateau of sixty home runs in '27, and the Yankees won the World Series. Afterward, Ruth got to tour the country with playmate Lou Gehrig. On that trip, he was treated like a god and made a ton of money. But was he better then than six years earlier? No way!

In 1921, Babe batted .378 and slugged .846 with 59 home runs, 44 doubles, and 16 triples. His slugging percentage led the league by an unthinkable 240 points. He drove in 171 runs and scored 177 times. These extraordinary statistics have amazed fans and historians for decades, but they don't tell the whole story. We now know that Babe Ruth was significantly better than even those Olympian numbers suggest. Consider this: he hit more 450-foot home runs (sixteen) and 500-foot homers (nine) in this season than anyone in baseball history in any other year. That's a total of twenty-five homers of 450 feet or more in 1921 alone. Babe also slugged about a dozen other 450-footers that resulted in triples, doubles, fly outs, or foul balls. Along the way, Babe recorded the single longest official homer in Major League annals. Essentially, Ruth hit baseballs so consistently hard that comparisons to anyone else are rendered pointless.

And here's the final piece of the 1921 puzzle: through careful analysis it is possible to determine that Babe Ruth was substantially hindered by the circumstances of the era in which he played. Both that assertion and the title for this book, *The Year Babe Ruth Hit 104 Home Runs,* will be addressed in detail in the final two chapters.

Part Two
The Analysis

5

Hidden Career

NOW THAT BABE RUTH'S Major League career has been summarized, it's time to take a closer look at his so-called hidden career. All players in Ruth's era participated in exhibition games that were not part of their official schedules, and Babe started just like everyone else. A few weeks after the start of his first professional season with Baltimore in 1914, the Orioles had an open date on Sunday, May 3. Jack Dunn and Connie Mack, respective owner-managers of the Orioles and Philadelphia A's, arranged a game at Back River Park near Baltimore. Ruth didn't even get into the game. But it was the start of a twenty-two-year process that would take Babe around the world and to the center stage of some of the greatest sports pageants ever witnessed.

Every Major Leaguer, past and present, participates in exhibition games near their annual spring-training sites. What sets Ruth and his teams apart is the intense level of travel and competition due to the Babe's presence. From around April 1 until opening day a few weeks later, Ruth and New York toured all through the South, Southwest, and Midwest in some of the most ambitious scheduling that anyone could conceive. In addition, Ruth played in a remarkable number of exhibition games during the season on off days. Lastly, Babe's post-season barnstorming activities remain unparalleled and will be a large part of the discussion of Ruth's hidden career.

If you add up all such games during Ruth's historic 1927 season (including spring tour games, mid-season exhibition games, and barnstorming appearances), the total comes to forty-one. The actual grand total of games played by Babe (including standard spring training games, the regular season, and the World Series) was 207 that year. That's a lot of baseball. In some years, Ruth didn't play quite so much (occasionally, he didn't barnstorm), but that number represents a typical annual amount of competitive contests.

In 1919, when Babe Ruth became a full-time outfielder and slugger, he also took over as the premier player in Major League baseball. Not coincidentally, that was the season when Ruth's hidden career took off like a Saturn rocket. Because of Babe's burgeoning popularity, the Red Sox arranged more exhibition games than normal during the regular season. They then stayed together after the regular season for a few contests in New England in early October. But Ruth had blasted the astounding total of twenty-nine home runs that year, and every sports fan in the country wanted to see him.

So Babe decided to cash in on his rising star, arranging several more solo appearances in the Northeast. The experiment was a success, and plans were made for a trip to California. Arriving in Los Angeles on October 28, he was greeted as a visiting potentate. The next three months were a whirlwind of events that changed Ruth's life forever. He played his first game on the Pacific Coast on November 1 as a member

of Weaver's All-Stars against Killefer's All-Stars. On that day, Babe walloped a line drive into the fourteenth row of the right field bleachers
and also hit a pop-up so high that he was stepping on second base as
it was caught. It was a propitious beginning to a new life that would
provide mutual thrills to Ruth and his countless fans.

Besides playing in Los Angeles, Babe also participated in games in
San Francisco, Oakland, and Sacramento. In each city, he clubbed at
least one home run. At that same time, Ruth was also learning his value
as a wage earner. On Christmas Eve, he returned his contract to the Red
Sox office demanding $20,000 per annum. The problem was that the
agreement still had two years to run at 10K per year. That seemingly
exorbitant request prompted Babe's sale on January 5, 1920, to the New
York Yankees, who quickly agreed to pay him the $20,000. He stayed
in Los Angeles for another month savoring the southern California
lifestyle and acting the part of Babe Ruth. At one point, he announced
that he was quitting baseball to become a movie star. When those
laughs wore off, Babe claimed that he would switch to boxing or
wrestling. He appeared just about everywhere, but nobody seemed to
get tired of him. He learned to play golf and somehow managed to get
in about fifty-four holes each day.

When he finally did make it back to Boston, Ruth did promotions for
a local cigar factory, accepted an honorary degree at a dinner in his
honor at the Brunswick Hotel, and crammed in as much miscellaneous
activity as was humanly possible. He arrived for spring training with
the Yankees in Jacksonville, Florida on February 29 without ever
pausing long enough to take a deep breath. During those off-season
months, Babe had earned $15,000. As he joined the Yankees, he had
become more than a deluxe home run hitter; he was a one-man circus.
And now he was on display in New York City, where entertainment
and sports were interwoven like nowhere else.

It didn't take long for the Yankees to test their new investment on
the exhibition market. They enjoyed large turnouts working their way
north through the Carolinas after leaving camp and then played the

Dodgers in three games at Ebbets Field. But the official schedule kept them in the East until June. Both the American and National Leagues were comprised of eight teams in those days, the bulk of the franchises being near the East Coast. In the American League, half the teams were aligned in a narrow corridor, including Boston, New York, Philadelphia, and Washington, D.C. The National League also had teams in Boston and Philadelphia as well as two in New York. The result was a glut of Big League games in the eastern states, but not much anyplace else. In fact, the Major Leagues in 1920 were represented in only ten cities situated from the Mississippi River to the Atlantic Ocean.

That left a lot of fertile ground in between, where the Yankees intended to reap the biggest harvest of needy baseball fans. Logistically, the best opportunities were found traveling between the East and the Midwest, and it was there that they scheduled their first in-season exhibition game of the Ruthian era. After completing consecutive four-game series in each of the four Midwest cities on June 23, the Yanks left St. Louis for New York. They had a single open date before meeting the Red Sox at Yankee Stadium on the 25th. If they could schedule a game somewhere in between and still arrive in New York on time, they could add to the all-important bottom line. The ideal place turned out to be Columbus, Ohio.

After traveling all night by train, the Yankees pulled into Columbus in the morning hours amidst a carnival atmosphere. The place was in a frenzy because Babe Ruth was coming. There were festivities all over town, and Ruth was besieged with requests for appearances at every local institution. He did all that was humanly possible, while trying to retain enough energy to perform at the Herculean level that would be expected of him at the ballpark. The actual game was played at 3:00 P.M. at Neil Park against a semipro team known as the Panhandles before a crowd of 6,020. Ruth started things off satisfactorily by smashing six impressive batting practice homers and signing innumerable autographs. During the contest, Babe played right field and went 2 for 3 with a double, home run, and a walk. His homer was a savage line drive over the fence in right center, but it wasn't quite as imposing as a shot he launched over the right field bleachers that went just foul. Along the way, he also stole two bases and pitched the final inning in a 10–1 victory. Predictably, Ruth left Columbus with the townsfolk singing his praises. Just for the record, the Yankees played their game against Boston the next day in New York, and Babe blasted two home runs.

There were only two cities in the Major League circuit where the Yankees were not scheduled for official games. They were Pittsburgh and Cincinnati, obvious destinations for exhibition appearances. New York targeted Pittsburgh first, and played the Pirates at Forbes Field on their last western swing of the 1920 season. Traveling between New York and Cleveland with a day off on September 8, the Yankees had no problems scheduling this game. The park's towering right field grandstand had not yet been constructed, and Ruth belted a homer far over the right field wall. It was hailed as the longest ever in the Steel City by the sellout crowd of 25,000. Since Pirates fans did not ordinarily get a chance to see Babe, the Yanks capitalized on their interest by organizing a game about every other year. They soon adopted a similar policy in Cincinnati.

After completing consecutive series in Cleveland and Detroit on September 14, 1920, New York had another day off before playing in Chicago. This time they stopped at Toledo's Swayne Park for a contest with the local minor league team. Ruth belted a pair of homers in front of 12,000 appreciative fans before the Yankees left town to face the White Sox. From there, they went to St. Louis for three more games before returning home to finish the year in the East. However, they had two days off due to the League's practice of keeping some days open for the rescheduling of rainouts late in the season. Since the Yankees were already caught up, they made the most of the opportunity by playing the Indianapolis Indians at their local site (Washington Park) on September 22 and the Orioles the next day in Baltimore. They drew 15,000 in both places. These games were contested on the level. It should be noted that New York lost both of these outings by one run.

So far, 1920 was a fascinating year in Babe Ruth's "other" career, but it was still far from over. By October 1, the Yankee season had ended, which signaled the beginning of Babe's barnstorming activities. He played a series of games in the East, including several against various Negro League teams. Ruth gave an especially amazing performance facing the Pittsburgh Colored Stars on the 13th in Buffalo. While playing first base, right field, catcher, and pitcher, Babe belted two long home runs. But that is only part of the story. He also flied out to the center field fence and crashed two monstrous foul homers that might be ruled fair today, coming within a whisker of recording five home runs in this single contest.

He then ventured to Oneonta, where he pounded another homer while fracturing a small bone in his left wrist. Of course, the injury put his upcoming trip to Cuba in jeopardy. But he played through the pain during the next two weeks and sailed from Key West on October 29 having healed only partially. Ruth joined John McGraw and the Giants to play a series of ten games. That was an event in itself, since McGraw didn't like Babe. He resented the way Ruth had changed the game from the old style of strategy and guile to raw animal power. But Babe was huge box office, and McGraw wanted to make a buck like everyone else. He encouraged Cuban promoter Abel Linares to make Ruth an offer that Babe couldn't refuse.

They played the first game versus the Almendares Blues at their home park in Havana on the 30th before a gathering of 10,000 islanders. Overcoming seasickness from the rough crossing earlier that same day, Babe went 2 for 3 with a long center field double and right field triple. Playing center field, Ruth also had an assist to home plate as the Americans won 4–3. However, the Giants and Ruth soon discovered that Cuban baseball was played at a very high level; the series was intensely competitive. As for Babe, he played in nine of the ten games staged in Havana, and then participated in two more in Santiago. There is no box score from the second Santiago game, but he went 11 for 32 in the ten documented contests. He recorded two homers, three triples, three doubles, and slugged at an .839 pace. On November 6, he had to take a backseat to Cristobal Torriente, the black "Cuban Babe Ruth," who hit three home runs. But, all in all, Ruth had a good time.

The Cubans cheered him passionately wherever he went, which was just about everywhere on the island. He showed up at the race-track, jai alai matches, cigar factories, golf courses and, of course, at the side of some very attractive señoritas late at night. And on November 8 in Havana, Babe launched an imposing home run to left center field that local officials estimated at 550 feet (although it was probably more like 520). According to Cuban historians, that blow is still revered today. It wasn't until Christmas Eve that Ruth finally returned to the States. Legends abound that Babe returned home flat broke, that he lost all his earnings gambling on jai alai and the horse races. Most of them are probably true. At that stage in his life, Ruth did enjoy gambling, and he certainly liked spending his money. Either way, he didn't miss any meals, and no permanent harm was done. It had been a breakthrough year in Babe's alternate career, and he saw no reason to slow down.

In 1921, Ruth and the Yankees did more of the same. They made their first visit to Redland Field (later known as Crosley Field) in Cincinnati on July 25, where Babe bombed two gigantic home runs before 16,361 very happy witnesses. It was a banner year all around until October, when Ruth injured himself in the World Series. The Yan-kees lost to the Giants, and Babe then tried to forget his troubles by barnstorming despite his restriction as a Series participant. The 1921 chapter has already addressed the consequences of that mistake. It's a real loss to baseball history that the scheduled tour was canceled, because Ruth was at the height of his athletic prowess. That cross-country trip would certainly have created some amazing memories for thousands of would-be fans.

Undaunted, Babe resumed business as usual the following spring, leaving folks gaping all over the state of Texas with his prodigious power, incredible energy, and unparalleled showmanship. When he came to bat for the first time on March 31 at League Park in San

Antonio, people were still talking about his monstrous homer two days before in Galveston. That shot cleared a cigar sign in right field by more than 100 feet. On this occasion, the game was delayed by the Knights of Columbus, who presented Ruth with a silver bat and ball. It was an expensive gift that probably taxed the resources of that well-intentioned organization, but they shouldn't have bothered.

Babe received dozens of these tokens every season, and he couldn't possibly keep them all. The Knights went home happy anyway, because Ruth responded to their gift by slamming the first pitch a record distance beyond the fence in right center field. Despite his early-season suspension, Babe was as much in demand as ever, and the Yanks squeezed in as many extra games as they could. Ruth's best exhibition outing of the season was played in Baltimore's Oriole Park on September 3 between games in Philadelphia and New York. Playing against the Third Army Corps, Babe hammered three straight massive homers, continuing his lifelong success in the city of his birth. The Yankees lost again in the World Series, but the ban on barnstorming had been lifted, which resulted in the oddest of all of Babe Ruth's many baseball adventures.

Babe paired with teammate Bob Meusel and went on a barnstorming tour that included appearances in some of the most unlikely places that anyone could imagine. The first game was played in Perry, Iowa. Not Des Moines, but Perry. The date was October 13, and the weather was cold and windy. A grand total of 800 frigid souls showed up. On successive days, games were next played in Lincoln and Omaha, Nebraska, which, at least, were places that most Americans knew. Then on October 16, Ruth found himself actually playing baseball in freezing sleet in a location that most Easterners couldn't find with a map. The place was Sleepy Eye, Minnesota, and, with respect to the folks who still live there, it's a puzzle why Babe Ruth was in their town in the middle of October. The only conceivable explanation is that they had asked him to come, and Ruth apparently loved seeing new places and meeting new friends. Despite the horrific conditions,

Babe managed to hit two home runs and left the 500 shivering witnesses with stories that are still being retold by their great-grandchildren. And this was just the beginning of a trip that doesn't seem possible in retrospect.

From Sleepy Eye, Ruth journeyed to Sioux Falls, South Dakota, and Sioux City, Iowa, before appearing in the renowned metropolis of Deadwood, South Dakota. It's hard to believe that the world's premier athlete would willingly submit to the logistics involved in these games. Ruth had to travel by train and automobile to get to Deadwood, and then underwent the same regimen the very next day by agreeing to play in Scottsbluff, Nebraska. In truth, he wasn't making much money in these small towns; the weather and the limited populations pretty much precluded that. And he was working extremely hard for anything that he got. At each place, he was asked to visit schools, hospitals, old-age homes, and institutions of every sort, and he rarely said no to any of them. Ruth rode in parades, opened new stores, spoke at banquets, and did just about anything to please these people, who would probably never see him again. He was human, though.

After playing the Negro League Monarchs in Kansas City on October 22, Babe resumed his small-town trek. When he appeared in Pratt, Kansas, on the 27th, he seemed exhausted. Ruth failed to hit a home run, and in three innings on the mound gave up ten runs. The *Pratt Daily Tribune* described the game as a "farce," which may have been unnecessarily harsh, since fans usually appreciated Babe's level of effort. On the rare occasions that he failed competitively, he still left a good impression by virtue of his sincerity and showmanship. The rebuke remained somewhat a mystery for years until more research revealed that Ruth had paid a price for playing a black team, since some white folks didn't approve of interracial activity. Citizens of the region who held that peculiar racial philosophy excoriated Babe for the game with the Monarchs. This issue will be discussed in more detail later. Predictably, Babe rebounded two days later in Denver by taking the town by storm.

Ruth arrived about 9:00 P.M. on Saturday, October 28, but still managed to attend three different functions before calling it a day. When he awoke the next morning, Babe toured the local Rocky Mountains, but was at Merchant's Park in time to put on his customary batting practice display. He pounded five tremendous drives out of the lot, and two of them landed on the far side of an adjoining field. They were regarded as the longest blows ever struck in Denver. For the game, Ruth played for a hometown group called the Whiz Bangs against the Denver Bears. Babe was at first base, which was his usual exhibition position when he wasn't pitching. Finally, Ruth and Meusel were in a big city. But the temperatures were frigid, a condition that plagued the entire tour, and only 700 teeth-chattering fans attended.

By then, Babe Ruth was a show-biz trouper and always acted on the adage that the show must go on. Ruth took immense personal pride in these appearances and tried valiantly to please everyone who came to see him. He almost always succeeded. And so he did on this occasion by going 5 for 5 with two home runs and a stolen base. When he arrived back in New York on November 7, he reported that he had played seventeen games (there were also two rainouts) and had hit twenty homers. When asked about the financial returns, Babe just smiled and said that he had a lot of fun. Over the years, Ruth made a small fortune on these games, but he knew a few days into this trip that the weather would not allow any real monetary success. Anybody else probably would have canceled the remainder of the tour. But Babe trudged on day after day in icy weather before tiny audiences simply because he didn't want to disappoint anyone who had been told that he was coming. He was like that.

As indicated in the season review, 1923 was a remarkable year in many ways for Babe Ruth. He won his first World Series as a Yankee. He compiled his highest-ever batting average and played his best all-around brand of baseball. He also raised the level of his alternate career to an even higher plane. After a rigorous spring training camp in New Orleans, Ruth and the Yankees tuned up for the regular season by touring through the states of Mississippi, Louisiana, Texas, Oklahoma, Illinois, and Missouri. They then played three final games against the Brooklyn Dodgers at Ebbets Field before opening day. Once the regular season was underway, they stopped in Paterson, New Jersey, on Sunday, April 29, for their first exhibition game while en route from Boston to Washington. It may now be difficult to believe, but it was one of fifteen such exhibition games in which Babe Ruth played during this championship season. In the ninth inning versus the Dougherty Silk Sox, he walloped the park's longest-ever home run and was mobbed by an overly exuberant swarm of fans. It seemed like a big deal, but, in fact, it was routine business for the Bambino.

Without exaggeration, it would be possible to fill an entire book on Ruth's hidden career during 1923 alone. We will settle for a few examples. After completing a series in Boston on June 26, the Yanks stopped in Haverhill, Massachusetts, for an encounter with a group of college All-Stars. Babe sent everyone into fits of wonder with his usual pregame batting demonstration, including one drive that almost cleared the football stands in right field. He then went 4 for 5 in the game, while stealing two bases and pitching four innings. During his mound work, Ruth wrenched a knee. Despite the pain, he was able to play the next day against the Athletics at Yankee Stadium. Although not catastrophic in nature, it was another example of the physical attrition Ruth sustained in these performance-oriented appearances. Over the next two months, Babe and the Yanks made return trips to Pittsburgh and Cincinnati and also visited Grand Rapids, Michigan, Indianapolis, Toronto, and Buffalo. At Toronto, he not only blasted a homer into the bay, but launched a pregame fungo off a clock beyond the center field fence. The following afternoon in Buffalo on August 29, Ruth clobbered a home run over a house in right center field, while scoring five times against the Bisons.

Before leaving the 1923 season, there are two other events that should be discussed. After clinching the pennant, but before the season ended, the Yankees went to Baltimore to play three straight exhibition games against the Orioles. Apparently, it was another planned break in the schedule for making up rainouts, but the Yanks were up to date. Ruth had a sprained ankle and should have been resting for the upcoming World Series, which New York had yet to win. Nevertheless, he played the first two games. Babe reinjured the ankle and came to the ballpark for game three using a cane. He sat that one out, but, almost unbelievably, played the next day, when the Orioles came to New York. And guess who he played with? The New York Giants.

That's right, the archrival Giants, who had defeated Ruth and the Yankees in the last two World Series and would be their opponents again in a bitterly anticipated rematch. Injury, rivalry, and the World Series notwithstanding, there was Babe Ruth at the Polo Grounds on October 3, 1923, playing for the hated Giants against his beloved Orioles. He even bombed a homer over the grandstand roof. The game was arranged for charity, and, as discussed, Ruth was a soft touch for just about any worthwhile cause. But this one stretches the credibility of someone looking back from the twenty-first century. No harm was done, since the Yanks won the Series, and Babe was the hero. However, can anyone even imagine any injured modern superstar playing charity ballgames on the eve of the World Series?

As soon as the Series ended, the triumphant Bambino departed on his annual barnstorming tour. This time he stayed closer to home, traveling through western New York and northern Pennsylvania, which was an area that he loved. Needless to say, the trip was filled with much derring-do, but we will limit our review to one day, which pretty well represents the whole two-week saga. On October 29, Babe arrived in Wilkes-Barre, Pennsylvania, at 5:00 A.M. by overnight train from Erie. He wolfed down a huge breakfast, and then went to his hotel, where he slept for a few hours. Shortly before noon, Ruth proceeded to City Hall for the customary honors. From there, he visited a sick child, but showed up at the ballpark in time for batting practice. One of his six BP homers sailed over the center field fence and established the local distance record. Then, in the game against Larksville, Babe went

3 for 5 with a competitive home run to center. On defense, Ruth tickled the crowd with a performance that was unusual even for him. He not only pitched two innings, but also played all nine positions, including catcher. After signing hundreds of autographs, Babe returned to the hotel and then attended two evening banquets. Late that night, Ruth asked about the prospects of finding time to squeeze in a little hunting. Before the Energizer Bunny, there was Babe Ruth.

In 1924, Ruth made his usual number of appearances in unofficial games, and one played in Buffalo on September 12 should be singled out. The Yankees headed west to Chicago after completing a series in Boston. They stopped in Buffalo along the way, although the use of the word "they" may be inappropriate. Manager Miller Huggins, as well as most of the starters, simply bypassed western New York and headed for the Windy City. In so doing, "they" were able to rest a little, while Babe Ruth and some lesser teammates went through the grueling paces of the standard exhibition ritual. Today, it is the opposite. It is the super-star who gets the preferential treatment, which might include an exemption from an unofficial game. But not Babe Ruth. He was the one player that everyone wanted to see, and there would have been no game without him. Babe belted two homers for the 9,000 paying customers, who would mostly have stayed home without the prospect of seeing him.

Ruth then concluded his '24 season with a spectacular barn-storming tour. After starting in Kansas City, most of the games were played in California. Babe began in the northern counties and worked his way south to San Diego. Along the way, he bashed a slew of leviathan homers and performed sensationally in every place he visited. But the best was saved for last. Walter Johnson and the Senators had just won their first World Series, and the Big Train was swimming in a nationwide wave of glory. Southern California was his home turf, and he was much in demand there. Promoters scheduled a game on October 31, which was the last allowable day for a barnstorming contest, and invited Ruth to pitch against Johnson. It was almost too good to be true, and the local folks anticipated the day like a child does Christmas. Of course, the two men had dueled in the past, but never under these circumstances. Johnson had belatedly reached the pinnacle of baseball success and was more popular than at any other time in his storied career. Ruth had been an outstanding pitcher when the two had faced each other man-to-man in earlier years. Now he was a symbol of unbridled power and the personification of the sport itself.

They crammed 15,000 lucky spectators into Anaheim's Brea Bowl as Ruth's All-Stars took the field against Johnson's Anaheim Elks. Long Bob Meusel (Ruth's barnstorming sidekick) hit a homer for Anaheim, and legendary Sam Wahoo Crawford did the same for the All-Stars. When the dust settled, Babe had a complete game 11–1 victory by allowing only six hits and striking out five. An understandably worn-out Walter Johnson departed after five innings, but not before Ruth had tagged him for two stupendous home runs. According to Johnson's biographer, Henry Thomas, the second homer was judged to have flown the astounding distance of 550 feet. However, all was not lost for the Big Train. In Babe's third and final at-bat against Walter, he struck out on three pitches. It is difficult to imagine a baseball game with more appeal than this one, and it has since taken on the mantle of mythology. But it really happened.

Unfortunately, 1925 was the year of Babe Ruth's terrible stomach ailment, and, among other things, it resulted in a temporary cutback to his "hidden career." He started out by playing sensationally in his annual spring tour, but fell ill before opening day. Ruth spent the rest of the season trying to recuperate, and was too weak to take on any extra duties. But by 1926, he was fully recovered, and renewed his efforts to play where no man had gone before. Babe began his barnstorming tour the day after the World Series ended, hopscotching all over the East before heading into the Midwest. Even by Ruthian standards, the itinerary for this trip was brutally difficult. From October 10 until October 24, Babe played a game in a different state (or Canadian province) every day. In South Bend, Indiana, he finally stayed put long enough to participate in the same place on consecutive days. This was at the height of the Knute Rockne era at Notre Dame, and organizers made sure that the Fighting Irish were out of town when Ruth played the first game on Saturday the 23rd. It turned out to be a great day. Notre Dame won their meeting against Northwestern in Evanston, Illinois, and Babe Ruth briefly replaced Rockne as the town's hero.

Ruth appeared on the field before any of his teammates and loosened up by playing with a group of children. As usual, Babe was teamed with a bunch of local semipros against the best area team, which in this case were the South Bend Indians. The contest was held at Playland Park, where there were no outfield fences. That allowed the Indian outfielders to position themselves as deep as they wanted, thereby practically precluding the chance for a Ruthian homer. But, of course, it didn't matter. In the sixth inning, despite nearly freezing temperatures, Babe did what everyone wanted him to do and connected with all his might. This is the way that the *South Bend Tribune* described the result: "the ball sailed and ascended to what seemed dizzy heights and dropped somewhere near the racetrack on the other side of the diamond, a distance of nearly 600 feet." They offered no details as to how they arrived at that estimate, and it may have been an exaggeration.

But it was pure Babe Ruth, and certainly farther than anyone thought that a mortal man could hit a baseball. A curious touch was added before the game the next day when Babe diplomatically asked the organizers if they could obtain better balls. He advised them that he was losing some distance on his shots and wondered where they might obtain some regulation Major League horsehides. That afternoon he contented himself with a 450-foot center field double and a complete game 3–3 tie on the pitcher's mound. By that time, Rockne was back in town, and Babe Ruth headed west to finish the remainder of his tour.

In 1927, everything seemed to work out perfectly for Babe Ruth. The baseball year began with a highly successful spring tour through the southern states, where people demonstrated that Ruth was more popular than ever. Traveling between Knoxville and Chattanooga on April 5, Babe's train made a water stop in Etowah, Tennessee. When he stepped onto the platform to say hello, practically the entire town was waiting in a steady rain just to get a look at him. Two days later in Nashville, the Tennessee House of Representatives adjourned early in an unprecedented procedure to watch Ruth play ball in their city. When the season started, Babe was healthy, and the Yankees were in top form. The results are now part of baseball history. Ruth broke his own home run record by blasting sixty, and the Bronx Bombers demolished all their competitors on the path to winning the World Series. Along the way, the Yankees scheduled eleven extra games, including an experimental night game in Lynn, Massachusetts, on June 24 under the lights. Unfortunately, that one was rained out, and Babe had to wait until 1931 to play under artificial illumination. Before the season ended, Ruth announced plans for his fall barnstorming trip, and it promised to be a humdinger.

The tour started at Kinsley Park in Providence, Rhode Island, on October 10, and concluded in Long Beach, California, on October 31. In between, there were enough heroics to last most Major League stars a lifetime. Lou Gehrig accompanied Ruth and usually played against him on a local team that was called the "Larrupin Lous." Babe dressed in black as opposed to Gehrig's light gray, and his assigned team took the name "Bustin Babes." Occasionally, they met a squad that had enough status to retain their own name, and that was the case on October 11 against the Brooklyn Colored Giants. The game was played in Trenton, New Jersey, at the city's high school field, which was the best ballpark in town. Ruth started slowly, and it is no wonder. He was facing Dick "Cannonball" Redding, who was one of the top pitchers in the Negro League.

In his first two at-bats, Babe popped up, but vowed on the bench to do better against Redding's imposing fastball. In the sixth inning, he did. Ruth reached out and poked a towering drive over the right center field fence, but he wasn't satisfied. Redding wasn't giving him anything in his wheelhouse, and Babe really wanted to tag one with all he had. Cannon Ball finally tired in the seventh, and Ruth got the pitch that he had been waiting for, a belt-high fastball, and he didn't miss it. The ball sailed far over the fence in right center, cleared a three-story house, and landed on the opposite side of Chambers Street for the longest homer ever hit in Trenton. Babe then duplicated this amazing feat the very next inning, finishing the contest with three home runs. And that brings us to an important issue that needs to be discussed. It has been suggested that Ruth benefited from less than an opposing pitcher's best efforts in these exhibition games, that they deliberately laid them right down the middle to help Babe look good for the fans. It is a reasonable theory for consideration. However, that prospect has been painstakingly researched, and, in the majority of cases, it just wasn't true.

It seems likely that Ruth and Gehrig provided each other with soft pitches when they occasionally faced one another from the mound during such games. It may even be possible that a friendly Major League pitcher did the same in certain infrequent situations. An example might be found late in a game where Ruth had not homered and would be called back to bat out of turn. In such an instance, everyone knew what was going on, and it was assumed that Babe would get a batting-practice fastball right down the middle. But that was it. Part of the allure of these games was for local fans to see their favorite native son pitch against Babe Ruth. He never asked for any favors, and didn't get any. The only oddity was that he rarely walked. Ruth knew that nobody came to the ballpark to see him trot to first base, and he would deliberately swing at ball four just to get another chance to hit the homer that everyone coveted. Dozens of amateur pitchers have gone on record and confirmed that they were expected to pitch their hearts out against Ruth.

Regarding the Trenton game, someone once said that Redding was asked by the promoters to take it easy on Babe. That just doesn't jibe with the facts. There are detailed contemporary accounts of the game, and it is obvious that Redding was doing everything he could to vanquish

Ruth. Babe was retired in early at-bats on really nasty pitches. If Redding was trying to make Ruth look good, what was he waiting for? Just as important, I had the privilege of befriending William "Judy" Johnson, and we discussed this issue at length. Johnson is one of the great figures in Negro League history and a Hall of Famer with an impeccable reputation for honesty. He scoffed at the suggestion that Babe Ruth was given any type of preferential treatment in games against Negro League teams. Judy personally managed several games against Ruth and stated that he had no knowledge that any Negro League pitcher ever lay down for him. If there was a difference in their approach, it was that they tried even harder against him. More will be said on this topic in a later chapter.

The tour then wound its way through the Midwest and the Rocky Mountains before reaching California, where many of Ruth's barnstorming trips concluded. Arriving on October 21, Babe and Lou played in San Francisco, Oakland, Marysville, Stockton, Sacramento, San Jose, Santa Barbara, Los Angeles, San Diego, and Long Beach. Naturally, the highlights were many and varied. Babe almost always put on a tremendous show in batting practice, but, in San Francisco on the 23rd, he outdid even himself. Warming up for the afternoon game (after playing in Oakland in the morning), Ruth bombed seventeen balls out of the park. He saved something for the game too, and went 4 for 5 with two competitive home runs. The next day he played two more games.

In the morning in Marysville, he slugged two homers, including a grand slam, despite a sore back. In the afternoon in Stockton, Ruth went 5 for 6 with a circuit shot into some far-off trees beyond the right field scoreboard. On October 27 in Santa Barbara, Babe teamed up with the crew from the U.S.S. *Colorado* at Peabody Field and thumped a titanic homer over the street in left center field and halfway across the high school parking lot. Nearing the end of the tour, Ruth appeared at the other Wrigley Field in Los Angeles, and stole the show from the many Hollywood stars in attendance. He clubbed a series of record batting practice drives and then whacked a double in the game, while also pitching two scoreless innings. There were 28,000 ardent fans crammed into the park on that occasion, and Ruth's share of the take was $10,500. That was a princely sum in those times. When Babe arrived home in New York on November 9, he estimated that he had traveled 8,000 miles, hit twenty home runs, drawn 200,000 paying fans, signed 5,000 autographs, and earned $70,000. It would prove to be his greatest post-season experience until his tour of the Orient in 1934.

The year 1927 was a tough act to follow, but the next season was just about as zany and successful. The spring tour was as hectic as ever, and the Yankees played eleven more exhibition games during the regular season. The most interesting vignette from the unofficial 1928 schedule came at the conclusion of a home stand at Yankee Stadium on June 25. That was a Sunday, and New York's next league game was set for Wednesday in Philadelphia. That meant two days without a scheduled game, and, naturally, the Yankees took the opportunity to showcase Babe and his buddies. They played at Municipal Stadium in John-stown, Pennsylvania, on Monday, where there had been no right field home runs in the two-year history of that ballpark. Ruth took care of that little oversight by knocking two balls far beyond that barrier, while going 4 for 5, and playing first base and pitcher. The Yanks then hopped on a train and arrived in Harrisburg around midnight.

After ostensibly sleeping the night away at the Penn Harris Hotel, Babe awoke to a huge breakfast of ham and eggs. At 11:00 A.M., Ruth met Governor Fisher at the State Hospital and toured the facility as they visited with patients. By 1:00 P.M., Babe was umpiring a boys' baseball game, which meant that he had to hustle to the clubhouse at "The Island Ballpark" for the 3:00 P.M. start of the game with the Har-risburg Senators. In between, he also signed 500 baseballs for charity and put on his customary batting practice display. In the game, the busy Bambino belted a homer and two singles, the second of which resulted in a 6–6 tie. Taking a quick shower, Ruth then had dinner as a guest at the Elks Lodge before departing for his 7:07 P.M. train to Philadelphia. He very nearly missed it when he was ambushed by a bunch of kids waiting for more autographs and handshakes. Fortunately, Babe made the train, and was finally able to relax for a few hours. At the game, there had been 4,212 paying customers, and the Yankees' share of the gate was $2,676. In retrospect, it hardly seems worth the bother from a business perspective (costs must be factored in), but the folks in central Pennsylvania certainly valued the experience.

Ruth's barnstorming journey at the conclusion of another World Series victory was the usual mix of perspiration and pageantry. Babe worked very hard, and the results were sensational. Starting against the Bushwicks just across the Brooklyn Bridge two days after the Series ended, Ruth ventured into Canada and then back into upper New York State. Following his normal pattern, he then turned west and finished at the end of October in Denver. The stop in Louisville on the 24th best exemplifies the month. Babe arrived from his prior appearance in Columbus, Ohio, at 1:40 A.M. and went to the Kentucky Hotel for a little sleep. As soon as he awoke, he was besieged with demands for his time and spent the next several hours stopping all over town in an effort to please everyone. At 2:00 P.M., Ruth gave a speech supporting Democratic Presidential candidate Al Smith, which was an activity that he repeated many times until the November election.

At the usual hour of 3:00 P.M., the game commenced at Parkway Field with Babe at first base for the Epps-Cola team. However, before it started, Ruth blasted two of his signature BP drives. The first one hit the Thompson Oil Station on one bounce, and the second landed on the middle of a warehouse roof beside the Station. Such descriptions are a little fuzzy, but both drives sailed over 500 feet. Once the competition got underway, the game evolved into a slugfest. Babe went 5 for 6 with two doubles and two home runs; one to left center and the other to right center. He also pitched the final three innings, preserving a 13–12 win to the delight of the crowd. When it was over, Ruth bade his farewells and headed for much the same kind of day on the morrow in Dayton. It was grueling, but he made a lot of money and made a lot of people very happy.

However, as discussed in the 1929 section, the years of excessive activity finally caught up to Babe Ruth in June of that season. The combination of personal tragedy and a particularly oppressive spring schedule were the straws that broke the camel's back. Ruth broke down physically and emotionally and rested for three weeks, but, upon his return, the Yankees went right back to the old ways of scheduling exhibition games every chance they got. Luckily for Babe, he had remarried earlier in the year, and his new wife vowed to watch over him. When the season ended, Ruth attended the World Series as a guest journalist, but did not schedule a barnstorming tour at its conclusion. He played in only two local exhibition games and enjoyed some long-sought domestic tranquility. Babe relaxed that autumn by hunting and fishing.

Although the spring tour in 1930 was extremely demanding, there were slightly fewer exhibition games during the regular season. Essentially, Babe then repeated the same post-season scenario as the year before, attending the World Series but not barnstorming. He did play in a few October ballgames, but they were arranged close to home. It was not as if Ruth had it easy those two years; he still had it tougher than any other player simply because he was Babe Ruth. But by cutting back just a little bit, he may have prolonged his career, and he certainly improved his health. And by 1931, Babe was ready to resume his old schedule, even if it was just for a few more years.

Ruth stopped in all the predictable places on the way from spring training to opening day in New York. It was a routine that never changed. Occasionally he didn't barnstorm, and the number of mid-season exhibition games varied, but Babe always played about fifteen contests all across the South or Midwest just prior to the start of the season. In 1931, he was particularly effective in these events, and, at one point, hit home runs in four consecutive days. During the official campaign, Ruth appeared in eight exhibition games, and, as always, tried to make each one of them memorable. Of course, the need to live up to his own image was bittersweet. Babe loved the adulation he received, but it was impossible to perform at Ruthian levels in every situation. A sequence of these games in 1931 demonstrates the monster that had been created.

On July 30, Ruth played in Albany and hit two homers. Then on August 4 in the middle of a seven-game series (that's right, seven games!) at Fenway Park, the Yankees headed for Springfield, Massachusetts, where Babe smacked two more home runs. In Scranton, Pennsylvania, on August 27, Ruth didn't hit a four-bagger, but his center field double flew about 450 feet. Babe next played the Colts of the Middle Atlantic League in Cumberland, Maryland, on September 3, where he somehow blasted yet another long home run. It was an amazing streak of distance hitting, but it had to end sometime. When the Yankees stopped in Wilkes-Barre, Pennsylvania, to play the Barons on September 8, Ruth ripped a shot into deep right field, but it stayed in the park. That was his only base hit for the afternoon, making his bid for a home run unsuccessful. After the game, Babe apologized repeatedly for his failure and seemed genuinely racked with guilt. Feeling an obligation to hit a home run every time he took the field must have been very stressful, but he never complained. Ruth had good common sense. He knew that the rewards of being Babe Ruth were considerable, and he just accepted the corresponding liabilities.

After attending the World Series, Ruth went west for one of his typical barnstorming trips. The first game in Kansas City against the Monarchs was rained out on October 13. That was a pity, since the contest was much anticipated. Babe moved on to Denver for one game and then focused on California for the remainder of the month. The first contest on the 18th featured the Babe Ruth Stars versus the George Burns Stars at Wrigley Field in Los Angeles. Ruth started things off with an awesome array of twelve BP homers and then recorded a single and home run in the game. He played first base and pitched, but lost the contest, when his bases-loaded moon shot was caught at the deepest center field angle.

The next night, Babe moved south to San Diego for his first game ever under the lights. Babe not only homered in that game, but did it again the next night back in L.A. Some Californians had wondered how Ruth would function in artificial light. In his first two games, he blasted two long home runs. They had their answer. During his few remaining years as an active player, Babe continued to play occasional games under the lights, and he performed very well. There seem to be no facets of competitive baseball that ever seemed to hinder Ruth in any significant manner.

As the 1931 post-season tour continued, Babe revisited most of his favorite West Coast destinations. Along with Los Angeles and San Diego, the tour included San Francisco, Oakland, Fresno, San Jose, Ventura, and Long Beach. Ruth was virtually unstoppable everywhere he appeared with one interesting exception. Playing against a team of local merchants in Ventura on October 30, Babe faced a nineteen-year-old Junior College pitcher named Gould Taylor. For the day, Ruth went 0 for 4 and had nothing but praise for the young man's efforts. Since he destroyed just about every other hurler he saw on the trip, Babe could afford to be magnanimous. Ruth's fall schedule concluded with two games (day and night) on the 31st, but he stayed in Hollywood to make a series of short baseball films. When he finally arrived back in New York, two predictable results of the trip were reported. Babe's wallet was thicker, and he had made a lot of new friends.

In 1932, Babe Ruth was thirty-seven years old, and it seems logical that the Yankees would have made it easier on their aging icon. But that wasn't the case. He played the entire game in each of their Midwest spring tour appearances and then played in eleven exhibitions during the regular season. On May 4 in Bridgeport, Connecticut, Babe played the whole game despite a painful injury to his right knee. If that sounds like a bad idea, it pales next to the folly of what happened in Binghamton, New York, on September 6. Ruth took the field that day feeling very ill and still hit a home run. By the time he checked into the

Book-Cadillac Hotel later that night in Detroit, he had gone from feeling bad to awful.

So, back to New York he went, where it was determined that he was probably suffering from appendicitis. Before he was properly treated, his condition had deteriorated to the point that he almost missed the World Series. Fortunately, he didn't. Think what the base-ball world would have missed, since that was the time that Babe hit his legendary "called shot" home run. This is one of many examples of how Ruth was not given the kind of protective care that modern ath-letes receive from their organizations. When the Series ended, Claire Ruth again intervened. She wisely suggested that Babe refrain from barnstorming, since he was not fully recovered from his illness. He lis-tened to her and was soon playing golf instead of hopping from town to town all over the country.

Ruth played eight more exhibition games during the 1933 season, but he was no longer seemingly able to hit home runs upon demand. Accordingly, Babe tried to make up for his inability to function like a superman. Each one of those appearances still entailed as much show business as athleticism and required that Ruth serve as master of cere-monies. He still did that better than anyone else. It had never been easy, but, at age thirty-eight, it was becoming extremely burdensome. In that year, the Yankees visited Jersey City, Binghamton, Indianapolis, Wheeling, Newark, Albany, New Haven, and Pittsburgh. At each stop, Babe was at the center of a swirl of activities involving local politi-cians, charities, institutions, and causes. By season's end, Ruth had usually done more promotional work in the prior six months than the average star did in a career. That was still the case in 1933. As a result, he really didn't have enough gas left in his tank to engage in a cross-country barnstorming tour.

Instead, Babe settled for attending the World Series as a reporter, and then headed for Hawaii with his family on a working vacation. As already discussed, he played only three games, but made them count. Ruth blasted three home runs and played great baseball. Of course, playing ball was just a small part of the overall experience of a Babe Ruth visit. Upon his arrival in Honolulu, Ruth was greeted by a cheering throng of 10,000 well-wishers before meeting with the governor. He went on to play charity golf matches, do radio shows, speak at banquets, ride in parades, and visit schools. It was the same bill of fare that Babe had been serving for the past fifteen years. And if Ruth could have kept going for another fifteen, the American public would have kept coming to see him. They never got tired of their beloved Bambino. But nothing lasts forever, and Ruth was nearing the end of the line. Fortunately, he had some magic left inside of him, and Babe's farewell to his "hidden career" in 1934 may have been his finest moment.

With all the amazing experiences that occurred during Babe Ruth's storied career, it is impossible to identify any one as the most remarkable. The World Series victories certainly rank as highly as his numerous record-breaking performances. Babe hit the first home run in Yankee Stadium the day it opened and belted the first All-Star Game homer the day it was first played in Chicago. He defeated Walter Johnson in classic man-to-man pitching duels and sometimes made Ty Cobb look small and ineffectual. Ruth set both long-distance hitting and attendance records just about everywhere he played. He hit his "called shot" home run during the 1932 World Series and thrilled millions of fans by appearing in more places than any other great American athlete. Yes, it is tough to talk about anything being the best of everything that Babe Ruth ever did. But his trip to Japan after the 1934 season is somewhere near the top of any list.

Since those events happened on foreign soil, they tend to be underrated by sports fans and historians in the United States. That is a mistake. Everything that Ruth did and everywhere he went in the Orient was marked by extraordinary deeds and corresponding adulation. In those days, Japanese culture was largely influenced by hero worship in different forms. As a kind of warrior-athlete, Ruth embodied one of those forms. Before he arrived, Babe was perceived almost like a deity. He had a virtually impossible task ahead of him. No mortal man could fulfill such expectations, but Babe Ruth came as close as humanly possible.

First and foremost, he was expected to play baseball better than anyone on the planet. Despite the fact that he was far past his athletic peak (Babe turned forty before returning home), he somehow became the best again for the duration of this tour. And remember that Ruth was vying for that distinction with Lou Gehrig and Jimmie Foxx in their primes. He was also expected to act like a king and convey an image of benign power, which he managed magnificently. When he departed, the Japanese were more enthralled with him than before he had arrived. Considering the unnatural anticipation that preceded him, such results are almost miraculous. If this was not Babe Ruth's finest hour, it was at least good enough to serve as a fitting climax to his unique alternate career.

Actually, Babe played very well in exhibition games throughout the entire 1934 season. He and the Yankees appeared in Albany, Rochester, New Haven, West Point, Norfolk, and Wheeling. In those outings, Ruth smacked four homers, batted .577, and slugged 1.077! Even though he had a subpar season, Babe knew that he could still rise to special occasions as he prepared to leave. The American team assembled in Vancouver on October 19 and scheduled a practice game to keep in baseball shape.

When a torrential rain turned Athletic Park into a quagmire, most of the players wanted to back out. Not Babe Ruth. He took note of the 2,000 local fans who had endured the horrible weather for a once-in-a-lifetime look at the great American entourage. He insisted that his prestigious teammates play, and so they did . . . all nine innings. Babe officially went 0 for 2, but also smashed two tremendous foul homers that were hailed as the longest ever struck in Vancouver. More important, he set the standard for professional conduct that would serve as the behavioral benchmark for the entire tour. During a brief stopover in Hawaii, the men played another practice game at Honolulu Stadium on October 25. This time, Ruth smacked a pair of 400-foot doubles in the team's final competitive tune-up. When they arrived in Tokyo on November 2, 1934, the reception for the American All-Stars was tremendous, and it set the tone for the entire one-month visit.

Babe Ruth 1934 tour team: The American team that toured the Orient in 1934. Ruth and Connie Mack are in the middle. Lou Gehrig is on the bottom row, second from the left. Jimmie Foxx is on the bottom row, third from the right. *(Philadelphia Athletics Historical Society)*

The crowds were large and enthusiastic, and they directed their greatest passion toward Ruth. In return, he awed them with his amazing power, which they regarded as superhuman. Although Japan did not have professional baseball at that time, they had a thriving baseball culture with huge stadiums. And the fences were surprisingly distant. At Meiji Shrine Stadium in Tokyo, it was 350 feet down the foul lines, and the barriers angled out sharply. When a different group of American Big

Leaguers first visited Japan in 1931, none of the U.S. players recorded a single homer there. But in batting practice before the first game at Meiji, Babe sent the sellout crowd into rhapsody by slugging six drives high into the seats. In later games, Ruth added three official homers in Tokyo. He also won a distance-hitting contest at Meiji on November 17 by smashing a ball near the top of the right field bleachers. When Ruth cleared the bleachers at Kokura on the 26th, the Japanese thought they had witnessed a miracle. During the eighteen-game tour, Babe slugged thirteen competitive home runs as well as dozens of batting practice or demonstration homers. He also amassed a .408 batting average.

The Bambino also made the fans laugh at his antics in the field, where he usually played first base. Once, in the rain, he fielded his position while holding a parasol over his head. Everything he did as either an entertainer or as an athlete seemed to please the Japanese, who referred to Ruth as Beibu Rusu. Along the way, Ruth clearly outshone his younger American teammates. At the conclusion of the trip, Babe was awarded three vase trophies offered by the tour organizers: one for the most home runs, one for the highest batting average, and the last for winning the aforementioned distance-hitting contest. Team U.S.A. won every game (mostly by large differentials), but, nevertheless, the hosts enjoyed themselves immensely. Overall, the trip was a huge success, and Babe Ruth became somewhat of a Japanese institution. He remains very popular there to this day. I can personally attest to that fact, since a Japanese television network sent a crew to my home a few years ago while making a documentary about Ruth. The deference and respect those reporters evidenced in discussing the Bambino bordered on religious reverence. It was a revelation.

After departing from Japan, the group sailed to Shanghai for a single game on December 5. The weather was so frigid that the contest was almost canceled. But Babe bundled up in gloves and a bulky sweater with two layers of long underwear, and went on with the show. He hit only one double, but also recorded three long fly outs. In general, the international community was well satisfied as the Americans sailed to the Philippines for three final games. Those contests were played at Rizal Stadium in Manila. Ruth somehow summoned one last measure of wizardry, lashing five hits including a farewell four-bagger. Before game two, he also set the national distance record by walloping a BP drive onto a scaffold above the tennis arena over 450 feet away. Before sailing west around the globe for New York, Babe squeezed in two rounds of golf at the local Caloocan Club. Learning that there were venomous cobras wondering around the course, some of the guys said, "No thanks." Ruth just shrugged and shot seventy-eight and seventy-nine, while wowing the members with several 300-plus-yard drives. Heading for home, even the mighty Bambino must have been content with what he had accomplished during the last six weeks.

Although they were climactic, the games in the Orient were not the final exhibition appearances by Babe Ruth. In 1935, even after his sudden retirement, Babe still participated in several such games. And so things went for several years as Ruth played occasional exhibition contests, while waiting unsuccessfully for a Big League managerial job. Counting the three types of unofficial games identified for discussion (spring training tours, mid-season exhibitions, and barnstorming events), the total comes to about 800. In those contests, Babe smashed over 300 home runs, while playing every position and pitching hundreds of innings. Altogether, he competed in six countries, forty-two states, and about 200 cities, towns, and villages. But by World War II, it was basically over. Yet, near the very end, there was one final moment, not even a game, that is worth mentioning.

On August 23, 1942, eight months after Pearl Harbor, the Yankees staged a fund-raiser for the Army-Navy relief program. The central event was a batting exhibition between games of the doubleheader that featured forty-seven-year-old Babe Ruth facing fifty-four-year-old Walter Johnson. The capacity crowd of 70,000 went wild at the sight of the two legends strolling onto the field. The fans then went positively bonkers as Ruth knocked the fifth pitch into the right field lower deck. A few swings later, Babe almost reached the center field bleachers, and then, on his twentieth and final swing, launched one into the upper deck in right. The ball was actually a little bit foul, but Ruth, the consummate showman, sensed the moment was right for an exit and trotted around the bases. The ovation was deafening. As he and Johnson walked off the field together, the scene magically represented all the drama, pageantry, and splendor that Babe Ruth's "hidden career" had created for millions of people around the world.

6

Power Incarnate

MUCH HAS ALREADY BEEN said about the extraordinary power of Babe Ruth, but where did it come from? Obviously, Ruth was an amazingly gifted athlete in every way. He was blessed with exceptional coordination; he had excellent speed; his eyesight was functionally perfect; he had stamina and durability. But, most of all, he swung a baseball bat with incredible power. There is no way to know exactly why. Babe was a large man; standing 6 feet, 2 inches and weighing about 225 pounds (depending on the particular stage of his career). But, if you look closely at photographs of Ruth in a swimsuit, you don't see much muscular definition. He appears big and strong, but *not that big and strong*. How is it possible that he could swing a baseball bat with more power than anyone who has ever played Major League Baseball? And don't doubt that he did. There are specific comparisons coming later in this chapter between Babe and all the other great sluggers. Those comparisons will identify Ruth as the mightiest batsman ever, but they will not explain how it happened. We can discuss this daunting issue forever and offer suggestions. But, in truth, we will never know the answer with certainty.

Essentially, batting strength is the ability to swing the bat at a high rate of speed. The faster the bat is traveling at the moment it meets the ball the faster (and farther) the ball will fly. Obviously, the weight of the bat is also a factor. If a 33-ounce bat (common in today's game) and a 54-ounce bat (often used by Ruth in 1921) are swung at 90 mph, the heavier bat will propel the ball farther. In the formula for the physics of hitting, velocity has more of an impact on the force applied to the ball than the mass of the bat does. On the practical level, repetitive experience has taught players that they can hit a ball harder and farther by using a lighter bat. Simply put, they can't swing a heavy bat fast enough to generate optimum power. So, over time, they have tended to reduce bat weight in order to increase bat speed. They achieve greater power by swinging a 33-ounce bat 90 miles per hour rather than a 54-ounce bat significantly slower. Certainly, a guy as big and strong as Mark McGwire could swing a 54-ounce bat, but he chose not to. Why? Because, by swinging the bat tens of thousands of time over many years, he determined that he could do better by swinging a significantly lighter bat. That is basically the same conclusion that almost every modern slugger has reached through the same process.

What does that tell us about Babe Ruth? It's difficult to say. Certainly, it tells us that, despite appearances, he was very strong. It also suggests, almost incomprehensibly, that Ruth would have been even better if he had used modern technology and equipment. It's frightening to contemplate anyone consistently striking a baseball harder than Babe did, but careful analysis suggests that probability. Is there more to this equation than already discussed? It appears that way to me. Is it possible that Babe Ruth's personal physiology and musculature were uniquely efficient for swinging a heavy bat at a high rate of speed? It seems improbable that he could be stronger in general than guys like McGwire, Sammy Sosa, and Barry Bonds. Just look at these contemporary stars and you see muscles upon muscles. They are the product of generations of scientific advancement in various fields of human performance. They lift weights; they stretch; they eat a better diet and possibly ingest substances that were unknown to Ruth. Who is the stronger batsman, then? Babe Ruth or a modern guy like Mark McGwire?

Well, first you have to determine what you mean by strong. If you mean total strength from head to toe, my money would be on Big Mac. But what about the single specific function of swinging a 54-ounce piece of carved wood? Since Mark McGwire left a legacy of hitting baseballs farther than just a rare few individuals, I must assume that he could swing a bat of any weight faster than almost anyone. But could he swing a 54-ounce bat faster than Babe Ruth? Apparently not. McGwire and a few historic others approach Ruth in raw batting power, but the record shows that Babe is still the strongest batsman of them all. It shouldn't be that way, but it is. I can't explain it, but the facts are undeniable.

What exactly do we know about the physiology of Babe Ruth? Not much, really. But we will discuss what little there is. In 1919, when Ruth was in the process of breaking Buck Freeman's season home run record, Freeman was quite gracious. First, he readily acknowledged that Babe was much better than he had ever been. Second, he offered an informal explanation about the source of Ruth's already legendary power. According to Buck, who was then working as an umpire in the American Association, Babe had abnormally thick wrists and forearms. Anyone who knows anything about hitting realizes the importance of lower-arm strength. Next, Ruth was comprehensively tested at Columbia University during the 1921 season. After playing a demanding ballgame at the Polo Grounds, Babe acquiesced to writer Hugh Fullerton's entreaties and agreed to act as a guinea pig for two faculty scientists.

They did everything that was possible back then to determine the reason for their subject's mysterious superiority. Their findings were limited by the technology of their time, but they still arrived at some interesting conclusions. According to Fullerton's subsequent article in *Popular Science Monthly,* Babe Ruth scored significantly higher than average in every test. That included coordination, eyesight, hearing, "nerves," reactions, and perceptual intelligence. They also established that Babe's swing achieved maximum power when directed at a pitch about two inches above his knees. But, unfortunately, there was no data to explain the musculature that could wield a 54-ounce bat so swiftly. I have heard suggestions that Babe Ruth possessed a high percentage of so-called fast-twitch muscle fiber, which would also add another piece of the puzzle. But there is no way to confirm this.

When Babe turned to Artie McGovern several years later to supervise his annual winter workouts, Artie would announce the results of his pupil's labors just before spring training. That announcement always included Ruth's body measurements. In general, those numbers were unremarkable . . . with one exception. The average person has only a two-inch increase in chest size when fully expanded. With the Babe, the difference was between six and seven inches, which might be an indicator of explosive athletic power. One final factor relates to the length of Ruth's arms and legs. From photographs, they appear to be unusually long. If that is true, he certainly benefited from an efficient "lever system," which is particularly useful in the sport of baseball. None of this is scientifically definitive, but it is the best we can do. My suggestion is that we simply accept Ruth as a freak of human genetics, a biological aberration. After all, who can explain Leonardo da Vinci or Albert Einstein? They also defy analysis, but they were real nonetheless. The human species occasionally produces anomalies, and Babe Ruth was one of them. So let's move forward to the actual historical comparison between Ruth and his batting-power competitors.

Proceeding chronologically, we could simply skip the entire period before Ruth because there were no serious challengers to his supremacy from those early days. However, there were some extremely potent batsmen from the late nineteenth and early twentieth centuries that should at least be acknowledged. They were the best of their times, and it would be both unnecessarily disrespectful and historically irresponsible to completely ignore them. The list of those pioneers of power hitting includes (but should not necessarily be limited to) Roger Connor, Harry Stover, Buck Ewing, Jocko Milligan, Ed Delahanty, and Big Dan Brouthers. They all hit a stream of long drives throughout their respective careers, but none of them consistently powered balls 450 feet or more. In fairness to these great players, we must recall that they played in the depths of the so-called Dead Ball Era.

The issue of the relative liveliness of the baseball will be discussed in more detail in the chapter relating to Ruth's career degree of difficulty. However, we can acknowledge here that the Major League baseball has tended to improve in its ability to travel farther over time. As a result, earlier players used balls that were less efficient for distance hitting than the players who followed them.

The era of true long-distance hitting began on July 21, 1915, in St. Louis, when Ruth blasted one over the right field bleachers that landed about 475 feet from home plate. Until that moment, no Major League home run is known to have flown nearly that far. It was an epiphany in the course of the National Pastime. From that time forward, the game would tilt increasingly and inexorably toward a preoccupation with power. Baseball continues to feed that obsession. The players keep getting bigger and stronger, the equipment continues to improve, and the ballparks are starting to resemble fancy Little League setups. Many observers, myself included, think it's too much of a good thing and wish it would stop. But there is no end in sight. However, back in 1915, no one had reason to think such thoughts, since they were witnessing something completely new and exciting. How could a twenty-year-old pitcher hit a baseball so far?

Sportsman's Park, St. Louis: Babe Ruth hit the first true "tape measure" home run in Major League history in St. Louis in 1915. The ball landed on the far side of Grand Avenue, where Ruth sent several more drives during his subsequent career. *(Philadelphia Athletics Historical Society)*

Actually, most fans considered Ruth's St. Louis bomb a fluke, and assumed they had witnessed an entertaining oddity that would probably not be repeated. But repeat it he did, and, by 1919, that enormously successful pitcher had been switched to the outfield in order to repeat it more often. Ruth kept hitting home runs farther and with more frequency, and fans flocked to the stadiums to watch. Predictably, the owners caught on quickly, telling their scouts to focus on prospects with pure power instead of skill and guile. Oddly enough, it was the Yankees who came up with the first real challenger to Ruth's supremacy. When they signed hometown strong boy Lou Gehrig, they harnessed the power of an extraordinary athlete. The Iron Horse went on to blast 493 home runs and almost certainly would have surpassed 600 if not struck down prematurely by a fatal disease. But what about absolute power? How did he compare with his renowned teammate and mentor for pure distance hitting?

As strong as Gehrig was, there really was no contest. Everywhere they played together, Gehrig's best shots fell about fifty feet short of Ruth's best. A useful illustration, of course, is Yankee Stadium, where there was no right field grandstand in Ruth's day. It wasn't built until 1937, when the Babe had been retired for two years. In Ruth's time, he aimed at a towering expanse of open bleachers that rose about seventy rows above the playing field. The furthest that Gehrig ever ventured into that area with a batted ball was on June 18, 1929, when his homer settled in about the fortieth row. Babe, on the other hand, often visited the top ten rows, including his moon shot of May 24, 1930. That drive landed in the seventieth row, one of at least eight Ruthian blows of similar magnitude. And yes, the Bambino did hit fair balls completely out of Yankee Stadium in batting practice. That fact was confirmed by former *New York Daily Mirror* reporter Charley Segar, who saw Ruth do it more than once. Getting back to Gehrig, he hit mighty drives everywhere he played, especially in Chicago, Cleveland, and Philadelphia. His record for pure power is remarkable, but, like everybody else, he just couldn't keep up with Ruth. Also, Lou swung on an unusually level plane, which meant that many of his hardest hits were line drives that didn't reach optimum distance. They scared the hell out of infielders, but couldn't fly as far as balls lofted at a higher trajectory.

The next of the great power hitters was Jimmie Foxx, who became a regular for the Philadelphia Athletics in 1928. Jimmie has almost been forgotten by modern fans, but Double X was the real deal. Of all the aspirants to Ruth's throne atop the slugging world, Jimmie probably came the closest. In the first half of his career, he played his home games at Shibe Park, where the left field grandstand stood 65 feet high. It was also 334 feet distant and 44 feet in depth. Foxx cleared the roof of that structure twenty-four times, and deposited another twenty-nine onto it. Later, as a member of the Red Sox, Jimmie hit dozens of homers in one of the few places where we can still judge firsthand. Home plate is still essentially in the same place at Boston's Fenway Park, and so are the buildings across Lansdowne Street. Foxx routinely bombarded the garage roof across the street in left center field, and we are blessed with visual documentation about the exact landing points. The *Boston Post* employed an artist who actually drew pictures of where he saw Foxx's homers return to earth. As a result, there is a documented legacy of amazing power hitting on the part of the genial farm boy with the bulging biceps. But, once again, the key question is whether he hit the ball as far as Ruth. The answer: not quite.

Most of Foxx's best blows in Boston went just left of center field, where they landed on the aforementioned garage. Jimmie was a right-handed hitter, and one would expect his longest drives to travel left of center. But what if someone, somehow, were found to match Foxx in that direction, but from the left side of the plate? Almost incredibly, Babe Ruth could make such a claim. On June 20, 1921, June 22, 1927, and September 6, 1927, Ruth blasted balls just left of center field that struck the garage across the street. Then on July 23, 1928, he miraculously hit one in the same direction that landed on top of the garage. No other left-handed hitter in the ninety-plus year history of Fenway Park has come close to that target. For a perspective, this paragraph was originally drafted during the early evening hours of Sunday, July 20, 2003, with the television turned on. As I wrote, ESPN showed a Nomar Garciaparra homer that landed in Fenway's center field bleachers just left of dead center. The announcer specifically noted that it was a "long" home run. But Ruth's drive, struck three-quarters of a century earlier, was still climbing where Nomar's was landing. Babe's ball traveled about a hundred feet farther, and he hit it from the opposite side. And that's the point. Whether it was Jimmie Foxx in the 1930s or any player since then, nobody . . . and I mean nobody . . . has hit the ball 500 feet to the opposite field. Except Babe Ruth.

Fenway Park brings us to the next great distance hitter for comparison with the Babe. That would be Ted Williams, who some regard as the greatest hitter ever. I favor Ruth, but a reasonable argument can be made on behalf of Teddy Ballgame. But not for pure power. That's not to say that Williams wasn't historically strong with a bat in his hands, because he was. Like everyone else, he just wasn't Babe Ruth. The best example for comparison is found at Fenway and is accompanied by a story. In 1986, I interviewed Reggie Jackson, who was nearing the end of his own historic tape measure career. I mentioned to him that the longest ball that Ted Williams ever hit on his home field was on June 9, 1946, when he reached the thirty-third row of the distant right field bleachers. Reggie was visibly impressed, since, as a career American Leaguer, he had never seen anyone come close to that level. I waited a moment for the Williams tale to sink in and then gave him the follow-up. On May 25, 1926, Babe Ruth launched one to the forty-fifth row of that fifty-row structure. Consider that Jackson is one of those rare living players who really cares about his sport's history. Arguably, he was also the strongest left-handed hitter in the American league in the past half-century. But when Reggie heard about the landing point of this Ruthian blast, he was flabbergasted. For twenty years Jackson was the man who wowed historians and fans with demonstrations of power. But on that day, Reggie Jackson was wowed.

Fenway's modern concrete bleachers weren't around in 1926, but the original wooden structure was situated in almost the exact same place with almost the exact same dimensions. Then, as now, the seats were placed just to the center field side of the original right field grand-stand about 400 feet from home plate. Both the old and the relatively new seats (erected in 1934) were fifty rows high, and it is a rare day in Beantown for anyone to hit a ball even halfway up. As far as anyone knows, Ted Williams's best shot went farther into that area than anyone else's, save Ruth. In measuring physical performance, the incremental difference between the best and second best is normally slight, especially in cases with thousands of variables over many years. The difference in this case: twelve rows or thirty feet. Ruth also struck the next five mightiest drives ever in that direction by belting a few others at least thirty rows deep. Those blasts were made on July 8, 1918, May 27, 1920, June 23, 1921, September 8, 1925, and June 22, 1927 (actually landed between bleacher sections, but would have landed near top).

Further on the matter of Ted Williams, I had the honor of interviewing him during spring training in 1986 at Winter Haven, Florida. Ted was born and raised in San Diego and first played professionally in the Pacific Coast League in 1936. He was an immediate sensation, shocking everyone with his remarkable power. Everywhere he went, up and down the West Coast, he left folks talking about his long drives. This is what he had to say on the subject: "When I first came up in the Pacific Coast League, I'd hear stories about long home runs. They'd point to a house across the street, and say that's where Lou Gehrig hit one. Or a wood pile, and say that's where somebody else hit one. And then they'd point to a factory across another street farther from the house, and say that's where Babe Ruth hit one. I'd hear stories like that everywhere I went." Williams was sixty-seven years old at the time, and had seen a lot of baseball. It was hard to impress him. But on the subject of Babe Ruth's power, he gushed like a rookie.

Proceeding chronologically, there were other great distance hitters during the '40s and early '50s, such as Hank Greenberg, Ralph Kiner, Lary Doby, and Luke Easter. However, as great as they were, none of them rivaled Babe Ruth for power. That didn't happen until Mickey Mantle came to the Yankees in 1951. Like almost all the great sluggers, Mickey got down to business right away. He blasted monstrous drives from both sides of the plate on March 26, 1951, in an exhibition game against Southern Cal University at Bovard Field in Los Angeles. Soon after, in Major League competition, he kept going with a 455-foot line drive homer to right center at Comiskey Park in Chicago. Three days later on May 4, Mantle ripped one over the right field bleachers in St. Louis that sailed about 490 feet. He was only nineteen at the time, but he was already stronger than anyone playing Big League ball. Such has been the case with all the truly legitimate sluggers in baseball history. If they were old enough to make it to the Big Show, they were old enough and strong enough to make their peers blink when they arrived.

Just two years later, at age twenty-one, Mickey hit one of the two most noteworthy drives of a career distinguished by extraordinary power. On April 17, 1953, Mantle struck the only ball in the history of Washington's Griffith Stadium that cleared the left field bleachers. It has been talked about ever since as a 565-foot drive. I liked and admired Mickey Mantle as do all true baseball fans, but, as an historian, I am obligated to tell the truth, which means I must sometimes point out what players have not done along with what they have done. In this case, Mickey didn't hit the ball nearly 565 feet, but more likely about 510 feet. The fact is that Yankee publicist Red Patterson went in search of the ball as soon as it left the premises and found a ten-year-old boy holding it in a backyard across the street. Patterson did his job too well when he announced that it was 563 feet (2 feet were soon added for the thickness of the outer stadium wall) to the point where the ball was located. The media went crazy, reporting that the ball had flown 565 feet. When I interviewed Patterson thirty years later, he stated in a rather bemused fashion that he had wondered all those years why nobody had ever challenged the reputed distance. He readily acknowledged that he had no idea where the ball actually landed.

Mantle personally told me that he hit that ball well, but "I hit about five or six balls a lot better." The truth is that it was 462 feet to the point where the ball left the stadium. The horsehide was also about fifty feet above ground level and on a rapidly declining trajectory. Plus, the ball actually glanced off an advertising sign as it left the lot. My conclusion, which is backed by computer analysis, is that this drive flew about 510 feet. That in itself is an historic blow. Keep in mind that nobody else ever cleared that thirty-two-row stand of bleachers, and some of the strongest right-handed hitters had plenty of chances. Jimmie Foxx played close to 150 games there and never did it. Legendary Negro League slugger Josh Gibson played there about as often as Foxx, and he never made it over the top either. That was confirmed to me by teammate

Buck Leonard, who explained that Josh's best shot (including batting practice) landed about three-quarters of the way up. Any way you look at it, what Mickey did in 1953 was very special; it just didn't go 565 feet.

That brings us to Mantle's other most famous long ball, and, since he hit it left-handed at Yankee Stadium, it aptly facilitates comparison with Babe Ruth. It was delivered on June 22, 1963, and sped on a line to the point where it collided violently with the roof façade over 100 feet above field level. The ball was about 370 feet away from home plate linearly and certainly would have flown well over 500 feet. Mickey told me that this was the hardest ball he ever hit. He had also reached the roof façade in 1956, although not with the same velocity, and has always been given appropriate acclaim for his achievements. He is the only player who ever reached that structure in its thirty-seven-year history. But that's where some folks lose touch with the historical perspective. As noted earlier, Babe Ruth never reached the roof façade because it simply didn't exist during his career. However, by entering the dimensions of Yankee Stadium from both eras into a computer, you can start an interesting process. By eventually plugging in all the relevant data, including the landing points of Ruth's longest right field Stadium homers, you get a revealing conclusion. Almost certainly, any balls landing above the sixtieth row of the Ruth-era bleachers would have landed on the Mantle-era rooftop. That means that the Bambino would have reached the roof at least eight times if he had played in the same Yankee Stadium as Mickey.

Another interesting comparison between these two giants is found in their opposite field prowess. Mantle reached the distant left center field bleachers three times as a right-handed batsman, but never as a left-hander. Once again, you need to compare the ballpark from generation to generation in order to get the real story. Those bleachers were a ridiculously distant 460 feet in Ruth's day (at their closest point!), and nobody ever reached them, not even Babe. But the relocated bleachers of Mantle's time were positioned just about at the outer edge of the running track situated in the outfield of Ruth's day. Babe cleared that track on the fly about ten times (including two fly outs), thereby surpassing Mickey by a pretty significant margin. Mantle was fabulously strong as a hitter, right there with Jimmie Foxx and a few others, but not quite in Ruth's unique class.

The 1960s were the Golden Age in the history of the "Tape Measure Home Run." Baseball has never seen such an array of remarkably strong hitters and probably never will again. Let me be more specific. There are more strong hitters now than ever (guys with 400- or even 450-foot power), but "remarkably" strong hitters (guys with 500-foot power) were a feature of the '60s. Admittedly, this is an oddity, much like the Ruth phenomenon, but it is a fact nonetheless. This decade was privileged to witness the Herculean efforts of Frank Howard, Willie Stargell, Harmon Killebrew, Willie McCovey, and Dick Allen. There were other great distance hitters active at that time (like Joe Adcock, Dick Stuart, and Boog Powell), but that Fab Five were the cream of the crop.

Each of them hit the ground running, and produced epic home runs early in their careers. They all got better too, staying strong until they retired. Precise comparisons with Ruth are difficult, but we can establish a reasonable semblance of relative batting strength.

At 6 feet, 7 inches and about 280 pounds, Frank Howard was the largest slugger of them all. As a late season "call-up" in 1958 and 1959, Hondo managed to hit only one homer in each of those first two years. But both were beauties, traveling about 450 feet. Then as a full-time rookie with the Dodgers in 1960 he blasted one far over the left field wall in Pittsburgh's Forbes Field that landed about 520 feet away. Howard was as large in deed as in stature. Through 1964, he left a trail of awesome homers everywhere in the National League. Moving to the American League as a Washington Senator in 1965, he did more of the same. The upper deck surrounding the outfield fences at RFK Stadium was a difficult and remote target, but Frank reached it twenty-four times. In Anaheim, where Howard was an occasional visitor, the stadium was not yet enclosed, and long home runs were measured for exact distance. Frank recorded drives at this single location of 452 feet, 468 feet, 485 feet, 495 feet, and 506 feet! He was a monster. But he could not hit them as far as Babe Ruth. Howard never reached the roof at Chicago's Comiskey Park, which is probably just a coincidence, but, in five full seasons in Los Angeles, he never hit a ball out of Dodger Stadium. Since we know this is doable, that omission is significant. Frank also fell far short of Ruth in opposite field power. All in all, Frank Howard was magnificent, but he didn't equal Babe Ruth.

Willie Stargell joined the Pittsburgh Pirates in 1962, and immediately had something in common with Babe Ruth. Stargell played in Forbes Field, which had a short right field boundary at 309 feet. As a left-handed hitter, Willie was usually thought to have an easy touch at his home park. That was a false premise. Of course, Stargell recorded a few cheapies down the right field line each year, but, like Ruth, he lost more than he gained by playing in a park with prohibitive dimensions every-where else. In fact, until Willie moved into Three Rivers Stadium during the 1970 season, he hit only 41 percent of his homers in Pittsburgh. But many of them were epic. Five times, Stargell landed balls atop the eighty-six-foot-high right field grandstand, and twice cleared it com-pletely. He also overcame the 465-foot distant center field wall in 1967 and 1969. After relocating to Three Rivers, Willie not only hit a lot more homers, he kept hitting them far. Before retiring, he reached the top or fourth deck four times, and the elevated center field seats just as often.

On the road, Stargell was equally lethal. At Philadelphia's Veterans Sta-dium, he was the only left-hander to ever reach the sixth level. In Los Angeles's Dodger Stadium, only four game balls have ever left the sta-dium, and Willie accounted for two of them. Stargell hit the ball as hard as any man of the modern era, ranking in the all-time top ten for power. About ten of his career blasts flew more than 500 feet. But Ruth bests him. At Forbes Field, where he rarely played, Babe still outdistanced the great "Pops." While Willie cleared the grandstand roof twice, there is no evidence that these balls reached the far side of Boquet Street as did Ruth's final career homer at age forty. The University of Pittsburgh's School of Engineering graciously measured Babe's shot and determined that the front of the targeted home was 529 feet, 6 $9/64$ inches from home plate. Ruth also reportedly topped the distant center field wall with ease in an exhibition game.

Harmon Killebrew was just an eighteen-year-old kid when he hit his first Big League home run for the Washington Senators in 1955. The ball landed in the twenty-fourth row of the distant left field bleachers at Griffith Stadium, a drive of about 470 feet for the burly right-handed Idaho country boy. He was on his way to long-distance immortality. Killebrew played most of his career in Minnesota, and, predictably, blasted many historic drives at Metropolitan Stadium. The two longest came in consecutive games on June 3 and June 4, 1967. The first landed in the far-off upper deck in left field, traveling an estimated 522 feet. The second hit a point on the upper deck façade, calculated at 510 feet from home plate. There were no American League ballparks during his era where Killebrew did not hit legitimate tape measure home runs. He was sensational, but he didn't rate with Ruth.

During Harmon's two full seasons at Griffith Stadium (plus parts of five others), he smacked three balls into the bleachers just left of dead center, but none over the thirty-one-foot wall in straightaway center. Babe cleared that imposing barrier on May 7, 1921, and deposited five balls into the adjoining bleachers, which were 441 feet away in Ruth's time. The one that Babe launched on July 3, 1927, landed in the twentieth row. Both logged hundreds of at-bats at symmetrical Comiskey Park in Chicago, and Killebrew did just fine. He reached the left field roof in 1972 and hit eight other balls into the upper deck. But he never reached the upper deck to the opposite field, which Ruth did twice in one series in 1928. Similarly, Harmon never reached the center field bleachers, where Babe left balls in 1922 and 1926. And, of course, Ruth flew one far over the towering grandstand roof in 1927 when it was much farther away than in Killebrew's time.

Willie McCovey came to the San Francisco Giants in 1959. He stood

6 feet, 4 inches, with a lean but muscular physique. Batting left-handed, he frightened pitchers with amazing power that ranks him as one of the mightiest batsmen ever to play. Willie knocked dozens of balls between 450 and 500 feet to right field at Candlestick Park, where he played most of his career. Some were aided by the prevailing right field wind, but not all. McCovey was no fair-weather fluke. He also smashed prodigious homers in every National League stadium regardless of the wind patterns. Among the longest were upper-deckers in St. Louis in 1966 and Atlanta 1969. The best place to compare McCovey and Ruth is Connie Mack Stadium (aka Shibe Park) in Philadelphia. Babe batted at that ballpark about one and a half times as often as did Willie, but the results more than offset that advantage for Ruth. McCovey reached the housetops across Twentieth Street in right field in 1964 and 1967, whereas Ruth did it twelve times. Willie also launched one over the 410-foot sign just left of dead center in 1969. That ball landed in the upper deck and would have traveled about 455 feet. But Babe's shot on September 9, 1921, followed the exact same route and landed on the far side of Somerset Street, about 55 feet farther.

That brings us to Dick Allen, the last of the Sixties supermen. Bud Ogden once pitched against Babe Ruth and swore that he would never see such power again. But decades later, he was scouting for the Philadelphia Phillies in western Pennsylvania where he saw Allen. Until he died years later, Ogden then swore a different oath: eighteen-year-old Allen hit two 500-foot homers the day Ogden scouted him. Perhaps some hyperbole crept into Ogden's memory, but Allen's verifiable Major League career suggests that almost anything was possible. On March 24, 1964, in Tampa, while preparing for his rookie season, Allen blasted a rising line drive that crashed into a light tower 96 feet above the 360-foot mark in left field. It's impossible to know how far the ball would have flown, but 500 feet is conservative. Dick went on to play for fifteen controversial years in the Big Leagues, where his character and work ethic were often questioned. Nobody ever questioned his power.

At just under 6 feet in height, Allen was 200 pounds of rippling muscle. He batted from the right side and swung his 40-ounce war club like a plastic Wiffle ball bat. In six seasons at Connie Mack Stadium, Allen cleared the 65-foot-high left field grandstand eighteen times. He also topped the scoreboard of the same height in right center field on two occasions, which was considered virtually impossible for a right-handed hitter. When Dick switched to the American League in 1972, he kept hitting tape measure shots everywhere he went. The best occurred at Detroit's Tiger Stadium in 1974. Allen smashed a sizzling liner that caromed off the roof façade at its farthest point in deep left center field. It was yet another blow of over 500 feet. And how did Dick Allen compare to Babe Ruth? He simply didn't hit enough homers (total of 351) to merit a real comparison. But those he did hit were as close to Ruth for pure power as anyone ever. His best balls to left field fell about twenty feet short of those pulled to right by Ruth. However, Dick lost only a small percentage of his power when hitting to the opposite field, and, in this way, he compared favorably with Babe. No one else can make that claim.

Three of baseball's mightiest hitters (left to right): Lou Gehrig, Jimmie Foxx, and Babe Ruth. *(Philadelphia Athletics Historical Society)*

The names Henry Aaron, Willie Mays, and Frank Robinson have not been mentioned in these batting-strength comparisons with Babe Ruth. On the matter of optimum power, they do not rank in the top fifteen on the all-time list. However, no discussion on the topic of power hitting should ignore these great sluggers. If the "pure power" list is extended to the top thirty, each would be included. Besides being fabulous all-around players, these three legends hit the ball ferociously hard throughout their long and distinguished careers. Their greatness resided in consistency, longevity, discipline, and superb overall athleticism. The specific topic of this chapter does not provide the proper forum to pay them the homage that they deserve.

Moving into the Seventies and Eighties, Greg Luzinski and Dave Kingman deserve recognition, since they rank in the top fifteen distance hitters in baseball history. Cecil Fielder, Mike Schmidt, George Foster, Darryl Strawberry, and Bo Jackson can make a case for being included in the top twenty-five. But only Reggie Jackson makes the top ten, which qualifies him for a specific Ruthian comparison. Certainly, Reggie's awesome 1971 All-Star homer off the light tower in right center field at Tiger Stadium is one for the ages. So were his two 1969 shots in Kansas City and Minnesota that nearly cleared towering scoreboards in deep right center field. But despite playing his entire career in the American League, Reggie never reached either the grandstand roof or center field bleachers at old Comiskey Park in Chicago. And by his own admission, he couldn't come close to the balls Babe Ruth hit at Fenway Park. Jackson also hit some mighty blows at Yankee Stadium, but they fell short of those authored by Ruth. Reggie Jackson was one of the strongest ever, but he couldn't bust them like the Babe.

In the 1990s and into the early 2000s, José Canseco, Ken Griffey Jr., Frank Thomas, Fred McGriff, and Adam Dunn have all made their marks on this story, but not as much as Sammy Sosa, Mark McGwire, and Barry Bonds. Normally, Canseco wouldn't merit specific discussion since he ranks in the top fifteen, not the top ten. However, now that José has publicly admitted taking steroids during his entire career,

he has created a particular area of interest. Many of the modern sluggers have undergone sudden and dramatic increases in strength, which
suggests the belated ingestion of steroids at some point in mid-career.
Since Canseco started using performance-enhancing drugs before his
rookie season at age twenty, you wouldn't expect any of those sudden
power spikes. And that's exactly what happened. José arrived in the
Big Leagues in September 1985, when he hit five home runs. And the
first three were missiles! Number one on September 9 in Oakland flew
deep into the center field bleachers for a 450-footer. He then reached
the left field rooftop at old Comiskey Park on the 22nd with a drive
estimated at 480 feet. Then back in Oakland on September 26, Canseco
smashed two homers, the first of which was special. It cleared the 372-
foot sign in left center field, eventually landing in the thirty-fourth row
of the bleachers. When interrupted, it had already traveled 474 feet; so
it probably would have flown around 500 feet. Jose went on to blast
many more long homers in his seventeen-year career, but he never hit
any farther in a Big League game.

Sammy Sosa has hit a few just over 500 feet, but each has been
wind-aided at Wrigley Field. Away from the "friendly confines," he is
still potent, but less so by about twenty feet. Sammy hit comparable
480-foot rockets in San Francisco on August 10, 1998; in Pittsburgh on
April 12, 2002; and in Florida on July 20, 2003. The 500-footers in
Chicago were launched on August 20, 1999; June 7, 2000; and June 24,
2003. It may be of interest to note that none of those drives were struck
until Sosa was in his thirtieth year.

Mark McGwire always hit a lot of homers when healthy, but he didn't
become a true distance freak until relatively late in his career. Most folks,
including Mark himself, assert that he was always a tape-measure
master. However, careful research proves this notion to be one of the
biggest misconceptions in recent sports history. Big Mac maintained an
optimum distance of about 455 feet until age thirty-one in 1995. He lifted
weights, did stretching exercises, ingested creatine and androsteindione,
and added volumes of muscle mass. By 1997, McGwire finally reached

the magic plateau of 500-foot power. For the next few years, he almost equaled the mighty Bambino for raw batting strength. But therein lies the biggest difference. McGwire maintained his 500-foot capacity for about four years, whereas Ruth did so for at least eighteen. However, during that relatively brief time, Mark recorded about a dozen drives of 500 feet or more. His two longest came four days apart on May 12 and May 16, 1998. The first landed deep in the left center field upper deck in St. Louis, while the second hit the upper deck façade in dead center in the same park. I estimated both at 535 feet. And that brings us to Barry Bonds for the final comparison with the Babe.

Some dramatic buildup would be nice, but, in truth, there is no comparison. For pure power, Babe dwarfs Barry. For a recent newspaper interview, a writer came to my house and reviewed my research records. He noted that I had placed a red star in the left margin of all my home run logs to indicate where the subject hit a drive of 450 feet or more. He asked me to add up the "red star" homers for both Babe Ruth and Barry Bonds. I had never done this, but I agreed to give it a go. The final tally surprised even me: Bonds had 36 red stars and Ruth had 198! And that did not include the approximately eighty other shots that Babe hit toward center field for doubles, triples, and fly outs. In this area, Bonds had none, since there are no current stadiums with 450-foot home run dimensions. For anyone interested in this count, Mark McGwire had 74.

Actually, upon taking a close look at the power performance curve over the course of Barry Bonds's entire career, one winds up blinking. If Mark McGwire arrived late for the tape measure party, Bonds almost missed the whole shindig. Before the 2000 season when he turned thirty-six, Barry hit only three balls known to have flown more than 450 feet. And all three were significantly wind-aided. In 1988 at Wrigley Field, Bonds hit one high into the center field bleachers with a 25–30 mph tail wind. His 1995 moon shot deep into Candelstick Park's right field upper deck had a helping breeze of 20–25 mph. Then in 1997, Barry's right center field drive at Candlestick was assisted by 15–20 mph air currents. In each case, as the data from the official U.S. Department of Commerce weather records indicates, the wind was blowing in the same direction as his batted balls. Since 2000, when Bonds was belatedly adding muscle mass he didn't have before, he has gone on a long-distance rampage. Still, his longest to date has been listed at 491 feet. That leaves him so far behind Babe Ruth that I envision the Bambino somewhere in homer heaven indulging in a mischievous wink.

It would be negligent not to at least mention steroids in an analysis of Barry Bonds. I would prefer to avoid it. This book is meant to honor Babe Ruth, not to direct controversy at someone else. But I realize that readers will expect me to tell them what I know. So this is what I have to say: whereas I do not have definitive proof that Bonds or anyone else has used performance-enhancing drugs, I have significant suspicions. Barry increased both his muscle mass and his power at a time in his career when he should not have been able to do so by natural means. If Bonds had not engaged in state-of-the-art strength training prior to 2000, a somewhat plausible argument could be made in support of nonuse. However, during my study of Barry's career, I have encountered multiple personal acknowledgments of his intense participation in weight lifting and conditioning. This is to his credit. Barry Bonds has always worked hard to be the best player that he can be. But there is a scientifically established performance curve that demonstrates the limitations of what a person can do. Once an athlete has engaged in optimum training, beyond about age twenty-five he or she can not significantly increase either strength or muscle mass.

In his first year with the San Francisco Giants on May 23, 1993, Barry Bonds gave a pregame talk to a group of Little Leaguers at Candlestick Park. An integral part of Bonds's message was the importance of his off-season conditioning regimen. Barry explained that he took a three-week rest, but spent the remainder of the winter working out five to six hours a day, five days a week. For those who don't know, that exercise schedule represents the maximum workload for achieving optimum strength. In other words, Barry was already doing everything humanly possible to gain power as far back as 1993. Bonds was just shy of his twenty-ninth birthday and weighed about 195 pounds. Barry's weight during the 2003 season was unofficially estimated at 240 pounds. I then contacted Dr. Charles Yesalis (Professor Emeritus, Penn State University) for some scientific assistance in this analysis. Yesalis is one of the nation's leading experts in the field of drug use in sports. I provided him with the facts about Bonds's belated power surge in the context of Barry's personal exercise history. Yesalis concluded that it was "virtually impossible" to accomplish those results through natural means. That is the essence of my research, and I will leave it to the readers to make their own judgments.

So much for the other guys; let's refocus on the Babe. There are a few remaining Ruthian drives that should be identified. One occurred on October 14, 1924, in Kansas City as Babe began his fall tour. For days before he arrived at Muehlebach Field, the locals wondered if Ruth could clear the formidable right field wall. It stood 423 feet down the foul line from home plate at a height of 45 feet. Organizers arranged a pregame hitting exhibition for Babe to challenge that previously insurmountable target. As Ruth prepared to take his first swing, most of the witnesses felt that not even the great Babe Ruth could hit a baseball so incredibly far. Commissioner Landis had also joined the debate, predicting that nobody would ever clear that imposing barrier. Then Babe took *his first cut.* Booommm! There it went toward right center field, where the wall was actually 440 feet away. The ball cleared the seemingly inaccessible obstacle by a considerable distance as fans gasped. Before he finished, Ruth powered two more beyond the "Great Wall," which suddenly looked a lot closer than a few minutes earlier.

An occurrence two years earlier in New Orleans was remarkably similar. The Yankees were training in the Big Easy for the first time, using Heinemann Park as their headquarters. The ballpark had a 14-foot-high center field fence situated 486 feet away from home plate. Naturally, it had never been cleared. As usual, Babe was a little late in joining his teammates for spring training. Following his normal practice, he first stopped in Hot Springs to lose some excess winter poundage. As of March 9, Ruth was still in Arkansas working out and playing golf. But New York had scheduled their first exhibition games for the 11th and 12th, and wanted their star attraction to participate. Babe hopped on a train and rolled into town at 11:00 A.M. on March 10 to a raucous welcome from 3,000 admirers. He then went directly to the stadium to take some much-needed batting practice for the morrow's contest with the New Orleans Pelicans. After walking through the dugout and selecting a bat (his personal war clubs had not yet arrived) Babe approached home plate. He limbered up with a few practice swings and then prepared to take his first 1922 cut at a pitched ball. A few seconds later, that ball was clearing an EAT RICE sign in remote dead center field. According to the New Orleans *Times-Picayune,* Pelican owner A. J. Heinemann "swallowed a couple of times, [and] moistened his lips to bring back the power of speech."

Among the many odd discoveries made during my long research of Babe Ruth is the existence of a phenomenon that I call "Bambino Alley." It is a nickname that I have given to a narrow and unlikely strip of space where Ruth hit many of his longest drives: a five-degree radius that extends from just left of dead center field to deep left center field. It is a peculiar place for a left-handed hitter to direct a high proportion of his mightiest blows. As incredible as it may seem, Babe is confirmed to have hit at least a dozen balls in competition that flew over 475 feet in that remote corridor. The longest was his historic shot in Havana, Cuba, on November 8, 1920, which landed about 520 feet away. The lengthiest in a Major League game was probably his home run at Fenway Park in Boston on July 23, 1928. That ball landed on top of the building across Lansdowne Street, traveling about 515 feet in the air. Babe's missile into a tree at Philadelphia's Shibe Park on September 9, 1920, was almost as long.

Also on this implausible list is a 500-footer in Knoxville, Tennessee, on April 6, 1925, as well as three more at Fenway Park. They were hit on June 20, 1921; June 22, 1927; and September 6, 1927. They all collided with the building across the street and flew close to 500 feet.

During Ruth's first season at Yankee Stadium in 1923, he hit three Bambino Alley balls inside the grounds that landed about 475 feet from home plate. He hit triples beyond the cinder running track left of the flagpole in successive days on April 19 and 20. Those were just the second and third games that Babe played in the new Bronx ball yard. He then bombed one to almost the same place on August 11, but was able to circle the bases for an inside-the-park home run. At League Park in Cleveland, Ruth reached the top of the wooden bleachers just left of the center field scoreboard on May 14, 1921, and June 15, 1930. They were both in the 480-foot range. On September 11, 1926, the Bambino blasted the ball about 485 feet into Cherry Street at Navin Field in Detroit. That drive left the premises about halfway between the left center field scoreboard and the center field corner. There were several others almost as far in Washington, Chicago, and St. Louis, but they fell a little shy of the 475-foot plateau. They all combine to establish

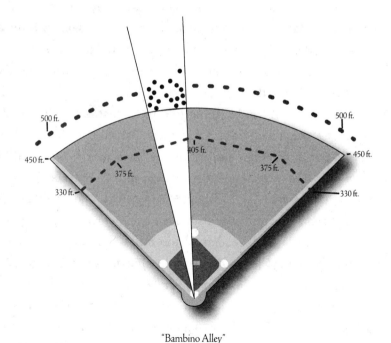

"Bambino Alley"

The approximate landing points of some of Babe Ruth's long drives to a narrow corridor in deep left center field.

an extraordinary pattern of batted balls. There must have been some subtle dynamic in Babe Ruth's swing that generated so many tremendous drives into such an improbable target area. Only the Babe could have created such a wondrous abnormality.

All this talk about long home runs leads inexorably to one specific question. What is the longest homer in Major League history, and who hit it? Unfortunately, that question can never be answered with certainty, but there is one that clearly has the best credentials. It is Babe Ruth's titanic center field blast at Navin Field (aka Tiger Stadium) in Detroit on July 18, 1921. The Yankees were touring the four "western cities" in the American League circuit and had already played series in Chicago and St. Louis. The 18th marked the third game in a four-game set, and the Yanks still needed to stop in Cleveland before returning home. New York had won six straight after losing their first three of the road trip, and Babe had belted four homers.

By the eighth inning of this game, Ruth's mood was turning sour. He had no hits in the series thus far, and his nemesis Ty Cobb was smirking from the Tigers' dugout. Ruth had already lost two potential home runs with mighty fly outs to center field in the earlier games. Plus, the Tigers had walked him four straight times, and Ruth hadn't yet lifted the bat from his shoulders during the game. Not surprisingly, when he did see a strike, Babe flailed away. But he fouled it back. He then waited until pitcher Bert Cole ran a 1 and 1 count, and came in with a fastball. The moment was perfect. Babe Ruth was ready to release his pent-up energy, and the wind was blowing about 18 mph toward center field. When wood met horsehide, the sound echoed around the stadium, and the ball rocketed heavenward.

On and on it soared toward the deepest corner of the ballpark, beyond the flagpole, where the wooden bleachers met a concrete wall. Center fielder Chick Shorten had long since given up when the ball cleared the 15-foot wall by about 10 more feet. By a rare coincidence, Tiger slugger Harry Heilman had struck what had been regarded as the city's longest home run just ten days prior. The head groundskeeper had personally measured that one at 512 feet, and everyone assumed they would never see its equal. But Heilman's drive had passed out of the grounds four panels to the left of the dead center location where Babe's had just exited. The crew chief knew right where to go and quickly produced the stadium's blueprints showing the distance to the center field corner at 560 feet. Exactly how far did Ruth's ball fly? Despite years of study, research, and analysis, I still don't know for sure. But this I do know: there are no other home runs in Major League history that have been confirmed to have flown so far. As often happened with Ruth's displays of particularly unnatural power, there were conflicting reactions from the spectators. Some cheered wildly and threw their hats high into the air. Others just stared in numb silence.

Is it possible that the groundskeeper's records were inaccurate? Maybe, but that appears unlikely. Expert analysis of aerial photographs from that era essentially confirms his assertions. Plus, if you simply take the right and left field foul line distances and apply the Pythagorean Theorem, you arrive at a diagonal of about 550 feet. The fifteen newspapers that offered firsthand accounts all agreed where the ball went. Most of them also referred to the documentation regarding the 560-foot distance to the outer corner. Unhappily, none of them carried subsequent coverage regarding an exact measurement. But something curious happened soon after. When Ruth smashed a Homeric drive at Shibe Park on September 9, the *Philadelphia Inquirer* compared it to the Detroit record breaker. According to the *Inquirer,* that blow in the Motor City had flown 601 feet. Not 600 feet, but specifically 601 feet. Where did that figure originate? Nobody now knows. However, over the intervening years, there have been other similar references. For example, the 1964 *Street and Smith Baseball Yearbook* recalled this blow as a 602-footer. So, if Babe's July 18 drive had not been actually measured (instead of estimated), why would anyone say 601 feet or 602 feet instead of 600?

Either way, this ball has a significantly longer confirmed linear distance than any other in Major League history. All other reputed 550-foot drives have been carefully studied and debunked. The usual cause for the exaggeration is the common tendency to credit extra distance to drives interrupted high in mid-flight. Mickey Mantle's roof façade homer at Yankee Stadium in 1963 and Mark McGwire's Seattle upper-decker in 1997 are prime examples of this phenomenon. Only Babe Ruth has hit a baseball over 550 feet in a Big League setting. My best judgment concludes that this Detroit homer flew about 575 feet.

Navin Field, Detroit: Babe Ruth hit the longest home run in Major League history at Navin Field (aka Tiger Stadium) on July 18, 1921. *(Burton Historical Collection, Detroit Public Library)*

How about spring training, exhibition and barnstorming games? Is it possible that Ruth, or anyone else, has hit a ball even farther in an unofficial game? How about 600 feet? Certainly, there have been occasional reports of such drives, and I have investigated every one of them. One by one, the accounts were proven to be false. Babe was personally reputed to have hit 600-foot home runs in Chicago, Grand Rapids, Pittsburgh, San Francisco, South Bend, and Winston-Salem. I checked them out as well, but could not arrive at any confirmations. For more than twenty years, I assumed that such a blow was humanly impossible. So, when I read a wire service report out of Wilkes-Barre,

Pennsylvania, from October 12, 1926, saying Ruth hit a 650-foot homer, I regarded it as bogus. Of course, I was obligated to investigate, and, when I did, things got very interesting.

Two days after losing the seventh game of the 1926 World Series to the St. Louis Cardinals, the irrepressible Bambino came to northeastern Pennsylvania to play an exhibition game. He had visited Scranton and Wilkes-Barre before, and had grown to love the people and the area. On this day, Babe also stopped at Mercy Hospital to cheer up the patients and attended a banquet, while squeezing in a radio appearance. In between, he played for Hughestown versus Larksville in an afternoon game at Artillery Park. The field derived its name from the adjoining National Guard Armory and was situated inside a large municipal tract of land known as Kirby Park. The beautiful facility had been created in 1924 as a gift from Fred Kirby, one of the founders of the Woolworth Corporation. Frederick Law Olmstead, the architect of Central Park, designed the grounds before his death in 1903. Ruth went 0 for 2 in the game, which was called off after six innings due to lengthy delays while Babe signed autographs. Ruth pitched and played first base, but everyone was there to see the big guy belt one. So, running short of time, Babe challenged all the local pitchers to strike him out. All four complied, and the scene was set.

Hurlers Tyson, Bartlett, and Delaney took turns pitching to Ruth. They did reasonably well, limiting Babe to one opposite field homer. Then Ernie Corchran of Pittston came to the mound, and Ruth challenged him to throw his best fastball. Like most ballplayers of that era, Corchran was no fool, and he first tried a few curveballs. But Babe knew that a fastball would be coming soon, and, when it did, he was ready. Swinging with all his formidable strength, Ruth made perfect contact and sent a rising line drive far over the right center field fence. The ball traveled so high and so far that many onlookers literally lost sight of it. Those with the best view saw it land on the far side of a running track in the direction of the Susquehanna River. Babe knew instantly what he had done. He simply dropped his bat and walked off the field. Moments later in the clubhouse, while autographing more baseballs, Ruth said: "When I hit that ball, it felt as if it was going to be the best clout I ever took. . . . I'd like to know just how far that traveled and some of the club officials said they would have it measured in the morning and let me know." When asked how it compared with his recent confirmed 530-footer in the World Series, Babe said: "I believe the ball I hit here this afternoon went a lot farther."

This is an aerial view of Artillery Field in Wilkes-Barre, Pennsylvania. It was taken sometime after 1926 when Babe Ruth hit his historic demonstration home run on this field. The bottom arrow shows the location of home plate as of October 12, 1926, and the top arrow shows the approximate landing point of Ruth's drive on that same date. (The Citizen's Voice, *Wilkes-Barre, Pennsylvania*)

Just how far did it fly? Sadly, once again, we will never know for sure. Unaccountably, there were no follow-up articles in the local papers about the promise to measure this historic drive. The field had to be altered to host an important college football game scheduled a few days later, and it appears that Ruth's request for a measurement went unfulfilled. However, this much we do know: the *Wilkes-Barre Record* stated that the ball flew over 600 feet. The Associated Press claimed 650 feet, and the *Scranton Republican* said 700 feet. What about surviving witnesses? There are a few, and their testimony is compelling. The most reliable recollection comes from Joe Gibbons, who was there as a ten-year-old with his father and uncle sitting about halfway up the grandstand beside first base.

At age eighty-seven on October 1, 2003, Mr. Gibbons accompanied me back to the ballpark, which remains in use under the ownership of Wilkes University. He described the events in vivid detail and then confidently walked to the point where he personally saw the ball land beyond the corner of the old running track. Home plate has been moved slightly over the years, but sequential photographs make it relatively easy to locate it to within a few feet of its original position. According to Gibbons's location, Babe Ruth's drive on October 12, 1926, flew almost 650 feet. How reliable a witness is he? He seemed completely lucid to me. Joe Gibbons survived a German prison camp in World War II and was hearty enough to play golf every day in his eighties. I spoke to his daughter, and she assured me that his mind was first-rate. She added that her father had talked about the proportions of

Mr. Joseph Gibbons on October 1, 2003, standing on the spot where Babe Ruth's great drive landed in Kirby Park in 1926.

that batted ball in reverential tones for as long as she could remember. His account has never changed.

How far do I think Babe's blast traveled? For years, I have steadfastly insisted that no man could hit a baseball 600 feet or more. My instincts and common sense still say the same thing. But this event has been comprehensively investigated, and the findings strongly point to this one as a 600-footer. The accumulated data is very convincing. Ruth's drive was hit toward the southeast, and the official weather records show that the ball got a little help from the wind. It was blowing to the south at about 5 mph. The Babe was at or near the peak of his physical powers. We know the circumstances. It was a hitting exhibition in which he had nothing to lose by swinging for maximum distance. And by his own admission, he hit this ball in absolutely perfect fashion. How far did it go? Obviously, I don't know for sure. But despite my innate reservations, my best estimate says somewhere in excess of 600 feet. If it were anyone else, I wouldn't believe it. However, with Ruth, there is a performance curve that repeatedly flirted with that seemingly unattainable distance. And in this single instance, I think he did it.

7
Comparative Difficulty

IT HAS BEEN MORE than seventy years since Babe Ruth retired, and much has changed in the game of baseball. A natural question arises as to whether Ruth's career production would be different if he played now. In the past, when I looked at those gaudy offensive statistics from his era, especially batting averages, I thought that Babe benefited from comparatively benign circumstances. However, now that I have scrutinized Ruth's career in such minute detail, I feel otherwise. This chapter will compare and contrast multiple aspects of the Ruthian and modern eras. This comparison will include logistics, ballparks, rules, equipment, caliber of competition, and so forth. Anything that affects the relative productivity of the players will be addressed. After each discussion, an evaluation will be made regarding the comparative difficulty for Babe Ruth and a player from the present. These evaluations will fall into one of five levels for each subject factor: much harder for Ruth, a little harder for Ruth, about the same, a little easier for Ruth, or much easier for Ruth. This process is admittedly speculative, but it is based on twenty-eight years of intense research and careful analysis. More important, it should be fun.

FACTOR ONE: CALIBER OF COMPETITION

This issue has been discussed by other historians, and I will not repeat the volumes of raw numbers relating to U.S. population and Major League Baseball expansion. In Ruth's day, there were sixteen Major League teams as opposed to the current number of thirty. However, the population of the United States has more than doubled. Plus, we now have more foreign players than in Babe's day. A minor exception is the current absence of Latin players from Cuba, who have been mostly barred since Fidel Castro came to power. When Ruth was playing, several Cuban Latinos made it to the Big Leagues. This is a case of point-counterpoint. The next counterpoint is that gifted athletes in Ruth's time could only make real money as professionals by playing baseball or boxing. As a result, a higher percentage of great athletes made their way into baseball as opposed to other sports.

I have heard it argued that the 300-pound linemen now in the NFL would not have been athletically suited to baseball. Accordingly, they would never have been a factor in the baseball talent pool. That is probably true, but what about all the quarterbacks and other so-called skill players now competing on the football field? Certainly, at least some of them would have been baseball players if born a hundred years earlier. In the 1920s, pro football was in its infancy and did not offer an attractive livelihood. Essentially, the same could be said about basketball, soccer, golf, hockey, track and field, and other sports. Consider Lou Gehrig in this context. He grew up poor and was anxious to take advantage of his great athleticism. At Columbia University, he excelled at both football and baseball. But when he decided to make a buck from his powerful, indestructible body, he had no real alternative to baseball. If pro football had been a viable option, he might have taken it.

Now, let's talk about Babe Ruth and the race issue. Some modernists claim that Ruth's numbers are inflated because he didn't play against black ballplayers. If all other factors remained the same over time, the inclusion of blacks certainly would have made it tougher for Babe or anyone else in the Majors of his era. But, as already discussed, other factors have not stayed the same. Plus, there is a common misunderstanding that Ruth had no experience with black athletes. The fact is that the Bambino had a rich and vibrant history of competition against the best black players of his era. He played often against Negro League All-Stars across the United States and Cuba (1920) in fall barnstorming tours. In those games, Ruth far exceeded his Major League statistics in batting average, slugging average, and home run percentage. It is an insult to Negro League players to ignore this aspect of their careers. For the most part, they enjoyed playing against Ruth and greatly admired and respected him. They knew that Babe paid a price for competing with them.

On October 22, 1922, Ruth and friend Bob Meusel joined a group of white semipros to play the Monarchs at Association Park in Kansas City. Batting against the renowned Bullet Joe Rogan and Rube Currie, Babe lined four base hits in four at-bats in a 10–5 losing cause. He then resumed his normal schedule versus white teams in small towns across Kansas and Oklahoma, where his press coverage was surprisingly unfavorable. Ruth was immensely popular, so this perplexed me for many years. Finally, a kindly reference librarian from that area patiently reminded me that the Ku Klux Klan had been very active in those parts at the time. She implied that Babe was lucky that bad press was the only result of his game with the Monarchs. I personally doubt that Ruth's life was actually endangered, but it is apparent that some white folks were displeased with him.

Hall of Fame Negro Leaguer Judy Johnson told me that Babe Ruth was one of his heroes. He added that he often played against Ruth and that his teams "could never seem to get him out no matter what we did." Also, at the closing of the Babe Ruth seminar at Hofstra University in 1995, Negro League luminary Buck O'Neil recalled the time that Ruth faced the legendary Satchel Paige sometime around 1938 in Chicago. Babe was about forty-three at the time and had already retired. Nonetheless, he launched a tremendous home run to center field in his first at-bat that left Paige speechless for perhaps the only time in his life. Further on this point, John Henry "Pop" Lloyd needs to be mentioned. Lloyd is often regarded as the greatest player in Negro League history. Pop also happened to be a personal friend of Babe Ruth (as was dancer Bill "Bojangles" Robinson).

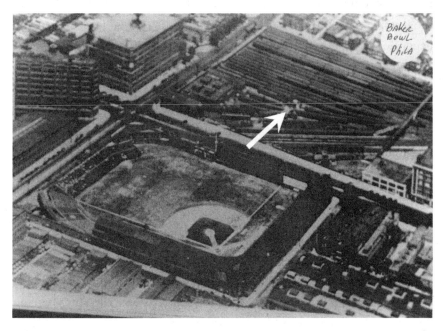

Baker Bowl, Philadelphia: Hall of Fame Negro League player-manager Judy Johnson saw Babe Ruth hit two mammoth home runs over the railroad tracks across from Baker Bowl in a barnstorming game around 1929. *(Philadelphia Athletics Historical Society)*

In his 1994 book *Turkey Stearns and the Detroit Stars,* Richard Bak had this to say: "Ruth demonstrated no racial bias on or off the field, which helped make him a favorite of black players and fans." He added: "Babe Ruth, affable to a fault, was adored by Negro leaguers." After he retired in 1935, Ruth agreed to play one final time against a black team. The game was scheduled for September 29 at Dyckman Oval near Harlem, and it was hyped in advance by the *New York Amsterdam News* (a well-known black newspaper). In part, the *News* said: "The Babe is all set for the game, and, as his popularity knew neither race, creed or color, the 'Oval' should present the most animated scene." So please, let's put the fiction to rest that Ruth had no personal history with black players.

The question is: what effect would there be on Babe's career output if those men had played in official Major League games? In my opinion, those effects would be minimal. It's not that I don't recognize the exceptional athleticism of modern black players; it is rather that I don't see how that ability could have significantly hindered Babe Ruth. Baseball is not football or basketball, where there is constant body-to-body contact. In those other sports, superior athleticism on the part of one athlete will prevent another athlete from succeeding. Baseball just isn't like that. Sure, if Cool Papa Bell had played center field for one of the American League teams, he would have occasionally raced into the gap to take away a double or triple from Ruth. But he would not have stopped Babe from hitting home runs.

Even if Cool Papa had a higher vertical leap than the average white outfielder, it wouldn't have done him much good. There were no eight-foot (or lower) fences in right or center fields in the American League back then. They ranged from ten feet to forty feet. In studying the landing points of all 714 Ruthian home runs, it is apparent that Bell, along with other black outfielders, could have prevented only one or two (if any) of them. The Ruth versus black player conundrum devolves into one simple matter. If the best black pitchers had played in the Major Leagues, what effect would they have had on Babe's production?

Since baseball integrated in 1947, batting, fielding, and base-running standards have been pushed higher and higher by black players. That is not the case with pitching. There have been many outstanding black pitchers in that time, but they have not had the same impact as the black position players. Twenty men have hit 500 or more home runs, and ten of them are black. Nine of the twenty-six players with 3,000 or more hits are also black. Of the fifteen men who have stolen 600 or more bases, eight are men of color. In the outfield, eight of the fifteen men with 5,000 or more putouts are black. Those are imposing numbers for a group of athletes who did not start playing until the second half of Major League Baseball's history.

However, when you look at the pitching benchmarks, the names of black hurlers are not as prominent. Of the twenty-two 300-game winners, none are black. In saves, two of the four men with career totals of over 400 (Lee Smith and Mariano Rivera) are men of color, but there are only four others in the top fifty. The top thirty career strikeout list features only three black men (rated 11, 13, and 15). In E.R.A., only three of the top hundred are men of color, but a clarification is necessary. Almost all the top fifty pitched prior to 1947, since runs were harder to score in the old days. There are only sixteen men of any color on the E.R.A. list of those who pitched after MLB was integrated. And, of all the Cy Young Award winners since 1947 (either official or Ex Post Facto as listed by the Baseball Encyclopedia), less than 10 percent have been of African American descent. Such awards are somewhat subjective, but they are not irrelevant.

I repeat that this doesn't mean that there aren't great black pitchers. Of all the mound performers that I have personally seen, I would give the ball to Bob Gibson if my life depended upon winning one specific game. Ferguson Jenkins, Doc Gooden, and Vida Blue were almost as good. Juan Marichal and Pedro Martinez have been terrific, but they are Latino. So are Luis Tiant and Rivera, but all four are dark-hued to the point that they could not have played in the Major Leagues prior to 1947. Functionally, therefore, they belong in this discussion, and they all have been magnificent. But the ability of these men is not the point. The point is how they would have done against Babe Ruth. Since they are all great pitchers, we can safely assume that they would have done reasonably well. But would they have significantly lowered his final statistics? Not likely.

Babe Ruth is known to have batted fifty-five times against the top black pitchers of his era. In those at-bats, he connected for twenty-five base hits and blasted twelve home runs. That works out to a batting average of over .400 and a slugging percentage of over 1.000. Ideally, we should be working with more variables, but that is all that I can find. And, for the record, I personally contacted every top Negro League historian that I know in 2006 and urged them to provide me with any data relating to this issue. Every one of them told me that they had no knowledge of any other documented games. We know that Ruth batted more than fifty-five times against black teams, but it is extremely difficult to pinpoint the exact dates and locations. There is both blame and shame on both sides of the racial aisle for this lack of specific records.

As already stated, many so-called white newspapers simply refused to report on games played between the races. For example, both the *Baltimore Sun* and *Kansas City Star* were reluctant to cover games contested by black and white players. But their selective reporting was not unique. On October 7, 1920, Ruth played against Hilldale in Philadelphia's Baker Bowl, and went 0 for 3. The *Philadelphia Tribune* (a so-called black newspaper) made a big deal out of that result. In their edition on October 16, 1920, the *Tribune* stated that Babe had been a "rank failure" in that contest. However, Ruth played the same team in the same place the very next day (October 8) and belted a home run. There was not a single word in the *Tribune* regarding that event.

Would black ballplayers have made it tougher for Babe Ruth? Of course. That fact can't reasonably be debated. But would they have significantly compromised his production? I don't think so. Most importantly, as Major League Baseball became more competitive with the arrival of blacks, it became weaker due to other factors. All in all, I believe that we have more than enough objective data to conclude that Babe Ruth played against competition that was at least equal to that of modern players.

There is one last factor that should be included in anyone's consideration of this "Caliber of Competition" debate. I have come to refer to it as the "cultural imperative" of baseball in Ruth's day. It is a simple recognition of the fact that baseball was much more important to American culture in those times. As a result, a much larger percentage of men played baseball, and they spent much more time honing their skills. I recall looking at the third sports page of the *Philadelphia Inquirer* one day from the 1920s. It included eight columns of local baseball results with each report limited to about two inches of column space. There were dozens of games between communities, factories, churches, and civic organizations all over the Delaware Valley. And these were games played by adults, not children. Kids had their own contests that just didn't make it into the newspapers. I came to realize that this scenario was played out the same way in every city, town, and village across the nation.

Folks often wonder why the Latin American countries, especially the Dominican Republic, produce such a disproportionate number of world-class players. The answer is not difficult to come by. They now have the same pervasive commitment to baseball that America had in the 1920s. That is what I mean by the cultural imperative of baseball. All the men were playing it, and all the women were watching it, if not at Big League ballparks, then in the fields of their own communities. It just isn't that way anymore. Life is much more complex, and we have more ways to spend our time, which is good. But as it relates to the quality of baseball, the result is not so good. Today's players are bigger and stronger than the players of the past, but they are not as skilled. They can't be. By the time they arrive in the Major Leagues, they have played thousands fewer hours of baseball than their earlier counterparts. In Babe Ruth's day, baseball was at the zenith of its popularity relating to participation, and ballplayers were generally more skilled than at any other time.

Admittedly, however, this thesis does not apply to the best players of this or any other generation. Almost by definition, the top athletes of each era arrive at that status by evolving through optimum conditions. Modern superstars like Ken Griffey Jr., Cal Ripken Jr., and Barry Bonds were all sons of professional baseball fathers (either players or coaches). As a result, they grew up in a baseball-rich environment in which they played as much as any kid from Babe Ruth's time. Their skill level, therefore, matched the skills of ballplayers of any age. Their culture may not have focused as much on baseball as in the past, but the specific circumstances of their individual lives nurtured optimum development. It is the great body of average Major Leaguers that lack the skill level of the older guys. It's not their fault. They grew up with video games, personal computers, DVDs, and so forth. They may be smarter and more sophisticated, but they don't play baseball with the same finesse as their predecessors. How could they? They simply don't play as much. They are definitely bigger and stronger, but, if my belief about declining skill is correct, they probably can't play baseball any better. I don't think anyone knows for sure.

Conclusion about caliber of competition: about the same for Babe Ruth.

FACTOR TWO: BALLPARKS

The use of artificial turf has influenced the game, but its effects are varied. Although there has never been a comprehensive study on the physical attrition to the human body by playing on turf, there is plenty of anecdotal evidence to suggest that it is harmful. Specifically, turf is harder than grass and causes significant jarring to the ankles, knees, and backs of those who play on it, which includes many current Major League players. Any player striving for historical greatness is somewhat less likely to attain longevity on such surfaces. The counterpoint in this issue is that the ball bounces faster on turf, thereby allowing fielders less time to react. As a result, anyone playing on turf is better able to accrue higher offensive statistics than one who doesn't. Someone playing all his home games on turf has a significant statistical advantage. Happily for baseball purists, there are only three ballparks in the Major Leagues that still use artificial turf. That is down from a total of twelve at the high point of its usage in the 1980s.

All Major League stadiums now have backgrounds or so-called batting eyes in center field that aid the batter in seeing the ball as it's released from the pitcher's hand. That was not the case in Ruth's time. On most days, when the center field bleachers were not occupied, the lack of a batting eye was not much of a factor. But on holidays and weekends, when the stadiums tended to fill, it could be brutal. Fans, who would be milling around directly in the hitter's line of vision, tended to wear white clothing in the summertime. There were regular reports from Yankee Stadium, Busch Stadium, Fenway Park, Griffith Stadium (when a right-handed pitcher was throwing), and Comiskey Park that it was dangerous to bat under such conditions. Batters simply couldn't distinguish the white ball from the white background quickly enough to react to the pitch. It certainly had an adverse effect on offensive production. On this topic, we have an example of exactly how Babe Ruth felt.

In 1938, Babe agreed to coach first base for the Brooklyn Dodgers. He was told that it might lead to the manager's job, whenever skipper Burleigh Grimes's tenure ended. Sadly, Ruth was again being duped, since the Dodgers had no intention of ever hiring him as their manager. Basically, they wanted him to help attendance by taking batting practice and appearing on field in uniform. That reality was explained to me by Grimes himself near the end of his long and interesting life. Either way, Babe took his duties seriously and quickly figured out why Brooklyn slugger Dolph Camilli wasn't hitting well. The green center field backdrop at Ebbets Field had been removed, leaving stands occupied by white-clad fans, and Dolph just couldn't see the ball. Ruth urged Dodger boss Larry McPhail to put it back up. This may have been the only time that McPhail actually listened to the Babe, and, when the screen was re-installed, Camilli readily acknowledged that his vision improved.

This issue should not be underestimated. Proof of the functional importance of the batting eye is the fact that every current stadium has one. In old parks, like Wrigley Field and Yankee Stadium, many of the original seats have been removed to facilitate batting eye installation. Auspiciously, there was a green screen at the Polo Grounds, when Babe played there from 1920 to 1922. But it was taken down whenever there were large enough crowds to fill the center field bleachers. When the Giants renovated the ballpark in 1923, they left an opening between the seats to create a good background. Whether old or new, each ballpark now does business without using that prime center field seating space. If the owners have been unanimously willing to reduce revenue for this purpose, you can be sure that it was a much-needed change.

The amount of foul ground in any ballpark can alter a player's batting record. In places with large areas outside the foul lines, fielders can range far into foul territory to catch pop flies. It could be an important issue in a cross-generational comparison like this, if there were large differences in the average amount of foul ground. But that is not the case. The amount of foul ground in today's stadiums appears to be about the same as for Ruth. Consequentially, this issue is not a factor in a comparative study.

Most Major League games are now played at night under artificial light, a state of affairs totally different than in Ruth's day. Babe never played an official game during evening hours. But what is the comparative difference relating to offensive output? The answer may be counterintuitive. Most modern players acknowledge that they can see the ball better at night than during the day. Of course, that is a tribute to the engineers who have developed the lighting systems in use today. It wasn't always that way. When night baseball originated in the 1930s and 1940s, most players hated it. They simply couldn't see well enough to follow the ball, and they thought that it was dangerous. But one aspect of night ball has always been appealing. It is a lot cooler at night, making the physical attrition of play significantly less than during day games. Most players prefer night ball for that reason alone.

Over the course of their careers, modern players avoid massive exposure to the harmful qualities of midday sunlight, extending their athletic lives in the process. Babe and his contemporaries took a beating
on this one.

The home run boundaries of Major League ballparks keep getting
smaller and smaller, which makes it much easier for modern sluggers
to hit home runs. The average distance from home plate to the outfield
fences in American League stadiums has decreased by about twenty-
eight feet from Ruth's era to today. That incorporates the five measurements to left, left center, center, right center, and right fields.

These dwindling distances should cause a scandal in the athletic
world. There are no other modern sports where the dimensions of the
playing area have deliberately been changed to make it easier to perform. Consider how NBA scoring would skyrocket if the height of the
basket was lowered. Or what if the field was shortened in the NFL? In
fairness, there has never been a uniform code for the distances to the
outfield fences. That is odd in itself. It almost certainly reflects back to
the origins of baseball, when home runs were not foreseen as an important part of the game. But somewhere along the way, a comprehensive
effort should have been made to achieve competitive continuity.

I'm not talking about adhering to the so-called cookie-cutter mentality of building every ballpark the same way. Designing those
delightful idiosyncratic nooks and crannies into each individual stadium is good for baseball. But doing so does not exclude the capability
to make them competitively consistent with other ballparks. Major
League baseball has demanded some accountability from its teams for
a long time now. They have the power to overrule any franchise that
plans to install fences that they deem to be either too far away or too
close. But they have never tried to maintain the same degree of difficulty for home run hitting from one era to the next. As a result, it has
become progressively easier to hit home runs. Of course, there have
always been drastic differences from ballpark to ballpark within any
given era. For example, Joe DiMaggio was acutely handicapped by

playing at Yankee Stadium. Every time he batted in his home field
during his entire career, he did so knowing that it was physically
impossible for him to hit a home run to the half of the field directly in
front of him. That's right! If you look at a baseball field from foul line
to foul line, it has a 90-degree radius. From the power alley in left
center field (430 feet in Joe's time) to the fence in deep right center field
(407 feet), it is 45 degrees. And Joe DiMaggio never hit a single home
run over the fences at Yankee Stadium in that 45-degree graveyard. It
was just too far. Joe was plenty strong; he routinely hit balls in the 425-
foot range. But that just wasn't good enough in cavernous Yankee Stadium. Like Ruth, he benefited from a few easy homers each season due
to the short foul line distances. But he lost many more than he gained
by constantly hitting long fly outs toward center field. Whereas most
sluggers perform better on their home fields, Joe D hit only 41 percent
of his career home runs in the Bronx. In his day, DiMaggio recorded
148 homers at Yankee Stadium. If he had hit the exact same pattern of
batted balls with a typical modern stadium as his home, he would have
belted about 225 homers during his home field career.

This point should be taken to its natural conclusion by inverting the
process. How would a modern player fare in the original Yankee Stadium configuration Babe Ruth faced? Who better to analyze than Barry
Bonds, the best of all contemporary sluggers? In 2004 (his last great
season), Barry hit forty-five homers. But what would have happened if
he had played all his games at the old Bronx ball yard? The answer is
sobering. Twenty-two of Bonds's home runs that season would not
have been out of the park in Ruth's Yankee Stadium! In fairness to
Barry, approximately four other batted balls that were not homers in
2004 would have cleared the short right field fence in the House That
Ruth Built. That would give him a total of twenty-seven for the year.

However, we all know that Barry Bonds is a highly intelligent athlete, and he would certainly adjust his hitting techniques if playing in
such odd circumstances. He would do what Babe Ruth was obliged to
do . . . pull the ball whenever possible. But how many more homers

would he then add to his total of twenty-seven? Nobody can know for sure, but I would judge not more than six or seven. If pitchers knew for certain that Bonds was physically incapable of driving the ball over either the left center field fence or center field fence, they would throw a steady stream of outside pitches. And make no mistake about the premise; Barry Bonds has *never* hit an official home run that would have cleared the original Yankee Stadium fences in those directions. Barry could do everything in his power to overcome the challenge, but his efforts would be futile.

How can we know for sure? It's simple, really. Every home run that Bonds ever hit has been plotted on the old Yankee Stadium grid, and none of them would have left the field in either center field or left center field. And consider this. Joe DiMaggio wasn't the only slugger who had a hard time with those daunting dimensions. Whereas Joe D lost about 45 degrees of home run territory in New York, the mighty Bambino himself lost about 30 degrees of viable target space. By the time DiMaggio played his second season in the Bronx, the ballpark was being renovated. The left center field bleachers, although still daunting, had been moved much closer to home plate. Ruth played all twelve of his Yankee Stadium seasons when the fences were at their most prohibitive.

In that time, he never hit a ball in a game that cleared either the left center field fence or dead center field fence. If Babe couldn't do it, when we know that he hit the ball significantly farther than Barry, than Bonds certainly couldn't do it. American League hurlers consistently challenged Ruth with outside pitches, daring him to pound it toward center field. He regularly drove them 450 feet or more, and would simply wind up with F-8 in the scorebook. The nastiest of those was probably the one on July 8, 1931, when Babe had already reached second base as his rocket was caught two steps shy of the 490-foot mark.

When Barry Bonds hits one of his best shots to center field, he gets to trot around the bases. From 1923 through 1934, when Yankee Stadium was home to Babe Ruth, the Bambino hit fifty-seven official home runs over various left center field and center field fences. A grand total of one of those came in New York. And that one barely qualifies. On May 31, 1924, Ruth launched one about five degrees to the right field side of straightaway center. The ball landed well up in the bleachers near the scoreboard, reportedly 525 feet away from home plate. And that's the only one he ever hit out of the park to the one-third of the field extending from the center field end of the scoreboard to the left field grandstand. All the old ballparks were tough on Babe Ruth, but to carry that anchor around his home turf for twelve years? That was a ponderous burden.

Let's look at another city as it relates to the issue of the shrinking modern stadiums. In 1971, the Philadelphia Phillies moved from Connie Mack Stadium into Veterans' Stadium. The players instantly recognized The Vet as a softer touch for home runs. That was the case even though the old park (aka Shibe Park) had seen its center field fence moved in sixty-five feet since Babe Ruth played there. After hitting a long home run at The Vet on June 17, 1971, Roberto Clemente acknowledged that it was easier to hit there for power than at Connie Mack Stadium. He said that he felt like he was "looking downhill" when he stood at home plate. Clemente wasn't alone. When it opened in 1971, Veterans' Stadium was one of the easiest places in the Major Leagues to hit a home run. However, by the time it closed after the 2003 season, it was regarded as middle of the road for homer hospitality. And guess what? When the Phillies players started hitting at new Citizens' Bank Park in 2004, they unanimously agreed that it was easier for homers than at The Vet. It's no surprise. While the other dimensions were comparable, the power-alleys were about thirteen feet closer.

In 1995, I wrote an article for *Baseball Weekly* (now *Sports Weekly*) that addressed this issue relating to Babe Ruth. I created a field with average home run dimensions of the '90s: 330-foot foul lines, 375-foot power alleys, and a 405-foot center field boundary. I then plotted all of Babe's known batted balls from 1927, when he recorded sixty home runs. The results astonished most readers. If Ruth hit the same pattern of balls in 1995 that he did in 1927, he would have recorded more than eighty-five home runs. The so-called 1927 pattern included a combination of doubles, triples, foul balls, and fly outs that were not homers then, but would be now. There was also a proportional adjustment for the newer, expanded 162-game schedule.

In that year alone, the long outs included four of 450 feet or more to center and left center at Yankee Stadium. They occurred on June 10, July 30 (two), and August 7. On the road, Babe was retired on prodigious center field drives of similar length in St. Louis on July 16 and Detroit on August 24. On May 5 in Washington, Tris Speaker caught Ruth's blast at the flagpole, and Ty Cobb did pretty much the same thing in Philadelphia on August 9 and September 27. To me, it is absurd that all those balls were outs for Ruth, but would be noteworthy home runs for a slugger of today. An integral part of baseball's appeal has always been the inclination to compare and contrast players from the past and present. Baseball produces numbers that invite statistical analysis. But how can we do that if the basic performance parameters are always being lowered? It is a form of cultural suicide to allow this to happen, but that has been the case.

Conclusion about ballparks: much harder for Babe Ruth.

FACTOR THREE: LOGISTICS

It amuses me to hear it suggested that modern players have it tougher than their predecessors due to scheduling and travel. The mantra is that the current 162-game schedule and the requirement to travel from coast to coast make their athletic lives tougher. We've already talked about this, but some additional discussion is in order. First, despite the official schedule, Ruth and his compatriots played more games annually than their successors. Second, the travel demands of baseball's early days are staggering compared to those of today. Modern players take first-class or charter flights cross-country, which takes about five hours. Ruth's longest trip took him only from New York to St. Louis, but what a difference in degree of difficulty.

When the Yankees and Cardinals played the 1926 World Series, they left St. Louis together on a train for New York to play Game Six. They obtained special routing privileges. As a result, the journey was made in record time: 23 hours and 35 minutes. During the first half of Babe's career, it was even worse. A train ride in his rookie season on April 13, 1915, from Cincinnati to Richmond took more than 24 hours. It's true that players of today experience some jet lag, which the old guys never knew. But if anyone wonders which is tougher, occasional jet lag or regular all-day train rides, just ask a modern player which he would rather endure.

Don't forget that those old-time trains were not air conditioned. Neither were the Ruth-era locker rooms, hotels, and restaurants. That modern comfort was not in general use until after Ruth finished playing. It is difficult to judge the additional physical hardship that the older guys endured by not having access to AC, but it is considerable. On hot days, contemporary players frequently escape into the locker room from the bench and get some much-needed relief. Babe Ruth could never do that. His favorite remedy for the heat was to place a piece of wet cabbage under his hat as he ran onto the field. In the summertime, St. Louis and Washington can be brutally hot and humid. Oftentimes, Babe and his teammates were unable to sleep in their ovenlike hotel rooms. Instead, they would haul their mattresses onto the outdoor balconies or even sleep in a nearby park.

And, oh those Blue Laws! In Philadelphia and Boston, certain commercial activities were prohibited on the Sabbath. Sunday games were banned in those two cities for most of Ruth's career. Some of the scheduling nightmares caused by that situation seem bizarre today. Babe's teams had to leave Philly and Beantown more than forty different times to play a one-day series somewhere else (usually in Washington or New York). They would then return to Shibe Park or Fenway Park to resume the prior series. Ruth did not play a Sunday game in Boston until May 26, 1929, and not in Philadelphia until June 3, 1934. A typical sequence occurred in late August 1931. As of Saturday, August 29, the Yankees had already played thirty games that month. That day, they played the Athletics in Philadelphia and then traveled overnight to play in Boston on Sunday. The Yanks then finished the month on Monday in New York, thereby playing in three cities in three days! It was pretty tough stuff, but it was the norm for Ruth and the Bronx Bombers.

Connected to the issue of travel is the topic of fan interaction, which was a particularly difficult logistical hurdle for Ruth. When 11,000 fans crammed into 4,000-seat Katy Field in Waco, Texas, on April 4, 1929, everyone knew that things would get hectic. They surely did. According to the *New York Times,* just as the game started, "some 300 youngsters, most of them barefooted and in overalls, charged out on right field and surrounded Ruth." Repeated efforts were made to hold back the crowd, but, eventually, the officials just gave up. The *Times* continued: "After the fifth inning the Yanks were forced to play with their distinguished right fielder completely engulfed in humanity." The world's most valuable athlete was simply handed over to a group of loving but unruly kids. The game was contested with Ruth and the children cavorting on the field as play unfolded. The *Times* added: "He gamboled on the grass, rolled on his back, and let the kids climb all over him."

Games followed in Dallas and then in Oklahoma City on April 6 and 7. It was in the eighth inning in the second Oklahoma City game (attendance: 18,000) that several youngsters ran into right field to obtain Babe Ruth's autograph. That was common enough. However, the *New York Times* again observed that things got out of hand: "This at once became the signal for a general stampede and in no time the Babe scarcely could be seen in the midst of a milling mob of several thousand." And that was just the beginning.

The fans in the stands hoped that Ruth would bat again in the ninth inning and didn't want to see the game called. So, they started hurling seat cushions. The *Times* summed up the riotous scene: "All the while the Babe was making frantic efforts to extricate himself from the crowd on the field which held him in a viselike grip. Umpire Campbell had called the game. He also made one attempt to reach the Babe, but quickly thought better of it. Three policemen, less cautious, tried it and got themselves well trampled on for their pains. After fifteen minutes of intense struggling, during which a perfect barrage of cushions flew out of the stands, the Babe, still beaming good-naturedly though his uniform was almost in shreds, gained the exit aisle and rushed for his automobile."

In a peculiar way, the issue of crowd interaction is a little like Ruth's unique power. We need to remind ourselves not to become desensitized to extraordinary events because we keep hearing about them. These phenomena may be common in the life of Babe Ruth,* but they are exceptional nonetheless. Regular 500-foot home runs didn't happen with anyone else in baseball history. And, similarly, no player has ever been mobbed on the field as the Babe was. Certainly, a few star players have received rowdy treatment from time to time, but none of them were ever subjected to what Babe Ruth had to endure, over and over again, year after year. If you really want to accurately compare Ruth's degree of logistical difficulty to everyone else, please linger over the prior few passages. They will help you to understand the truth.

On the matter of media relations, the demands of the press are generally more demanding today. But then one must take into account the "Babe Ruth Factor." No player in baseball history had media and public relations responsibilities like Ruth. Radio coverage didn't begin until Babe was well into his Big League tenure, and television didn't arrive until after he retired. But he had to answer to about twenty newspaper reporters every day, and he was never shielded from any of them. Many were actually his personal friends, and, although they genuinely cared for him, they made constant demands on his time and energy. He never seemed to say no to any of them. Both the team management and the media concocted a never-ending stream of personal appearances, stunts, promotions, goodwill missions, and charity events. He was inundated for as long as he played.

Before leaving the media issue, one other factor warrants consideration. When Barry Bonds was in the process of passing Ruth's home run total in 2006, there was a predictable focus on Babe's life and times. Several alleged "experts" opined that Ruth's legend has somehow been exaggerated because of preferential treatment from the press. I wonder if any of them actually did any research. Regarding the alleged tendency to overlook Ruth's individual peccadilloes, they are categorically wrong. I have personally read over one thousand contemporaneous articles relating to Babe's various behavioral indiscretions. That includes speeding tickets, traffic accidents, paternity suits, fishing and hunting without a license, violations of child labor laws (he brought a child on stage during a vaudeville show), and so on and so on. When Ruth's first wife died in a fire in 1929, the press hounded Babe relentlessly for details that he couldn't provide. They had been separated for years and he just didn't know anything.

These same experts claim that modern writers cover the personal problems of today's athletes in ways that Ruth's contemporaries did not. That may be true, but, if so, the difference is only marginal. If you want to test this matter, ask yourself a question. When is the last time that a Major League "beat writer" broke a story about a player's sex life or substance abuse? Essentially, it just doesn't happen. Occasionally, when a player is publicly involved in an illegal incident, their paper will be compelled to cover it. But, in almost every case, the assignment will be given to a different reporter. Why? Because contemporary writers are forced to coddle modern ballplayers. It's really not their fault. They know that if they cross that personal line and report honestly, the player will no longer talk to them. No interviews, no job. Sure, there are some gutsy sportswriters who will take on anybody, but they existed in Ruth's day as well.

Check into Joe Vila's coverage of Babe Ruth during the 1921 World Series for the *New York Sun*. Vila basically accused Babe of choking (and/or quitting), but didn't give fair recognition to the extent of Ruth's disabling arm injury. Vila was brutal. And try reading the game accounts of the *Washington Post*'s Frank Young during Babe's career. You will probably wince. The truth is that things have changed very little. None of Babe's press buddies wrote about his womanizing, but hardly any of the modern writers ever breathe a word about the same topic. The old reporters did tend to use flowery prose that wouldn't fit into today's culture. But it had little effect on how Babe Ruth was perceived. Human beings haven't become smarter in the last eighty years. Folks in the 1920s knew the difference between stylized description and factual reality. Ruth did what he did on the field. No writer could change a 0 for 4 into something else. And a 500-foot home run was an extraordinary event regardless of how it was described. Whether it was press relations or travel or whatever, Babe Ruth's logistics were uniquely demanding.

And that brings us to one of the classic questions in baseball history. It does not directly involve Babe Ruth, but it is relevant and has been asked of me on many occasions. Who had a higher degree of difficulty in establishing his consecutive game streak? Lou Gehrig or Cal Ripken Jr.? And the truth is that I just don't know. They were both literally extraordinary. Like Ruth, I firmly believe that Gehrig had tougher logistics to overcome. But he was a first baseman, whereas Ripken was a shortstop for most of his career. It's no easy task playing first base at the Major League level, but playing shortstop in the Big Leagues is one of the most demanding functions in the world of sports. Plus, Cal Ripken Jr. was unusually large for a shortstop, standing 6 feet, 4 inches and weighing about 230 pounds. For him to continuously lunge, leap, and execute the double play day after day, year after year, without ever missing a game, borders on the incredible.

Also, Ripken's media responsibilities were harder to bear than the Iron Horse's. For most of Gehrig's career, he was largely shielded from the press by Ruth's presence. Even after Babe's departure from the Yankees in 1935, most writers tended to respect Lou's desire for privacy. And besides, Joe DiMaggio arrived in 1936 and became an immediate media darling, which further lightened some of Gehrig's burden. Throughout his long career, Cal rarely refused interviews. I know; I was one of the guys who used to request them. As Ripken's streak approached Gehrig's, his public relations duties became almost unbearable. But he never complained; he just kept marching on. One final point: Cal's streak ultimately surpassed Lou's by more than 500 games, which must be considered. Who had it tougher: Lou Gehrig or Cal Ripken Jr.? Frankly, I am in awe of both accomplishments.

On the topic of logistics, I want to share one final thought. It originates from a family member, and I believe it to be important. My Aunt Mary, who was born in 1907, worked for Western Electric on Glenwood Avenue in North Philadelphia. She recalled many occasions when the Yankees came to town by way of the North Broad Street train station. She would hear: "Babe Ruth is coming! Babe Ruth is coming!" and leave her desk to stand at the window. All the Yankee players would soon come into view as they walked the five blocks from the station to Shibe Park. And most of them carried luggage or equipment. But not Babe Ruth. And why was that? Was it because he got special treatment due to his unique stature? No. It was because he always led a group of neighborhood children who gathered around him as though he were the Pied Piper. On most occasions Ruth actually carried one of the kids on his shoulders or in his arms, while laughing and waving to the adults. That is the way Babe Ruth arrived at the ballpark.

Conclusion about logistics: much harder for Babe Ruth.

FACTOR FOUR: EQUIPMENT

In the discussion about equipment, we are referring to bats, balls, gloves, and uniforms. Ruth used a hickory bat as heavy as fifty-four ounces in the early years of his career. Little by little as the seasons passed, he swung lighter and lighter bats. By the time he retired, Babe swung a club made of white ash that weighed about 38 ounces. Modern sluggers swing bats that are designed by computers and generally weigh about 32 ounces. The barrels are thicker and the handles are thinner than in Ruth's time. Plus, the barrel ends are hollowed out. Why? Because science and technology have taught us that players can hit the ball harder and farther that way. Just by hitting a few balls in a batting cage, most hitters know right away that they get better results with the newer type bats.

I once saw José Canseco take a few swings in batting practice with an old bat that someone handed him. He disgustedly threw it down, and said: "I don't know how those old guys hit with those things!" Ruth played in a time when it was considered proper, even manly, to use a heavy bat. He, too, intuitively understood that he could do better by progressively dropping down in weight. But he started at such an extreme that he never really adjusted enough to maximize his ability. Putting it simply, Babe never used the right tools. What he might have done with more efficient equipment, we can only guess.

However, we do know about one specific event that is very revealing. Entering the game in St. Louis on May 25, 1921, Ruth was unhappy about his recent 2 for 22 slump. He impulsively grabbed teammate Aaron Ward's 32-ounce bat, while discarding his regular 54-ounce war club. So, what happened? Babe lined a double to right center, launched a 460-foot fly out to the center field fence and then blasted an epic 535-foot home run into the center field bleachers. Those results pleased Ruth, but they also confused him. Afterward, he mockingly referred to Ward's bat as a "toothpick" and wondered how far his homer would have flown if he had used his normal tree trunk. My belief is that the ball would not have traveled as far. Babe was so saddled with the contemporary bias about sluggers using heavy bats that he had a hard time getting past it. He went right back to his 54-ouncer.

It should be noted that Hillerich and Bradsby (the manufacturer of

Louisville Slugger bats) has stated that they have no record of Babe Ruth ever ordering bats weighing more than 52 ounces. Considering their stature over the decades, their position must be given serious consideration. But, so must the words of Ruth himself. There are dozens of documented statements from Babe saying that he swung a 54-ounce bat in his early years and used a 44-ouncer during his record 1927 season. Either way, he certainly competed with bats that were significantly heavier than he would have used today.

We have already talked about the baseballs used then and now. The National League ball was rendered livelier for the 1925 season, but then it was deadened somewhat in mid-season. Then it was livened up again, and then slowed down once more. And so on and so forth. In the simplest terms, the balls used today are better for offensive production than those used seventy-five to one hundred years ago. There are few official data sources for this conclusion, but every anecdotal source confirms this thesis. The balls are more resilient and the stitches are sewn closer to the surface, thereby making them more aerodynamically efficient. When a baseball manufactured in 2007 is hit, it will fly farther than a ball made in 1920 struck by the same force.

However, in this context, we are referring only to the quality and specifications in the manufacturing of the ball. In the subsequent section relating to pitching, there will be a detailed discussion on the maintenance and use of the ball. The central theme in both cases is that a ball that has been in play a short period of time is easier to hit than a ball that's been in play for a longer period of time. Babe probably would have had a higher E.R.A. in his days as pitcher with the modern baseball, but his offensive numbers would also have been higher.

Now we come to the topic of baseball gloves. I am admittedly shocked that more has not been said over the years about this matter. This is the area in which Babe Ruth derived the most comparative advantage over his modern counterparts. Sure, he might have accrued fewer errors if he had used a better glove in the field. And his E.R.A.

which would have ballooned a bit with the newer ball, would probably have balanced out if his fielders had better fielding mitts. But we judge Babe mostly on his offensive statistics, and he got a big break by not facing fielders with the large, superbly crafted gloves of today. People often wonder why all other offensive numbers have risen over time, but batting averages have decreased. In my opinion, better fielding equipment is the reason, pure and simple.

We should also mention the protection that modern hitters have available to them. Babe Ruth never wore a protective batting helmet, nor did he have any of the so-called body armor that today's players sometimes wear. Babe was an eyewitness to the pitch that struck Ray Chapman on the side of the head, killing him, in 1920. Not even a fearless competitor like Ruth could completely dismiss those images. Babe had to be very careful about getting hit by a pitch. Even if he didn't worry about sudden death, he certainly had to be concerned about debilitating injuries. Ruth hated missing games, and he managed to limit his career HBP total to forty-three.

Over the years, all power hitters have been pitched much the same way. Major League hurlers throw a steady diet of outside balls and then occasionally "bust" one inside to keep the batter from moving on top of the plate. Barry Bonds certainly doesn't enjoy being hit by a pitched ball, but he doesn't have to worry about the likelihood of a catastrophic result in the way that Ruth did. Barry wears a protective helmet as well as shielding on his right arm (the one exposed to the approaching pitch). If he gets hit, he will feel some pain, and he might even get injured. However, the chances of serious injury are remote. As a result, he can crowd the plate, negating some of the effectiveness of the pitchers who are trying to avoid his power. In his career, Bonds has been struck by 100 pitches, but has never been seriously incapacitated by any of them. This is another case where improved equipment has made it easier to perform.

The matter of uniforms is not as important as the other elements of equipment. However, there are differences that should be noted. Those old wool uniforms that Ruth wore were itchy and hot. Any middle-aged man who wore them as a kid in Little League can attest to that. Were they a factor in wearing down the older players? Probably. Were they a big factor? I'm not sure, but probably not. But I'd bet that Cal Ripken Jr. would not have wanted to play 2,632 consecutive games wearing them.

Conclusion about equipment: a little harder for Babe Ruth.

FACTOR FIVE: TRAINING AND MEDICAL CARE

I doubt that anyone needs much help figuring this one out. Both the training practices and the medical care applied to Babe Ruth seem medieval in retrospect. A major problem was the lack of weight lifting or other effective strength-enhancing regimens. Players did some push-ups or threw a medicine ball for a few minutes, but exercise physiology did not exist as we know it today. Players couldn't significantly increase their strength regardless of their determination to do so. Cardiovascular conditioning wasn't much better. There were experts in those days, but for whatever reasons, they didn't run in baseball circles.

When Babe Ruth was a young pitcher with the Boston Red Sox, he got some pretty good direction on the "cardio" issue. During spring training at Hot Springs, he and his teammates often arrived at practice by hiking over the mountains. That was good stuff, certainly helping Ruth to log those huge inning totals. But when he became a famous slugger with the Yankees, spring training was virtually worthless in the area of fitness. Babe would work intensely a few times early in camp, sometimes pitching batting practice in the broiling sun. But then he would be encouraged to cut back and limit himself to a little BP while jogging around the field a couple times. Essential cardiovascular con-tinuity was nonexistent.

By spring 1925, Ruth was a fat physical wreck, and his severe col-lapse on April 7 was inevitable. We're still not certain what specifically ailed him. It was reported that he had a stomach abscess (whatever that is), and there were rumors of syphilis. Whatever it was, it certainly was exacerbated by Babe's deplorable physical condition. He arrived at camp the month before in St. Petersburg claiming to weigh 225 pounds. In truth, it was probably more like 255. In reviewing this whole sorry episode, it is apparent that neither Ruth nor his bosses had any coherent plan regarding physical fitness. Considering his playboy mentality, it is fair to wonder if Babe would have followed an intense workout schedule if provided with one. The answer is an unequivocal yes. Probably the biggest misconception about Babe Ruth is the notion that he didn't work hard. That idea is absolute folly. It is doubtful that any Major League player ever worked harder than Ruth. Partying hard and working hard are not mutually exclusive. Babe Ruth did eat, drink, and womanize, but he also worked like a demon at whatever he was told to do. He just didn't know how to train for physical fitness. Babe also accepted his role as baseball's preeminent personage with a profound sense of commitment.

During the next off-season, Ruth sought out New York's toughest exercise guru. He was former boxer Arthur McGovern, who ran a no-nonsense gym in Manhattan. Babe worked out all winter, and, by all contemporary accounts, McGovern was merciless. The key points are that Ruth sought him out and then obeyed his directives completely. When he reported to camp in 1926, Babe was in excellent condition.

Ruth reaped the benefits from his hard work with a great season. Capitalizing on his restored popularity, he set out to make some big money during the off-season. Those efforts included an October barn-storming trip followed by a three-month vaudeville tour. He concluded with a month of moviemaking in Hollywood. But Babe had learned something from his 1925 disaster and arranged for McGovern to join him in Los Angeles on February 3, 1927. Artie only had one month to whip his pupil into shape, but was successful. Again, Ruth worked tirelessly and parlayed those efforts into his record sixty home run season. Artie McGovern was great for Babe Ruth. If he had always supervised Babe's training, Ruth would have set records that would never be broken. But Artie was not the Yankee manager, and in those days, it was the manager who oversaw official training. For the next several years, Babe continued to work out during the off-season. But much of what McGovern did for Ruth in the winter was undone in the spring. Miller Huggins meant well, but he wasn't qualified as a trainer. Huggins certainly wanted Ruth to keep in shape; he hounded him to moderate his lifestyle. Unknowingly, however, he oversaw a spring schedule that decreased Babe's physical vitality.

The older Ruth got, the more he needed aerobic exercise. Under Huggins's supervision, Babe did less and less running as he aged. It wasn't Huggins's fault. No manager of that era knew any better. Ruth was instructed to "save his legs" by running as little as possible in spring training. Not much of this made sense, since Babe often headed for the golf course as soon as he left the practice field. At least he did some walking there, but it wasn't the same as running. Spring training in 1928 is a good example of the problem. Babe arrived in St. Petersburg on February 26, reportedly in good condition. For over a week, he ignored baseball and played about fifty-four holes of golf each day. Up to a point, that was okay, since he was doing a lot of walking. Then on March 6, Ruth showed up at Crescent Lake Park to play some ball.

He appeared under a blistering sun in a long-sleeve sweatshirt and rubber jacket. He proceeded to push himself to the point of exhaustion. After an intense batting practice session, Babe felt that he hadn't labored hard enough. So he took the mound to pitch fifteen minutes of BP to his teammates. By the time Ruth finished, he could barely walk back to the dugout to get a desperately needed drink of water. According to the *St. Petersburg Times,* Babe was pouring "rivulets" of sweat onto the field, and "tottered" into the dugout. He was so unsteady on his feet that he "knocked over the water cooler trying to get a drink." Babe Ruth very well could have died right then from heatstroke. Among the many training deficiencies faced by athletes of the Ruthian era, the misunderstanding about hydration was arguably the most hazardous. It wasn't until the Seventies that players were actually encouraged to drink liquids during periods of high exertion. Babe exercised throughout his entire career without properly replacing essential bodily fluids.

The subsequent spring schedule further demonstrates the ignorance applied to Ruth's training. When Babe played in the Yankees' first intra-squad game on March 9, he was at first base for the "Yanigans" (the name given to the team made up of rookies and backups). Lou Gehrig played first base for the regular first team. That practice continued throughout all the spring "squad" games. Why? Ruth was at first base in order to "save his legs." When Babe blasted the ball almost into the lake in the next squad game, he could easily have circled the bases for a home run. Instead, he merely jogged to third base for a triple. Why? He was saving his legs!

The same exact thing happened three days later. One paper stated that the Bambino stopped briefly at second base "to get wind up for a thrilling dash to third." When the Yanks traveled to Avon Park to play the Cardinals on the sixteenth, Ruth was in right field. Against other teams, Babe had to play his regular outfield position because he and Gehrig couldn't play first base at the same time. But the policy of not running was still in effect. Ruth walloped a prodigious center field drive, but there were no fences. There could be no automatic homers, which would allow Babe to simply jog around the bases. Again, Ruth settled for a triple. Virtually the same thing happened during exhibition games in Montgomery and Knoxville. The only spring home runs that Babe recorded were in Chattanooga, Nashville, and Charlotte, where there were fences.

In fact, there are no known examples of Babe Ruth sprinting around the bases or the equivalent of 360 feet during that entire spring. As a result, he may literally have lost the capability to perform this specific physical exertion. In his career, Ruth recorded ten inside-the-park home runs, but it is interesting that only one of them occurred after 1927. That one happened on July 15, 1929, in Detroit, and it required special circumstances. Babe's towering drive was pursued to deepest center field near the flagpole, where it struck a low concrete wall. The ball bounced far back toward the infield, allowing Ruth to amble all the way home. But despite his dozens of other monumental blows to the remote center field corners around the American League, Babe Ruth sprinted around the bases only once after age thirty-two. That should tell us something.

By 1929, Ruth had clearly slipped backward again. Artie McGovern knew what was going on, but was powerless to intervene. Babe's first wife died tragically in January of that year, and Ruth took it pretty hard. The Yankees then put Babe through what might have been the most punishing spring schedule in baseball history. By May, he was physically and mentally exhausted. By June he broke down completely. He suffered a nervous collapse as well as cardiac irregularities. The Yankees shipped him off to the Chesapeake Bay for a two-week rest, but resumed their abusive manipulation within a month. Meanwhile, McGovern was in New York explaining to reporters that Ruth desperately needed more intense physical exercise. No human being, not even Babe Ruth, could undergo such a grueling lifestyle without training for it. Babe needed more exercise interspersed with proper rest intervals, but the Yankees saw that he got neither. All his professional time was spent playing baseball and signing autographs. Over the years, he held up magnificently, but Babe Ruth could and should have accomplished even more.

The culmination of this folly occurred in April, 1932. As discussed in the section on Ruth's 1932 season, Ruth played a lot of golf upon arriving for spring training two months earlier. But when the Yankees returned to New York to start the regular season, they announced that their legendary player would stay off the links until that season ended. The reason? You guessed it; they wanted him "to save his legs" for baseball. As of 1931, Ruth had already slipped a lot as an all-around star player. He was no longer the "whirling dervish" of 1923, when he seemingly spent six months sprinting and leaping everywhere at once.

But he was still a decent fielder and base runner, as well as a great hitter. In 1932, Babe Ruth suddenly became an old man. Of all the years Ruth spent in the game (except for his 1925 illness), 1932 was the season that he manifested the most physical deterioration from the year before. It was not a coincidence.

Babe desperately needed to walk around golf courses for the exact opposite reason that the Yankees wanted him not to. By then, it was the only way that he maintained any leg strength. By forcing him to give up golf, the Yankees unwittingly pushed him into a downward spiral of premature physical atrophy. Just the year before, there were reports of Babe playing thirty-six holes at Winged Foot Country Club on an off day in August. The Yanks didn't know it at the time, but that activity was holding Ruth together as a professional ballplayer. Once it stopped, Babe only masqueraded as an athlete. He could still swing a bat like no one else, and his offensive numbers tended to hide the sad truth. In reality, he was only a hollow shell of the human dynamo that he once had been. What might Babe Ruth have accomplished if he had trained with the scientific oversight that is afforded modern players?

Whenever an athlete's physical status is discussed, there is an overlap between training and medicine. And, unfortunately, there is a tragic example of this crossover that needs to be discussed before moving into the realm of pure medicine. On January 31, 1929, Ruth came to St. Petersburg, one of his earliest-ever arrivals for spring training. Almost certainly, he did so to avoid the New York press, who still wanted more information about the death of Babe's wife. He immediately settled into a comfortable routine of golf and sociability. However, a peculiar photograph appeared in the *St. Petersburg Times* on February 18. It showed Ruth and Yankee manager Miller Huggins sitting side by side in a newly installed solarium atop the roof of the Princess Martha Hotel. There are supporting articles in other issues explaining that Huggins intended to install one at the Yankee training facility.

He had become convinced that massive exposure to the direct rays of the sun was an ideal way for his players to prepare for the season. One caption stated: "The idea of this shanty is to sit in it for hours and hours and have the sun cure all human ills." Within seven months, fifty-year-old Miller Huggins died of erysipelas, which is an infection of the skin and underlying tissue. As just discussed, Babe Ruth also suffered major health problems a few months before that. Is there a connection? Who knows for sure? But one thing is certain: Ruth's annual spring training regimen did him considerably more harm than good. No other baseball immortal ever needed to overcome such a handicap.

So far, we have focused primarily on training, but the medical issue is just as relevant. In essence, Babe Ruth's doctors were only marginally more useful than his trainers. Again, it was a matter of the times rather than anyone's negligence. Physicians had little of the knowledge and few of the tools that are now taken for granted. This part of the story may best be told by way of examples, some of which have already been mentioned, but when put together they illustrate the message.

On May 19, 1918, Babe went to the beach on one of his rare real off-days and developed a "sore throat." This was one of countless times that the absence of antibiotics severely affected his career. Ruth came to the ballpark the next day with a 104 degree temperature. The official Red Sox remedy was to swab his throat with silver nitrate, which promptly sent him to the Massachusetts Eye and Ear Infirmary with acute edema of the larynx. Babe did not start in the next eleven games as a result of that medical misadventure. Two years later, when Ruth was with the Yankees, he showed up at the Polo Grounds on May 18 not feeling well. He was diagnosed with "the grippe" and forced to sit out for five days. They later said that Babe might have had the measles, but acknowledged that they really didn't know. Later that season on August 27, Ruth was suffering from an infected insect bite (probably a mosquito), and the team doctor made a three-inch incision in his lower right arm. That bit of medical magic cost Babe six games.

Then on October 6, 1921, Ruth scraped his elbow sliding into third base in game three of the World Series. Today, that injury would amount to nothing. But back then, it became infected and considerably tarnished Babe Ruth's reputation. Doctors ordered him not to play the remainder of the Series, but he gamely tried anyway. He was so weak that he could barely walk; his play suffered dramatically. Eventually, the physicians prevailed, and Ruth sat on the bench (except to pinch-hit once) during the final three games. When the Giants defeated the Yankees, Babe received most of the blame. Oddly (at least by modern standards), the same kind of injury happened the very next year. This time, Ruth was sliding into second base in Detroit on August 8, when he skinned his right ankle. He wound up with another infection, requiring surgery and more missed games.

To me, the most interesting medical horror story originated from May 31, 1924, when Ruth collided violently with a teammate while chasing a fly ball. He was knocked unconscious for several minutes. The team doctor and trainer conferred on the best method for aiding the world's preeminent athlete and came to a highly scientific and sophisticated solution. They tossed a glass of water in his face! Today, he would have been immobilized and taken by ambulance to a hospital for a series of comprehensive tests. In the sports world of 1924, upon reviving, Babe was given a pat on his butt and told to "Go get 'em." And indeed he did. A few innings later, Ruth blasted a monstrous home run deep into the center field bleachers at Yankee Stadium. But at what price? How much additional neurological damage resulted from Babe's continued athletic activity? Perhaps none, but it certainly didn't do him any good.

On July 2, 1926, Manager Miller Huggins announced that Babe Ruth was suffering from blood clots in his right leg and water on his left knee. Both legs had been bothering him for weeks, but, as usual, Ruth had tried to play through the pain. Now that the full extent of the problem was known, he was expected to be out of the lineup indefinitely.

But a funny thing happened later that same day. Trailing 6–5 in the ninth inning in Washington, Huggins sent his invalid outfielder in to pinch-hit. Babe skied out to left field, and the Yankees lost. The next day, Ruth not only pinch-hit again, but spent most of the game on his feet by coaching on the base paths. Two days later in Philadelphia, Babe pinch-hit against Lefty Grove in the first game of a doubleheader, which New York lost 2–1.

Having dropped three of their last four, Ruth was inserted in the starting lineup for game two. When a fourth-inning cloudburst turned the field into a "swamp" and delayed the contest for thirty minutes, Babe kept playing. He slipped and fell flat on his back while fielding a ball in the sixth inning. All of this sounds like bad fiction, but that's the way it happened. Press accounts made it clear that Ruth could barely run, but he was thrown back into action nonetheless, and in extremely hazardous conditions. These events now seem incomprehensible.

We've already talked about Babe's health problems in 1925 and 1929. In both cases, he was a crisis waiting to happen, but no one intervened to save him. Would he have listened if anyone had tried? Perhaps not in 1925, since he wasn't ready for a lifestyle makeover. But by 1929, he was definitely seeking help. However, even if those breakdowns could not have been avoided, they shouldn't have been nearly as ruinous as they ultimately were. From a medical perspective, the 1925 episode was the worst. Ruth first collapsed from his mysterious malady on April 7, and, upon reviving in his hotel room, insisted on playing the afternoon exhibition game in Asheville. A local doctor resorted to the prevailing medical catch phase of the time. He diagnosed a "severe case of grippe," and advised his patient not to play.

By the next day, Babe still felt lousy, and he was sent home to New York. After being examined at St. Vincent's Hospital, the conclusion remained pretty much the same. There were vague references to influenza, a cold, fatigue and a poor diet. Regardless of the exact problem, it was reported as "not serious." It was not until April 16 that doctors announced the presence of a "stomach abscess." It was surgically removed the next morning, whereupon Babe was expected back in the lineup within three weeks. When he finally returned more than six weeks later on June 1, Ruth was not even close to being physically fit. Upon making a diving catch at the fence in the fifth inning, he had to be helped to his feet by center fielder Earle Combs. In reviewing events after the fact, it is clear that Babe Ruth, whose medical treatment was completely incompatible with modern standards, did not return to full physical vigor until the end of the year.

The 1929 fiasco was basically a matter of complete exhaustion, both emotional and physical. The decision to rest Ruth in a remote place was a good one. But did he really have to return to action in a pressure-packed, critical five-game series with the archrival Philadelphia Athletics? The three-time defending American League champion Yanks were already several games behind the A's, and Babe was summoned from his sickbed to save them. He played all but one inning of the five games, which spanned only fifty-two hours (there were two double-headers). The *New York Times* referred to the fourth game as "fourteen innings of nerve racking play." In that crucial victory, Ruth tied the game in the eighth inning with a surprise RBI bunt single. The crowds at Yankee Stadium were predictably huge, and they were relying on Babe Ruth to vanquish the hated enemy. Was that a medically prudent way to manage a man who had suffered a breakdown just three weeks prior? For the record, Babe played errorless ball in that five-game crucible, while going 7 for 21 with three walks, two home runs, and eight runs-batted-in.

When Ruth missed eight games with a leg injury in April, 1931, doctors originally diagnosed a torn ligament in his left thigh. By the next day, they attributed the problem to a paralysis of the nerve center. Can anyone today make any sense out of that? In September 1932, Babe was absent for fifteen contests due to appendicitis that was subsequently diagnosed as an undisclosed "stomach ailment." One month later, the *Chicago Daily Tribune* opined that Ruth's recent disability was probably a recurrence of his 1929 cardiac abnormality.

A tragic occurrence in December 1932, which only indirectly involved Babe Ruth, further dramatizes this somewhat unpleasant but important topic. While Babe was hunting in North Carolina, he received word that his forty-four-year-old longtime personal physician had died. Ruth was incredulous. He had attended a football game with Dr. Edward King only two weeks before, where the renowned surgeon had appeared hale and hearty. Now he was dead, and it wasn't the result of a heart attack, stroke, or sudden trauma. This previously healthy medical-care expert had died of plain old-fashioned pneumonia within twelve days of contracting a "bad cold." It was basically the same problem that Babe endured every spring, without the fatal conclusion. In this appalling context, it is less problematic to understand the extreme difficulty that Ruth experienced with his annual bout with so-called chest colds.

On June 10, 1944, just a few years before Babe Ruth died of throat cancer, he had cartilage removed from his right knee in an operation at New York Orthopedic Hospital.

On that occasion, Babe explained that the original injury had occurred during an exhibition game in 1918. Although I have been unable to identify that specific game, I have confirmed multiple incidents of knee problems suffered by Ruth beginning in that year. On July 9, 1918, Babe "threw his knee out." Nine days later, the knee was X-rayed due to continuing pain along with fear of potential permanent injury. On June 5, 1919, Ruth caught his spikes on third base, and the *Boston Globe* reported the incident with the following language: "slipping of a ligament near the knee . . . until it is replaced." Five subsequent knee injuries have been documented (not including the incident in July 1926), and, in at least one instance, the pain was so excruciating that Babe actually fainted. What if MRIs and arthroscopic surgery had existed then as they do now? What if Babe had had the original injury repaired in 1918 and not played on a bad knee for the next seventeen years?

There were dozens of other illnesses and injuries, but career athletes of every era experience them. Not every game missed by Ruth was the result of the times in which he played. He was just a man and certainly would suffer various forms of debilitation if he were here now. But how much of a reduction in total production resulted from these factors as compared to modern athletes? I suspect quite a lot, but there is no way to know for sure. However, one thing I believe strongly: Ruth was forced into a premature retirement that could have been avoided today. And that is a shame. That issue has been discussed in the 1935 chapter and need not be repeated. Suffice to say that if antibiotics and modern exercise physiology had been around at the time, Babe Ruth would have played a lot better for a lot longer.

Before moving on, we should speak briefly about nutrition. Considering Ruth's nature, it is unlikely that he would ever have been a fruit-and-salad man. But would he have eaten more wisely if a professional nutritionist had been there to help him? I bet that he would have. Babe Ruth loved being the world's greatest baseball player; he always strived to improve his craft. He tended to get into trouble by working too hard, partying too much, and simply not knowing what to do. If alive today, he probably would have been just as wild for just as long. But he almost certainly would have acted on any positive advice that would have helped him as a player. In other words, Ruth would likely indulge in the same negatives, but he would benefit from some positives that were not available to him. For example, he might gorge himself on fast food and pizza, but would also ingest supplements to improve his overall nutrition.

Conclusion about training and medicine: much harder for Babe Ruth.

FACTOR SIX: PITCHING

Despite an unavoidable crossover with both Factor One (Competition) and Factor Four (Equipment), we will further compare the quality of pitching between the past and present. Today's hurlers are bigger and stronger than their predecessors, which implies that they can throw harder. But can they? Consider the following argument that has been offered by so-called traditionalists. In the old days of sixteen teams and four-man rotations, baseball needed only 64 starting pitchers. Now, with thirty teams and five-man rotations, they need 150 starters. That's a big difference. The argument suggests that there used to be enough talent to allow teams to push their pitchers harder. If they burned out their arms, so what? They would just go out and get another. In so doing, they created a pass-fail system, whereby any pitcher who survived would be very strong. This theory is akin to the one that says that any challenge that doesn't kill you makes you stronger. I don't believe that, but the baseball corollary is interesting. Because of the injury factor, modern pitchers certainly are spoiled compared to their forerunners. Whether that ultimately makes them stronger or weaker, I don't know. And we have no empirical data to say if any generation threw harder than another.

How about the science of pitching? I believe that it would be foolish to say that it hasn't advanced. The split-finger fastball is relatively new, and it is nasty. Babe Ruth didn't have to deal with it. But he did have to face a lot more screwball pitchers than modern hitters do. Because of the reverse twist to the elbow in throwing the "scroogie," it has caused more arm damage than any other pitch. As a result, almost nobody throws it today. But it was common in Ruth's day. Fortunately for Babe, he rarely faced the two best-ever screwball pitchers, since Christy Mathewson and Carl Hubbell were both National Leaguers. Ruth never dealt with the legendary "fadeaway" thrown by "Big Six" in an official game, and he only matched up with Hubbell on a few occasions. He did, however, bat against personal nemesis Hub Pruett along with many other screwball pitchers.

Babe Ruth also had to face legalized spitballs for most of his career along with "shine balls," "emery balls," and their like. In fact, the balls thrown to Ruth in general were in relatively lousy condition. No modern hitter has to worry about that stuff. If a ball even touches the dirt, the home plate umpire throws it out of play. Batters are paranoid about the purity of the balls that are thrown to them. They think that the slightest defect or imperfection will cause them to flutter or "dance" on the way to home plate. Ruth logged the majority of his career at-bats with balls that would be considered unplayable today.

On May 2, 1951, the *Philadelphia Bulletin* published an interview with Frank "Home Run" Baker that was particularly revealing on this topic. Baker, who earned his nickname by hitting the now seemingly modest total of ninety-six career homers, was sixty-five at the time. Since his career overlapped Ruth's for eight years, he served as a good observer. According to Baker: "Sometimes the same ball would stay in play for several innings. And between coloring it with tobacco juice, licorice and rubbing it in the grass, it was really black." He identified the use of "a nice, shiny white ball" as a big advantage to current hitters. And that was back in 1951, when the balls weren't nearly as scrupulously maintained as they are now. Baker then described the techniques of several of his contemporaries, but his insights into White Sox ace Eddie Cicotte were most informative.

The legendary Baker stated: "Cicotte rubbed melted paraffin on the front of one trouser leg and had a lot of talcum powder in his pocket. First, he'd rub the ball in the paraffin and load the seams with wax. Then he'd put the talcum powder on the other side of the ball and shine it against his pants. He held the paraffin one way and the shined spot the other. Then the ball would break whichever way the paraffin was held. The longer the ball stayed in the game the heavier the paraffin side became. And, of course, the break became sharper and wider." It's true that Cicotte was one of the Black Sox expelled from baseball after the 1920 season. But Babe Ruth compiled many at-bats against him before his departure. Baker also identified Dave Danforth as another hurler who was in Cicotte's class for doctoring pitches, and he stayed in the American League through 1925.

It is important to acknowledge that Major League Baseball tried to outlaw all "freak pitches" as early as 1920. Deliberately defacing the ball in any way was ruled illegal. However, at those February meetings in Chicago, many new rules were enacted. In fact, there were too many. As a result, the umpires wound up rebelling, since they concluded that the standards imposed by the owners were impossible to enforce. One such new rule was that a home run was to be judged fair or foul according to where the ball passed over the outfield fence. Before that time, the ruling was based on where the ball either landed or was last seen by the umpire. This change would have benefited Babe Ruth immensely. However, the umps simply refused to apply the new rule, and it was rescinded on June 25, 1920. It was not permanently put in place until December 12, 1930.

What may have been even more important was the enforcement of the new pitching standards. Originally, as a result of the new agreements enacted in February 1920, the spitball was to be allowed for only the remainder of that year. However, there was such an outcry from pitchers and old-timers that, in December 1920, the rule was significantly softened. A total of seventeen Major League spitball pitchers would be permitted to continue throwing their specialty until they retired. That list included such American League stalwarts as Stan Coveleski, Red Faber, Dutch Leonard, Jack Quinn, and Urban Shocker. Ruth accumulated hundreds of at-bats against these guys, who had an aggregate career E.R.A. of 3.16 in the years they pitched against him. They were tough dudes. For example, Coveleski allowed just one home run per forty-six innings pitched.

The owners may have wanted trick pitches abolished in 1920, but what could they really do from up in their offices? The umpires were the ones down on the field with the responsibility to control the games. They knew that they couldn't force veteran pitchers to abruptly give up their sole means of staying in the Big Leagues. The umps may not have publicly refused to enforce the new standards, but they certainly weren't inclined to apply them in any immediate and/or literal fashion. As a result, the new rules were "grandfathered in" over time.

The same thing happened with the Major League's 1921 intention to keep a clean white ball in play. It was in 1920 that Ray Chapman was killed by a pitch from Carl Mays. Since that tragic incident occurred in the same year that trick pitches were outlawed, the owners lumped the two related issues together. Events converged, which made the physical integrity of the ball very topical. All these improvements came to pass, but not right away. In fact, it evolved into a seventy-year process. For example, during the middle of the 1921 season, MLB decided to retreat again on the issue of ball maintenance. Pitchers would once more be permitted to rub them with dirt if they thought that they were too new and slippery. Can you imagine a modern pitcher trying a stunt like that? That practice continued for the remainder of Babe Ruth's playing career.

As late as the 1980s, Mike Schmidt could regularly be seen stepping out of the batter's box whenever a pitch hit the dirt and short-hopped into the catcher's mitt. Schmitty appeared to pause and politely say: "Ball Please?" Those words were framed as a question because he was actually asking the umpire to either check the ball or remove it from play. In almost every instance, the ump did what was requested. The point is that *he had to ask*. Not anymore. Modern hitters don't have to bother. All balls are routinely replaced whenever they touch the ground.

As discussed, the issues of outlawing trick pitches and using better quality balls have interwoven over time. And they have essentially followed the same evolutionary track: slow but sure. It wasn't that long ago that Gaylord Perry and Phil Niekro were pitching their way into the Hall of Fame by allegedly throwing "doctored" baseballs on a regular basis. At present, there are no premier Major League pitchers who are suspected of doing that. They can't. With improved enforcement and multiple TV camera angles, it's pretty tough to get away with rubbing saliva or Vaseline on a baseball in the middle of a ballgame. A few guys still occasionally try, but not often. It took a long time, but Major League Baseball finally got it right. Let's put it this way: if Ted Williams had inspected the balls that Babe Ruth had to hit, he would have been horrified. If Mike Schmidt had examined the balls that Ted Williams played with, he would have been dismayed. And if Alex Rodriguez looked at the balls thrown to Mike Schmidt, he would be surprised. Enough said.

The cultural imperative of baseball also has to be factored in here. If guys were pitching more back in Ruth's time, assuming again that they didn't wreck their arms, wouldn't they tend to get better? Old-timers always say that pitchers of their day were craftier and more sophisticated. But that probably reflects a natural bias in human nature to honor and value the experiences of one's youth. They might be right, but they can't prove it. I just don't know if starting pitching was better then or now. But I am certain that relief pitching has improved dramatically. The catch for this particular discussion is the reemergence of the "Babe Ruth Factor." Nothing was ever the same for Ruth compared to everybody else of his day, and so it was with relief pitching.

Connie Mack was most proactive in finding ways to circumvent Ruth. As long as it was legal, Connie would try it. It was Mack who forbade his pitchers to throw Babe a fastball strike until Lefty Grove came along. And it was Connie Mack who formulated the most advanced relief pitching strategies to deal with the Bambino. Mack liked Ruth, but he felt obligated to try to stop him. By 1921, Connie was tired of losing to Ruth, so he appointed a specific man to pitch in relief against him. That man was lefty Dave Keefe, and Mack used him to relieve his starter in the fourth inning on August 11 in Philadelphia for the sole purpose of retiring George Ruth. Babe liked Connie right back, but not as much as he liked hitting homers. So he knocked Keefe's trademark forkball to the top of the left field bleachers, and that was the end of this particular experiment.

In 1922, the St. Louis Browns tried a pair of tricky lefties to face Ruth in key situations. The first was Bill Bayne, whose curveball drove Ty Cobb nuts. He did okay, but the next day on May 22, Hub Pruett used his screwball to fan Babe in the tenth inning. Ruth looked so pitiful against Pruett that the Browns then used him to start against the Yankees, even though he wasn't particularly effective against anybody else. Hub's subsequent success against the Bambino is now legendary. Then, something really odd happened on April 22, 1923. Trailing Washington 4–3 in the ninth inning, Babe was due to face Walter Johnson. The Big Train was past his prime, but he was still one of the best. Plus, he was Walter Johnson, who backed down from no one. Nevertheless, he was yanked in favor of lefthander George Mogridge, who saved the game for Johnson. It's not that Ruth was the only hitter to face relief pitchers during his era; it's just that he had to do it more often than anyone else. Just as Lefty Grove eventually became a great occasional closer against all teams, he was used most often against Ruth.

Specialized relief artists were essentially unknown in Babe's time, and the art of relief pitching has improved substantially. As usual, it is difficult to judge the impact of the "Babe Ruth Factor" in assessing comparative difficulty. We know that Ruth faced considerably tougher relief pitching than anyone else in the Twenties and Thirties. But was it as tough as it is today? I don't think so. This is one aspect of the pitching puzzle where Babe got a break. But there is an extremely important counterpoint to this issue that few people talk about.

There are only so many great pitching arms in the baseball world at any given time. If some of them are now channeled into the relief role, their abilities cannot be included in the group of qualitative starting pitchers. All batters face good starters many more times than good relievers. The counterpoint-to-the-counterpoint, of course, is that not all good contemporary closers would necessarily have become good starting pitchers. But, in talking to scouts and personnel experts, their consensus is that most would be good either way. Is it possible, therefore, that the current focus on relief pitching has had the opposite effect on career offensive output than we usually suppose? Certainly, Babe Ruth or any other hitter would tend to achieve fewer late-inning successes against better talent. For example, their legacy of "walk off" home runs would likely be diminished, but would their overall career production be lower? So far, no one has offered any proof of that common assertion.

We also need to consider one other detail of the "Babe Ruth Factor" before moving on to the next topic. In general, did pitchers provide Ruth with as many balls within the strike zone as other sluggers? Of course, the answer is no. How far did that tendency extend? Is it possible that Babe received a lower percentage of hittable balls than anyone else who ever played Major League baseball? I say yes to this question.

We've all seen the way pitchers have been cowering away from Barry Bonds in recent years and walking him in record numbers. It is hard to blame them; the man is that dangerous. Bonds occasionally gets frustrated and swings at a bad pitch. But, for the most part, he remains patient and accepts his bases-on-balls. Barry has decided to take the Ted Williams approach. Williams once told me that he never intentionally swung at a bad pitch. As much as he loved to hit, he felt that he lost too much efficiency to go out of the strike zone. Babe Ruth felt differently. He knew that walks were often his best alternative, but he also felt that there were times when he had to hit. As a result, he deliberately swung at hundreds of bad pitches during his long career. I don't know if it was a good idea or not. Statisticians will tell you that any man who walked every time up in his lifetime would be the greatest offensive player ever. If Ruth had waited for good pitches, he would have hit fewer homers and driven in fewer runs. But he certainly would have had a higher on-base percentage and scored more runs. I suspect that his batting average and slugging percentage would have increased as well.

Just how bad were the pitches that Babe Ruth swung at? On July 10, 1926, he got so frustrated after two earlier bases-on-balls that he swung at a pitch during an intentional walk. He was ruled out, compounding the stupidity of the move. On the other hand, Ruth hit home runs on pitches far out of the strike zone at least on the following occasions: April 19, 1919; July 18, 1919; April 16, 1921; May 14, 1921; May 17, 1921; May 25, 1921; June 11, 1921; June 12, 1921; September 3, 1921; July 3, 1922; May 10, 1924; May 5, 1926; September 30, 1927; May 10, 1928; August 1, 1930; July 2, 1931; and April 21, 1934.

The number of other base hits off bad pitches is beyond count. On June 12, 1919, Babe ripped a double off the left field wall at Fenway Park to drive in runners from second and third base. After the game, the pitcher acknowledged that he had tried to walk Ruth and that the costly pitch had been a foot outside. Two months later, the White Sox refused to allow something like that to happen, deliberately walking Ruth with the bases loaded. They lost 1–0. No one can quantify this issue with exactitude. However, after reviewing multiple firsthand accounts of every game that Babe Ruth played, I can state with certainty that he swung at bad pitches regularly throughout his career. Since I have studied all the home runs of every other great slugger, I can also confirm that none of them shared the same experience.

In the archives of *Baseball Magazine,* there are many interesting quotes on this subject. According to veteran pitcher Urban Shocker, Ruth's titanic center field home run off him on May 25, 1921, was hit on a pitch that was "at least a foot outside." Hall of Fame hurler Ted Lyons elaborated: "There are other times when you can't put the ball within two feet of the plate with any safety, if he wants to go after it. He waits out a lot of balls and gets his base, but he also goes after a lot of bad balls." The great Walter Johnson added: "I once saw Babe swing at a ball that struck the ground before it reached the plate. No doubt, he'd made up his mind to go after the ball. The fact is he can hit any kind of a ball that comes within his reach, and he can reach a foot and a half outside the plate."

Of the many statements made by Ruth's contemporaries on this issue, one of the most telling came from left-handed pitcher Sherrod Smith. Babe knew "Sherry" very well since he defeated him 2–1 in that classic fourteen-inning pitchers' duel in the 1916 World Series. Smith stayed with the Dodgers until the end of the 1922 season, where he often played preseason games against Ruth. He then joined the Cleveland Indians, pitching regularly for the Tribe for the next four years. In the process, Smith faced Babe many times, including June 11, 1923. In the first inning of that game, Ruth's double was the key hit in a two-run rally. Babe made four more plate appearances that day and Smith walked him each time. Here is the heart of the matter: Sherrod Smith pitched a complete game 4–3 victory on that occasion. Sherry had this to say about the pitches that came Ruth's way: "If Babe got balls somewhere near where he liked to hit them, he would bat .450. He seldom gets a good ball. A pitcher is foolish to give him a good ball."

Was Smith overstating his case? Probably not. When Ruth hit sixty homers in 1927, Sherrod was in decline and playing his final season. But teammate Joe Sewell was in his prime. Sewell competed with the Babe for eleven years as a star infielder with Cleveland and eventually joined the Yankees from 1931 through 1933. Years later, Joe had this to say about the pitches that came Ruth's way: "When Babe hit sixty home runs in 1927, no one even pitched to him. I played for the Indians back then, and we threw the ball in the dirt, behind his back, over his head, anywhere but over the plate. If everyone pitched to him, he would've hit 1.000."

If Babe Ruth had waited for strikes, he would rarely have swung the bat. That's just the way it was. There seemed to be an unwritten contract that, if Ruth wanted to hit, he would have to function in a considerably expanded strike zone. Everybody, including Babe, just accepted it and moved on. The quality of pitching may or may not have improved in the last seventy-five years; we simply don't know. But the combined overall degree of difficulty for every pitch thrown to Babe Ruth probably exceeds that faced by any other hitter.

Conclusion about pitching: a little harder for Babe Ruth.

FACTOR SEVEN: RULE CHANGES

Most baseball rules have remained the same, but there have been some significant changes. As already discussed, one of the more important is the so-called Fair-Foul home run rule, known as Paragraph 48. Until 1931 (except for seventy days in 1920), balls hit over the fence were judged fair or foul depending on where they landed or were last seen by the umpire. In subsequent years, the determination was made according to whether they were fair or foul when they passed over the outfield fence. Babe was asked about the new rule changes early in spring training in 1931. Sitting on the bench, he responded in part: "Another rule that's going to make the pitchers mad is the one which says a home run shall be judged at the point where it passes the pole. A lot of them curve foul directly after passing the pole fair. It's okay with me. But you'll hear a lot of pitchers moaning." Ruth's exceptional power worked against him in this context. He lost at least fifty home runs due to this rule, a highly significant number.

One "old rule" that might have helped Babe is the one that formerly allowed balls to bounce over the fence for a home run. Now they are doubles. If old stadiums all had warning tracks, off which balls bounce higher, it would have made a difference. But they didn't. Similarly, if artificial turf and eight-foot walls had commonly been in place, it would have made a big difference. But they weren't. Yankee Stadium had a low left field wall, but it was the only place in the American League where one could be found. On May 30, 1927, Ruth bounced a ball off the railing there, but it stayed in play for a double. That was the closest he ever came to benefiting from that old rule. In his entire career, Babe never hit a home run that bounced over the fence.

During Ruth's twenty-two-year career, the pitcher's mound (officially referred to as the "pitcher's box") was elevated fifteen inches above home plate. Before the 1969 season, the rule was changed to lower the mound to ten inches of elevation. It has stayed that way until the present. Obviously, that five-inch decrease helps the hitter and assists modern sluggers in establishing optimum career production. But rule changes are never made in a vacuum. The offensive numbers were way down in 1968, and it was apparent that the science of pitching was outpacing that of hitting. Of course, Babe would have benefited from the lower height, but we must weigh this factor in the context of the related pitching issue.

That brings us to the Designated Hitter rule. It didn't exist in Ruth's day. If it had, Babe almost certainly would have played longer and hit more home runs. That was the case with Hank Aaron, as well as many other historically significant players. How much longer would Babe have played with that rule, and how many more homers would he have hit? Nobody knows, but it is interesting to speculate.

There have been other minor rule changes in the intervening years, but none of them appear to be a factor in the matter of comparative difficulty. But there is one change that is tremendously important. It may not be the result of an official rule change, but it is a dramatic change in how the game is played and functions as a rule change. I'm referring to the way that the strike zone has become progressively smaller and smaller over the years. Along with the improvement in the quality of baseball gloves, this is the most underappreciated factor in assessing comparative difficulty.

When the strike zone was bigger, players almost unanimously agreed that the high fastball was the hardest pitch to hit. Now that it has been lowered at its highest point by about twelve inches, some hitters would identify the low-and-away breaking ball as the toughest. The modern guys will never know how difficult it is to hit a fastball passing over the plate at chest level. Babe Ruth did. He had to deal with Walter Johnson and Lefty Grove throwing 100 mph heaters just under his armpits. It was practically a biomechanical impossibility to level the bat squarely on a pitch like that. If Roger Clemens or Randy Johnson threw a fastball above Sammy Sosa's waistline, he just watched it pass. It was called a ball.

While watching or listening to games, we will often hear an announcer say that a pitcher is getting hit because "he is up in the strike zone." Let's clarify what is meant by that reference. The human body is constructed so that it can most easily strike a thrown object at mid-body height. A little higher or a little lower makes it more difficult. Pitchers can no longer take advantage of the "little higher" area, because it isn't in the strike zone. Naturally, therefore, they mostly aim for the "little lower" area around the knees. They're fine if they stay there, but, when they move "up in the strike zone," they get hit. By referring to "up," it means that the pitcher is throwing from the mid-thigh to the beltline level. That is right where the average human body functions best, and pitches in that area usually get hit. If pitchers could go "up" even higher, from the waistline to mid-chest, they would do just fine. They could do that during Babe Ruth's era, but now they can't.

During the early stages of a game against Ted Williams and the Boston Red Sox on August 20, 1946, pitcher Ellis Kinder fared pretty well. But in the eighth inning, Williams blasted one of his fastballs 450 feet to right field for a home run. After the game, Williams told reporters that as long as Kinder threw his fastball at chest level he (Williams) could not hit it squarely. He added that he expected Kinder to eventually make a mistake and throw his heater around belt level. Ted was right, and we just described the result. That story effectively illustrates the point under discussion, but how about an example directly from Babe Ruth's career? No problem.

In the second game of a doubleheader versus the White Sox on July 19, 1920, Ruth broke his home run record set just the year before. He smashed his thirtieth homer into the Polo Grounds bleachers in the fourth inning off a Dickie Kerr curveball. Then, Babe hit his thirty-first off another curveball in the ninth inning as Kerr was finishing his complete game victory. But, in between, Ruth struck out on three chest-high fastballs. Just a coincidence? That's highly doubtful. Fastballs thrown at chest level were once a hitter's nightmare. Today, they are merely a respite, since they can be ignored. Babe Ruth had an uppercut swing and always hit low pitches better than high ones. If he could have narrowed his focus to balls thrown where he most liked to hit them, it is hard to imagine what he might have done. Make no mistake; the shrinking strike zone has been a major boon to modern hitters.

Conclusion about rule changes: much harder for Babe Ruth.

In summarizing this chapter, there are no broad areas of comparative difficulty that were easier for Babe Ruth than for modern players. Those are the conclusions of my research, and that is what I believe. In a few limited areas, Ruth got a break. He got a lot of help from the inferior fielding equipment of his era. He derived moderate benefit from avoiding the specialized relief pitching of today. Other than that, he was at a disadvantage. It is my conviction that he would be much more successful if he played in the modern era. Just how much more successful will be addressed in the final chapter.

8

Conclusions and Projections

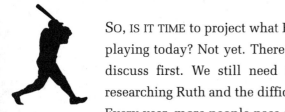SO, IS IT TIME to project what Babe Ruth would do if he were playing today? Not yet. There are still a few other points to discuss first. We still need to talk about the process of researching Ruth and the difficulty in trying to quantify him. Every year, more people pass away who had actual personal experience with him. As of now, there are very few men alive who took the field with or against him. Essentially, we are left with individuals who merely watched him play when they were children. Can we count on what they say? Are childhood memories historically reliable? We have a natural tendency to imbue our lives with romanticized importance, especially as we grow old.

What, then, is the role of oral history in a treatise like this? Should it be ignored? No. But it needs to be considered only as a starting point for evaluation and investigation. The story being told may be apocryphal. Then again, it may be true. In the case of Babe Ruth, this is particularly relevant. There is so much oral history relating to him that it is almost overwhelming. The man's persona has incredible staying power, and his legacy endures in the countless locations that he visited. There is a specific 1923 incident in Philadelphia that is particularly revealing. I first heard about it from an aging area resident and was then able to corroborate the details from documented primary sources.

After playing the Athletics at Shibe Park on September 4, 1923, Babe went directly to a waiting cab that sped across town to the Kensington section of the city. The Catholic parish of Ascension of Our Lord had a top amateur baseball team, but had gone into debt providing them with a quality field on which to play. Assistant Pastor William Casey was an unofficial chaplain to the Athletics and had asked Ruth on a prior visit if he would consider playing a few innings as part of a fund-raiser. Of course Babe consented, but with one condition. He wanted to play the entire game. So plans were set in motion, and the game was scheduled for 6:00 P.M. the day after Labor Day, when the Yankees returned to Philadelphia.

An Ascension uniform was specially made for Ruth and placed in a local store window as a promotion. Word spread around the neighborhood that Babe Ruth was coming; all 7,000 tickets were sold. Thousands of other requests went unfulfilled. Upon arrival, Ruth quickly changed uniforms and stepped onto a field that buzzed with electric anticipation. There may have been 7,000 anxious fans crammed into the small ballpark, but about that many more were situated everywhere within view of the field. People stood on housetops, hung out of windows, perched in trees, and congregated on factory roofs to watch the world's premier ballplayer perform in their backyard. At least 2,000 more lined up along the Pennsylvania Railroad tracks beyond left field to watch from a distance. Babe played first base and batted fourth for

Ascension, who took the field against Lit Brothers, a department store team and one of the best amateur nines in the area.

When the day began, the Ascension club was $6,500 in debt. But Father Casey knew in advance that Ruth's participation would guarantee a financial windfall. So he presented Babe with a diamond stickpin at home plate before the Bambino's first at-bat in the second inning. Ruth flied out to left field. The Lit Brothers pitcher was a tough lefthander named Gransbach, who performed like a pro the entire game. Ruth batted again in the fourth frame with his squad trailing 2–0, and this time he really connected. His rising line drive sailed high over the nearby right field fence and disappeared so far in the distance that nobody saw where it landed. Father Casey, who had played college ball at St. Bonaventure's, blinked in disbelief from the bench. When he was finally able to speak, the beloved cleric said in reverential tones: "That ball has left our parish." To this day there are still neighborhood people talking about that drive, and it wasn't even a homer. The right field fence was too close to award four bases for any ball clearing it. There was a flagpole about 100 feet from the foul line, and anything to the right of it was limited to two bases. Babe's blast passed about two feet to the right of the Stars and Stripes. A bemused Ruth was sent back to second base.

Ascension could have used the run, because they lost the game 2–1. Later in the game, Babe grounded out, but did score his team's only run after his ninth-inning fly went so high that the leftfielder got dizzy trying to catch it. When the game ended, Babe was covered in dirt and sweat from his exertions. His team had lost, but nobody cared. Ruth had been magnificent. He dove for balls in the field, and ran the bases like a demon. Between innings, he signed baseballs (about five dozen), which were then auctioned for five bucks apiece. Standard autographs were given by the hundreds. Babe also hit fungos over the left field fence to the kids waiting by the train tracks. As usual, he was mobbed trying to leave the field and carried by the happy throng to Father Casey's automobile. Instead of being in the red by thousands of dollars, the Ascension club was in the black with plenty to spare. As they rode away, the grateful clergyman asked Ruth how he could repay him. Babe responded: "Say, Father, are you kidding me?"

For me, this story is pure joy. Finding people who remember being there has become tougher as the years have passed. But locating folks whose parents saw those events and passed on their memories is not difficult. There are still bars and corner shops that resonate with anecdotes about the time that the great Babe Ruth came into their community to save their financially troubled parish. But the story wouldn't have the same poignancy without that personal interaction. Geographic proximity in concert with oral history allowed me to truly understand what happened back in 1923. If it weren't for my roots in Philadelphia, I probably wouldn't have even heard about it. Then, personally interacting with the folks telling the story added that intangible dimension. Telephones and e-mails are very helpful in communicating amongst ourselves, but they do not give the same depth and clarity as do face-to-face interviews.

Then there are the two barnstorming games that Babe played in Trenton, New Jersey, in 1927 and 1928. Trenton is the state capital and only about an hour's drive from where I live. When I did research at the state archives, a staff member told me that the field on which Ruth had played was still in place. I drove ten minutes across town and found a ballgame in progress. Within thirty minutes, I met dozens of people who wanted to talk all night about the home runs that Ruth hit there almost eighty years earlier. None of them actually saw those homers, but they had heard about them and considered themselves experts. Of course, there was some outrageous exaggeration. One guy swore that Ruth hit a ball that landed at the corner beyond center field, which is over 700 feet away. I smiled and thanked him for his help. That type of hyperbole is common in oral history, and all historians are aware of the pitfalls inherent in the oral research process. The counterpoint is that these tales can't be simply ignored. Often, amidst the fiction are kernels of truth waiting to be developed and clarified. And so it was in this instance.

As is often the case, the events of Ruth's '27 and '28 games have interwoven over time. My sources in the neighborhood knew that Babe hit some great homers, and most believed that the long balls all happened in one day. Newspaper coverage confirms that Ruth hit three long homers in the 1927 game, but none in 1928. The documented record shows that all of Ruth's drives carried to right or right center field. So, is the legend of a monumental center field blast completely baseless? Not necessarily. I visited the neighborhood several times, finally meeting some fairly reliable sources. A middle-aged fellow who grew up in the neighborhood told me about his father, who had watched Ruth take batting practice from the top of the family garage. He had gathered there with other family members to get a free view. In the process, Babe pounded a ball completely over their heads, a blow that left a lifelong impression. The garage is still there, as is home plate, and I measured the distance between the two at 497 feet. I accept this account, since both the source and the specificity are convincing. I believe that the competitive home runs from the 1927 game and this batting practice drive (either in 1927 or 1928) have been mixed together across the years. I thoroughly enjoyed the investigative experience, but it wouldn't have happened if not for geographic coincidence and oral history.

Another of my personal favorites is the tale of Babe Ruth at Shibe Park on May 22, 1930. And why not? My own father was there, and told me about it when I was a child. Decades later, while I did the formal research, I felt as though I had been there myself. According to my dad, he went to the doubleheader with his uncle, who didn't have much money in those Depression times. Dad was fourteen and a passionate fan of the World Champion Athletics. He knew that Ruth had belted three home runs the day before and couldn't wait to see the rematch between Babe and his beloved A's. So he was crushed when his uncle opted to buy the fifty-cent rooftop seats across Twentieth Street from right field. He wasn't even inside the stadium. His malaise lasted until the third inning, when Ruth batted for the second time.

Then he saw the ball leap from Babe's bat, followed closely by a gunshot-like sound. On and on the ball sped directly toward him, but, in an instant, it whizzed far over his head. I can still picture my father closing his eyes, reliving the moment, and yanking his head backward as he pantomimed his attempt to follow the improbable flight of the ball. This was the Ruthian home run that landed on Opal Street, after flying well over 500 feet. Until that moment, Dad felt disconnected from the events inside the ballpark. He was just too far away to feel any sense of the action. But Babe Ruth and his powerful swing changed things instantly. Dad said to me; "That big sonovabich just pulled me inside the park with him. All of a sudden, it was like I was in the infield." What son of a baseball family wouldn't cherish a story like that?

Ruth's post-season trip to Wilkes-Barre, Pennsylvania, in 1926 has been discussed in the chapter dedicated to Babe's great batting power. But the entire story is still untold. It is a fitting climax to the point presently in consideration. I read the original wire service report about a 650-foot drive, while at the Philadelphia Public Library sometime in the late 1990s. Since I didn't think such a blow was possible, I put verification efforts on the back burner. I finally got around to the follow-up research on February 2, 2002, when I made an appointment to visit the Luzerne County Historical Society. Once there, the more I read, the more interested I became. By the time the office closed and the staff asked me to leave, I knew that I was onto something. Four days later was Babe's birthday, and I usually make a pilgrimage to the Babe Ruth Museum on this date. During the two-hour drive, I told my wife Marie about my recent findings in Wilkes-Barre, and suggested that I might be on the trail of the home run Holy Grail. Over the years, she has helped me with my research, and knew the implausibility of a 600-foot batted ball. So, when I said that I might have identified one, she looked at me wistfully.

Later, during the festivities at the museum, Director Michael Gibbons introduced me to the guests, and invited me to say a few words. Motivated by my recent work, I made a few generalized remarks about Babe's tremendous batting strength. The folks seemed to enjoy it, but it was no big deal. Afterward, an elderly gentleman approached my wife and me, and asked: "Is there any chance that you ever heard about a long home run by Ruth in Wilkes-Barre back in the twenties? I had a friend who just died recently and he spoke about it right before he passed." My wife and I turned to each other with our mouths open.

The man's name is Dan Corchran and his deceased friend was Joe Drugash, who was born in Wilkes-Barre around 1916. He was one of many children in attendance at Artillery Field on October 12, 1926, when Ruth made his historic blow. Apparently, the sight of Babe's blast was so awe-inspiring that Drugash literally reminisced about it until the day he died. According to Corchran, Drugash said that the ball passed far over the right center field wall and hit a fence at the far side of a running track in adjoining Kirby Park. I kept investigating and eventually made arrangements with officials at Wilkes University (the current owner) to allow me inside Artillery Park to take some measurements. This was in August 2003. Frankly, I considered it a minor miracle that the field was still in existence. When I arrived, there were a few reporters, who later wrote articles about my visit in the local papers. One of those articles identified a few surviving witnesses to the subject event. That was what led me to Joe Gibbons who was alive and well (and still in town). Mr. Gibbons and I went back to the park two months later, and he showed me where the ball landed.

Along the way, I also heard from Mrs. Joan Lavery. After the third inning during the game in 1926, a group of boys came out of the right field stands to gather around Babe Ruth. As was often the case, their excitement led to unintentional unruliness. Ruth was knocked to the ground, and several policemen raced over to rescue him. When they sorted through the pile of humanity, Babe popped up grinning and holding onto a four-year-old child. Most of the kids were much older and bigger than the youngster, and Ruth's primary concern was to protect the little guy from being trampled. His name was Frank Lavery, and, when he grew up, he married Joan. Mrs. Lavery had also read about my visit to Wilkes-Barre and decided to contact me. By sheer good luck and the effort of an enterprising photographer, a photo was taken of Babe and Frank as the two untangled from the pile. A copy of that picture became Frank Lavery's most cherished possession until the day he died.

Babe Ruth and young Frank Lavery during 1926 barnstorming game in Wilkes-Barre. (Wilkes-Barre Record *and Mrs. Joan Lavery)*

We've just discussed a few events in Babe Ruth's life that were confirmed and enriched by direct contact with witnesses to those events. But there are fewer and fewer of these folks with each passing year. Very soon, there will be none, and the impact on Ruthian research will be debilitating. Much of this book has been devoted to Babe Ruth's unique batting power. We have just discussed his amazing 1926 Wilkes-Barre drive, which he categorized as his longest immediately after he hit it. With the assistance of surviving witnesses, the tale evolved into living history. But while doing research at the Library of

Congress in 2004, I discovered an old newspaper interview in which Babe identified a different blow as his longest. That event has never been confirmed. I decided that this book would be better balanced if I shared an example of an unsuccessful investigation. Ruth was serving as the first base coach for the Brooklyn Dodgers when he gave an interview to the *Chicago Daily News* on July 20, 1938. In the process, he was asked to name his longest home run. This was his response: "That must have been the one at Pittsburgh. I really tagged that one. They told me afterward—after the exhibition game with the Pirates—that it was the first time a ball had been hit out of the park over the center field wall. That Waner said to me: 'Babe, when that ball sailed over me, it was just starting to move.'"

When Babe referred to "Waner," we don't know if he meant Paul or Lloyd. They were brothers. Paul (nicknamed "Big Poison") began play with the Pirates in 1926, and Lloyd ("Little Poison") started the following year in 1927. Since Lloyd was a center fielder and Paul was a right fielder, Ruth probably was referring to Lloyd. The key then is to find exhibition games between the Yankees and Pirates in Forbes Field beginning in 1927. I found one on May 3, 1929, but Babe went 1 for 4 with a single. Interestingly, the *Pittsburgh Post Gazette* mentioned in its game coverage that Ruth hadn't been there since the 1927 World Series. It also said that Babe had not hit a homer at Forbes Field since his exhibition appearance in 1923. That meant that the great blow must have been delivered from 1930 to 1934 (after which, Ruth left the Yankees). Right?

The problem is that I have never been able to identify any Yankee-Pirate exhibition games during that time. Additionally, when Ruth blasted his final career home run as a National Leaguer at Forbes Field in 1935, it was monstrously long. The descriptions in the local papers were very inclusive. Isn't it natural that they would have compared that homer to any recent Ruthian drive of similar magnitude? But, there was no mention of any such event. None of it makes much sense. Perhaps, looking backward, Babe just made a mistake. If so, it would be the only time to my knowledge that he made such an error. I have been able to confirm every other deed that the Bambino is known to have referenced. At least for the present, this Ruthian claim remains unconfirmed.

But what if I had read the original newspaper account in 1984 instead of 2004? When I was unsuccessful in using newspaper resources, I might have succeeded in locating a witness. I did try, but it was too late. I called my contacts in Pittsburgh and then spoke to a few area SABR members (Society for American Baseball Research), but the trail was cold. As recently as 2003, I met Joe Gibbons, who had seen Babe's Wilkes-Barre drive and helped to confirm the occurrence. However, when I tried to recontact Mr. Gibbons in 2006, his daughter told me that he had lost his memory and was living in a home for the elderly. If I had tried to track down the Wilkes-Barre event in the same time frame as the Pittsburgh event (just a few years' difference), I would never have met Joe Gibbons. Researchers from this time forward will be severely handicapped by the lack of eyewitnesses. Therefore, I encourage anyone with firsthand memories of Babe Ruth to step forward now and go on record with their stories. They are part of American history, and their efforts would be appreciated. Any local historical society, situated in most counties, would likely be pleased to hear from them.

The good news is that there are still enough authenticated Babe Ruth stories to fill five books like this. Whether talking about his twenty-two years of official baseball, his long list of unofficial games, his raw power, or his commanding personality, there is always more to say. Remember the second time that Babe broke down? First, he collapsed from that mysterious stomach ailment in 1925, and then he suffered a nervous breakdown in 1929. We have already discussed much of what led to Ruth's 1929 problem, but the strangest link in that chain is now ready for review. It will also assist us in a final evaluation of Babe Ruth's greatness. On May 19 at Yankee Stadium, Babe was involved in an incident that may be the oddest and most tragic that ever occurred in a Major League ballpark.

Two innings after Ruth lined a home run into the right field seats, an explosively violent thunderstorm rumbled through the Bronx. Frightened fans in those open bleachers stampeded toward an exit that simply could not accommodate the volume. Within seconds, those rushing from the upper rows collided with those who got there first, knocking many of them down. Before another minute had elapsed, a grotesque pile of human flesh formed inside the overtaxed exit. By the time the suffering horde had been separated, more than one hundred fans had been injured. Tragically, one man was already dead, and seventeen-year-old Eleanor Price was mortally injured. Most of the 50,000 folks inside the stadium didn't even know what had happened. By then, almost all the players had retreated into the locker-room, but Babe Ruth had remained in the dugout. He recognized that a crisis was unfolding and called for doctors from the stands. When Babe saw a police officer carrying Ms. Price across the field, he ran out to assist. Ambulances were hurriedly summoned, but they would take twenty minutes to arrive. What should be done in the meantime? It was decided to convey the stricken teen to the Yankee clubhouse. When the emergency personnel rushed into the locker-room, it was already too late. There lay Eleanor in the arms of Babe Ruth, who was devastated by his inability to save her.

But how could this scene have happened? Why was a critically injured person being held by an uneducated athlete? Doctor S. Greenwald had responded to Ruth's summons and was tending to her. But he had no equipment. There was little that he could do, except raise her spirits. That's where Babe Ruth came in. Babe intuitively understood that his uncanny gift for imbuing people with hope was her best chance. It was an impossible task, but he willingly accepted it. So, he knelt on the floor and gently stroked the girl's head in a desperate effort to save her life. And when he failed, he paid a heavy price. The four previous months since his first wife had died in a fire had been emotionally draining for Ruth. This intimate encounter with senseless death was the final straw. Three days later, Babe visited the seriously injured at Lincoln Hospital, but he was a shell of his usual effervescent self. Ten days after that, Ruth was broken in body and spirit.

I believe that almost anyone else would have been through for the season. But not Babe Ruth. Before the month of June ended, he was the same invincible warrior of old, personally vanquishing the great Lefty Grove. This bizarre one-month episode is actually Babe Ruth in microcosm. It tells us why he was so transcendent as both an athlete and a personality. Yes, he was supremely physically gifted, but Ruth was more than an athletic machine. Regardless of his humble and sometimes troubled youth, Babe grew up unafraid to try anything—even holding a dying girl in his arms in the faint hope that he could help her.

As I completed this book, I did what I suppose all authors do. I reviewed everything to make sure that I had been as accurate as possible. In that wrapping-up process, I again contacted Dr. Charles Yesalis, who had helped me with various issues relating to sports, medicine, and the performance of elite athletes. He believes that there are only marginal physical differences, if any, between the top tier of world-class athletes and those rare individuals who become the absolute best. He theorized that Babe Ruth did what he did by way of both neurological superiority and behavioral uniqueness. I couldn't comment on the neurological aspect of his thesis, but I asked him about the aforementioned incident with the dying girl at Yankee Stadium. He responded by saying: "That's exactly what I'm referring to. That behavior would have to carry over to his on-field performance."

In fact, a similar event had occurred with Ruth on a train ride through the Midwest during his 1928 barnstorming tour. A passenger suffered a heart attack between towns, and Babe spent thirty minutes trying to revive him. This was before formal CPR training, and Ruth probably had no idea of exactly what to do. But he tried anyway. Then there was the time in 1932 when Ruth went alligator hunting in central Florida prior to spring training. He and his three companions were hip deep in swamp muck when a poisonous water moccasin attacked them. The others tried to flee, but Babe simply addressed the threat by shooting the snake through the head with a single shot from his .30-.30 rifle.

The two on-field events that first come to mind are Babe's World Series moments in 1926 and 1932. In '26, his attempt to steal second base resulted in failure, thereby ending the season. The '32 event was Ruth's "called shot" when he blasted an unforgettable home run under considerable duress. Whether he won or lost, succeeded or failed, this unique man always responded to critical situations in the same way. He simply acted without any apparent fear or consideration of failure. Yesalis believes that it was an innate gift, something that Babe Ruth could not have been taught. Regardless of its origin, this rare trait was crucial in achieving his extraordinary athletic success.

Combining courage, indomitable spirit, and exceptional ability made Babe Ruth the greatest athlete in American history. Oddly, however, it was Babe's limitations that helped make him so popular. If people only saw extraordinary natural gifts, they certainly would have admired Ruth, but they would not have related to him. Instead, they saw a flawed man with a bloated physique. He was intemperate, coarse, and profane. But he was also generous, loyal, and kind. Babe could be the proverbial bull in the china shop. Other times, he was gentle as a kitten. Life had a way of knocking him down, but he never stayed down for long. Babe always got up and swung for the fences. And people everywhere loved him for it. The rich and powerful flocked to him because he was the most celebrated person in the country. And despite the wealth, fame, and privilege that he earned for himself, common folk felt connected to him. They didn't just care for him; they were one with him.

Would he be so wildly popular if he were alive today? I don't see why not. It's true that he played at a time when America desperately needed heroes. The Great War (now known as World War I) had sapped the nation and the world of much of its joy and innocence. The sports stars of that era remain among the most beloved ever. Men like Jack Dempsey, Red Grange, and Bobby Jones reside in that pantheon reserved for only our favorite few. And who today can truly comprehend the nearly hysterical reaction to Charles Lindbergh's solo flight across the Atlantic Ocean in 1927? It was a time made for Babe Ruth. But are things really so different now?

For whatever reasons, we again live in an age when we look to the athletic world to find our heroes. Our political leaders should satisfy that need, but we won't allow them to. Our political climate is so partisan and biased that our presidents are routinely vilified by half the population. So, we look elsewhere. Babe Ruth would fit perfectly into our time. We are willing to forgive athletes for personal weakness as long as we perceive them as essentially good people. If they are honest and offer us great on-field performance, we have a track record of overlooking behavioral flaws. Ruth was so naturally genuine, inherently likeable, and athletically magnificent that he would capture the hearts of modern fans like no one else.

In the preceding chapter, I have outlined reasons why Babe Ruth would do well if he played today. Just how well is an important and provocative issue. In order to project, we must first establish a frame of reference. Babe started as a pitcher and then switched to the outfield. That mid-career change rarely happens today, but it hardly occurred in Ruth's day as well. He was unique then and would be unique now. So, we first have to determine what position a contemporary Babe Ruth would play. Let's assume that Babe would follow the same career path and start as a pitcher before eventually switching to the outfield. At what age would he first arrive in the Major Leagues? Given Ruth's personality and temperament, he almost certainly would have signed a professional contract at the conclusion of high school. We know how successful he was as a teenage baseball player, and he would have been offered college scholarships. But Babe would likely have shunned the classroom and headed straight into the minor leagues.

The summer after his eighteenth birthday would find him flourishing in an Instructional League somewhere. He was such an overwhelming athletic force that he would not stay there for long. By the next season, he would probably excel at the Double A level, where he would be called up for a September look by the parent club. By age twenty in 1915, Babe Ruth was a full-time Big Leaguer in his rookie season with the Boston Red Sox. I see no reason why a performer of his vast ability would take longer today. Dwight Gooden, Ken Griffey Jr., and Alex Rodriguez all played virtually full time in the Major Leagues at an equivalent age.

Defensively, Babe Ruth has always been underrated. He tends to be remembered as an aging, overweight athlete who was a defensive liability. In his last few seasons, those pejorative claims were valid. However, for most of his career, Babe was a superior outfielder with the statistics to prove it. In fact, Tris Speaker, the greatest defensive outfielder of his era, had this to say in the October, 1928 edition of *Baseball Magazine:* "I will say without hesitation that Babe Ruth is one of the half dozen greatest outfielders I ever saw. This is aside from his slugging ability, which is unrivaled, and his base running ability which is much greater than is commonly supposed. Purely as an outfielder, Babe will rank among the game's greatest. . . . He covers a lot of ground, primarily because he plays the batter correctly. He has a sure pair of hands, a wonderful throwing arm and he always knows exactly what to do with the ball when he gets it." And Ruth evolved into a good first baseman due to years of service at that position during exhibition games.

On the bases, Babe had one demonstrated weakness. Consistent with his personality, he sometimes was overly aggressive. Ruth was thrown out trying for extra bases more than the average Major League player. And that fact weighs against him. However, we have no statistics to tell us how many errors, balks, and assorted other defensive missteps he caused the opposition. I can say with certainty that the number was considerable. Game accounts are replete with references to the problems that Babe generated for the defense when he was on base. And, oh those collisions! Ruth was always barreling into somebody. But he wasn't dirty, as was Ty Cobb with his flying spikes. Babe's opponents respected him as a base runner, and, with few exceptions, regarded his roughneck style as suitable for the age in which he played. Although he made some mistakes, all in all, Babe was a better than average Major League base runner. He would be essentially the same in the modern era.

As a starting pitcher, I believe that Babe Ruth would be approximately as successful today as he was in his own time. Since the game has changed, his statistics would reflect those changes. His E.R.A. would be higher but so would his strikeout totals. His innings would be lower, but his win-loss percentage would be about the same. Remember how well he pitched at the conclusion of the 1930 and 1933 seasons as a relatively old man? Ruth was terrific, even though he hadn't thrown at the Big League level for a decade. Babe had won sixty-seven games before he was twenty-three years old. At a comparable age, Greg Maddox had won twenty-six, Roger Clemens sixteen, Nolan Ryan twelve, and Randy Johnson none. There is every reason to believe that Ruth would have won more than 300 games if he had continued on the mound. He pitched effectively in hundreds of exhibition and barnstorming games as he aged, never developing a sore arm.

What about a modern-day Ruth's offensive statistical legacy? I believe that it would be awesome! Batting averages tend to be lower now, and Babe Ruth would be affected accordingly. Those modern baseball gloves would deprive Ruth of many base hits, and I estimate that his career average would drop about twenty points from .342 to about .322. But that's the only area in which he would depreciate. Of course, he would strike out more, since everyone does, but that would not adversely affect his home run totals or slugging percentage. Babe's numbers would go right through the roof in those two categories. Turning Ruth loose in our small modern ballparks would be an invitation to offensive mayhem. Then, factor in the shrunken strike zone, improved equipment, the current fair-foul rule, and an exercise-induced stronger Babe Ruth, and his production would boggle the mind.

I believe that Babe would average about twenty-five more home runs per year over the roughly seventeen full seasons he was an everyday player. That translates into about 1,150 career home runs. Specifically, there is a year-by-year chart in Part III that lists the projected total at exactly 1,158. And, of course, that does not include his 300-plus unofficial homers from exhibition and barnstorming games. On the matter of a projected slugging percentage, we must first deduct about 234 total-bases due to a reduced batting average. However, we then need to substitute those extra homers for a proportionate number of outs and extra-base hits. In this way, Ruth accrues many more total bases than he loses. The result is a career slugging percentage of .807. Are those numbers realistic? I think so; they may even be conservative.

If Babe could have played his entire career as a modern-day outfielder, who can even guess what might have happened? He unquestionably would put on a Big League uniform already possessing prodigious power. In 1914, as a nineteen-year-old professional neophyte, Ruth set distance records in three different locations. As a twenty-year-old rookie pitcher the next season, Babe smashed drives of record length in St. Louis and Boston. And he did it without ever lifting a single weight. Just imagine Babe Ruth initiating formal strength training in high school (as almost all modern athletes do), and then starting his Major League career as a twenty-year-old outfielder. How many career home runs would he hit? Who has a calculator?

Even if I'm wrong in my analysis of every subjective area of comparative difficulty, there is compelling objective data pointing to at least 390 additional homers. If Ruth played with the modern "fair-foul" rule, he would hit at least fifty more home runs. If he played with a 162-game schedule instead of his 154-game calendar, he would record no fewer than forty additional homers. If he played with the same outfield dimensions as current sluggers, Babe would add about 300 home runs. Remember the discussion in the "ballpark" section in the preceding chapter about "Comparative Difficulty?" Research indicates that Babe Ruth would have hit 91 home runs in 1927 if he had played under modern circumstances. The same research methodology has now been used to project his home run totals for every year. Since Babe was at his most potent in 1921, it was particularly intriguing to determine the findings for that season. The results? Under today's conditions, Babe would have hit the mind-numbing total of *104 home runs!*

Officially, Ruth hit fifty-nine four-baggers during that nearly incredible campaign. With today's dimensions, he probably would have lost about five of those. In away games, there was only one homer that might not have counted today. It was Babe's towering fly over the forty-foot-high wall and screen in Cleveland on August 23. That boundary was just 290 feet down the right field line, and the newspaper accounts don't tell us how far from that line the ball left the playing field. So, in order to be conservative, that one is taken away from Ruth. None of his other twenty-six "away" home runs could possibly be discounted now. Only St. Louis had another short right field target, but all four of Babe's homers at Sportsman's Park flew way beyond those outfield walls. Twenty-six of Ruth's twenty-seven blows hit outside the Polo Grounds were blasted very hard and very long.

At home, Babe recorded thirty-two circuit shots, several landing in the nearby right field grandstand. It was absurdly close along the foul line at 257 feet, but it angled out radically at 135 degrees. For those who need a little help with their geometry, if you drew a line from home plate through second base into center field, the right field grandstand wall would parallel that line. Not even halfway from the foul pole to straightaway center, the grandstand ended at a spot about 400 feet distant from home plate. Beyond that point, there were open bleachers from right center to left center, which created dimensions that were much farther away than in any modern ballpark. Again, the problem in a projection like this is to find precise descriptions as to where Ruth's drives landed in the grandstand. In some instances, those exact details are not available.

A few of the grandstand homers are easy to evaluate. On June 11, Babe lined one into the lower deck near the foul line. No problem. Obviously, that blow would not be a home run today. On July 2, Ruth drilled a ball into the upper deck at the far end near right center. This case is another no-brainer, but with a different conclusion. This drive would be an easy four-bagger in any of the current thirty Major League stadiums. But what about Babe Ruth's home run on September 7, 1921? Multiple newspaper accounts confirm that it was lined viciously into the right field lower deck. But exactly where? Near the 257-foot foul line? Into the center field end at a 400-foot distance? Or somewhere in the middle? We just don't know. But in order to proceed with the projection, we must do something.

I have chosen to apply statistical probability and make an educated estimate. There are only five such nebulous drives in Babe Ruth's 1921 resumé. By examining Babe's established directional pattern, I believe that about half of any undetermined grandstand drives would not clear today's outfield fences. Therefore, three of those five unknown drives are subtracted from Babe's total. Adding those to the foul-line hugger of June 11 along with the Cleveland homer on August 23, we reduce Ruth's season total to fifty-four dingers. But this is where the fun starts!

On the matter of the old "fair-foul" rule, four lost home runs have been identified. On April 16 and July 2, Babe smashed prodigious drives far over the eighty-foot-high grandstand that were clearly fair until just before they faded from view. Also, on June 11, Ruth bombed one almost over the left field bleachers that was ruled foul. Babe was so disgusted by the umpire's decision that he broke his bat on the ground. All three of these balls would readily be judged fair under the current rule. At present, there is only one other confirmed example of a lost "fair-foul" Ruthian homer in 1921. On August 21 in St. Louis, Ruth blasted a drive far over the right field bleachers in fair territory. As it flew to the far side of Grand Avenue, the ball drifted foul, and that's the way it was judged.

Certainly, there are a few others. Knowing what we know about Babe's batting pattern, it's ridiculous to assume that he hit no other such drives as a visiting player. We just don't know where or when or how many. On May 3, Ruth slammed one far over the right field grandstand roof at Fenway Park, but it was ruled foul. It was a truly prodigious drive of epic length, but we have no way to determine if it passed over the right field fence on the fair side of the "foul pole." Babe also cleared the distant right field fences in Washington (May 6) and Chicago (July 10). Back at home, he blasted one over the left field bleachers at the Polo Grounds on July 31. These may have been homers today, but we have no definitive proof. In all, Ruth belted twelve *apparent* foul homers during the 1921 season. So, what next? Since this projection is based on the philosophy of erring on the side of conservatism, we will add only the four certain cases to Ruth's cause. Accordingly, he has bobbed back up to fifty-eight home runs.

We may be finished with the "fair-foul" concept, but we're not finished with the peculiar role of the Polo Grounds' right field grandstand. He hit singles off that twelve-foot-high outfield wall on April 13 and September 2, and doubles on April 26, June 6, June 15, July 5, September 1, and September 23. Babe also lifted fly outs against that barrier on April 17 and September 27. Almost certainly, Ruth hit many other outs that would have struck that wall if left untouched, but we have no data on them. Once more, we will make no effort to give Babe Ruth unsubstantiated credit. So, of the ten confirmed drives against the right field wall, how many would have passed over modern fences? By again studying patterns and probability, it seems likely that about one-in-four such balls would be present-day homers. Accordingly, Babe adds two more home runs to raise his total to sixty.

But 60 is a long way from 104. Where are the remaining forty-four would-be home runs? Actually, it's rather simple. In 1921, Babe Ruth hit a combination of at least forty triples, doubles, and fly outs in various American League parks that would easily soar over twenty-first-century fences. A good barometer of the distance to the Polo Grounds bleachers in right center is that only two balls landed there from 1909 until 1920. And remember that two teams played there (Giants and Yankees) for much of that time. For the record, Ruth did it thirteen times from 1920 through 1922 when the Polo Grounds served as his home turf. It was a long way out to both power alleys, and the green screen in center field ranged from 440 feet to 475 feet. Babe routinely bombed balls all over that expansive real estate without recording home runs. And for the Doubting Thomases, here is the list:

April 13: Double to base of center field screen

April 16: Fly out to center field screen

April 16: Fly out to exit gate in deep right center field

April 26: Fly out to bleacher fence in right center field

June 2: Triple off exit gate in deep right center field

June 3: Triple off screen on one bounce just left of dead center field

June 4: Line drive out to deep right center field

June 5: Triple off bleacher fence just left of center

June 9: Fly out to Tris Speaker at exit gate in deep right center field

July 27: High fly out to deep center field

July 28: Towering fly out near bleacher fence in right center field

July 31: Triple off bleacher fence in right center field

August 4: Double to deep left center field in front of bleachers

September 1: Double off top of bleacher fence just right of center

September 7: Triple on one bounce off bleacher fence in right center field

September 14: Fly out to deep center field near Grant Memorial

September 15: Triple off center field screen on short-hop

September 18: Triple landed between Grant Memorial and screen in center

September 26: Double off left center field bleacher fence

October 2: Fly out to deep right center field near bleacher fence

In the seven other American League stadiums, there were many more Ruthian nonhomers that would clear present-day fences. Here is the catalog for everyone to ponder:

April 21, Philadephia: Double off bleacher wall just left of center

May 12, Detroit: Triple to bleacher fence in deep right center field

May 13, Detroit: Triple off center field fence (against wind)

May 16, Cleveland: Triple off bleacher fence in deep left center field

May 20, Chicago: Triple to base of center field scoreboard

May 25, St Louis: Fly out to center field bleacher fence

June 20, Boston: Double off top of high left field wall

July 10, Chicago: Fly out to center field fence

July 11, Chicago: Fly out to just left of center field scoreboard

July 16, Detroit: Fly out to center field fence

July 24, Cleveland: Triple to deepest center field corner

August 11, Philadelphia: Double off fence in deep right center field

August 13, Philadelphia: Fly out to deepest right center field (near
old scoreboard)

August 19, Chicago: Triple to deep center field on towering high
drive

August 20, St Louis: Triple on line drive off center field fence

August 25, Cleveland: Double off high screen in deep right center
field

August 26, Detroit: Fly out to top of fence in deep right field

August 30, Washington: Double on line drive off top of high right
field wall

Sept 5, Boston: Triple to base of right center field bleacher fence

Sept 5, Boston: Fly out to bleacher fence in deep right field

Lastly, we must factor in today's lengthened schedule. Ruth's 100 projected homers in his 154-game schedule translates into an additional
5.2 four-baggers in the current 162 game format. As always, we won't
give Babe any breaks, so we will add just four home runs instead of the
more numerically probable five homers.

Well, there it is. The total comes to 104 home runs. Do I think this
analysis is reliable? Of course; the facts are undeniable. Please refer to
the list of two primary sources for every confirmation, which can be
found at the end of Part III. If anything, Babe's final output would be

higher if we possessed the complete data. Take a close look at the two corresponding coded spray charts for the 1921 season (also in Part III). You will notice that most of the marks (long drives that did not result in home runs) are plotted close to the outfield walls. This is especially true for Ruth's home games at the Polo Grounds. Anyone educated in statistical probability will wonder about the absence of plot points closer to the dotted line that represents the average position of modern fences. Didn't Babe Ruth hit any balls in the 390-to-415-foot range?

Of course he did. But, when they were hit between the power alleys from right center field to left center field, they were almost always caught for outs. And unless they scored a run from third base as a sacrifice fly, sportswriters were not likely to describe them in their articles the next day. Why would they? There was no television or radio coverage in 1921, and newspapers were essentially the only way for folks to get details about the games. The writers needed every line of available column space just to describe the scoring along with any items of particular human interest. Would a 390-foot out to right center or a 415-foot out to center motivate a competent journalist to write about it? Remember that the center field fences in the American League that year ranged from 455 feet to 488 feet. There was no drama to a 415-foot fly ball that was caught routinely by center fielders, who positioned themselves at about that distance before Ruth even hit the ball. My belief is that Babe Ruth almost certainly hit another ten or twelve fly outs during the 1921 campaign that would be homers today. But we will never know about them because there are no specific records. However, we do have our common sense. What does yours tell you?

The intellectual and emotional impact of these numbers should not be minimized just because we haven't known them until now. For anyone genuinely interested in baseball history and/or our American cultural heritage, this is a powerfully compelling story. Its significance and uniqueness are absolute. No other player has ever come even remotely close to this level of nearly superhuman performance.

Assuming I'm in error about the caliber of competition and the effects of modern relief pitching, Ruth would still arrive in today's game with huge objective superiority. Any naysayers have the burden of proof. If pitching has improved slightly (which I doubt), would the newer version of The Babe be significantly less effective? That seems highly implausible to me. I have studied an average of five firsthand accounts (often more) of every official game that Ruth ever played. I have also reviewed at least three primary sources for nearly all of his approximately 800 unofficial games. In so doing, the certain realization has evolved that Babe Ruth was gifted beyond rational expectation. He really was that transcendent. And along the way, he uplifted an entire nation with optimism, joy, and hope. Everywhere he went, Babe left people happier than before they met him. His natural passion and spontaneous bliss were beacons to those whose lives were not so blessed.

Is there anything else left to say? Only this: there has never been a baseball player like Babe Ruth, and we will never see his like again.

Part Three
The Facts

Don't tell me about Ruth; I've seen what he did to people. I've seen them, fans driving miles in open wagons through the prairies of Oklahoma to see him in exhibition games as we headed north in the spring. I've seen them: kids, men, women, worshippers all, hoping to get his name on a torn dirty piece of paper, or hoping for a grunt of recognition when they said, "Hi ya, Babe." He never let them down; not once. He was the greatest crowd pleaser of them all.

—Waite Hoyt, New York Yankee pitcher
1921–1930, in *I'd Rather Be a Yankee* by John Tullius

9
Projected Home Run Totals

As ILLUSTRATED IN THE forthcoming series of spray charts (Chapter 11), Babe Ruth hit many balls in his twenty-two-year career that were not home runs then, but would be now. The following list shows a comparison between his official annual home run totals and the totals that are projected under modern conditions. The differences primarily reflect the smaller ballparks in use today. These projections also include the 1931 change in the fair/foul rule as well as additional homers that Ruth would have accrued with an expanded 162-game schedule.

Year	Official HRs	Projected HRs
1914	0	0
1915	4	9
1916	3	8
1917	2	9
1918	11	42
1919	29	66
1920	54	86
1921	59	104
1922	35	62
1923	41	67
1924	46	71
1925	25	43
1926	47	70
1927	60	91
1928	54	76
1929	46	75
1930	49	73
1931	46	60
1932	41	51
1933	34	46
1934	22	36
1935	6	13
Regular Season	**714**	**1,158**
World Series	**15**	**23**
Total	**729**	**1,181**

10
Babe Ruth's Career Home Runs

THE FOLLOWING IS A listing of all known competitive home runs hit by Babe Ruth as a professional baseball player. Ruth also hit many as a teenage amateur while attending St. Mary's School in Baltimore, but those homers are not listed here. By "competitive home runs," I refer to four-base hits achieved in contested games. Accordingly, any known home run struck by Babe Ruth in any type of ballgame after turning pro in 1914 will be listed. That includes spring training games (including intra-squad games), spring tour contests, in-season exhibition games, and post-season barnstorming games. It does not count batting practice or demonstration homers, which Babe hit by the hundreds. Of course, all 714 official Major League four-baggers as well as his World Series and All-Star home runs are included.

It should be emphasized that no single source will ever include literally every competitive home run hit by Babe Ruth. The official homers are not the problem; they are a matter of established record. It is the unofficial deeds of The Bambino that will always defy total reckoning. Ruth simply played in too many relatively unknown and remote places to establish any thoroughly definitive record. On occasions, he even played games in rather spontaneous fashion that prohibited significant media coverage. It is believed that the following log is, by far, the most inclusive established to date. It is estimated that about 98 percent of all Ruthian home runs (approximately 1,100) are noted here. The remaining few may never be known.

Some further discussion is necessary for a complete understanding of this document. In a few instances, so-called ground rule doubles have been included in the list of unofficial home runs. That is only the case when there is clear and compelling documentation that certain Ruthian drives should be counted as home runs. He played many games in settings where balls hit in some directions were ruled doubles (or even singles) regardless of their extraordinary distance. A prime example occurred on October 11, 1926, in Bradley Beach, New Jersey. Babe was in town to play the Brooklyn Royal Colored Giants and belted two tremendous drives over the street in right field. They were limited to two-base hits due to a local ground rule. Apparently, the distance down the right field line was too short to allow any ball landing there to merit four bases. But, in Ruth's case, all the local newspapers confirmed that both of Babe's blows would have been homers in any park in the country with a right field fence. So, for the purpose of understanding Babe Ruth's accomplishments, those few drives are included in this log.

It should also be understood that many of Ruth's unofficial games were played on fields with no fences at all. As a result, he hit numerous drives of stupendous length that had no realistic chance of resulting in a home run. A good example of this scenario was his game at the Crampton Bowl in Montgomery, Alabama, on March 29, 1925.

Babe blasted one against the Brooklyn Dodgers that landed on a cinder track in distant right center field that went for a double. It was impressive enough to induce the local officials to measure it. The result: 497 feet! Right fielder Dick Cox then played Ruth about 450 feet away on his next at-bat, whereupon Babe knocked one over his head anyway. That result, however, was just another double. None of these amazing drives are included in this home run log. It is estimated that if Babe Ruth had played all his unofficial games with fences of standard dimensions, he would have added about another 100 homers.

In the listing of Ruth's Major League homers, there are brief descriptions and estimates of flight distances. The estimates are just that. However, they are based on multiple firsthand accounts that have been integrated with official stadium dimensions. Most of the estimates are probably accurate to within ten feet. On the matter of the descriptions, there were changes in ballparks that should be acknowledged. For example, the double-deck grandstand at Chicago's Comiskey Park was not constructed until 1927. Before then, the outfield fences were surrounded by open bleachers. As a result, the descriptions of Babe's homers reflect those stadium differences. Similar changes occurred in most of the Big League ballparks during the course of Ruth's career. There is one final point on the stadium issue. During the twelve years that Babe Ruth played at Yankee Stadium (1923–1934), there was no grandstand in right field. All his home runs in that direction were aimed at a vast expanse of open bleachers that extended upward for about seventy rows.

HOME RUN LOG ABBREVIATIONS

I	inning
MOB	men on base
Dst	distance

N.B. The occasional insertion of a superscript numeral 1 or 2 in the "I" (for inning) column denotes either the first or second game of a doubleheader.

1914 HOME RUN LOG—1

Date	City	Team	Pitcher	I	MOB	Description	Dst
9/5	Toronto	Toronto	Johnson	6¹	2	Far over right field fence	410

SPRING TRAINING HR:

3/7 Fayetteville, NC

1915 HOME RUN LOG—4

HOME FIELD: BOSTON'S FENWAY PARK

Date	City	Team	Pitcher	I	MOB	Description	Dst
5/6	NY	NY	Warhop	3	0	Into right field upper deck	375
6/2	NY	NY	Warhop	2	1	Line drive high into right field upper deck	435
6/25	Bos	NY	Caldwell	2	2	Deep into right center field bleachers	445
7/21	St.L	St.L	James	3	0	Far over right field bleachers; landed across Grand Ave.	475

SPRING TRAINING HR:

3/23 Hot Springs, AR

1916 HOME RUN LOG—3

Date	City	Team	Pitcher	I	MOB	Description	Dst
6/9	Det	Det	Dubuc	3	0	Deep into bleachers just right of dead center	465
6/12	St.L	St.L	Park	7	2	Into right center field bleachers; pinch-hit	365
6/13	St.L	St.L	Davenport	3	0	Into right field bleachers	340

BARNSTORMING HR:

10/17 Laconia, NH

1917 HOME RUN LOG—2

Date	City	Team	Pitcher	I	MOB	Description	Dst
8/10	Bos	Det	James	5¹	0	To 8th row in center field bleachers	465
9/15	NY	NY	Munroe	9	1	Line drive high into right field upper deck	440

1918 HOME RUN LOG—11

Date	City	Team	Pitcher	I	MOB	Description	Dst
5/4	NY	NY	Russell	7	1	Into upper deck near right center field; plus 2 HRs just foul	410
5/6	NY	NY	Mogridge	4	1	High into right field upper deck	385
5/7	Wash	Wash	Johnson	6	1	Towering drive far over right field wall	395
6/2	Det	Det	Erickson	6	0	To top of right center field bleachers	430
6/3	Det	Det	Dauss	1	0	Deep into right center field bleachers	420
6/4	Det	Det	James	6	1	Deep into right center field bleachers	420
6/5	Clev	Clev	Enzmann	6	1	Far over right field wall and through window across street	405
6/15	St.L	St.L	Rogers	7	2	Into right field bleachers	335
6/25	NY	NY	Russell	1	1	Rising line drive deep into right field upper deck	445
6/28	Wash	Wash	Harper	7	0	Over high right field wall	380
6/30	Wash	Wash	Johnson	10	1	Far over high right field wall	440

1918 UNOFFICIAL HOME RUN LOG

7/8 Home run ruled as triple due to 1918 rules limiting Ruth to the base he arrived at when the winning run crossed the plate:
• Boston off Cleveland's Coveleski in the tenth inning of game one, one man on base.
• Line drive thirty rows into distant right field bleachers, 490 feet.

SPRING TRAINING HRs:
3/17 Hot Springs, AR (two)
3/24 Hot Springs, AR
3/30 Little Rock, AR (two)

EXHIBITION HRs:
8/18 New Haven, CT

BARNSTORMING HRs:
9/14 New Haven, CT

1919 Home Run Log—29

Date	City	Team	Pitcher	I	MOB	Description	Dst
4/23	NY	NY	Mogridge	1	1	Line drive to short center field; inside-the-park	215
5/20	St.L	St.L	Davenport	2	3	Far over right field bleachers into Grand Ave.	425
5/30	Phil	Phil	Perry	8^2	1	Over right center field fence and onto rooftop across 20th St.	485
6/7	Bos	Det	Dauss	5	2	Line drive to 10th row in right center field bleachers	440
6/17	Bos	Clev	Morton	6^2	0	Line drive 20 rows into right field grandstand	450
6/24	Bos	Wash	Robertson	7	0	Halfway up bleachers in right center field	460
6/30	NY	NY	Shawkey	6^1	3	Into right field upper deck	330
7/5	Bos	Phil	Johnson	8^2	1	Deep into right field bleachers	415
7/5	Bos	Phil	Johnson	10^2	0	Over high left field wall	370
7/10	St.L	St.L	Shocker	6^2	0	Into right field bleachers	350
7/12	Chic	Chic	Danforth	3	2	Into left field bleachers	400
7/18	Clev	Clev	Jasper	4	1	Over high right field wall and across street	395
7/18	Clev	Clev	Coumbe	9	3	Over right field wall and onto house across Lexington Ave.	425
7/21	Det	Det	Ehmke	9	0	Over right field fence into Trumbull Ave.	385
7/24	Bos	NY	Shawkey	8	1	Line drive to 20th row in right center field bleachers	455
7/29	Bos	Det	Leonard	9	1	Line drive to 5th bleacher row in deep right center field	440
8/14	Chic	Chic	Kerr	7	1	Deep into right field bleachers	405
8/16	Chic	Chic	Mayer	5	1	Towering drive far over right center field bleachers	500
8/17	St.L	St.L	Shocker	1^2	1	High into right field bleachers	325
8/23	Det	Det	Dauss	3	3	Over right center field bleachers; landed across Trumbull Ave.	510
8/24	Det	Det	Ayres	1	1	Over bleachers in deep right center field	460

8/24	Det	Det	Love	6	1	Over right field fence into street	390
8/25	Det	Det	Leonard	6	0	To top of right center field bleachers	420
9/1	Bos	Wash	Shaw	7^2	1	Line drive halfway into right field bleachers	455
9/5	Phil	Phil	Noyes	3	1	Over right center field fence into 20th St.	410
9/8	NY	NY	Thormahlen	8^1	0	Line smash into far end of right field lower deck	440
9/20	Bos	Chic	Williams	9^1	0	Over clock in left center field; through window across street	415
9/24	NY	NY	Shawkey	9^2	0	Line drive far over right field roof near center field end	505
9/27	Wash	Wash	Jordan	3^1	1	Far over 45-ft. wall in deep right field	435

1919 UNOFFICIAL HOME RUN LOG

SPRING TRAINING HRs:
4/1 Tampa, FL
4/4 Tampa, FL

SPRING TOUR HRs:
4/15 Richmond, VA
4/17 Richmond, VA
4/18 Baltimore, MD (four)
4/19 Baltimore, MD (two)

EXHIBITION HRs:
6/1 Paterson, NJ
9/7 Baltimore, MD (two)
9/21 Bristol, CT

BARNSTORMING HRs:
9/28 Hartford, CT (official ground rule 1b)
9/30 Portland, ME
10/1 Sanford, ME
10/3 Lynn, MA
10/5 Rutland, VA
10/10 Beverly, MA
11/1 Los Angeles, CA
11/8 San Francisco, CA
11/9 Oakland, CA (A.M.)
11/9 San Francisco, CA (P.M.)
11/11 Sacramento, CA
12/28 San Diego, CA

1920 HOME RUN LOG—54
HOME FIELD: NEW YORK'S POLO GROUNDS

Date	City	Team	Pitcher	I	MOB	Description	Dst
5/1	NY	Bos	Pennock	6	0	Far over right field roof at 4th flag from foul line	505
5/2	NY	Bos	Jones	6	1	Liner between grandstand and bleachers in right center field	450
5/11	NY	Chic	Wilkinson	1	1	Line drive into distant bleachers in right center field	435
5/11	NY	Chic	Kerr	5	0	Into right field upper deck; plus 440-ft. right center field triple	355
5/12	NY	Chic	Williams	5	0	Line drive into right field upper deck near foul line	390
5/23	NY	St.L	Weilman	6	1	Rising line drive 40 feet over 3rd flag on right field roof	520
5/25	NY	Det	Leonard	1	1	Line drive into right field upper deck	395
5/26	NY	Det	Dauss	2	0	Line drive into right field upper deck	400
5/27	Bos	Bos	Harper	6	0	To 40th row in distant right center field bleachers	525
5/27	Bos	Bos	Karr	8	0	Over high wall in left center field	380
5/29	Bos	Bos	Bush	4^1	1	Far over high wall and clock in left center field	410
5/31	NY	Wash	Johnson	8^2	1	Line drive off right field roof façade	430
6/2	NY	Wash	Zachary	1^1	1	Into upper deck near right center field	405
6/2	NY	Wash	Carlson	8^1	0	Deep into right center field bleachers	445
6/2	NY	Wash	Snyder	8^2	0	High into right center field bleachers past exit gate	480
6/10	Det	Det	Okrie	3	1	Line drive deep into right center field bleachers	410
6/13	Clev	Clev	Myers	6	0	Over right field wall and over house across street	470
6/16	Chic	Chic	Faber	8	1	High drive into right field bleachers	375
6/17	Chic	Chic	Williams	4	2	Far over right field bleachers against 20 mph wind	445

6/23	St.L	St.L	Shocker	6	0	High drive into right center field bleachers	355
6/25	NY	Bos	Pennock	1	1	To top of right center field bleachers	485
6/25	NY	Bos	Pennock	9	0	Line drive off far end of right field roof	500
6/30	Phil	Phil	Bigbee	9^1	0	Line drive to right field; hit chimney across 20th St.	440
6/30	Phil	Phil	Perry	4^2	1	Deep into left center field bleachers	380
7/9	NY	Det	Oldham	5	0	Line drive off pillar in right field upper deck	405
7/10	NY	Det	Dauss	3	0	Into right center field alley between grandstand and bleachers	435
7/11	NY	Det	Ehmke	3	0	Line drive into right field lower deck	305
7/14	NY	St.L	Davis	2	0	Into right field lower deck	285
7/15	NY	St.L	Burwell	1^1	2	Line drive off façade at far end of right field roof	495
7/19	NY	Chic	Kerr	4^2	1	Near top of right center field bleachers	465
7/19	NY	Chic	Kerr	9^2	0	Line drive into right field lower deck	320
7/20	NY	Chic	Faber	5^1	0	Line drive over 2nd pole on right field roof	455
7/23	NY	Clev	Morton	6	0	Into right field upper deck near foul line	350
7/24	NY	Clev	Bagby	4	0	Hit 4th flag from foul pole on right field roof	460
7/25	NY	Bos	Hoyt	5	1	Line drive into right field lower deck	340
7/30	St.L	St.L	Vangilder	9	1	Over right field bleachers; hit street light across street	505
7/31	St.L	St.L	Shocker	8	0	Over right field bleachers into Grand Ave.	390
8/2	Chic	Chic	Williams	4	1	Line drive to top of right field bleachers	435
8/5	Det	Det	Ehmke	2	0	Over right field fence and hit back wall	375
8/6	Det	Det	Dauss	3	0	To top of bleachers in deep right center field	475
8/6	Det	Det	Dauss	6	2	Over right center field bleachers & across Trumbull Ave.	500

8/14	Wash	Wash	Shaw	1	0	Line drive onto house past right field wall	435
8/19	NY	Clev	Caldwell	4	0	Over right field grandstand roof	450
8/26	NY	Chic	Kerr	1	1	Line smash into right field lower deck	365
9/4	Bos	Bos	Jones	3^1	0	Into old left field bleachers	320
9/4	Bos	Bos	Bush	6^2	0	Line drive into first row of right center field bleachers	405
9/9	Clev	Clev	Coveleskie	3	0	Over high right field wall; hit porch across street	410
9/10	Clev	Clev	Caldwell	1	1	Over high right field wall; plus 455-ft. center field fly out	335
9/13	Det	Det	Ehmke	6	1	High into right center field bleachers	415
9/24	NY	Wash	Acosta	1^1	0	Off right field grandstand roof façade	405
9/24	NY	Wash	Shaw	1^2	0	Line drive into right center field bleachers	420
9/27	Phil	Phil	Rommel	1	1	Over right field fence & house across 20th St.	470
9/27	Phil	Phil	Rommel	6	0	To right field; thru screen door across 20th St.	415
9/29	Phil	Phil	Keefe	9^1	1	Over right field fence into 20th St.	360

1920 UNOFFICIAL HOME RUN LOG

SPRING TRAINING HRs
4/1 Jacksonville, FL

SPRING TOUR HRs:
4/8 Winston-Salem, NC (three)
(official ground rule
doubles; see 1920 season summary)

EXHIBITION HRs:
6/24 Columbus, OH
9/5 Haverstraw, NY
9/8 Pittsburgh, PA
9/15 Toledo, OH (two)

BARNSTORMING HRs:
10/3 Bronx, NY (three)
10/4 Philadelphia, PA
10/5 Dover, DE
10/8 Philadelphia, PA
10/10 Bronx, NY (two)
10/13 Buffalo, NY (two)
10/14 Rochester, NY
10/15 Oneonta, NY
10/16 Jersey City, NJ
10/17 Bronx, NY
11/8 Havana, Cuba
11/14 Havana, Cuba

1921 HOME RUN LOG—59

Date	City	Team	Pitcher	I	MOB	Description	Dst
4/16	NY	Phil	Harris	6	0	High drive into right field upper deck; plus 2 foul HRs	340
4/20	NY	Bos	Russell	7	1	Vicious line drive off right field upper deck façade	385
4/21	Phil	Phil	Moore	9	1	Line drive over right field fence; hit house across 20th St.	435
4/22	Phil	Phil	Rommel	4	1	To top of left field bleachers	410
4/25	NY	Wash	Johnson	1	0	Line drive off façade of right field grandstand roof	460
5/2	Bos	Bos	Jones	9	0	Line drive to 15th bleacher row in right field	450
5/6	Wash	Wash	Erickson	3	0	Line drive far over high scoreboard in right center	490
5/7	Wash	Wash	Johnson	8	0	Far over 40-ft. wall in deepest center field corner	520
5/10	Det	Det	Middleton	1	1	High into bleachers just right of center field	460
5/12	Det	Det	Dauss	1	1	Over scoreboard in left center field into Cherry St.	405
5/14	Clev	Clev	Bagby	8	2	To top of bleachers just left of center field	480
5/17	Clev	Clev	Uhle	9	0	Far over high wall in deep right center field	470
5/25	St.L	St.L	Shocker	7	2	Into distant center field bleachers; plus 460-ft. center field fly out	535
5/29	NY	Phil	Keefe	3	0	Far over right field grandstand roof near foul line	455
5/31	Wash	Wash	Zachary	9	2	Line drive over high right field wall	405
6/3	NY	St.L	Davis	6	0	Liner into right field lower deck; plus 430-ft. center field triple	365
6/10	NY	Clev	Bagby	3	0	Rising line drive into right field upper deck	420
6/11	NY	Det	Middleton	7	2	Liner into right field lower deck near foul line	275
6/12	NY	Det	Sutherland	5	1	Into right field upper deck	365
6/13	NY	Det	Ehmke	3	0	Line drive into right field upper deck	400

6/13	NY	Det	Ehmke	7	1	To 3rd row in center field bleachers near exit	480
6/14	NY	Det	Dauss	1	1	To top of left field bleachers	430
6/14	NY	Det	Dauss	3	1	To 7th row in center field bleachers right of backdrop	490
6/20	Bos	Bos	Myers	10	0	Over wall in deep left center field; hit garage across street	500
6/23	Bos	Bos	Thormahl'n	5	1	To 35th bleacher row in right field	510
6/25	NY	Wash	Johnson	5	1	Line drive into right field lower deck	330
6/26	NY	Wash	Mogridge	3^2	1	High into right center field bleachers	430
6/29	NY	Bos	Bush	1	0	Line drive into right field lower deck	380
7/2	NY	Bos	Russell	7^1	0	Line drive off upper deck façade in deep right field	415
7/2	NY	Bos	Myers	1^2	1	Over right field roof; plus 2 foul HRs over right field roof	440
7/5	NY	Phil	Hasty	6	0	Off right field roof façade at far end near right center field	445
7/11	Chic	Chic	Kerr	6	1	To top of right field bleachers	430
7/12	St.L	St.L	Davis	3	2	Line drive to top of right field bleachers	385
7/12	St.L	St.L	Davis	7	0	Over bleachers in deep right center field into street	470
7/15	St.L	St.L	Vangilder	6	1	Far over right center field bleachers into Grand Ave.	450
7/18	Det	Det	Cole	8	1	Over far corner of stadium in dead center field	575
7/30	NY	Clev	Coveleskie	6	0	Into bleachers in deep right center field	440
7/31	NY	Clev	Caldwell	6	2	Line drive high over roof at far end near right center field	560
8/6	NY	Det	Oldham	8	2	Rising line drive to top of right field upper deck	435
8/8	NY	Chic	Wieneke	3^1	1	Line drive against right field roof facade	465
8/8	NY	Chic	Kerr	1^2	0	Line drive into right center field bleachers	425
8/10	NY	Chic	Hodge	3	1	Deep into left field bleachers	370
8/11	Phil	Phil	Keefe	4	2	High into left field bleachers	385
8/12	Phil	Phil	Hasty	8	0	To top of left field bleachers	400
8/17	Chic	Chic	Wieneke	6	1	High over bleachers in deep right center field; landed in soccer field	550

8/18	Chic	Chic	Faber	7	2	Over left field fence near foul line; landed in park	395
8/23	Clev	Clev	Caldwell	1	1	Very high fly over right field wall	340
8/23	Clev	Clev	Caldwell	3	1	Far over right field wall; onto house across Lexington Ave.	460
9/2	NY	Wash	Erickson	7	1	Far over right field roof at far corner and into vacant lot	520
9/3	NY	Wash	Courtney	3	2	Into right field upper deck	355
9/5	Bos	Bos	Karr	9^2	0	Deep into center field bleachers	460
9/7	NY	Bos	Pennock	4^2	1	Line drive into right field lower deck; plus 430-ft. right center field triple	315
9/8	Phil	Phil	Rommel	4	0	Over right field fence into 20th St.	365
9/9	Phil	Phil	Naylor	4	1	Far over bleachers in deep left center field and into tree across street	510
9/15	NY	St.L	Bayne	5^1	1	Line drive into right field upper deck at far end near right center field	430
9/16	NY	St.L	Shocker	4	0	Over right field roof between 1st and 2nd flags	455
9/26	NY	Clev	Coveleskie	1	0	Deep into alley between right field grandstand and bleachers	440
9/26	NY	Clev	Uhle	5	1	Over roof in deep right field; plus 450-ft. left center field double	465
10/2	NY	Bos	Fullerton	3	2	To 8th row of upper deck in deep right field	390

1921 UNOFFICIAL HOME RUN LOG

SPRING TRAINING HRs:
3/8 Shreveport, LA
3/13 Shreveport, LA (three)
3/16 Lake Charles, LA
3/27 Shreveport, LA (two)

SPRING TOUR HR:
4/10 Brooklyn, NY

EXHIBITION HRs:
5/9 Toronto, Canada
7/22 Akron, OH
7/25 Cincinnati, OH (two)
8/14 Columbus, OH

BARNSTORMING HRs:
10/16 Buffalo, NY
10/17 Elmira, NY (two)
10/19 Warren, PA

1922 HOME RUN LOG—35

Date	City	Team	Pitcher	I	MOB	Description	Dst
5/22	NY	St.L	Vangilder	8	0	Line drive against right field roof façade	430
5/30	NY	Phil	Heimach	6	1	Line drive to lower deck in deep right field	390
6/4	NY	Phil	Heimach	5	2	Over right field roof between 3rd and 4th poles	505
6/8	Chic	Chic	Robertson	1	0	Over right center field bleachers	465
6/9	Chic	Chic	Courtney	9	0	Over fence in dead center	480
6/10	St.L	St.L	Shocker	3	1	Over right field bleachers into Grand Ave.	375
6/19	Clev	Clev	Mails	1	0	Over high right field wall	340
6/26	Bos	Bos	Quinn	5	2	Into distant right field bleachers	405
7/1	Phil	Phil	Rommel	3^1	1	Into left field bleachers	355
7/1	Phil	Phil	Heimach	4^2	0	Over right center field fence; hit awning across 20th St.	460
7/1	Phil	Phil	Heimach	7^2	0	Over right field fence; onto house across 20th St.	455
7/2	NY	Phil	Yarrison	8	2	Line drive into right field lower deck	325
7/3	Phil	Phil	Eckert	7	0	Into left field bleachers	370
7/6	NY	Clev	Mails	3^1	3	High fly into right field lower deck	290
7/17	NY	Chic	Robertson	7	1	Line drive into right field lower deck	335
7/26	St.L	St.L	Wright	7	0	Over right field bleachers into Grand Ave.	400
7/26	St.L	St.L	Bayne	9	1	Line drive to top of right center field bleachers	415
7/29	Chic	Chic	Hodge	7	0	Deep into right field bleachers	405
8/4	Clev	Clev	Mails	7	1	Over high right field wall	360
8/6	Det	Det	Johnson	6	1	Liner into right center field bleachers; plus 470-ft. center field double	415
8/9	Det	Det	Cole	9	0	To bleachers just right of center field; plus 450-ft. center field out	470
8/16	NY	Det	Johnson	5	0	Liner against right field roof façade; plus 435-ft. double	440
8/18	NY	Chic	Davenport	10	0	Into right field upper deck	365
8/19	NY	Chic	Leverette	3	0	Line drive against right field roof façade	445

8/20	NY	Chic	Faber	1	1	Deep into right center field bleachers	430
8/20	NY	Chic	Faber	9	2	Into right center field bleachers	420
8/29	NY	Wash	Johnson	4	0	To top of right center field bleachers	460
8/30	NY	Wash	Francis	1	1	Into right field upper deck	345
9/5	NY	Bos	Pennock	1^1	0	Against upper deck façade in right field	340
9/11	Phil	Phil	Naylor	5	0	Into left field bleachers; plus 2 doubles and 440-ft. center field fly out	360
9/11	Phil	Phil	Schilling	7	0	Into left center field bleachers	390
9/14	Chic	Chic	Leverette	4	0	Line drive deep into left field bleachers	415
9/17	St.L	St.L	Pruett	6	0	Over right field bleachers into Grand Ave.	425
9/19	Det	Det	Pilette	1	1	Into bleachers right of center field flagpole; plus 440-ft. triple	480
9/21	Det	Det	Oldham	7	0	Over scoreboard in left center field into Cherry St.	405

1922 UNOFFICIAL HOME RUN LOG

SPRING TRAINING HRs:
3/16 New Orleans, LA
3/18 New Orleans, LA
3/22 Bogalusa, LA
3/25 New Orleans, LA

SPRING TOUR HRs:
3/29 Galveston, TX
3/31 San Antonio, TX
4/7 Richmond, VA

EXHIBITION HRs:
4/16 Baltimore, MD
7/24 Cincinnati, OH
9/3 Baltimore, MD (three)
9/25 Buffalo, NY

BARNSTORMING HRs:
10/15 Omaha, NE
10/16 Sleepy Eye, MN (two)
10/17 Sioux Falls, SD
10/26 Fort Scott, KA
10/29 Denver, CO (two)

1923 HOME RUN LOG—41

HOME FIELD: NEW YORK'S YANKEE STADIUM

Date	City	Team	Pitcher	I	MOB	Description	Dst
4/18	NY	Bos	Ehmke	3	2	Line drive to 20th bleacher row in right field	400
4/24	NY	Wash	Russell	5	0	Line drive to the 55th row in right field bleachers	480
5/12	Det	Det	Pillette	6	0	To bleachers just right of center field; near flagpole	465
5/15	Det	Det	Collins	3	1	Over left field fence into Cherry St.; plus 440-ft. triple	360
5/17	St.L	St.L	Bayne	9	0	Deep into right center field bleachers	390
5/18	St.L	St.L	Wright	7	1	Line drive into bleachers in deep left center field	440
5/19	St.L	St.L	Pruett	1	1	Line drive into right field bleachers	350
5/22	Chic	Chic	Cvengros	15	1	Over right field bleachers	455
5/26	Phil	Phil	Hasty	3	2	Over right center field fence into 20th St.	390
5/30	Wash	Wash	Johnson	1^1	0	Far over right field wall; landed at back of house	435
5/30	Wash	Wash	Mogridge	3^2	2	Line drive over scoreboard in right center field	475
6/8	NY	Chic	Cvengros	3	1	To 30th row of right field bleachers	405
6/12	NY	Clev	Uhle	1	2	To 35th row in right center field bleachers	495
6/17	NY	Det	Dauss	2	0	To 30th row of bleachers in deep right field	430
7/2	NY	Wash	Zachary	1	2	To 40th row of right field bleachers	425
7/3	NY	Wash	Mogridge	15	0	Line drive into right field bleachers to win 2–1	330
7/7	St.L	St.L	Vangilder	1	0	Over right center field bleachers; broke window across street	505
7/7	St.L	St.L	Vangilder	8	0	Far over right field bleachers; cleared Grand Ave.	490
7/9	St.L	St.L	Davis	1	1	High drive into bleachers in left center field	390
7/12	Chic	Chic	Lyons	6	1	Line drive into bleachers in deep right center field	445
7/14	Clev	Clev	Metevier	8^2	0	Over right field wall; onto house across street	410

7/18	Det	Det	Holloway	7	0	High drive just over right field fence	375
7/24	Phil	Phil	Walberg	9	2	Line drive over right field fence; broke window across street	415
7/27	Phil	Phil	Naylor	1	0	Over right center field fence; hit awning across 20th St.	430
8/1	NY	Clev	Smith	9	1	High into right center field bleachers	460
8/5	NY	St.L	Kolp	1	1	Line drive into right field bleachers	350
8/5	NY	St.L	Kolp	6	0	Thru exit of bleachers in deep right field	380
8/11	NY	Det	Dauss	9^2	0	Past track in deepest left center field; inside-park	475
8/12	NY	Det	Johnson	1	0	High fly into bleachers near right field foul line	335
8/15	St.L	St.L	Shocker	8	1	Over right field bleachers; landed across Grand Ave.	475
8/17	St.L	St.L	Vangilder	1	1	Into right field bleachers; landed in water barrel	365
8/18	Chic	Chic	Cvengros	9	2	Over right field bleachers to win 6-5	460
9/5	Phil	Phil	Hulvey	6	0	Over right field fence; over house across 20th St.	480
9/9	NY	Bos	Murray	4^2	0	Misjudged high fly to deep center field; inside-the-park	420
9/10	NY	Bos	Quinn	4	0	Line smash to left center field; rolled far; inside-the-park	300
9/13	NY	Chic	Blankenship	1	1	Line drive into lower right field bleachers	320
9/16	NY	Clev	Uhle	7^1	0	High into right field bleachers	435
9/28	Bos	Bos	Ehmke	6	2	Into center field bleachers	450
10/4	NY	Phil	Hasty	1	1	High into right field bleachers	465
10/5	NY	Phil	Walberg	3	0	Liner that bounced past center fielder; inside-the-park	270
10/7	NY	Phil	Harris	1	1	Into right field bleachers	340

1923 UNOFFICIAL HOME RUN LOG

SPRING TRAINING HRs:
3/17 New Orleans, LA
3/22 New Orleans, LA
3/29 New Orleans, LA

SPRING TOUR HRs:
4/8 Fort Worth, TX

BARNSTORMING HRs:
10/26 Mahanoy City, PA
10/27 Oil City, PA
10/28 Erie, PA
10/29 Wilkes-Barre, PA
10/31 Williamsport, PA
11/1 Shamokin, PA
11/4 Long Island, NY

EXHIBITION HRs:
4/29 Paterson, NJ
6/21 Albany, NY
7/5 Pittsburgh, PA
7/20 Grand Rapids, MI (two)
8/14 Indianapolis, IN (three)
8/28 Toronto, Canada
8/29 Buffalo, NY
9/4 Philadelphia, PA
(official ground rule double)
9/30 Baltimore, MD
10/3 New York, NY

1924 HOME RUN LOG—46

Date	City	Team	Pitcher	I	MOB	Description	Dst
4/20	Wash	Wash	Johnson	9	0	Over high right field wall; plus 450-ft. right center field triple	380
4/23	NY	Bos	Howe	8	2	To 30th bleacher row in deep right field	445
4/25	NY	Bos	Piercy	3	2	To 20th row in right field bleachers	375
4/28	Phil	Phil	Harris	7	0	Far over fence in deep right center field into 20th St.	430
4/28	Phil	Phil	Baumgartner	8	0	Line drive deep into left field bleachers	395
5/5	NY	Phil	Hasty	1	2	To lower rows in right field bleachers near foul line	320
5/10	NY	Chic	Thurston	1	0	To left field bleachers near foul line	340
5/13	NY	Chic	Lyons	1	0	To 40th bleacher row in deep right center	515
5/15	NY	St.L	Wingard	6	0	To 15th bleacher row in deep right center	465
5/23	NY	Det	Cole	5	1	Just over right field fence; plus 430-ft. right center field fly out	325
5/26	NY	Det	Stoner	1	0	Line drive into bleachers in deep left field	415
5/30	NY	Phil	Harris	3^1	0	High into right center field bleachers	495
5/31	NY	Phil	Gray	9^2	0	Deep into bleachers just right of dead center	525

6/6	Chic	Chic	McWeeney	5	0	High drive into right field bleachers	400
6/12	Det	Det	Johnson	4	1	Over right field fence near foul line	385
6/17	Clev	Clev	Uhle	4	0	Just over high right field wall and screen	355
6/21	NY	Bos	Quinn	5^1	0	Deep into right field bleachers	390
6/25	NY	Wash	Marberry	1	0	To 60th row in right field bleachers	490
6/30	Phil	Phil	Meeker	1	0	Over right field fence; hit awning across 20th St.	420
7/1	Phil	Phil	Burns	9	2	To aisle at top of left field bleachers	405
7/3	Phil	Phil	Gray	8	1	Halfway into bleachers just left of center	470
7/6	Wash	Wash	Martina	8	0	To 10th bleacher row in deep left center	445
7/10	NY	Chic	Connally	7^1	1	High into right field bleachers	385
7/11	NY	Chic	Mangum	1	1	Into right field bleachers	345
7/14	NY	St.L	Wingard	7^2	0	Line drive deep into right field bleachers	440
7/14	NY	St.L	Wingard	8^2	2	Almost to scoreboard in deep right center	495
7/19	NY	Clev	Coveleskie	1	0	Line drive deep into right center field bleachers	435
7/20	NY	Clev	Metivier	2^2	2	Liner past pitcher to center field flagpole; inside park	475
7/23	NY	Det	Dauss	11	0	Halfway into right field bleachers to win	430
7/26	Chic	Chic	Connally	14	0	Into right field bleachers to win	405
7/28	Chic	Chic	Cvengros	1^2	2	Over bleachers in deep right center field	505
7/29	Chic	Chic	Thurston	5	2	Into left field bleachers; plus 450-ft. center field double	390
7/31	St.L	St.L	Danforth	6^2	0	Over right field bleachers into Grand Ave.	410
8/4	Det	Det	Collins	5	2	Over left field fence into Cherry St.	365
8/5	Det	Det	Stoner	5	2	Over fence in deep left field into Cherry St.	370
8/6	Det	Det	Whitehall	4	0	Over right center field bleachers and across Trumbull Ave.	485
8/8	Clev	Clev	Messenger	1	0	Over high right field wall; plus 460-ft. center field triple	345
8/8	Clev	Clev	Messenger	6	0	Over high wall in deep right field	365

8/24	NY	Det	Leonard	1	1	Line drive into right field bleachers; plus 455-ft. fly out	375
8/25	NY	Clev	Uhle	5	1	To center field flagpole past track; inside-the-park	475
8/28	NY	Wash	Zachary	4	0	Deep into right center field bleachers	460
8/28	NY	Wash	Russell	7	1	High into right field bleachers	425
9/6	NY	Phil	Meeker	6	1	Towering fly into right field bleachers	355
9/8	Bos	Bos	Fullerton	8	1	Halfway into bleachers in deep right center	500
9/11	Bos	Bos	Ehmke	8^1	1	Line drive halfway into center field bleachers	510
9/13	Chic	Chic	Lyons	8	1	Into right field bleachers	385

1924 UNOFFICIAL HOME RUN LOG

SPRING TRAINING HRs:
3/20 New Orleans, LA

SPRING TOUR HRs:
3/31 Mobile, AL
4/8 Knoxville, TN (two)

EXHIBITION HRs:
6/2 Louisville, KY
7/1 Delanco, NJ
7/25 Indianapolis, IN (two)
8/20 Utica, NY
9/12 Buffalo, NY (two))

BARNSTORMING HRs:
10/1 Springfield
10/3 Altoona, PA
10/14 Minneapolis, MN (two)
10/17 Spokane, WA
10/19 Seattle, WA (three)
10/21 Portland, OR
10/22 Dunsmuir, CA (two)
10/25 San Francisco, CA
10/26 Oakland, CA (A.M.)
10/26 San Francisco, CA (P.M.) (two)
10/29 Santa Barbara, CA
10/31 Anaheim, CA (two)

1925 HOME RUN LOG—25

Date	City	Team	Pitcher	I	MOB	Description	Dst
6/11	NY	Clev	Miller	7	0	Line drive into right field bleachers	370
6/14	NY	Det	Leonard	3	0	Line drive to 20th bleacher row in right field	420
6/16	NY	Det	Whitehill	3	1	Halfway up right field bleachers; plus 430-ft. right center field fly out	445
7/1	Bos	Bos	Fuhr	3	0	Into lower rows of right field bleachers	405
7/1	Bos	Bos	Ross	7	1	Deep into right field bleachers	430
7/2	NY	Phil	Rommel	5	0	Line drive through exit in right field bleachers	390
7/8	St.L	St.L	Davis	3	1	Over left field bleachers and hit scoreboard	450
7/11	Chic	Chic	Cvengos	6	2	Deep into left field bleachers	410
7/18	Det	Det	Stoner	1	1	High drive over right center field bleachers into street	425
7/20	Det	Det	Collins	7	1	Over scoreboard in left center field into Cherry St.	415
7/28	NY	St.L	Wingard	7	1	Halfway into right field bleachers	430
8/18	Det	Det	Stoner	8	0	High fly just over right field fence; plus 2 long outs	375
8/22	Clev	Clev	Uhle	4	1	Towering fly over high right field wall	325
8/23	Clev	Clev	Karr	6	0	High over 40-ft. right field wall	385
8/24	Clev	Clev	Miller	7	0	Far over right field wall and landed on roof across street	455
9/8	Bos	Bos	Ross	7^2	0	To 35th row in right center field bleachers	510
9/10	Phil	Phil	Gray	4^1	0	Over right field fence and hit house across 20th St.	420
9/10	Phil	Phil	Rommel	4^2	0	High fly over right field fence into 20th St.	350
9/12	Phil	Phil	Walberg	9^1	0	Over right field fence & hit porch across 20th St	415
9/18	NY	St.L	Giard	7	0	Halfway into right field bleachers near exit	440
9/24	NY	Chic	Connally	10	3	Far into right center field bleachers to win; plus 430-ft. right center field double	425
9/27	NY	Det	Whitehill	6^1	0	High into right field bleachers	415

Date	City	Team	Pitcher	I	MOB	Description	Dst
9/28	NY	Det	Holloway	3^1	0	To 50th bleacher row in right center field bleachers	500
9/28	NY	Det	Dauss	1^2	0	High drive just over right center field fence	380
10/3	NY	Phil	Willis	5	0	Into right field bleachers	330

1925 UNOFFICIAL HOME RUN LOG

SPRING TRAINING HRs:
3/24 St. Petersburg, FL

SPRING TOUR HRs:
3/30 Birmingham, AL
3/31 Birmingham, AL (two)
4/5 Chattanooga, TN (two)
4/6 Knoxville, TN

NO EXHIBITION HRs

NO BARNSTORMING HRs

1926 HOME RUN LOG—47

Date	City	Team	Pitcher	I	MOB	Description	Dst
4/20	Wash	Wash	Johnson	1	1	Line drive far over high right field wall	440
4/23	NY	Bos	Ruffing	7	0	Line drive to 12th bleacher row in deep right center field	455
4/24	NY	Bos	Lundgren	8	2	Almost to top of bleachers in right center	510
4/30	NY	Wash	Coveleskie	7	0	Very high fly to 2nd row in right field bleachers	315
5/5	Phil	Phil	Gray	3	1	Vicious line drive into left center field upper deck	445
5/7	NY	Det	Holloway	1	1	Line drive into bleacher exit in right field	370
5/8	NY	Det	Whitehill	5	2	High drive to 50th bleacher row in right field	460
5/10	NY	Det	Gibson	5	0	Line drive into bleacher exit in right field	375
5/13	NY	Clev	Shaute	1	1	To 60th row in right field bleachers	480
5/13	NY	Clev	Karr	8	0	Line drive deep into right field bleachers	435
5/14	NY	Clev	Levsen	1	1	Halfway (35 rows) into right field bleachers	445

5/15	NY	Chic	Thomas	8	1	Line drive into lower right field bleachers	330
5/19	NY	St.L	Zachary	3	2	To 58th bleacher row in right field bleachers	475
5/19	NY	St.L	Ballou	8	0	Line drive to 64th bleacher row in right field	515
5/20	NY	Bos	Gaston	5	1	Line drive just over right center field fence	365
5/25	Bos	Bos	Zahniser	7^1	0	To 45th bleacher row in deep right field	545
6/3	NY	Bos	Wiltse	1	1	Over exit in right field bleachers	415
6/3	NY	Bos	Wiltse	3	2	To 23rd bleacher row in right field bleachers	395
6/5	Clev	Clev	Buckeye	3	1	Far over right field wall; on roof across Lexington Ave.	425
6/8	Det	Det	Stoner	3	1	Far over right center field fence; hit taxi beyond Trumbull Ave.	520
6/8	Det	Det	Holloway	11	1	Line drive just over right field fence to win	385
6/14	St.L	St.L	Robertson	2	0	Line drive into right field pavilion	345
6/22	Wash	Wash	Palermo	3^2	1	Over wall near scoreboard in right center field	420
6/25	Bos	Bos	Russell	5^2	0	High drive to 6th row in right field bleachers	415
6/27	NY	Bos	Heimach	7	0	Line drive into left field bleachers	375
6/29	Phil	Phil	Gray	3	0	Into left field upper deck; plus 440-ft. center field fly out	365
7/9	NY	Clev	Smith	4	0	High into right field bleachers	390
7/20	NY	St.L	Ballou	3	0	To lower bleachers near right field foul line	310
7/21	NY	Chic	Blankenship	1^1	2	Halfway into right field bleachers	430
7/25	NY	Chic	Blankenship	6	1	Into right center field bleachers	395
7/27	St.L	St.L	Zachary	2	0	Onto bleacher pavilion roof in deep right center	440
7/30	St.L	St.L	Ballou	2	0	Far over right field pavilion roof into Grand Ave.	410
7/31	Chic	Chic	Edwards	8	0	Over center field fence at 450-ft. mark	470
8/5	Clev	Clev	Smith	1	1	Over right field wall; landed on roof across street	415
8/6	Clev	Clev	Levsen	5	0	Line drive over wall in deep right center field; landed across street	510

8/9	Det	Det	Johns	7	1	High into bleachers in deep right center field	455
8/11	Wash	Wash	Crowder	6^2	0	Far over high right field wall; plus 460-ft. center field triple	415
8/14	NY	Wash	Ruether	3^1	0	Line drive into right field bleachers	360
8/15	NY	Bos	Wingfield	3^1	0	Line drive halfway into right field bleachers	450
8/28	NY	Det	Stoner	8	0	Into right field bleachers near foul line	340
9/3	Phil	Phil	Grove	4^2	0	Towering drive over right field fence and across 20th St.	400
9/11	Det	Det	Stoner	9	2	Over fence just left of center field into Cherry St.	485
9/19	Clev	Clev	Levsen	7	1	Line drive to deep center; inside-the-park	430
9/21	Chic	Chic	Cox	9	1	High into right field bleachers	410
9/25	St.L	St.L	Vangilder	5^1	3	Onto right field pavilion roof	355
9/25	St.L	St.L	Ballou	6^2	1	Far over right field pavilion roof into Grand Ave.	435
9/25	St.L	St.L	Giard	9^2	0	Over right field pavilion roof into Grand Ave.	410

1926 UNOFFICIAL HOME RUN LOG

SPRING TRAINING HRs:

3/19 St. Peterburg, FL
(official ground rule double)
3/20 St. Petersburg, FL

SPRING TOUR HRs:

3/29 Birmingham, AL
4/3 Atlanta, GA
4/8 Charlottte, NC

EXHIBITION HRs:

6/4 Rochester, NY

BARNSTORMING HRs:

10/11 Bradley Beach, NJ (two)
(official ground rule doubles)
10/14 Scranton, PA (two)
10/15 Lima, OH (two)
10/17 Montreal, Canada (two)
10/21 Atlantic Highlands, NJ (two)
10/23 South Bend, IN
10/27 Des Moines, IA (three)
10/28 Iron Mountain, MI

1927 HOME RUN LOG—60

Date	City	Team	Pitcher	I	MOB	Description	Dst
4/15	NY	Phil	Ehmke	1	0	Halfway into right field bleachers	430
4/23	Phil	Phil	Walberg	1	0	Over right field fence; hit house across 20th St.	415
4/24	Wash	Wash	Thurston	6	0	Line drive over 40-ft. high right field wall and past alley	420
4/29	Bos	Bos	Harriss	5	0	Into distant right field bleachers	405
5/1	NY	Phil	Quinn	1	1	Line drive halfway into bleachers near right center field	465
5/1	NY	Phil	Walberg	8	0	Halfway into right field bleachers	430
5/10	St.L	St.L	Gaston	1	2	Into right field pavilion	340
5/11	St.L	St.L	Nevers	1	1	Towering drive into center field bleachers	465
5/17	Det	Det	Collins	8	0	Over scoreboard in deep left center field	415
5/22	Clev	Clev	Karr	6	1	Towering fly over high right field wall	320
5/23	Wash	Wash	Thurston	1	1	Into bleachers in dead center field	455
5/28	NY	Wash	Thurston	7^1	2	Line drive into bleachers in deep right center field	425
5/29	NY	Bos	MacFayden	8	0	Into farthest section of left field lower deck	410
5/30	Phil	Phil	Walberg	11^1	0	Into left center field upper deck	405
5/31	Phil	Phil	Quinn	1^1	1	High fly over right field fence into 20th St.	360
5/31	Phil	Phil	Ehmke	5^2	1	Far over right field fence; onto house roof across 20th St.	450
6/5	NY	Det	Whitehill	6	0	Line drive deep into right field bleachers	415
6/7	NY	Chic	Thomas	4	0	Into lower rows of right center field bleachers	400
6/11	NY	Clev	Buckeye	3	1	Into seats almost to scoreboard in deep right center field	490
6/11	NY	Clev	Buckeye	5	0	Near top of right field bleachers close to foul line	485
6/12	NY	Clev	Uhle	7	0	Halfway into right field bleachers	430
6/16	NY	St.L	Zachary	1	1	Halfway into right center field bleachers	465
6/22	Bos	Bos	Wiltse	5^1	0	Just left of center field; hit building across street	480
6/22	Bos	Bos	Wiltse	7^1	1	Far into alley; between bleachers in right center	515

6/30	NY	Bos	Harriss	4	1	High into right center field bleachers	425
7/3	Wash	Wash	Lisenbee	1	0	To 20th row in bleachers in dead center field	495
7/8	Det	Det	Hankins	2^2	2	Over fielder's head in deep center field; inside-the-park	440
7/9	Det	Det	Holloway	1^1	1	Into bleachers just right of center field	435
7/9	Det	Det	Holloway	4^1	2	Almost over bleachers in deep right center field	475
7/12	Clev	Clev	Shaute	9	1	Over right field wall; onto roof across Lexington Ave.	415
7/24	Chic	Chic	Thomas	3	0	Deep into right center field upper deck; plus 450-ft. center field triple	460
7/26	NY	St.L	Gaston	1^1	1	Over exit to 50th row in right field bleachers	470
7/26	NY	St.L	Gaston	6^1	0	High into right field bleachers	410
7/28	NY	St.L	Stewart	8	1	Deep into right center field bleachers near scoreboard	465
8/5	NY	Det	Smith	8	0	Liner just over right field fence; plus 480-ft. center field double	315
8/10	Wash	Wash	Zachary	3	2	Into bleachers just left of center	425
8/16	Chic	Chic	Thomas	5	0	Far over 75-ft. high right field double-deck grandstand roof	520
8/17	Chic	Chic	Connally	11	0	Into left field lower deck	375
8/20	Clev	Clev	Miller	1	1	Far over right field wall; over house across Lexington Ave.	480
8/22	Clev	Clev	Shaute	6	0	Line drive over high right field wall	350
8/27	St.L	St.L	Nevers	8	1	High drive far over right field pavilion roof into street	435
8/28	St.L	St.L	Wingard	1	1	Line drive onto right field pavilion roof	365
8/31	NY	Bos	Welzer	8	0	Almost to top of right field bleachers	495
9/2	Phil	Phil	Walberg	1	0	Line drive over wall just right of center field	440
9/6	Bos	Bos	Welzer	6^1	2	Over wall just left of center field; near flagpole	505
9/6	Bos	Bos	Welzer	7^1	1	High drive into lower seats in right field bleachers	400
9/6	Bos	Bos	Russell	9^2	0	Halfway into bleachers; just right of center field	475
9/7	Bos	Bos	MacFayden	1	0	Over left center field wall; near clock	380

9/7	Bos	Bos	Harriss	8	1	Into center field bleachers near flagpole	445
9/11	NY	St.L	Gaston	4	0	Line drive deep into right field bleachers	420
9/13	NY	Clev	Hudlin	7^1	1	Into right field bleachers	355
9/13	NY	Clev	Shaute	4^2	0	High into right field bleachers	380
9/16	NY	Chic	Blackenship	3	0	Line drive into right field bleachers	365
9/18	NY	Chic	Lyons	5^2	1	Line drive deep into right center field bleachers	425
9/21	NY	Det	Gibson	9	0	High into right center field bleachers	440
9/22	NY	Det	Holloway	9	1	To 60th row in right field bleachers	480
9/27	NY	Phil	Grove	6	3	Line drive deep into right center field bleachers	435
9/29	NY	Wash	Lisenbee	1	0	Line drive into lower right field bleachers	335
9/29	NY	Wash	Hopkins	5	3	Far into right field bleachers; plus 4 other long drives	430
9/30	NY	Wash	Zachary	8	1	Line drive halfway into right field bleachers near foul line	435

1927 UNOFFICIAL HOME RUN LOG

SPRING TRAINING HRs:
3/23 St. Petersburg, FL (two)

SPRING TOUR HRs:
4/7 Nashville, TN
4/9 Brooklyn, NY

EXHIBITION HRs:
5/6 Fort Wayne, IN
6/24 Springfield, MA (two)
8/12 Baltimore, MD
8/15 Indianapolis, IN

BARNSTORMING HRs:
10/11 Trenton, NJ (three)
10/13 Asbury Park, NJ
10/14 Lima, OH (two)
10/15 Kansas City, MO
10/18 Sioux City, IA
10/16 Omaha, NE (two)
10/19 Denver, CO (two)
10/23 San Francisco, CA
10/24 Marysville, CA (A.M.)
10/24 Stockton, CA (PM)
10/25 Sacramento, CA
10/26 San Jose, CA
10/27 Santa Barbara, CA
10/29 Fresno, CA

1928 HOME RUN LOG—54

Date	City	Team	Pitcher	I	MOB	Description	Dst
4/19	Bos	Bos	Wiltse	5^2	0	Halfway (25 rows) into bleachers in deep right	470
4/24	NY	Wash	Lisenbee	3	0	Deep into right center field bleachers	455
4/24	NY	Wash	Lisenbee	7	0	Into lower rows of right field bleachers	340
4/29	Wash	Wash	Lisenbee	5	2	Towering drive over high right field wall	375
5/1	Wash	Wash	Marberry	1	0	High into bleachers in dead center field past 441-ft. sign	505
5/4	NY	Chic	Cox	6	0	Deep into right center field bleachers; plus two long foul HRs	450
5/10	NY	Clev	Hudlin	6	2	Just under mezzanine in deep left field grandstand	465
5/12	NY	Det	Stoner	7	0	Line smash into right field bleachers; plus 435-ft. center field triple	360
5/14	NY	Det	Vangilder	7	0	Line drive into right field bleachers	350
5/15	NY	Det	Whitehill	5	0	Into right field bleachers	345
5/15	NY	Det	Smith	6	0	Into right field bleachers; plus 480-ft. center field triple	365
5/17	NY	St.L	Wiltse	5	0	To 50th bleacher row in right field bleachers	475
5/22	NY	Bos	Harriss	6	1	Into lower deck in left field grandstand	390
5/24	Phil	Phil	Orwoll	8^2	0	Over right field fence near foul line	380
5/25	Phil	Phil	Walberg	1^2	2	Over fence in right center field and hit porch across 20th St.	435
5/25	Phil	Phil	Rommel	7^2	0	Over fence just right of center field and across 20th St.	515
5/29	NY	Wash	Brown	4^2	0	Deep into right field bleachers	405
5/29	NY	Wash	Brown	7^2	0	Into lower deck in left field grandstand	380
5/31	NY	Wash	Hadley	3	0	Into right center field bleachers; plus 455-ft. left center field triple	390
6/7	Clev	Clev	Shaute	9	2	Over right field wall; landed on roof across Lexington Ave.	440
6/10	Chic	Chic	Faber	5	0	Line drive into right center field lower deck	415

6/10	Chic	Chic	Lyons	9	0	Into left center field upper deck	430
6/12	Chic	Chic	Adkins	5	1	Into left field upper deck	405
6/15	St.L	St.L	Crowder	3	1	Over right field pavilion; plus 455-ft. center field fly out	390
6/17	St.L	St.L	Ogden	7	0	Onto right field pavilion roof	370
6/23	NY	Bos	Settlemire 5[1]		0	Into right field bleachers	355
6/23	NY	Bos	MacFayden 4[2]		0	Into right field bleachers	345
6/24	NY	Bos	Russell	3	0	High into right field bleachers	430
6/28	Phil	Phil	Walberg	1	1	Line drive over scoreboard in right center field	395
6/28	Phil	Phil	Earnshaw	8	0	Over scoreboard in right center field; hit house across 20th St.	460
7/2	Wash	Wash	Braxton	6	0	Line drive over high right field wall	400
7/8	NY	St.L	Blaeholder 9[2]		1	Into bleachers below scoreboard in deepest right center field	465
7/11	NY	Det	Gibson	7	0	High into right field bleachers	410
7/15	NY	Clev	Grant	1[2]	1	Liner into right center field bleachers; plus 450-ft. left center field sac fly	405
7/16	NY	Clev	Bayne	3[1]	1	Line drive to 30th bleacher row near right field foul line	420
7/18	NY	Chic	Lyons	9	2	Line drive high into right field bleachers to win	400
7/19	NY	Chic	Thomas	1	1	Deep into right field bleachers	385
7/19	NY	Chic	Thomas	7	1	Into right center field bleachers	380
7/21	NY	Chic	Walsh	7	0	High into right field bleachers	390
7/23	Bos	Bos	MacFayden 6		0	Over wall just left of dead center field; landed on garage	515
7/30	Clev	Clev	Miller	6	1	Over high wall in right center field	375
8/1	St.L	St.L	Crowder	1	0	Onto right field pavilion roof	365
8/4	Chic	Chic	Adkins	5	1	Line drive off façade on right field upper deck	435
8/14	NY	Chic	Adkins	1	0	High into right field bleachers	410
8/15	NY	Chic	Faber	4	0	Almost to top of right field bleachers	505
8/25	NY	Det	Smith	4[2]	2	High into right field bleachers; plus 440-ft. right center field triple	405
8/30	Wash	Wash	Jones	7	0	Over high right field wall	395
9/8	NY	Wash	Braxton	7	2	Deep into right field bleachers	415
9/11	NY	Phil	Grove	8	1	To 40th bleacher row in right field to win	450
9/15	St.L	St.L	Crowder	1	1	Onto right field pavilion roof	385

9/27	Det	Det	Carroll	1^1	0	Over right field fence into Trumbull Ave.	395
9/27	Det	Det	Sorrell	1^2	0	Over right field fence; hit taxi building across Trumbull Ave.	485
9/28	Det	Det	Page	8	1	Far over bleachers in deep right center field and into Trumbull Ave.	505
9/30	Det	Det	Sorrell	5	1	Into right center field bleachers	400

1928 UNOFFICIAL HOME RUN LOG

SPRING TOUR HRs:
4/3 Chattanooga, TN
4/4 Nashville, TN
4/6 Charlotte, NC (two)
4/8 New York, NY

EXHIBITION HRs:
4/15 Baltimore, MD
5/27 York, PA
6/25 Johnstown, PA (two)
6/26 Harrisburg, PA
8/9 Everett, MA
8/28 Hartford, CT (two)
8/29 Providence, RI
9/13 Toledo, OH

RAIN OUT HR:
6/21 New York, NY

BARNSTORMING HRs:
10/17 Elmira, NY
10/20 Reading, PA
10/22 Watertown, NY (three)
10/24 Louisville, KY (two)
10/25 Dayton, OH
10/28 Milwaukee, WI
10/29 Des Moines, IA
10/30 Sioux City, IA

1929 HOME RUN LOG—46

Date Description	City	Team Dst	Pitcher	I	MOB		
4/18	NY	Bos	Ruffing	1	0	Line drive over 402-ft. sign into left field grandstand	420
4/28	Wash	Wash	Burke	7	0	Over 32-ft. wall in deep right center field	490
5/4	Chic	Chic	McKain	7	1	Into right field upper deck	425
5/5	Chic	Chic	Adkins	1	1	Into right center field lower deck	415
5/7	St.L	St.L	Crowder	4	2	Into right field pavilion	355
5/10	Det	Det	Sorrell	5	2	Over right field fence into Trumbull Ave.	405
5/19	NY	Bos	Russell	3	0	Line drive into right field bleachers	340

5/23	Bos	Bos	Gaston	5	0	Over high wall in left center field	385
5/26	Bos	Bos	Carroll	8	1	At Braves Field; deep into left field bleachers	375
6/1	NY	Chic	Adkins	8	1	To 25th bleacher row past 429-ft. sign in deep right center field	505
6/21	NY	Phil	Shores	7^2	2	Line drive into right field bleachers	370
6/21	NY	Phil	Shores	8^2	2	Deep into right center field bleachers	410
6/26	Wash	Wash	Marberry	5^1	1	Into bleachers in dead center field	460
6/29	Phil	Phil	Grove	5	1	Over fence just right of center field	450
6/29	Phil	Phil	Grove	7	0	High over right field fence near foul line	375
6/30	Bos	Bos	MacFayden	5	1	Braves Field; to top of bleachers in dead center field	475
7/3	NY	Bos	Ruffing	7	3	Line drive halfway up right field bleachers	440
7/9	St.L	St.L	Stewart	4	0	Over right field pavilion; plus 450-ft. 3B to center field flagpole	420
7/13	Chic	Chic	McKain	5^2	1	Towering drive into left field grandstand	390
7/15	Det	Det	Carroll	9	0	Against center field fence near flagpole; inside-the-park park	455
7/16	Det	Det	Sorrell	3	0	Line drive over left field fence into yard 400 across Cherry St.	
7/17	Det	Det	Whitehill	3	0	Into right center field bleachers	390
7/27	NY	St.L	Blaeholder	8	0	Line drive into right field bleachers	360
7/28	NY	St.L	Collins	12	0	To upper rows in right field bleachers to win	465
8/1	NY	Chic	Lyons	6	0	Deep into right field bleachers	385
8/6	NY	Wash	Burke	5^2	3	Halfway into right field bleachers	435
8/6	NY	Wash	Burke	7^2	1	Towering drive into right field bleachers	365
8/7	Phil	Phil	Ehmke	2^1	3	Line drive over scoreboard in right center field and across 20th St.	440
8/10	Clev	Clev	Shoffner	8	0	Far over right field wall & over house across wide street	470
8/11	Clev	Clev	Hudlin	2	0	Over high right field wall near foul line; Career HR 500	350
8/12	Clev	Clev	Shaute	3	1	Over the high right center field wall and screen	395
8/16	Det	Det	Uhle	1	1	Line drive high over left field fence	390
8/17	Det	Det	Sorrell	3	1	Far over left field fence and hit car in parking lot	415

8/25	St.L	St.L	Stewart	4	0	Far over right field pavilion; almost across street	455
8/25	St.L	St.L	Stewart	9	0	Onto pavilion roof just right of center field	475
8/28	NY	Phil	Walberg	1	0	Halfway into right center field bleachers	480
8/29	NY	Wash	Marberry	8^1	2	Line drive deep into right field bleachers	410
8/31	NY	Wash	Burke	1^2	2	Into bleachers in deep right center field	430
8/31	NY	Wash	Savidge	8^2	1	High into right center field bleachers right of scoreboard	480
9/1	Bos	Bos	Bayne	1	0	Braves Field; to top of bleachers in center field	470
9/7	NY	Det	Carroll	5^2	2	Line drive deep into right field bleachers	420
9/8	NY	Det	Sorrell	4	2	High into right field bleachers	415
9/10	NY	Det	Whitehill	4^1	0	Into right field bleachers	335
9/10	NY	Det	Carroll	9^2	2	To 9th bleacher row in right field	350
9/18	NY	Clev	Miller	1^1	1	Deep into right field bleachers	390
9/18	NY	Clev	Shoffner	8^2	1	Into upper rows in right field bleachers	465

1929 UNOFFICIAL HOME RUN LOG

SPRING TOUR HRs:
4/5 Dallas, TX
4/13 Brooklyn, NY (two)

EXHIBITION HRs:
5/16 Binghamton, NY
5/27 Hartford, CT (two)
5/31 Chambersburg, PA
8/9 Albany, NY
8/26 Columbus, OH (two)
9/5 Sing Sing Prison, NY (three)

BARNSTORMING HR:
10/27 South Orange, NJ

1930 HOME RUN LOG—49

Date	City	Team	Pitcher	I	MOB	Description	Dst
4/25	NY	Bos	Gaston	7	0	Deep into right center field bleachers; plus 465-ft. center field sac fly	420
4/27	NY	Bos	Russell	9	2	Line drive into right field bleachers	360
5/4	NY	Chic	Walsh	8	1	To 45th bleacher row in right field	465
5/7	NY	Clev	Miller	4	2	Very high fly into lower right field bleachers	315
5/11	NY	Det	Sorrell	1	0	High drive into right field bleachers	350
5/18	Bos	Bos	Morriss	1	0	Braves Field; liner to top of right field bleachers ("jury box")	490
5/21	Phil	Phil	Earnshaw	1^1	1	Over right field fence into 20th St.	365
5/21	Phil	Phil	Earnshaw	3^1	2	Far over right field fence & over house across 20th St.	505
5/21	Phil	Phil	Grove	8^1	1	Far over right field fence & onto roof across 20th St.	470
5/22	Phil	Phil	Ehmke	3^1	1	Far to right field; cleared 2 rows of houses to Opal St.	540
5/22	Phil	Phil	Rommel	4^1	1	Far over right field fence & onto roof across 20th St.	465
5/22	Phil	Phil	Quinn	2^2	1	Over right field fence into 20th St.	360
5/24	NY	Phil	Quinn	5^1	0	Deep into right field bleachers	405
5/24	NY	Phil	Walberg	4^2	1	To top bleacher row in deep right center field; into water barrel	535
5/30	NY	Bos	Lisenbee	1^1	0	Into right field bleachers	355
6/1	NY	Bos	Gaston	9	0	Into right field bleachers	370
6/3	Chic	Chic	Lyons	4	3	Into right center field lower deck	410
6/4	Chic	Chic	Caraway	7	2	Into right field lower deck	390
6/7	St.L	St.L	Stewart	1	2	Into pavilion in deep right center field	435
6/12	Det	Det	Sullivan	4	1	Just over right field fence	385
6/15	Clev	Clev	Bean	6	0	Into wooden bleachers just left of dead center	480
6/19	NY	Det	Uhle	7	1	Into right field bleachers	370
6/21	NY	Det	Hogsett	8	0	Line drive into right field bleachers	365
6/23	NY	St.L	Kimsey	2^1	0	Deep into right field bleachers	400
6/25	NY	St.L	Blaeholder	3^2	1	High into right field bleachers	415
6/25	NY	St.L	Holshauser	5^2	0	High into right field bleachers	420
6/27	NY	Clev	Miller	3	0	Into right field bleachers	340
6/28	NY	Clev	Holloway	4^2	0	Into right field bleachers	360
6/28	NY	Clev	Gliatto	7^2	0	Into right field bleachers	355

6/30	NY	Chic	Thomas	7	2	Far above 429-ft. sign into bleachers in deep right center field	495
7/2	NY	Chic	Henry	5^1	1	Into right field bleachers	375
7/4	Wash	Wash	Marberry	1^2	1	Over high right field wall	380
7/18	St.L	St.L	Gray	5	0	Onto pavilion roof just right of center field	490
7/20	Clev	Clev	Shoffner	4	0	Far over right field wall and onto house across street	440
7/21	Clev	Clev	Miller	3	1	Far over right center field wall and onto house across street	460
7/24	Det	Det	Cantrell	8	0	To top of bleachers in deep right center field	445
8/1	Bos	Bos	Lisenbee	1	0	Line drive to 13th row in center field bleachers	470
8/1	Bos	Bos	Gaston	9	1	Line drive over high right field wall	375
8/2	NY	Wash	Marberry	5^2	0	Into right field bleachers	350
8/3	NY	Phil	Walberg	4	0	Line drive high into right field bleachers	430
8/5	NY	Wash	Hadley	6^1	0	To 7th bleacher row just right of center field	470
8/10	NY	St.L	Coffman	4	1	Deep into right center field bleachers	425
8/12	NY	Det	Hoyt	3	0	High fly to 2nd bleacher row in right field	315
8/17	NY	Chic	Henry	7	0	Deep into right field bleachers	390
9/5	NY	Wash	Crowder	9	1	Into bleachers past 429-ft. sign in deep right center field	460
9/12	Det	Det	Wyatt	3	0	Over right center field bleachers	440
9/20	Chic	Chic	Thomas	7	0	Into left field lower deck	380
9/27	Phil	Phil	Earnshaw	3	0	Liner over scoreboard in right center field; hit porch across street	450
9/27	Phil	Phil	Earnshaw	4	3	Into upper deck in left center field	445

1930 UNOFFICIAL HOME RUN LOG

SPRING TRAINING HRs:
3/10 St. Petersburg, FL
3/22 St. Petersburg, FL

SPRING TOUR HRs:
3/29 Houston, TX
3/31 San Antonio, TX
4/3 Wichita Falls, TX (two)

EXHIBITION HRs:
6/2 Cincinnati, OH
6/18 Albany, NY (two)
7/11 Toronto, Canada (two)
9/8 Rochester, NY
9/22 Buffalo, NY (two)

NO BARNSTORMING HRs

1931 HOME RUN LOG—46

Date	City	Team	Pitcher	I	MOB	Description	Dst
4/14	NY	Bos	Durham	7	0	High into right field bleachers	410
4/20	NY	Phil	Earnshaw	4	1	Almost to top of right field bleachers	505
4/20	NY	Phil	Earnshaw	8	1	Deep into bleachers near right field foul line	415
5/6	NY	Wash	Fischer	5	1	High into right field bleachers	390
5/21	Clev	Clev	Hudlin	1	0	Far over high right field wall; plus 435-ft. center field triple	380
5/24	NY	Phil	Walberg	6	0	High into right field bleachers	385
5/26	Phil	Phil	McDonald	6	0	Over right field fence into 20th St.	370
5/28	Phil	Phil	Walberg	6	0	Over right field fence into 20th St.	375
5/31	Wash	Wash	Brown	7	1	High into left center field bleachers	425
6/5	NY	St.L	Gray	9	1	High into right field bleachers to win 8–7	405
6/6	NY	Clev	Miller	3	0	Into right field bleachers	350
6/19	St.L	St.L	Stiles	5	1	Into pavilion just right of center field	450
6/21	St.L	St.L	Stewart	3^1	2	Line drive into right center field pavilion	380
6/23	Chic	Chic	McKain	5^1	1	Deep into right field lower deck	400
6/24	Chic	Chic	Braxton	3	0	Over scoreboard into right center field lower deck	415
6/25	Chic	Chic	Thomas	1^1	0	Into right field lower deck	390
6/28	Clev	Clev	Hudlin	8	2	Over right field wall; onto roof across Lexington Ave.	455
6/29	Clev	Clev	Shoffner	6^1	1	Over high right field wall	360
7/2	Det	Det	Hoyt	8	1	Over left field fence and into tree across 415 Cherry St.	
7/4	NY	Wash	Fischer	1^2	1	Line drive deep into right field bleachers	395
7/8	NY	Bos	Russell	1	1	Into right field bleachers; plus 470-ft. center field fly out	330
7/16	NY	Clev	Brown	7	1	Deep into right field bleachers	385
7/17	NY	Clev	Ferrell	4	0	Into right field bleachers	355
7/22	NY	Det	Bridges	1^2	1	High into right field bleachers	400
7/22	NY	Det	Sullivan	6^2	0	Into right field bleachers	360
7/23	NY	Det	Whitehill	3	2	Into right field bleachers	345
7/27	NY	Chic	Frazier	6^1	2	Into right field bleachers	370
7/29	NY	Chic	Faber	3	1	High drive deep into right field bleachers	405
8/5	Bos	Bos	Lisenbee	3^2	1	To 7th row in center field bleachers	460

8/6	NY	Phil	Walberg	5	0	Towering drive into right field bleachers	390
8/14	Clev	Clev	Harder	9^1	0	Over high right field wall	365
8/15	Det	Det	Uhle	16	0	Far over right field fence; Ruth predicted this homer	410
8/16	Det	Det	Herring	5	1	Line drive into right center field bleachers	395
8/20	St.L	St.L	Hebert	9	3	Far over right field pavilion into street to win 7–3	430
8/21	St.L	St.L	Blaeholder	3	1	Far over right center field pavilion into street; Career HR 600	440
8/23	Chic	Chic	Moore	2^1	1	Liner to right field upper deck; plus 450-ft. center field double	420
8/24	Chic	Chic	Thomas	1	0	Line drive almost to grandstand roof in right center field	490
9/2	NY	Bos	Lisenbee	1	0	High into right center field bleachers	435
9/7	Phil	Phil	Hoyt	6^2	0	Over right field fence and landed on porch across 20th St.	410
9/7	Phil	Phil	Hoyt	9^2	1	Far over right field fence and over house across 20th St.	475
9/17	NY	St.L	Gray	3^2	0	Into right field bleachers	350
9/17	NY	St.L	Gray	5^2	0	Into right field bleachers	375
9/18	NY	St.L	Stewart	3	0	Deep into right field bleachers	385
9/20	NY	Clev	Connally	2^2	2	High into right field bleachers	390
9/25	NY	Wash	Crowder	6	0	Deep into right center field bleachers	435
9/25	NY	Wash	Crowder	8	0	Line drive into right field bleachers	370

1931 UNOFFICIAL HOME RUN LOG

SPRING TRAINING HR:
3/20 St. Petersberg, FL

SPRING TOUR HRs:
4/5 Nashville, TN
4/8 Asheville NC
4/9 Asheville, NC
4/10 Charlotte, NC
4/11 Brooklyn, NY

EXHIBITION HRs:
7/30 Albany, NY (two)
8/4 Springfield, MA (two)
8/10 Cincinnati, OH
9/3 Cumberland, MD
9/9 New York, NY (charity game)

BARNSTORMING HRs:
10/18 Los Angeles, CA
10/19 San Diego, CA (night)
10/20 Los Angeles, CA (night)
10/21 Fresno, CA
10/23 Oakland, CA (two) (night)
10/26 Oakland, CA
10/31 Long Beach. CA (two)
10/31 Los Angeles, CA (night)

1932 HOME RUN LOG—41

Date	City	Team	Pitcher	I	MOB	Description	Dst
4/12	Phil	Phil	Earnshaw	1	2	Over right center field fence and onto house across 20th St.	480
4/12	Phil	Phil	Earnshaw	4	1	Over right field fence and over house across 20th St.	480
4/16	Bos	Bos	Weiland	7	0	Into right center field bleachers	420
4/20	NY	Phil	Grove	3	1	Just over right field fence into lower bleachers	320
4/23	NY	Phil	Walberg	1	1	High into right center field bleachers; plus 455 ft left center field triple	425
4/30	NY	Bos	Lisenbee	8	1	To 45th bleacher row in right field	460
5/18	NY	Clev	Brown	10	0	Deep into right center field bleachers to win 3–2	430
5/19	NY	Wash	Fischer	1^2	1	Into right center field bleachers	380
5/21	NY	Wash	Brown	5^1	3	Line drive into right field bleachers	365
5/21	NY	Wash	Ragland	6^1	1	Into right field bleachers	355
5/24	NY	Phil	Walberg	1	0	High drive into right field bleachers	370
5/28	Wash	Wash	Brown	6^1	0	Over scoreboard in right center field	435
5/28	Wash	Wash	Weaver	6^2	0	Over high right field wall	390
5/29	Wash	Wash	Ragland	7	0	Over high right field wall	405
6/3	Phil	Phil	Earnshaw	5	0	Over fence just right of dead center field	475
6/5	NY	Bos	Weiland	1	0	Line drive into right field bleachers	365
6/8	Det	Det	Whitehill	1	1	Into right center field bleachers	395
6/11	Clev	Clev	Ferrell	1	1	Over high right field wall	400
6/12	Clev	Clev	Harder	4	1	Over high right field wall	380
6/12	Clev	Clev	Pearson	9	1	Far over right field wall and onto house across street	450
6/13	Clev	Clev	Russell	5	1	Over high right field wall	350
6/23	St.L	St.L	Hebert	7	0	Over pavilion roof in right center field into street	415
7/4	Wash	Wash	Brown	4^2	1	Deep into left field bleachers	420
7/9	NY	Det	Whitehill	6^1	0	Into right field bleachers	345
7/13	NY	St.L	Hebert	1	1	Deep into right field bleachers	410
7/14	NY	Clev	Brown	1	0	Into right field bleachers	365
7/28	Clev	Clev	Ferrell	6	1	Over high wall in deep right center field	420

7/28	Clev	Clev	Connally	7	2	Far over right field wall; landed	470
						on factory across street	
7/29	Clev	Clev	Brown	9	0	Far over right field wall and	440
						onto house across street	
7/31	Det	Det	Uhle	6	2	Over right field fence into	400
						Trumbull Ave.	
8/7	St.L	St.L	Stewart	3^1	0	Onto right field pavilion roof	360
8/9	St.L	St.L	Cooney	6	2	Over right field pavilion roof	405
						into Grand Ave.	
8/14	Wash	Wash	Weaver	4	0	Over high wall in right center field	420
8/17	NY	Det	Sorrell	5	0	Into right field bleachers	355
8/19	NY	Det	Bridges	3^2	1	Into right field bleachers	380
8/25	NY	Clev	Hildebrand	6	1	Line drive into right field bleachers	375
8/26	NY	Clev	Ferrell	4	0	Deep into right field bleachers	410
8/28	NY	Chic	Lyons	9^1	0	Into right field bleachers	370
8/28	NY	Chic	Gaston	5^2	2	Into right field bleachers	360
9/5	NY	Phil	Rommel	4^1	0	Into bleachers under scoreboard	485
						just right of center	
9/24	Bos	Bos	Michaels	9	0	To 25th bleacher row in right	480
						center field	

1932 UNOFFICIAL HOME RUN LOG

SPRING TRAINING HRs:
3/24 St. Petersburg, FL
3/26 St. Petersburg, FL (two)

SPRING TOUR HRs:
4/2 Memphis, TN
4/4 Louisville, KY

EXHIBITION HRs:
9/6 Binghamton, NY

NO BARNSTORMING HRs

1933 HOME RUN LOG—34

Date	City	Team	Pitcher	I	MOB	Description	Dst
4/15	NY	Phil	Cain	1	1	Deep into right field bleachers	405
4/21	Bos	Bos	Welch	5	0	Over left field wall and scoreboard	380
4/27	Phil	Phil	Cain	5	1	Over right field fence into 20th St.	370
4/28	NY	Wash	Stewart	6	1	Deep into right field bleachers	390
4/30	NY	Bos	Weiland	1^2	1	Into right field bleachers	355
5/23	NY	Clev	Hildebrand	1	0	Into right center field bleachers	385
5/28	NY	Chic	Jones	1^1	0	Into right center field bleachers	400
5/28	NY	Chic	Gaston	1^2	1	Over 429-ft. sign into bleachers in deep right center field	455
5/28	NY	Chic	Faber	7^2	0	Into right field bleachers	365
6/3	NY	Phil	Freitas	8	2	Into right field bleachers	395
6/6	NY	Bos	Weiland	7^2	1	High into right field bleachers	415
6/8	Phil	Phil	Coombs	9	0	Far over right field fence and over house across 20th St.	485
6/10	Phil	Phil	Grove	1^1	0	Far over right field fence and onto house across 20th St.	450
6/10	Phil	Phil	Grove	3^1	1	Over right field fence into 20th St.	375
6/20	Chic	Chic	Jones	6	1	Into right field upper deck	415
6/23	St.L	St.L	Coffman	4^1	1	Over right field pavilion roof into Grand Ave.	390
6/28	Det	Det	Frazier	8	2	Over 455-ft. sign in straightaway center field	475
7/4	NY	Wash	Stewart	9^2	0	High into right field bleachers	400
7/7	NY	Det	Frazier	1	1	Deep into right center field bleachers	420
7/9	NY	Det	Rowe	3^1	1	Line drive into right center field bleachers near scoreboard	475
7/9	NY	Det	Rowe	5^1	1	Into right field bleachers	335
7/9	NY	Det	Bridges	6^2	1	Into right field bleachers	370
7/15	NY	Chic	Gaston	5	1	Deep into right center field bleachers near scoreboard	470
7/15	NY	Chic	Wyatt	7	0	Into right field bleachers; plus 435-ft. right center field and 455-ft. left center field fly outs	405
7/29	Wash	Wash	Crowder	8	2	Line smash over high right field wall	410
8/7	NY	Wash	Stewart	8^2	0	Into right field bleachers	360

8/17	St.L	St.L	Blaeholder	3	0	Over right field pavilion roof into Grand Ave.	405
8/19	Chic	Chic	Kimsey	3	0	Into lower deck in right center field	410
9/17	NY	Clev	Pearson	6^1	0	Into right field bleachers	350
9/17	NY	Clev	Harder	5^2	1	Into right field bleachers	390
9/23	Bos	Bos	Welch	4	1	To 25th bleacher row in dead center field	510
9/28	NY	Wash	Stewart	4	0	Almost to top of right field bleachers	495
9/30	NY	Wash	Thomas	7	0	Into right field bleachers	365
10/1	NY	Bos	Kline	5	0	Deep into right field bleachers; also pitched 9-inning complete game win	400

1933 UNOFFICIAL HOME RUN LOG

SPRING TRAINING HR:
3/24 St. Petersburg, FL

BARNSTORMING HRs:
10/22 Honolulu, HI
10/29 Hilo, HI (two)

EXHIBITION HR:
5/12 Indianapolis, IN

1934 HOME RUN LOG—22

Date	City	Team	Pitcher	I	MOB	Description	Dst
4/18	Phil	Phil	McKeithan	8	0	Far over right field fence and through window across street	415
4/21	Bos	Bos	Weiland	1	1	Over high left field wall and scoreboard	380
4/29	NY	Bos	Weiland	8	0	High into right center field bleachers	420
5/4	NY	Det	Bridges	1	0	Line drive halfway up right field bleachers	450
5/5	NY	Det	Auker	4	2	To 50th bleacher row in right field bleachers	475
5/5	NY	Det	Rowe	7	0	Line drive into right center field bleachers	410
5/9	NY	St.L	Weaver	4	2	Into right center field bleachers	375
5/28	St.L	St.L	Knott	7	1	Inter right center field pavilion	370
6/3	Phil	Phil	Cain	8	0	Far over right field fence and onto roof across street	460

6/14	NY	St.L	Andrews	1	2	To 35th bleacher row in right field (above exit)	455
6/24	NY	Chic	Jones	2	3	Deep into right field bleachers	390
6/27	NY	Chic	Gaston	2	1	Line drive into right field bleachers	350
7/8	NY	Wash	Weaver	5	1	High into right field bleachers; plus 430-ft. center field double	400
7/13	Det	Det	Bridges	3	1	Far over right field fence; cleared Trumbull Ave.; Career HR 700	505
7/14	Det	Det	Auker	4	2	To top of right center field bleachers	435
7/22	Chic	Chic	Lyons	2^1	2	Into right field upper deck	405
7/31	NY	Bos	Ostermu'ler	7^2	0	Into right field bleachers	335
8/4	NY	Phil	Dietrich	5	2	Liner into right field bleachers; plus 470-ft. center field double	360
8/11	Bos	Bos	Ostermu'ler	8	0	Far into grandstand near runway in deep right field	440
9/1	NY	Wash	Stewart	1	0	Into right field bleachers	370
9/3	NY	Phil	Dietrich	1^1	0	High into right field bleachers	390
9/29	Wash	Wash	Cohen	7^1	2	Over high fight field wall	410

1934 UNOFFICIAL HOME RUN LOG

SPRING TRAINING HRs:
3/17 St. Petersburg, FL
3/22 Clearwater, FL (two)
3/24 Clearwater, FL (two)
3/25 St. Petersburg, FL

EXHIBITION HRs:
4/23 Albany, NY (two)
7/27 Wheeling, WV

RAIN OUT HR:
6/12 New York, NY

ORIENTAL TOUR HRs:
11/9 Sendai, Japan (two)
11/10 Tokyo, Japan
11/11 Tokyo, Japan (two)
11/13 Toyama, Japan
11/17 Tokyo, Japan (two)
11/18 Yokohama, Japan (two)
11/26 Kokura, Japan
11/29 Omiya, Japan (two)
12/9 Manila, Philippines

1935 Home Run Log—6
Home Field: Boston's Braves Field

Date	City	Team	Pitcher	I	MOB	Description	Dst
4/16	Bos	NY	Hubbell	5	1	Into runway between right field grandstand and bleachers	430
4/21	Bos	Brkln	Benge	1	0	Line drive to 6th bleacher row in left center	395
5/21	Chic	Chic	Carleton	6	0	Far over right field wall and landed in yard across street	440
5/25	Pitt	Pitt	Lucas	1	1	High fly into right field lower deck	385
5/25	Pitt	Pitt	Bush	3	1	Line drive high into upper deck in right center	500
5/25	Pitt	Pitt	Bush	5	0	Far over right field roof; hit house across Boquet St.	540

Unofficial Home Run Log

SPRING TOUR HRs:
4/4 Savanah, GA

4/7 Newark, NJ (two)

BARNSTORMING HR:
10/13 Long Island, NY

7/26/38 Albany, NY—Hit HR in exhibition game as Brooklyn Dodgers coach

World Series Home Run Log—15

Date	City	Team	Pitcher	I	MOB	Description	Dst
10/9/21	NY	NY	Douglas	9	0	Out of stadium in right center field between roof and bleachers	475
10/11/23	NY	NY	McQuiln	4	0	Far over right field grandstand roof	465
10/11/23	NY	NY	Bentley	5	0	Line drive into right field lower deck; plus 440-ft. fly out	305
10/15/23	NY	NY	Nehf	1	0	Line drive into right field upper deck	385
10/6/26	St.L	St.L	Rhem	1	0	High fly over right field pavilion near foul line	395
10/6/26	St.L	St.L	Rhem	3	0	Far over right center field pavilion; through window across Grand Ave.	515
10/6/26	St.L	St.L	Bell	6	1	Halfway up bleachers in dead center field	530

10/10/26	NY	St.L	Haines	3	0	Into right center field bleachers	390
10/7/27	NY	Pitt	Cvengrs	7	2	Line drive to 20th bleacher row in right field	385
10/8/27	NY	Pitt	Hill	5	1	Deep into right center field bleachers	405
10/9/28	St.L	St.L	Sherdel	4	0	Line drive over right field pavilion	410
10/9/28	St.L	St.L	Sherdel	7	0	Far over right field pavilion	425
10/9/28	St.L	St.L	Alexndr	8	0	Line drive onto right field pavilion roof	370
10/1/32	Chic	Chic	Root	1	2	Over right field wall; high into temporary seats	430
10/1/32	Chic	Chic	Root	5	0	Over center field fence to flagpole; "called shot HR"	490

ALL-STAR HOME RUN LOG—1

Date	City	Team	Pitcher	I	MOB	Description	Dst
7/6/33	Chic	NL	Hallahan	4	1	Line drive into right field lower deck	400

11

Babe Ruth's Home Run Spray Charts

THE FOLLOWING PAGES ARE composed of coded spray charts. They show the approximate landing points of every official home run hit by Babe Ruth, plus, the landing points of extra-base hits, fly outs, and foul homers that would result in home runs under modern conditions. Specifically, there are two charts for each year of Ruth's career: one for home games and one for away games. There are a few exceptions. Since Babe started as a pitcher, he had relatively few at-bats in his first few seasons. Accordingly, all his batted balls from 1914 through 1918 have been combined onto single charts for home and away games. They are followed by individual yearly charts for each season beginning in 1919, when Ruth became a full-time outfielder. The only other exception is for 1935, when Babe retired effective on Memorial Day. As a result, all of Ruth's drives for that abbreviated season are found on a single chart.

The first home field chart is, of course, for Fenway Park, where Babe Ruth began playing as a member of the Boston Red Sox. The solid line represents the dimensions of the outfield walls at Fenway as they existed in Ruth's era. There were no significant changes until 1934, when Babe's career was almost over. The dotted line depicts the dimensions of an average ballpark in modern times. Those "average" distances are 330 feet for foul lines, 375 feet for power alleys, and 405 feet to the center field fences. That standard dotted-line representation is found on every chart, both home and away. It would be impractical to display a chart for every "away park" for each year. So, all long drives in each of the seven parks visited by Ruth each season are consolidated into a single chart.

Every official home run has its landing point marked by a white plot point. There are also black plot points for balls that would fly over today's fences, but were doubles, triples, and outs for The Babe. Additionally, there are x-ed plot points for balls that landed just foul after passing over the fences in fair territory. Since the rule changed on this issue after the 1930 season, there are no x-ed points on the charts from 1931 through 1935.

The second home stadium chart is for the Polo Grounds, where Ruth played as a New York Yankee from 1920 until 1922. It has traditionally been reported that the length from home plate to the center field fence was 433 feet in those days. However, we now know that those figures are inaccurate. It was 433 feet to the angle in deep right center field, but it was 475 feet to the most distant point just right of center. It was about 460 feet to straightaway center field. Those dimensions were changed in 1923, but it was in that year that Babe Ruth began playing his home games in Yankee Stadium.

The charts for "The House That Ruth Built" represent a composite of the distances for Babe's time there from 1923 through 1934. There were minor changes in 1924 and 1928, but the single standardized outline is very close to the way Yankee Stadium was configured during the entire Ruthian era.

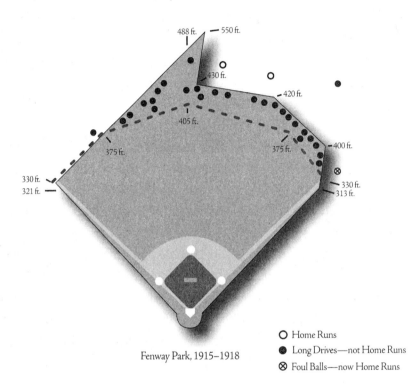

Fenway Park, 1915–1918

○ Home Runs
● Long Drives—not Home Runs
⊗ Foul Balls—now Home Runs

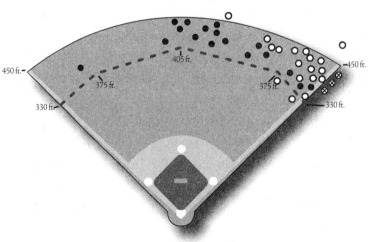

Away Games, 1915–1918

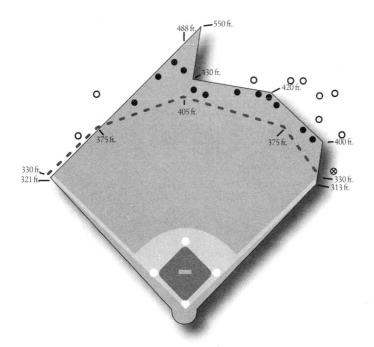

Fenway Park, 1919

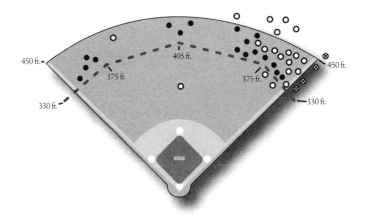

Away Games, 1919

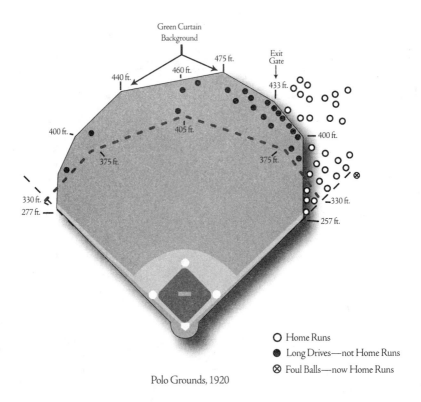

Polo Grounds, 1920

○ Home Runs
● Long Drives—not Home Runs
⊗ Foul Balls—now Home Runs

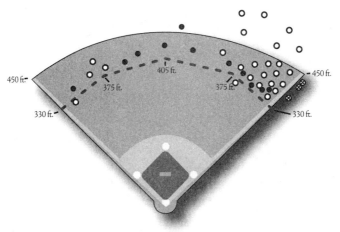

Away Games, 1920

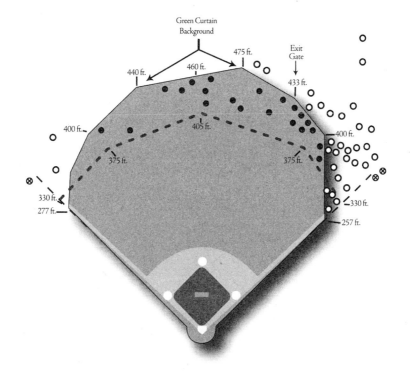

Polo Grounds, 1921

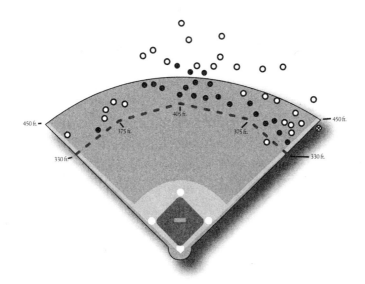

Away Games, 1921

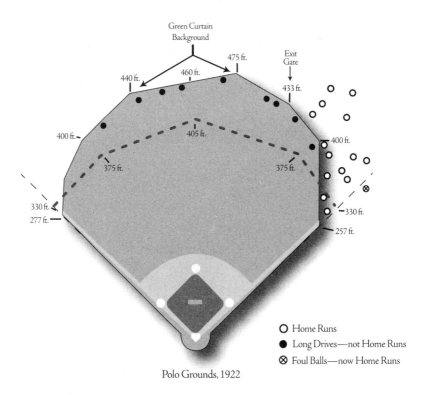

Polo Grounds, 1922

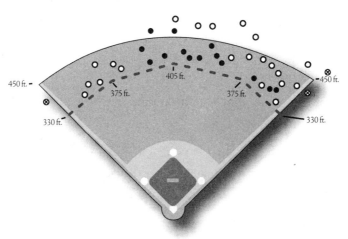

Away Games, 1922

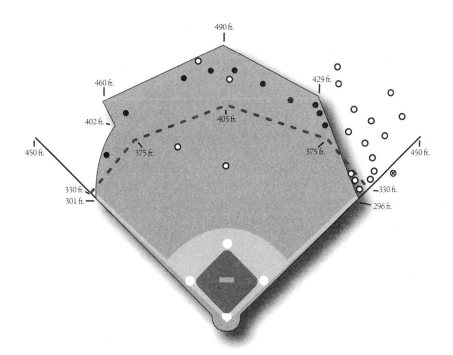

Yankee Stadium, 1923

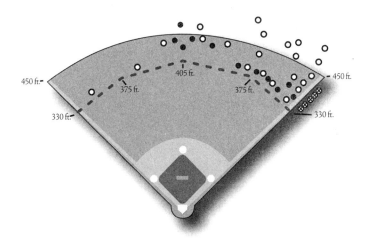

Away Games, 1923

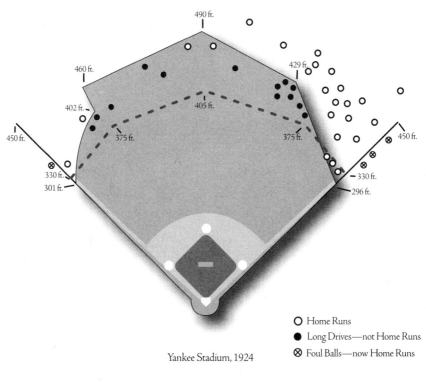

490 ft.

460 ft.

429 ft.

402 ft.

405 ft.

450 ft.

375 ft.

375 ft.

450 ft.

330 ft.

330 ft.

301 ft.

296 ft.

O Home Runs

● Long Drives—not Home Runs

⊗ Foul Balls—now Home Runs

Yankee Stadium, 1924

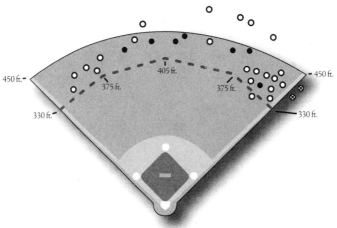

450 ft.

405 ft.

450 ft.

375 ft.

375 ft.

330 ft.

330 ft.

Away Games, 1924

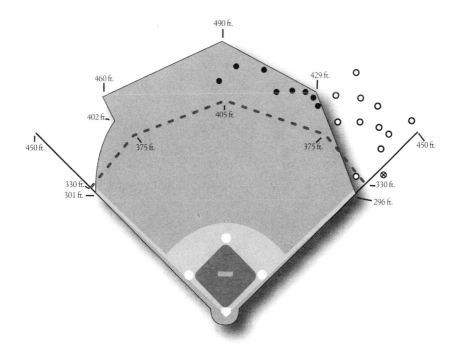

Yankee Stadium, 1925

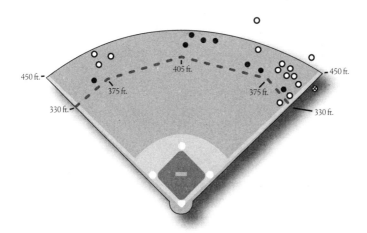

Away Games, 1925

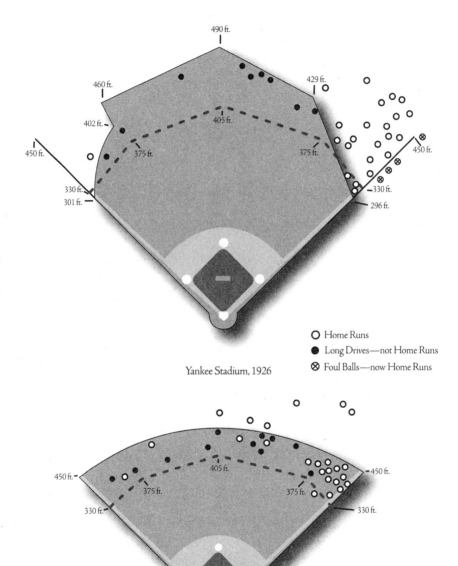

Yankee Stadium, 1926

○ Home Runs
● Long Drives—not Home Runs
⊗ Foul Balls—now Home Runs

Away Games, 1926

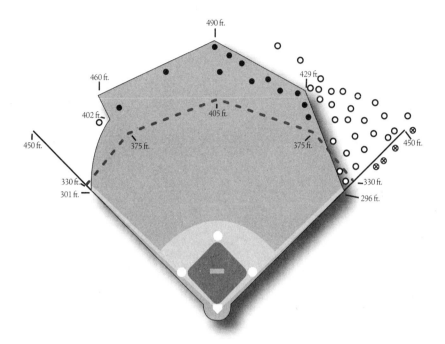

Yankee Stadium, 1927

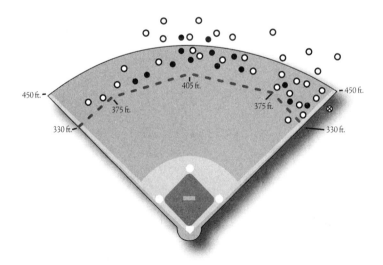

Away Games, 1927

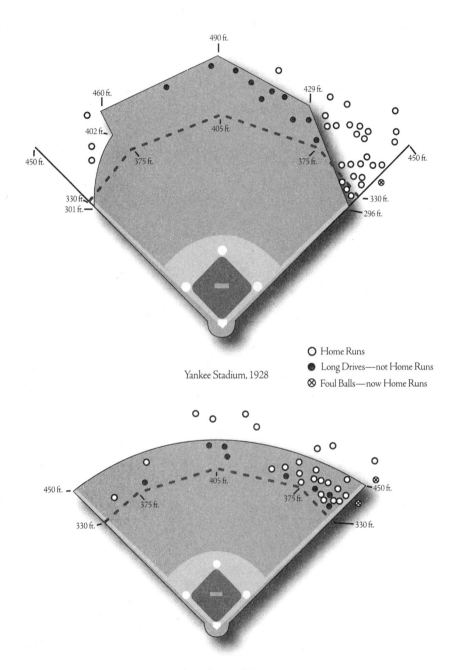

Yankee Stadium, 1928

○ Home Runs
● Long Drives—not Home Runs
⊗ Foul Balls—now Home Runs

Away Games, 1928

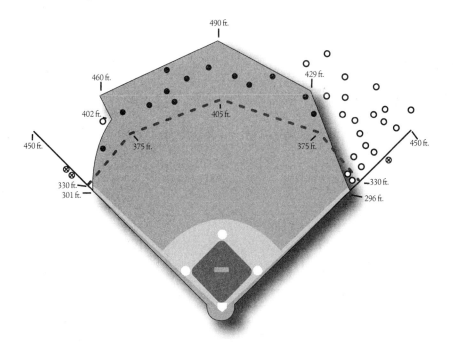

Yankee Stadium, 1929

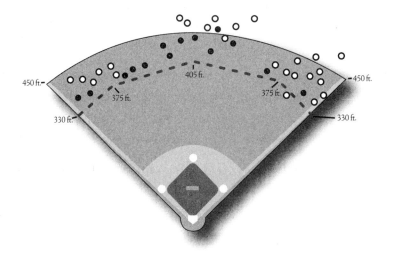

Away Games, 1929

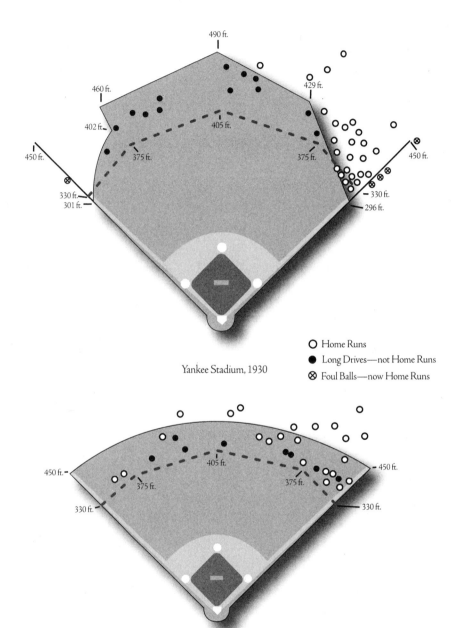

490 ft.

460 ft.

429 ft.

402 ft.

405 ft.

450 ft.

375 ft.

375 ft.

450 ft.

330 ft.

330 ft.

301 ft.

296 ft.

○ Home Runs
● Long Drives—not Home Runs
⊗ Foul Balls—now Home Runs

Yankee Stadium, 1930

405 ft.

450 ft.

450 ft.

375 ft.

375 ft.

330 ft.

330 ft.

Away Games, 1930

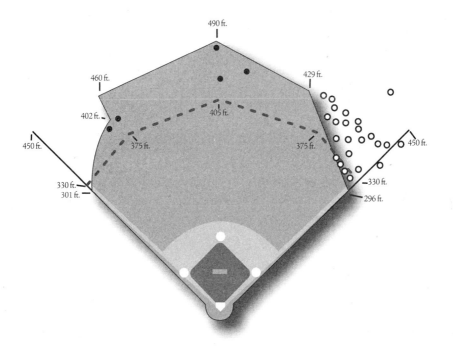

Yankee Stadium, 1931

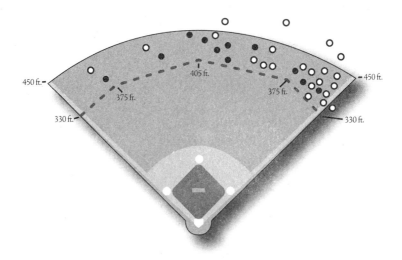

Away Games, 1931

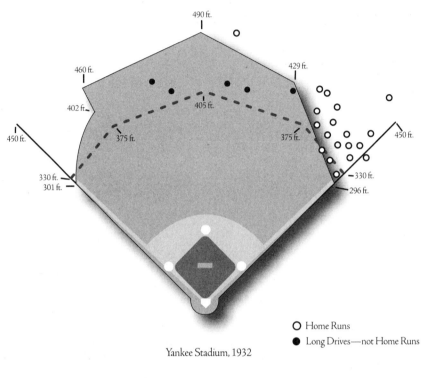

490 ft.

460 ft.

429 ft.

402 ft.

405 ft.

450 ft.

375 ft.

375 ft.

450 ft.

330 ft.

330 ft.

301 ft.

296 ft.

○ Home Runs
● Long Drives—not Home Runs

Yankee Stadium, 1932

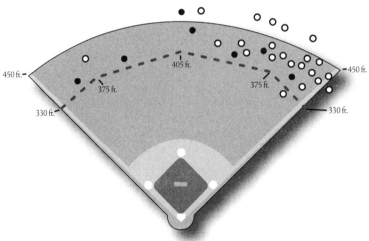

405 ft.

450 ft.

450 ft.

375 ft.

375 ft.

330 ft.

330 ft.

Away Games, 1932

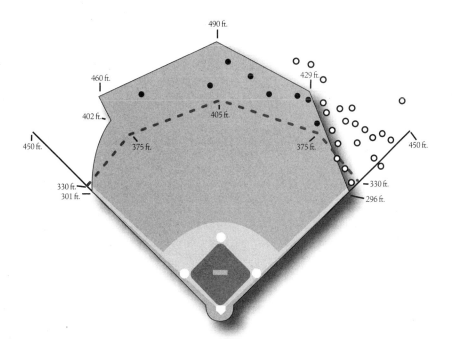

Yankee Stadium, 1933

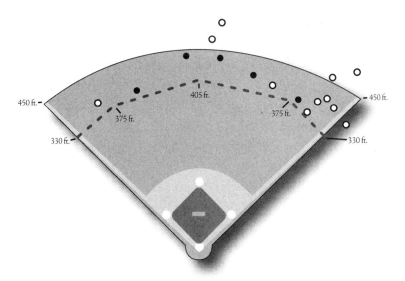

Away Games, 1933

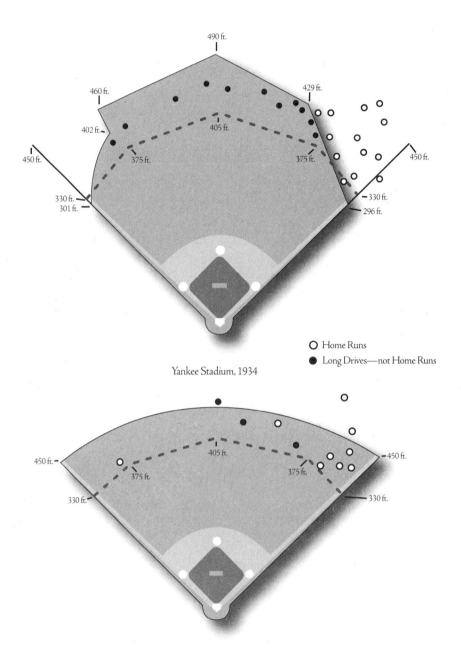

490 ft.

460 ft.

429 ft.

402 ft.

405 ft.

450 ft.

375 ft.

375 ft.

450 ft.

330 ft.
301 ft.

330 ft.
296 ft.

○ Home Runs
● Long Drives—not Home Runs

Yankee Stadium, 1934

450 ft.

405 ft.

375 ft.

375 ft.

450 ft.

330 ft.

330 ft.

Away Games, 1934

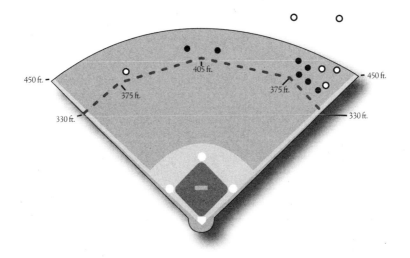

Home and Away Games, 1935

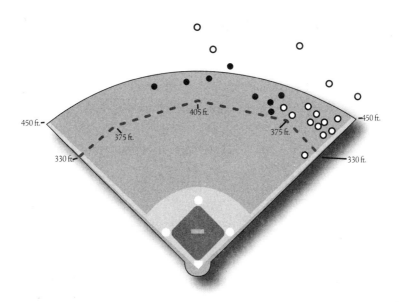

World Series and All-Star Games
Home and Away
O Career Home Runs
● Long Drives—not Home Runs

12
Stadium Photographs

THE NEXT SECTION INCLUDES photographs of the ten Major League ballparks where Babe Ruth played most often. Arrows have been positioned on the photos to show where Babe's longest drives landed in each stadium.

Included in the group of ten are:

- The Polo Grounds in New York, where Ruth played for the Yankees from 1920 to 1922. Babe also excelled in the 1923 World Series versus the Giants at this location.

- Yankee Stadium in New York, where Ruth played for the Yanks from 1923 to 1934.

- Fenway Park in Boston, where Ruth played for the Red Sox from 1914 to 1919.

- Braves Field in Boston, where Ruth played many Sunday games during the years that Fenway Park was unavailable due to the Sabbath blue laws. Babe also used Braves Field as his home park during his final, abbreviated season in 1935.

- Shibe Park (aka Connie Mack Stadium) in Philadelphia, where Ruth played against the Athletics from 1915 to 1934.

- Griffith Stadium in Washington, D.C., where Ruth competed with the Senators (aka The Nationals) from 1915 to 1934.

- League Park in Cleveland, where Ruth played the Indians from 1915 to 1934. A few of the Yankees–Indians games in 1932–1933 were staged at newly built Municipal Stadium.

- Navin Field (aka Briggs Stadium and Tiger Stadium) in Detroit, where Babe and the Tigers competed from 1915 to 1934.

- Comiskey Park in Chicago, where Ruth played the White Sox from 1915 to 1934.

- Sportsman's Park in St. Louis, where Babe took on the Browns from 1915 to 1934. Ruth also starred against the Cardinals in the World Series there in 1926 and 1928.

Not all of the photographs show the stadiums exactly as they were when Babe Ruth played in them. However, they have been chosen for the way they create functional panoramas of the landing points of Babe's longest homers in all directions.

This aerial photo of the Polo Grounds was taken in 1921 when it was Babe Ruth's home park. Starting from the right, we see a pair of arrows where Ruth hit homers into the center field bleachers on consecutive days. The first one on June 13, 1921, flew 480 feet, and the one the following day (at the far right) went about ten feet farther. Moving to the left, we see the landing point of a blow on June 25, 1920, that traveled about 500 feet to the top of the bleachers in right center field. Ruth blasted numerous drives over the 80-foot-high grandstand roof in right field, which was in place during his time at the Polo Grounds (1920–1922). Probably, his mightiest was struck on July 31, 1921, and the approximate spot where it landed is illustrated by the next arrow. It is believed that this amazing drive flew about 560 feet. The final arrow at the far left shows where Babe's drive on May 23, 1920, returned to earth about 520 feet from home plate. *(Associated Press)*

This photograph shows Yankee Stadium as it was for most of Babe Ruth's career. The left arrow shows the landing place of his longest opposite field home run, hit on May 10, 1928. The left-center arrow illustrates his longest center field home run, which occurred on May 21, 1924. The arrow at the right-center shows where Babe's drive on May 24, 1930, landed in a water barrel in the top row of the right center field bleachers. The right arrow shows the approximate landing point of several Ruthian drives. The open bleachers were seventy rows deep here, and Ruth consistently belted balls into the top few rows from 1923 through 1934. Perhaps, the best example took place on August 15, 1928. *(National Baseball Hall of Fame and Museum, Cooperstown, New York)*

Here we have the familiar site of Fenway Park in Boston; Babe Ruth's longest home run here was hit on May 25, 1926. That estimated 545-footer landed in the forty-fifth of the fifty bleacher rows and is indicated by the farthest right arrow. It is important to note that this photograph shows Fenway after the 1934 renovation. During most of Ruth's career, the bleachers did not extend all the way across center field to the spot where they joined with the high left field wall (later known as "The Green Monster"). *(Philadelphia Athletics Historical Society)*

However, the bleachers of Ruth's era in right and right center field were positioned in almost the same way as they are shown here. The old bleachers were made of wood and featured a breezeway in the center. But they also extended about fifty rows high, assuming basically the same dimensions as the newer concrete-and-steel bleachers. Moving from right to left from the first arrow, the second arrow shows the midpoint of approximately five Ruthian blasts landing anywhere from the thirtieth to the fortieth row of the old bleachers. These blows were struck on July 8, 1918; May 27, 1920; June 23, 1921; September 8, 1925; and June 22, 1927. They flew anywhere from 490 feet to 525 feet.

The next arrow, which centers in the middle of the modern bleachers, actually shows an area that was a triangle of open field prior to 1934. On May 18, 1918, Babe smashed a double over Ty Cobb's head to that point beyond the center field flagpole. The final arrow shows a building across Lansdowne Street, which still stands in the same place today. Ruth defied credibility by powering a ball to the spot depicted by the arrow on top of that two-story structure on July 23, 1928. He hit other balls in the same direction almost as far on June 20, 1921; June 22, 1927; and September 6, 1927. Each of those balls traveled anywhere between 480 feet and 515 feet.

This is Braves Field in Boston, where Babe Ruth played many games when he was not at Fenway Park. The top arrow shows one of Babe's homers that was powerfully struck, but not necessarily one of his longest.

It was delivered on April 16, 1935, on the festive occasion of his first game for the Boston Braves. It flew about 430 feet. Moving downward, we see where Ruth's vicious line drive collided with the top row of the right field bleachers (aka the "Jury Box") on May 18, 1930. Some observers felt that, if the ball had been left unimpeded, it would have struck the armory on the far side on the street. This drive would have flown at least 490 feet. The bottom arrow shows where two of Babe's homers landed during the 1929 season, when the Red Sox were using Brave Field for Sunday games. Ruth hit almost identical blows to the top of the center field bleachers on June 30 and September 1. It is believed that each of these blasts traveled in the 470-foot range. *(Philadelphia Athletics Historical Society)*

Here, we are looking at Shibe Park (aka Connie Mack Stadium) in Philadelphia. This photo was actually taken many years after Babe Ruth retired (note the light towers). However, it still represents an ideal overview of the area, where Babe blasted many memorable home runs. The right arrow shows where Ruth's mighty opposite field drive landed in a tree on September 9, 1921 (before the double-deck grandstand was built in 1925). Moving left, the next arrow illustrates the landing point of a classic blow to deep right center field on May 25, 1928. Continuing to the left, we see where Babe's majestic drive on April 12, 1932, landed on a house across Twentieth Street in right center field. The arrow at the extreme left identifies the point on Opal Street where Ruth powered one of his longest-ever homers on May 22, 1930. That blow has previously been pictured. But it should be noted that Babe also hit one the day before (next arrow to the right) that traveled almost as far. *(Philadelphia Athletics Historical Society)*

Shown here is Griffith Stadium, where Ruth played against the Washington Senators from 1915 through 1934. The lower arrow shows where Babe blasted balls near the top of the center field bleachers on July 3, 1927, and May 1, 1928. Moving upward, the next arrow shows the spot where Ruth's drive of May 7, 1921, landed near a house after clearing the high center field wall. Now, continuing to the right, we see where Babe blasted three homers far over the scoreboard in deep right center on May 6, 1921; May 30, 1923; and April 28, 1929. Lastly, the top arrow shows the direction of several long Ruthian blasts to right field. *(Philadelphia Athletics Historical Society)*

This is League Park (aka Dunn Field), where Ruth played most of his games in Cleveland. The first arrow at the far right shows the landing point of his two 480-foot drives into the center field bleachers on May 14, 1921, and June 15, 1930. Moving to the left, the next arrow shows the open space in deep center field, where Babe hit several 460-foot blows for both triples and fly outs. Next, we see where Ruth's home run on August 6, 1926, landed on the far side of Lexington Avenue in deep right center field. This blast flew about 510 feet. The last arrow shows a median point, where several of Babe's longest right field home runs landed on rooftops. A few examples include balls hit on June 13, 1920; August 23, 1921; August 20, 1927; and August 10, 1929. Each traveled at least 470 feet, but might have flown significantly farther. *(Barry Howe Photography)*

This is an aerial view of Navin Field (aka Tiger Stadium) in Detroit, where Babe Ruth hit an unusually high number of his longest drives. Since all sluggers had similar success in this ballpark, it is apparent that there were atmospheric conditions that were conducive to long hitting. Starting from the top, we see where Ruth's homer on September 27, 1928, struck the taxicab building across Trumbull Avenue in right field. This blow flew about 485 feet. Moving downward, the next arrow shows the landing point of an historic blast onto Plum Street on June 8, 1926, that traveled about 520 feet. We next see a point on the far side of Trumbull Avenue in front of a lumber company in right center field. Babe visited that approximate point four times, including August 23, 1919; August 6, 1920; August 6, 1924; and September 28, 1928. These drives flew from between 485 feet and 510 feet. Continuing downward, we again see Babe's longest-ever home run, which has already been pictured. Finally, we see Ruth's 485-foot drive to deep left center field, which landed in Cherry Street on September 11, 1926. *(Burton Historical Collection, Detroit Public Library)*

This is Comiskey Park in Chicago as it looked after the double-deck grandstand was built in 1927. Proceeding from left to right, the first arrow shows where Babe Ruth deposited two opposite field shots into the upper deck on June 10, 1928 and June 12, 1928. The next arrow locates where Ruth struck his two longest center field home runs at Comiskey on June 9, 1922, and July 31, 1926. Both of these balls traveled in the 475-foot range. Still moving to the right, the next arrow illustrates the landing point of one of Babe's mightiest career home runs. It was hit on August 17, 1921, and flew high over the open bleachers, which were in place prior to 1927. The ball landed in a soccer field in deep right center field about 550 feet from home plate. The final arrow indicates where Babe Ruth's historic blow cleared the right field roof on August 16, 1927. That home run was estimated at 520 feet. *(Philadelphia Athletics Historical Society)*

This is an overhead view of Sportsman's Park (later known as Busch Stadium) in St. Louis. Starting with the right arrow, we see where Ruth's first Major League "tape measure" home run landed on July 21, 1915. That drive flew roughly 475 feet, but was about 30 feet shorter than one he hit in the same direction on July 30, 1920. The next arrow, upward and to the left, shows where a couple of Babe's best right center field blows landed on the far side of Grand Avenue. The first occurred on July 7, 1923, and traveled 505 feet, while the second happened in the World Series on October 6, 1926. That majestic blow actually broke a window about 10 feet farther than the previous example. The next arrow to the left (in center field) illustrates where two of Ruth's lengthiest home runs came back to earth. Number one is dated May 25, 1921, while number two was recorded in the aforementioned World Series contest on October 6, 1926. The first soared approximately 535 feet, and the second flew only about five feet less. The final arrow identifies the spot where Babe dented the scoreboard atop the left field bleachers on July 8, 1925. That 450-foot drive was one of the longest opposite field homers ever struck. *(National Baseball Hall of Fame Library, Cooperstown, New York)*

13
Miscellaneous Data

THE FINAL PAGES OF this book include a kind of potpourri of lists relating to different aspects of Babe Ruth's career. They have been chosen to both inform and entertain.

LONG 1921 DRIVES NOT PROJECTED AS HOME RUNS

The following list includes Babe Ruth's long drives in 1921 that are not projected as modern home runs. However, there are two exceptions. Of Ruth's ten drives to the right field grandstand wall at the Polo Grounds, two would likely be homers in today's game:

April 13, NY: Line drive single off right field wall

April 14, NY: Towering fly out to deep left field

April 16, NY: Drive into right field upper deck that was barely foul

April 17, NY: Fly out to right field wall

April 26, NY: Line drive double off right field wall

May 2, Bos: Long foul drive into right field grandstand

May 3, Bos: Fly out to deep center field

May 3, Bos: Tremendous foul drive over right field grandstand

May 6, Wash: Line out to deep center field

May 6, Wash: Long foul drive over high right field wall

May 11, Det: Line drive double to deep right center field

May 18, Chic: Towering fly out to center field

May 30, Wash: Line drive out to deep right field

June 6, NY: Double off right field wall

June 12, NY: Drive over right field grandstand roof that was just foul

June 15, NY: Double off right field wall

June 22, Bos: Fly out to deep center field

July 3, NY: Towering foul drive over right field grandstand roof

July 5, NY: Double to top of right field wall (probable home run, but
    for fan interference)

July 10, Chic: Long foul drive over right field fence

July 10, Chic: High fly to deep center field dropped for two base
    error

July 12, St.L: Line drive double off right center field fence

July 13, St.L: Fly out to deep center field

July 16, Det: Fly out to deep center field

July 20, Clev: Line drive single off high right field wall

July 21, Clev: Long single off high wall in right center field

July 23, Clev: Line smash single off screen atop high right field wall
    (bounced back to first base)

July 24, Clev: Exceptionally high fly out to deep center field

July 31, NY: Tremendous foul drive over left field bleachers

August 7, NY: High fly out to deep left field

August 20, St.L: Double off right center field fence

August 31, Wash: Double off high scoreboard in right center field

August 31, Wash: Fly out to deep right field

August 31, Wash: Line drive fly out to deep left field

September 1, NY: Double off top of right field wall

September 2, NY: Line drive single off right field wall

September 6, Bos: Towering fly to deep left field dropped for error

September 7, NY: Sacrifice fly to deep left field

September 23, NY: Double off right field wall

September 27, NY: Fly out to right field wall

Babe's Fair/Foul Home Runs

When Babe Ruth began his professional baseball career in 1914, home runs were not ruled fair or foul according to where they passed over the outfield fences. Instead, they were judged according to where they landed or were last seen. At a Major League meeting in Chicago on February 9, 1920, the rule was changed. However, it was only one of many modifications on that date, and most umpires were unhappy with the new situation. Along with the home run rule, there were alterations to the standards for intentional walks, balks, spitballs, and so forth. The umpires felt that they had been given too much responsibility, and were being asked to enforce impractical rules. As a result, they tended to simply ignore the changes. On June 17 at Comiskey Park, after hitting one long homer, Ruth launched two prodigious right field drives into a strong crosswind. Both balls passed over the fence in fair territory before curving foul. According to the newly revised rule, these blows should have been regarded as home runs. But neither was. Eight days later, so-called Paragraph 48 reverted back to the 1919 wording and stayed that way until December 12, 1930. As a result, Babe Ruth lost many home runs during his career. Nobody knows exactly how many were lost, but it was at least fifty. The following list provides the dates and locations of seventy-eight long Ruthian drives that landed foul beyond the fences. These, of course, all happened before the permanent

May 4, 1918-NY-RF (two)	June 12, 1921-NY-RF	Aug 14, 1926-NY-RF
May 6, 1918-NY-RF	July 2, 1921-NY-RF (two)	Aug 27, 1926-NY-RF
Sept 2, 1918-NY-RF	July 10, 1921-Chic-RF	May 27, 1927-NY-RF
May 30, 1919-Phil-RF	July 31, 1921-NY-LF	July 12, 1927-Clev-RF
June 28, 1919-NY-RF	Aug 21, 1921-StL.-RF	July 29, 1927-NY-RF
June 29, 1919-NY-RF	June 6, 1922-Chic-LF	Sept 29, 1927-NY-RF (two)
July 9, 1919-St.L-RF	June 7, 1922-Chic-RF	Oct 1, 1927-NY-RF
July 15, 1919-Chic-RF	Aug 24, 1922-NY-RF	May 4, 1928-NY-RF (two)
June 17, 1920-Chic-RF (two)	Sept 22, 1922-Clev-RF	Sept 17, 1928-St.L-RF (two)
July 1, 1920-Phil-RF	May 18, 1923-St.L-RF	April 18, 1929-NY-LF
July 9, 1920-NY-RF	July 22, 1923-Det-RF (two)	April 19, 1929-NY-RF
July 20, 1920-NY-RF	Sept 2, 1923-Wash-RF	April 30, 1929-NY-RF
July 26, 1920-NY-RF (two)	Sept 9, 1923-NY-RF	May 17, 1929-NY-RF
July 31, 1920-St.L-RF	Sept 29, 1923-Bos-RF (two)	Aug 1, 1929-NY-LF
Aug 18, 1920-NY-RF	May 17, 1924-NY-RF	May 5, 1930-NY-RF
Aug 19, 1920-NY-RF	May 23, 1924-NY-LF	Aug 19, 1930-NY-RF
Aug 21, 1920-NY-RF	June 3, 1924-Chic-RF	Sept 5, 1930-NY-RF
Sept 12, 1920-Det-RF	June 3, 1924-Chic-RF	
Sept 18, 1920-Chic-RF	Aug 31, 1924-NY-RF	
Sept 26, 1920-NY-RF	June 1, 1925-NY-RF	
April 16, 1921-NY-RF (two)	Sept 7, 1925-Bos-RF	
May 2, 1921-Bos-RF	April 13, 1926-Wash-LF	
May 3, 1921-Bos-RF	May 13, 1926-NY-RF	
May 6, 1921-Wash-RF	May 20, 1926-NY-RF	
June 11, 1921-NY-LF	July 20, 1926-NY-RF	

rule was implemented, effective in 1931. Not every one would necessarily be a homer under modern conditions, but the majority would be. And how many others occurred that remain unknown, because they were not described in contemporary newspaper accounts?

BABE RUTH VERSUS NEGRO LEAGUE OR BLACK PITCHERS

As discussed, Ruth played many games against Black ballplayers during his career. Unfortunately, not all have been reliably documented. The two following lists provide data about those events. These games have been authenticated by contemporary primary sources:

September 14, 1918: New Haven vs. Cuban Stars-1 for 3-HR

October 4, 1920: Philadelphia vs. Atlantic City Bacharachs-2 for 4-1B & HR

October 7, 1920: Philadelphia vs. Hilldale-0 for 3

October 8, 1920: Philadelphia vs. Hilldale-1 for 4-HR

October 13, 1920: Buffalo vs. Pittsburgh Colored Stars-2 for 4-Two HRs

October 24, 1920: Buffalo vs. Pittsburgh Colored Stars-1 for 3-1B

November 6, 1920: Havana vs. Almendares-0 for 3

November 14, 1920: Havana vs. Almandares-1 for 2-HR

> *N.B. Some Almandares pitchers were Hispanic, but these at-bats were vs. black pitchers*

October 17, 1922: Sioux Falls, SD, vs. Emil Collins (city's best player)-1 for 1-1B

October 22, 1922: Kansas City vs. Monarchs-4 for 4- 4 Line Drive 1Bs

October 11, 1926: Bradley Beach, NJ, vs. Brooklyn Colored Giants-2 for 4-Two HRs

October 9, 1927: New York vs. Linclon Giants-Rained out

October 11, 1927: Trenton vs. Brooklyn Colored Giants-3 for 5-Three HRs (off Dick Redding)

October 13, 1927: Asbury Park, NJ, vs. Brooklyn Colored Giants-1 for 4-HR

October 14, 1928: Montreal vs. Chappies-2 for 3-2 1Bs

October 20, 1929: West New York, NJ, vs. Royal Giants-3 for 4- Two 1Bs & 2B

October 13, 1931: Kansas City vs. Monarchs-Rained out

September 29, 1935: New York vs. New York Cubans-1 for 4-2B

The remaining games have been reported by dependable individuals, but have not been confirmed by contemporary primary sources:

1928: Kansas City vs. Chicago American Giants—Two line hits according to Willie Powell

1929: Philadelphia vs. Hilldale—Hit Two long right field HRs according to Judy Johnson

1935-1938: Chicago vs. Satchel Paige—Hit long center field HR according to Buck O'Neill

Babe Ruth's Bunt Base Hits

Everyone recognizes Babe Ruth as a great power hitter, but few realize how well he executed even the most intricate baseball maneuvers. He is known to have bunted safely for base hits at least forty-three times during his career, while accumulating many more sacrifice bunts. Please note that there are no examples from 1923, when Babe played his best brand of "speed and finesse" baseball. It is possible that he bunted so often in that season that sportswriters didn't consider it necessary to mention it in their game accounts.

Here is the list:

9-14-1917: Boston vs. New York

8-22-1918: Boston vs. St. Louis

8-11-1919: Boston vs. St. Louis

8-8-1921: New York vs. Chicago

8-10-1921: New York vs. Chicago

8-13-1921: Philadelphia

8-31-1921: Washington

9-8-1921: Philadelphia

9-15-1921: New York vs. St. Louis

10-10-1921: New York vs. Giants in World Series

6-8-1922: Chicago

7-14-1922: New York vs. St. Louis (two)

8-17-1922: New York vs. Detroit

8-20-1922: New York vs. Chicago

9-29-1922: Boston

9-30-1922: Boston

5-5-1924: New York vs. Philadelphia

5-30-1924: New York vs. Philadelphia

6-12-1924: Detroit

7-12-1924: New York vs. St. Louis

8-1-1924: St. Louis

8-5-1924: Detroit

9-27-1924: Philadelphia

5-17-1926: New York vs. Chicago

6-13-1926: St. Louis

4-21-1927: Philadelphia

6-23-1927: Boston

5-4-1928: New York vs. Chicago

6-22-1929: New York vs. Philadelphia

8-16-1929: Detroit

4-30-1930: Washington

5-24-1930: New York vs. Philadelphia

5-27-1930: New York vs. Washington

6-22-1930: New York vs. St. Louis

7-4-1930: Washington

8-10-1930: New York vs. St. Louis

6-25-1931: Chicago

7-22-1931: New York vs. Detroit

7-26-1931: New York vs. Chicago

6-4-1932: Philadelphia

8-26-1932: New York vs. Cleveland

5-17-1933: New York vs. Detroit

A PARTIAL LIST OF GEORGE HERMAN RUTH'S NICKNAMES OR TITLES:

Abou Ben Ruth
Ace of Clubbers
Babe the Ruthless (or the Mighty)
Ball Mauling Majesty
Baltimore Adonis
Baltimore Behemoth (or Blizzard)
Bambino (aka Bambina)
Banzoi of Bingle
Battering Infant
Batting Babe (and Biffing, Burly Babe)
Battling, Busting, Bruising Babe
Bazoo of Bust
Behemoth
Behemoth Blaster
Behemoth of Bam (or Biff or Bust or Bash)
Big Bambino (or Bam or Slam)
Blistering Babe
Blunderbuss
Boston Mauler
Buster
Bustin' Bambino (or Behemoth)
Busting Brobodignagian
Caliph of Clout (or Crash)
Chief Cudgeler
Colossus
Colossus of Clouters (or Swat)
Czar of Crash (or Slam)
Demon Slugger (or Swatter)
Emperor
Goliath (or Goliath of the Bludgeon)
Grand Colossus of All Hitters
Harlem Catapult
Hercules
Heroic Figure of Our National Sport
His Royal Nibs (or Highness)
Human Howitzer
Infant Swatigy
Invincible Invalid (in 1929)
Juggernaut
Jumbo Jouster

Khedive of Klout
King of Clout (or Diamonds or Swat, etc.)
Kleagle of Klout
Maharajah of Maulers (or Mash)
Mandarin of Maul
Master Mauler (and Mastadonic Mauler)
Mauling Mandarin (or Menace or Marvel)
Menace, The
Mightiest of Maulers
Mightiest of the Mighty
Mighty Basso Profundo
Mighty Man of Baseball
Monarch of Maulers
Monarch of the Home Run
Oriole Infant
Oriole Sharpshooter
Potentate of Pounders
Prince of Pounders (or Pummelers)
Prince of Punch (or Punchers)
Rajah of Rap (or Swat)
Royce Rools of Diamond
Ruthless Ruth
Ruth the Rampant
Samson (Samson of Swat)
Smashing Infant (and Stalwart Infant)
Son of Swat
Sultan of Swat (or Swat Sultan)
Superman
Superswatsman
Swattingest Swatter of Swatdom
Sweet Swatter
Tarzan
Terror of Pitchers
Titan of Thump
Wali of Wallop
Wazir of Wham
Wazzoo of Wham
Wizard of Wallop (or Whack)
Wonder Man
Zeus

Bibliography

Alexander, Charles. *John Mcgraw*. New York: Viking Penguin Inc., 1988.

Alexander, Charles. *Ty Cobb*. New York, Oxford: Oxford University Press, 1984.

Bak, Richard. *Turkey Stearnes And The Detroit Stars: The Negro Leagues in Detroit, 1919–1933*. Detroit, Michigan: Wayne State University Press, 1994.

Canter, Len. *Babe Ruth*. New York: Baronet Books, 1996.

Considine, Bob. *The Babe Ruth Story*. New York: E. P. Dutton and Co., Inc., 1948.

Creamer, Robert W. *Babe: The Legend Comes to Life*. New York: Simon & Schuster, 1974.

Fleming, G. H. *Murderers' Row: The 1927 New York Yankees*. New York: William Morrow and Company, Inc., 1985

Holway, John B. *Black Diamonds: Life in the Negro Leagues from the Men Who Lived It*. New York: Stadium Books, 1991.

Holway, John B. *The Complete Book of Baseball's Negro League: The Other Half of Baseball History*. Fern Park, Fl., 2001.

Honig, Donald. *Baseball When the Grass Was Real*. New York: Coward, McCann and Geoghegan, Inc., 1975.

Honig, Donald. *The New York Yankees: An Illustrated History*. New York: Crown Publishers, Inc., 1981.

Kashatus, William. *Connie Mack's '29 Triumph*. Jefferson, North Carolina, and London: MacFarland and Company, Inc. 1999.

Lally, Richard. *Bombers: An Oral History of the New York Yankees*. New York: Crown Publishers, 2002.

Lane, F. C. *Batting*. New York: Baseball Magazine Company, 1925.

Meany, Tom. *Babe Ruth: The Big Moments of the Big Fellow*. New York: Grosset and Dunlap, 1947.

Miller, Ernestine. *The Babe Book: Baseball's Greatest Legend Remembered.* Kansas City: Andrews McMeel Publishing, 2000.

Montville, Leigh. *The Big Bam: The Life and Times of Babe Ruth.* New York: Doubleday, 2006.

Neyer, Rob, and Epstein, Eddie. *Baseball Dynasties: The Greatest Teams of All Times.* New York, London: W. W. Norton and Company, 2000.

Nicholson, Lois P. *Babe Ruth: Sultan of Swat.* Woodbury, Connecticut: Goodwood Press, 1994.

Peterson, Robert. *Only the Ball Was White: A History of Legendary Black Players and All-Black Professional Teams.* New York: Gramercy Books, 1970.

Pirrone, Dorothy Ruth. *My Dad, the Babe: Growing Up With An American Hero.* Boston Massachusetts: Quinlan Press, 1988.

Ribowsky, Mark. *A Complete History Of The Negro League, 1884–1955.* Secaucus, New Jersey: A Citadel Press Book, 1997.

Ritter, Lawrence, and Rucker, Mark. *The Babe: The Game that Ruth Built.* New York: Total Sports, 1997.

Robinson, Ray. *Iron Horse: Lou Gehrig in His Time.* New York, London: W. W. Norton and Company, 1990.

Rust, Art. *Get That Nigger Off the Field: An Informal History of the Black Man in Baseball.* New York: Delacorate Press, 1976.

Shaughnessy, Dan. *The Curse of The Bambino.* New York: Penguin Books, 1990.

Smelser, Marshall. *The Life That Ruth Built: A Biography.* Lincoln and London: University of Nebraska Press, 1975.

Smith, Curt. *Storied Stadiums: Baseball's History Through its Ballparks.* New York: Carroll & Graf Publishers, 2001.

Snyder, Brad. *Beyond the Shadow of Senators.* Chicago, New York: Contemporary Books, 2003.

Sobol, Ken. *Babe Ruth and the American Dream.* New York: Ballantine Books, 1974.

Sowell, Mike. *The Pitch That Killed.* New York: Macmillan Publishing Co., 1989.

Staten, Vince. *Ol' Diz: A Biography Of Dizzy Dean.* New York: Harper Collins Publishers, 1992.

Wagenheim, Kal. *Babe Ruth: His Life and Legend.* Chicago, Illinois: Olmstead Press, 2001.

Wood, Allan. *Babe Ruth and the 1918 Red Sox.* San Jose, New York, Lincoln, Shanghai: Writers Club Press, 2000.

Sources

BABE RUTH'S ACCOMPLISHMENTS WERE so extraordinary that any real-istic account of his career will likely be received with a healthy measure of cynicism. For that reason, the following list of sources is offered to any readers who want to pursue their own corroborative research. The primary sources for many of Ruth's most exceptional deeds have already been identified within the narrative text of the book. But serious students of baseball may want more; so here they are.

But some advice is offered first. The most implausible aspect of Babe's persona is his nearly superhuman power. These sources will help to confirm the premise that he is baseball's "mightiest ever" batsman, but they will not provide the entire explanation. In order to definitively understand the scope of Ruth's power, it is also necessary to know the ballparks in which he played. Knowing the distances to outfield fences is essential, but so is familiarity with the surrounding streets, buildings, and neighborhoods. That's where many of Babe's longest home runs landed. Phil Lowry's comprehensive book on stadium history (*Green Cathedrals*) will assist readers pursuing their own research.

As a general rule, two primary sources are listed for each event. If someone chooses to do his or her own research, it is suggested that both sources be referenced. It is often necessary to read at least two accounts of an athletic event in order to understand what actually happened. The more sources that are read, the more clarity will be achieved. In a few cases, additional sources are provided. The best example relates to Babe Ruth's historic home run in Detroit on July 18, 1921. Since this book identifies that blow as the longest in Major League history, all known sources have been itemized. Good luck and good hunting!

12. . . . **about 435 feet:** March 7, 1914. Sources—*Baltimore American,* March 8, 1914, and *Baltimore Sun,* March 8, 1914.

13. . . . **landed beside the flagpole on a hill in center field. . . . the longest drive they had ever seen:** August 22, 1914. Sources—*Providence Journal,* August 23, 1914, and *Rochester Democrat and Chronicle,* August 23, 1914.

15. . . . **Boston-area distance record with his third home run:** June 25, 1915. Sources—*Boston Herald,* June 26, 1915, and *New York Herald,* June 26, 1915.

16. . . . **landed beside the center field flagpole . . . would have been the stadium's longest drive:** July 21, 1915. Sources—*Boston Herald,* July 22, 1915, and *Boston Post,* July 22, 1915.

16. . . . **about 475 feet:** July 21, 1915. Sources—*St. Louis Globe-Democrat,* July 22, 1915, and *Boston Globe,* July 22, 1915.

18. . . . **about 460 feet from home plate. . . . the longest ever in Navin Field:** June 9, 1916. Sources—*Detroit Free Press,* June 10, 1916, and *Boston Globe,* June 19, 1916.

21. . . . **400-foot sacrifice fly:** May 7, 1917. Sources—*Boston Globe,* May 8, 1917, and *Washington Evening Star,* May 8, 1917.

22. . . . **about 465 feet:** August 10, 1917. Sources—*Boston Herald,* August 11, 1917, and *Boston Post,* August 11, 1917.

23. . . . **the longest drive of the year in New York except for a foul ball hit earlier that day by Ruth. That one sailed far over the grandstand roof, and would have been judged fair under today's rules:** September 15, 1917. Sources—*Boston Herald,* September 16, 1917, and *Boston Globe,* September 16, 1917.

23. . . . **won the pregame fungo contest with a drive of 402 feet:** September 27, 1917. Sources—*Boston Globe,* September 28, 1917, and *Boston Herald,* September 28, 1917.

24. . . . **was the longest hit ever made . . . in Hot Springs:** March 17, 1918. Sources—*Boston Post,* March 18, 1918, and *Boston Herald,* March 18, 1918.

24. . . . **evidence indicates a flight of about 500 feet:** March 24, 1918. Sources—*Boston Globe,* March 25, 1918. and *Boston Post,* March 25, 1918.

25.   . . . **about 430 feet into center field:** May 9, 1918. Sources—*Washington Evening Star,* May 10, 1918 and *Boston Post,* May 10, 1918.

25.   . . . **a drive of 460 feet:** May 18, 1918. Sources—*Boston Herald,* May 19, 1918, and *Boston Globe,* May 19, 1918.

26.   . . . **about 490 feet . . . the longest ever witnessed in The Hub. But it wasn't a home run:** July 8, 1918. Sources—*Boston Herald,* July 9, 1918, and *Boston Post,* July 9, 1918.

28.   . . . **445-foot double to center field:** August 31, 1918. Sources—*Philadelphia Inquirer,* September 1, 1918, and *Boston Globe,* September 1, 1918.

30.   . . . **likely distance was 552 feet:** April 4, 1919. Sources—*Boston Globe,* April 5, 1919; April 6, 1919; April 20, 1919; and September 9, 1919; and *New York World,* April 5, 1919; April 9, 1919; February 23, 1925.

30.   . . . **another local distance record in Richmond:** April 15, 1919. Sources—*Boston Herald,* April 16, 1919, and *Boston Post,* April 16, 1919.

31.   . . . **about 500 feet:** April 18, 1919. Sources—*Baltimore Sun,* April 19, 1919, and *Boston Post,* April 19, 1919.

32.   . . . **on the roof of a three-story house in right centerfield, and may have traveled farther than all the other homers:** April 19, 1919. Sources—*Baltimore American,* April 20, 1919, and *Boston Herald,* April 20, 1919.

32.   . . . **at the base of yet another house beyond the right field fence:** April 19, 1919. Sources—*Boston Post,* April 20, 1919, and *Baltimore Sun,* April 20, 1919.

33.   . . . **the longest ever at Shibe Park, but Connie Mack called it the longest he ever saw (up to that time) :** May 30, 1919. Sources—*Philadelphia Inquirer,* May 31, 1919, and *Philadelphia North American,* May 31, 1919.

33.   . . . **over the right field wall, cross Lexington Avenue, and crash onto the roof of a house:** July 18, 1919. Sources—*Cleveland Plain Dealer,* July 19, 1919, and *Boston Post,* July 19, 1919.

34.   . . . **broke a window across Lansdowne Street:** September 20, 1919. Sources—*Boston Post,* September 21, 1919, and *Boston Globe,* September 21, 1919.

34.   . . . **far over the right field grandstand roof:** September 24, 1919. Sources—*New York Tribune,* September 25, 1919, and *Boston Globe, September 25, 1919.*

35–36.   . . . **fence was 429 feet from home plate, and the ball touched earth about 75 feet past that point . . . the city's longest:** April 1, 1920. Sources—*New York World,* April 2, 1920, and *New York Herald,* April 2, 1920.

36.   . . . **somewhere close to 1,600 feet:** April 8, 1920. Sources—*Winston-Salem Journal,* April 9, 1920, and *Twin City Sentinal,* April 9, 1920.

37.   . . . **around 500 feet away:** May 1, 1920. Sources—*New York World,* May 2, 1920, and *New York Tribune,* May 2, 1920.

38.   . . . **occasion landed near the top of those bleachers just right of center field:** June 25, 1920. Sources—*New York Tribune,* June 26, 1920, and *New York Herald,* June 26, 1920.

39.   . . . **460 feet away:** September 10, 1920. Sources—*New York Herald,* September 11, 1920, and *Cleveland Plain Dealer,* September 11, 1920.

40.   . . . **more than 500 feet from home plate:** November 8, 1920. Sources—*Havana Post,* November 9, 1920, and *Diario de la Marina,* November 9, 1920.

42.   . . . **cleared the 486-foot sign in center field:** November 8, 1920. Sources—*New Orleans Times-Picayune,* March 11, 1922, and *New York World,* March 11, 1922.

42.   . . . **two of his typical "longest ever" pokes in Galveston and San Antonio:** March 29 and March 31, 1922. Sources—*New York World,* March 30, 1922; and April 1, 1922; and *New York Times,* March 30, 1922; and April 1, 1922.

43   . . . **just missed a home run as his huge drive drifted foul after clearing the right field bleachers in fair ground:** June 7, 1922. Sources—*New York Times,* June 8, 1922, and *Chicago Tribune,* June 8, 1922.

43.   . . . **about 480 feet:** June 9, 1922. Sources—*Chicago Daily News,* June 10, 1922, and *New York Times,* June 10, 1922.

45.   . . . **beyond the flagpole 470 feet away . . . It was ruled a double according to a prearranged agreement:** August 6, 1922. Sources—*New York Times,* August 7, 1922, and *Detroit Free Press,* August 7, 1922.

47.   . . . **a 450-foot shot to center field in the third game:** Game 3, World Series, October 7, 1922. Sources—*New York Times,* October 8, 1922, and Associated Press, October 8, 1922.

47.   . . . **a 500-foot double:** March 31, 1923. Sources—*New Orleans Times-Picayune,* April 1, 1923, and *New York Times,* April 1, 1923.

48.   . . . **a 475-foot drive:** April 19, 1923. Sources—*New York Herald,* April 20, 1923, and *Boston Globe,* April 20, 1923.

48–49.   . . . **triple landed past the running track in remote left center . . . a double in the ninth inning onto the track in direct center . . . three balls over 450 feet in those two days, and had no home runs:** April 20, 1923. Sources—*New York Herald,* April 21, 1923, and *New York World,* April 21, 1923.

52.   . . . **nearly 500 feet to the far side of that roadway, but Ruth then cleared it twice in the same series in actual games:** July 7, 1923. Sources—*St. Louis Globe-Democrat,* July 8, 1923, and *New York World,* July 8, 1923.

53.   . . . **a 440-foot fly out:** October 11, 1923. Sources—*New York Times,* October 12, 1923, and *New York World,* October 12, 1923.

54.   . . . **two 470–foot fly outs . . . two 490-foot doubles off the fence:** Spring Training, 1924. Sources—*New Orleans Times-Picayune,* March 16, 1924; March 23, 1924; March 26, 1924; and March 31, 1924; and *New York Times,* March 16, 1924; March 23, 1924; and March 26, 1924.

54.   . . . **450 feet:** April 8, 1924. Sources—*Knoxville Journal and Tribune,* April 9, 1924, and *New York Herald-Tribune,* April 9, 1924.

55.   . . . **476 feet:** May 30, 1924. Sources—*Philadelphia North American,* May 31, 1924, and *New York Times,* May 31, 1924; and June 1, 1924.

55.   . . . **estimated flight path was 525 feet:** May 31, 1924. Sources—*Philadelphia Record,* June 1, 1924, and *New York World,* June 1, 1924.

57–58.   . . . **flew over the center fielder's head, and landed beyond the flag-pole. It then bounded into the fence almost 500 feet away:** July 20, 1924. Sources—*New York Times,* July 21, 1924, and *New York Herald-Tribune,* July 21, 1924.

58.   . . . **two 500-footers:** September 8–11, 1924. Sources—*Boston Post,* September 9, 1924, and September 12, 1924; and *Boston Globe,* September 9, 1924, and September 12, 1924.

60.   . . . **over a gas station across the street, and was hailed as the longest ever hit in the Pacific Northwest. The third went even farther:** Seattle barnstorming stop, October 19, 1924. Sources—*Seattle Post-Intelligencer,* October 20, 1924, and *Seattle Daily Times,* October 20, 1924.

61.   . . . **497 feet:** March 29, 1925. Sources—*New York Herald-Tribune,* March 30, 1925, and *New York World,* March 30, 1925.

62.   . . . **an opposite field shot that topped the left field bleachers and hit the scoreboard. . . . only time that a left-handed batter accomplished this deed in a stadium that remained in use until 1966:** July 8, 1925. Sources—*New York Daily News,* July 9, 1925, and *New York World,* July 9, 1925.

63.   . . . **thirty-five rows into the bleachers in right center. It was his longest batted ball of the year:** September 7, 1925. Sources—*Boston Post,* September 8, 1925, and *Boston Globe,* September 8, 1925.

64.   . . . **a flight of 538 feet:** October 4, 1925. Sources—*Long Island City Daily Star,* October 5, 1925, and *Star-Journal,* August 27, 1925.

66.   . . . **flew 100 feet beyond the right field wall:** April 20, 1926. Sources—*New York Times,* April 21, 1926, and *New York Daily News,* April 21, 1926.

67.   . . . **two tremendous homers near the top of the right center field bleachers:** April 23 and 24, 1926. Sources—*New York World,* April 24, 1926, and April 25, 1926; and *New York Herald-Tribune,* April 24, 1926, and April 25, 1926.

67.   . . . **into the upper rows of the vast right field bleachers; the second of two hit on May 19 landed sixty rows high:** May 19, 1926. Sources—*New York Post,* May 20, 1926, and *New York World,* May 20, 1926.

67.   . . . **the mightiest ever in Beantown . . . traveled 512 feet horizontally,**

when it met a wooden bench 28 feet above field level: May 25, 1926. Sources—*Boston Post,* May 26, 1926, and *Boston Globe,* May 26, 1926.

67–68.　. . . longest liftoff on June 8 in Detroit. . . . across Trumbull Avenue in right field, and crashed onto the roof of a taxi on Plum Street . . . This particular drive by Ruth was terrific, flying about 520 feet: June 8, 1926. Sources—*Detroit Free Press,* June 9, 1926, and *Detroit Times,* June 9, 1926.

69.　. . . the fence at a distance of 450 feet. . . . passed over the 12-foot fence: July 31, 1926. Sources—*New York Times,* August 1, 1926, and *New York Herald-Tribune,* August 1, 1926.

70.　. . . on an awning on the far side of Twentieth Street: September 3, 1926. Sources—*Philadelphia Public Ledger,* September 4, 1926, and *Philadelphia Inquirer,* September 4, 1926.

72.　. . . cleared two fields located side by side: Wilkes-Barre barnstorming stop, October 12, 1926. Sources—*Wilkes-Barre Record,* October 13, 1926, and Associated Press, October 13, 1926.

74.　. . . into the center field bleachers, which were 441 feet from home plate: May 23, 1927. Sources—*Washington Evening Star,* May 24, 1927, and *New York World,* May 24, 1927.

74.　. . . onto the housetops across Twentieth Street: May 31, 1927. Sources—*Philadelphia Inquirer,* June 1, 1927, and *Philadelphia Public Ledger,* June 1, 1927.

74.　. . . almost to the scoreboard atop the right center field seats: June 11, 1927. Sources—*New York Times,* June 12, 1927, and *New York Herald-Tribune,* June 12, 1927.

74.　. . . the top of the towering right field bleachers and almost out of The Stadium: June 11, 1927. Sources—*New York Times,* June 12, 1927, and *New York World,* June 12, 1927.

75.　. . . hit a building across the street near the flagpole just left of center, and the second went through the opening in the old right center field bleachers before colliding with a garage on one bounce: June 22, 1927. Sources—*Boston Globe,* June 23, 1927, and *Boston Post,* June 23, 1927.

75.　. . . some 475 feet: July 4, 1927. Sources—*Washington Star,* July 5, 1927, and *New York Herald-Tribune,* July 5, 1927.

75.　. . . to the top of the bleachers just right of center field: July 9, 1927. Sources—*New York Times,* July 10, 1927, and *New York World,* July 10, 1927.

76.　. . . "the longest two-bagger ever." . . . hit the fence in dead center on the first hop, and flew about 480 feet: August 5, 1927. Sources—*New York World,* August 6, 1927, and *New York Herald-Tribune,* August 6, 1927.

76　. . . high over the right field boundary, and landed half a block away beside a coal car: August 15, 1927. Sources—*Indianapolis Star,* August 16, 1927, and *New York Times,* August 16, 1927.

76.   . . . **easily surpassed the grandstand roof . . . landed in an adjoining parking lot:** August 16, 1927. Sources—*New York Evening Journal,* August 17, 1927, and *New York Herald-Tribune,* August 17, 1927.

76.   . . . **another homer almost as far**: August 20, 1927. Sources—*New York Herald-Tribune,* August 21, 1927, and *Cleveland Plain Dealer,* August 21, 1927.

77.   . . . **425-foot fly out:** September 3, 1927. Sources—*New York Times,* September 4, 1927, and *Philadelphia Inquirer,* September 4, 1927.

77.   . . . **at least 500 feet:** September 6, 1927. Sources—*Boston Herald,* September 7, 1927, and *New York Times,* September 7, 1927.

78.   . . . **Babe also flied out to the right center field fence, blasted two balls just foul into the right field bleachers, and tripled off the fence in right center field. . . . six balls for home run distance in this single contest:** September 29, 1927. Sources—*New York Times,* September 30, 1927, and *New York World,* September 30, 1927.

79.   . . . **another first by actually blasting one of his two center field homers over the flagpole:** April 6, 1928. Sources—*New York Herald-Tribune,* April 7, 1928, and *New York World,* April 7, 1928.

80.   . . . **over the clock near center field and collided with a telephone pole:** April 15, 1928. Sources—*Baltimore Sun,* April 16, 1928, and *New York Times,* April 16, 1928.

80.   . . . **landed high in the bleachers in dead center, generating the usual debate about which of Ruth's many such blows was his longest:** May 1, 1928. Sources—*Washington Post,* May 2, 1928, and *New York Times,* May 2, 1928.

80.   . . . **may have hit the longest-ever opposite field home run on this occasion. . . . Look out to the center field end of the left field grandstand, and picture a line drive crashing into the seats just under the mezzanine. It's about 460 feet to that point, and the ball still had a little flight left in it:** May 10, 1928. Sources—*New York Herald-Tribune,* May 11, 1928, and *New York World,* May 11, 1928.

81.   . . . **about 460 feet away:** May 31, 1928. Sources—*Washington Evening Star,* June 1, 1928, and *New York World,* June 1, 1928.

81.   . . . **into the left center field upper deck:** June 10, 1928. Sources—*New York Times,* June 11, 1928, and *New York Herald-Tribune,* June 11, 1928.

81.   . . . **ball into the left center field upper deck:** June 12, 1928. Sources—*Chicago Tribune,* June 13, 1928, and *New York Telegram,* June 13, 1928.

82.   . . . **two homers over the scoreboard in right center field, but two others in the same direction missed:** June 28, 1928. Sources—*New York Times,* June 29, 1928, and *Philadelphia Bulletin,* June 29, 1928.

82.   . . . **Ruth's longest-ever center field homer in Boston . . . well over 500 feet:** July 23, 1928. Sources—*Boston Herald,* July 24, 1928, and *Boston Post,* July 24, 1928.

83. . . . came to rest in the uppermost rows of the right field bleachers: August 15, 1928. Sources—*New York Post,* August 16, 1928, and *New York World,* August 16, 1928.

84. . . . straight to the fortieth row of the bleachers in right field: September 11, 1928. Sources—*New York World,* September 12, 1928, and *Philadelphia Public Ledger,* September 12, 1928.

87. . . . the longest drive ever launched in Flatbush: Spring Training, April 13, 1929. Sources—*New York World,* April 14, 1929, and *New York Times,* April 14, 1929.

90. . . . about fifty rows into the right field bleachers: July 28, 1929. Sources—*New York Herald-Tribune,* July 29, 1929, and *New York World,* July 29, 1929.

91. . . . sailed 447 feet: July 31, 1929. Sources—*New York World,* August 1, 1929, and *New York Times,* August 1, 1929.

91. . . . a 460-foot triple: August 2, 1929. Sources—*New York Herald-Tribune,* August 3, 1929, and *New York Times,* August 3, 1929.

91. . . . twice in recent days Ruth hit comparable balls that had been caught for outs: July 28 and 31, 1929. Sources—*New York Herald-Tribune,* July 29, 1929, and August 1, 1929.

91. . . . clearing a house on the far side of Lexington Avenue. . . . this hit traveled a considerable distance past the houses, but we can never know just how far: August 10, 1929. Sources—*New York World,* August 11, 1929, and *New York Herald-Tribune,* August 11, 1929.

92. . . . 450 feet away and 30 feet up: September 1, 1929. Sources—*New York Herald-Tribune,* September 2, 1929, and *New York World,* September 2, 1929.

92. . . . at least 520 feet: September 5, 1929. Sources—*New York Times,* September 6, 1929, and *New York Herald-Tribune,* September 6, 1929.

94. . . . broke the wooden right field fence: April 8, 1930. Sources—*New York World,* April 9, 1930, and *Memphis Commercial Appeal,* April 9, 1930.

95. . . . 400 feet away and 20 feet high: April 15, 1930. Sources—*New York Times,* April 16, 1930, and *Philadelphia Inquirer,* April 16, 1930.

95. . . . almost reached the top of the right field seats: May 4, 1930. Sources—*New York Times,* May 5, 1930, and *New York Herald-Tribune,* May 5, 1930.

95. . . . to the top of the right field bleachers known as the "jury box." . . . 435 feet away, and the ball was still screaming at a height of about 40 feet: May 18, 1930. Sources—*Boston Herald,* May 19, 1930, and *Boston Globe,* May 19, 1930.

96. . . . a 500-foot monstrosity: May 21, 1930. Sources—*Philadelphia Daily News,* May 22, 1930, and *Philadelphia Bulletin,* May 22, 1930.

96. . . . into the fans watching from the rooftops across the street: May 21, 1930. Sources—*Philadelphia Public Ledger,* May 22, 1930, and *Philadelphia Bulletin,* May 22, 1930.

96.   . . . bypassed the right field fence, Twentieth Street, a row of houses, an alley with backyards, another row of houses, and ultimately returned to earth in Opal Street. . . . three different individuals provided confirmation. . . . Opal Street was a minimum distance of 505 feet from home plate, so this beastly thing flew somewhere in excess of that length: May 22, 1930. Sources—As above, May 23, 1930 and Waite Hoyt, Allen Lewis, Ken McKenzie, and William T. Jenkinson in later years by way of oral history. Also, in subsequent visits to Shibe Park, Babe Ruth was known to refer to Opal Street as the place where: "I dropped the big one."

97.   . . . near the top of the bleachers in right center field. . . . the ball landed in a barrel of water kept in the top row in case of fire. If true, this drive came as close to leaving Yankee Stadium as any that has ever been struck: May 24, 1930. Sources—*New York Times,* May 25, 1930, and Waite Hoyt in a 1958 radio interview preserved on a recording.

98.   . . . into the center field bleachers: June 15, 1930. Sources—As above, June 16, 1930, and *Cleveland Plain Dealer,* June 16, 1930.

98.   . . . broke the distance record in Hawkins Stadium: June 18, 1930. Sources—*Albany Knickerbocker Press,* June 19, 1930, and *New York Times,* June 19, 1930.

99.   . . . The ball hit the same exact loudspeaker that had been hit on opening day: September 26, 1930. Sources—*Philadelphia Inquirer* ("Short Strays on A's"), September 27, 1930, and *New York Times,* September 27, 1930.

102.   . . . so far over the right field fence that it also cleared an adjoining livery stable: April 5, 1931. Sources—*Nashville Banner,* April 6, 1930, and *Nashville Tennessean,* April 6, 1931.

102.   . . . nearly cleared the right field bleachers: April 20, 1931. Sources— *Philadelphia Public Ledger,* April 21, 1931, and *Philadelphia Inquirer,* April 21, 1931.

104.   . . . about 480 feet for an out: July 8, 1931. Sources—*New York Herald-Tribune,* July 9, 1931, and *New York Times,* July 9, 1931.

105.   . . . a 450-foot center field double: August 27, 1931. Sources—*Scranton Republican,* August 28, 1931, and *Scranton Times,* August 28, 1931.

107.   . . . about 480 feet: April 12, 1932. Sources—*New York World-Telegram,* April 13, 1932, and *Philadelphia Record,* April 13, 1932.

107.   . . . over a roof in right field: April 12, 1932. Sources—*Philadelphia Inquirer,* April 13, 1932, and *Philadelphia Public Ledger,* April 13, 1932.

110.   . . . landed on a house across Lexington Avenue: June 12, 1932. Sources—*Cleveland Plain Dealer,* June 13, 1932, and *New York Herald-Tribune,* June 13, 1932.

111.   . . . well past the 429-foot sign in deep right center: Labor Day, September 5, 1932. Sources—*Philadelphia Evening Public Ledger,* September 6, 1932, and *New York Times,* September 6, 1932.

112.   . . . Ruth revisited those same seats off Charlie Root for an early lead:

October 1, 1932. Sources—*New York Times,* October 2, 1932, and *Chicago Daily Tribune,* October 2, 1932.

112. **. . . almost 500 feet away:** October 1, 1932. Sources—*Chicago Daily News,* October 2, 1932, and *Chicago Daily Tribune,* October 2, 1932.

115. **. . . close to 500 feet from home plate:** May 12 and 15, 1933. Sources—*Indianapolis Star,* May 13, 1933, and *Wheeling Register,* May 16, 1933.

115. **. . . over the 429-foot sign in right center:** May 28, 1933. Sources—*Chicago Daily Tribune,* May 29, 1933, and *New York Times,* May 29, 1933.

116. **. . . well past the 455-foot marker in dead center field:** June 28, 1933. Sources—*Detroit News,* June 29, 1933, and *New York Daily News,* June 29, 1933.

116. **. . . deep left center field beyond the running track . . . snagged against the 429-foot sign in right center:** July 15, 1933. Sources—*New York Times,* July 16, 1933, and *Chicago Daily Tribune,* July 16, 1933.

117. **. . . off the top of the wall in center field at the 441-foot mark:** July 31, 1933. Sources—*Washington Post,* August 1, 1933, and *New York Times,* August 1, 1933.

118. **. . . halfway up the center field bleachers at Fenway Park:** September 23, 1933. Sources—*Boston Herald,* September 24, 1933, and *New York Times,* September 24, 1933.

118. **. . . about fifty rows into the right field bleachers:** September 28, 1933. Sources—*Washington Evening Star,* September 29, 1933, and *New York Herald-Tribune,* September 29, 1933.

119. **. . . home runs flew 450 feet and 475 feet:** October 29, 1933. Sources—*Honolulu Advertiser,* October 30, 1933, and Associated Press, October 30, 1933.

120. **. . . through a window across Twentieth Street:** April 18, 1934. Sources—*New York Herald-Tribune,* April 19, 1934, and *Philadelphia Inquirer,* April 19, 1934.

121. **. . . a 460-foot center field triple:** May 21, 1934. Sources—*New York Sun,* May 22, 1934 *and New York Herald-Tribune,* May 22, 1934.

122. **. . . about 505 feet:** July 13, 1934. Sources—*Detroit Free Press,* July 14, 1934, and *New York Herald-Tribune,* July 14, 1934.

126. **. . . a 460-footer:** Spring Training, March 20, 1935. Sources—*St. Louis Post Dispatch,* March 21, 1935, and *Boston Herald,* March 21, 1935.

126. **. . . a 500-foot shot . . . was longer by far than any other drive in city history:** April 4, 1935. Sources—*Boston Post,* April 5, 1935, and *Boston Globe,* April 5, 1935.

127. **. . . about 500 feet:** April 7, 1935. Sources—*Boston Post,* April 8, 1935, and *Newark Evening News,* April 8, 1935.

127. **. . . 430 feet away:** April 16, 1935. Sources—*New York Times,* April 17, 1935, and *Boston Post,* April 17, 1935.

128. **. . . a pair of 400-foot doubles:** April 22, 1935. Sources—*Knickerbocker Press* (Albany), April 23, 1935, and *Albany Times Union,* April 23, 1935.

129. **. . . about 440 feet:** May 21, 1935. Sources—*Chicago Tribune,* May 22, 1935, and *Chicago Daily News,* May 22, 1935.

129.   . . . two fly outs to Paul Waner in right center that traveled more than 400 feet: May 23, 1935. Sources—*Pittsburgh Press,* May 24, 1935, and *Pittsburgh Post Gazette,* May 24, 1935.

129.   . . . Waner again roamed to the wall near right center to catch Ruth's towering fly: May 24, 1935. Sources—*Pittsburgh Sun-Telegraph,* May 25, 1935, and *Pittsburgh Post Gazette,* May 25, 1935.

129.   . . . might have traveled 500 feet if not impeded in mid-flight: May 25, 1935. Sources—*Pittsburgh Press,* May 26, 1935, and *Pittsburgh Post Gazette,* May 27, 1935.

129.   ". . . surmounted the 86-foot-high grandstand by another twenty feet. . . . The occupants of 318 Boquet Street confirmed that the ball landed smack on the roof of their home. . . . well beyond 500 feet: May 25, 1935. Sources—*Boston Globe,* May 26, 1935, and *Pittsburgh Post Gazette,* May 27, 1935.

134.   . . . flew past the flagpole, which was 424 feet distant, and was instantly labeled as the longest in the city's history: Spring training, March 8, 1921. Sources—*Shreveport Times,* March 9, 1921, and *New York World,* March 9, 1921.

135.   . . . (one flying 455 feet): April 13, 1921. Sources—*Philadelphia North American,* April 14, 1921, and *New York World,* April 14, 1921.

135.   . . . two long fly outs (to center and right center) that would have easily cleared any modern fences: April 16, 1921. Sources—*New York Herald,* April 17, 1921, and *New York Tribune,* April 17, 1921.

135.   . . . one would certainly have been ruled fair under today's conditions: April 16, 1921. Sources—*Philadelphia Record,* April 17, 1921, and *New York Times* ("Curves and Bingles"), April 17, 1921.

135.   . . . airborne for about 490 feet: May 6, 1921. Sources—*Washington Post,* May 7, 1921, and *New York Daily News,* May 7, 1921.

136.   . . . over the 30-foot center field wall at a point 450 feet from home plate: May 7, 1921. Sources—*Washington Evening Star,* May 8, 1921, and *New York American* (article by Babe Ruth), May 11, 1921.

137.   . . . 480 feet to the top of the wooden bleachers just left of dead center field for yet another local distance record: May 14, 1921. Sources—*Cleveland Plain Dealer,* May 15, 1921, and *New York Tribune,* May 15, 1921.

137.   . . . three days later he blasted a comparable drive just right of center: May 17, 1921. Sources—*New York American,* May 18, 1921, and *New York Herald,* May 18, 1921.

137.   . . . a 460-foot shot to the center field wall just the inning before that was caught by Bill "Baby Doll" Jacobson: May 25, 1921. Sources—*New York American,* May 26, 1921, and *New York Herald,* May 26, 1921.

138.   . . . about 535 feet: May 25, 1921. Sources—As above, *St. Louis Globe-Democrat,* May 26, 1921, and *New York Times,* May 26, 1921.

139.   . . . in the upper deck in right . . . the first ever to reach the distant center field bleachers: June 13, 1921. Sources—*New York Herald,* June 14, 1921, and *New York World,* June 14, 1921.

139.   . . . almost cleared the left field bleachers (one of the longest-ever opposite field blows), and the second landed even higher in the center field seats than the record breaker of the previous day. . . . the two blows were estimated at 480 and 490 feet respectively: June 14, 1921. Sources—*New York World,* June 15, 1921, and *New York Tribune,* June 15, 1921.

141.   . . . on the two-story garage about 470 feet away . . . homer struck a bench 20 feet above field level at a linear distance of about 490 feet: June 20 and 23, 1921. Sources—*New York Tribune,* June 21, 1921, and *New York World,* June 21, 1921, and *Boston Post,* June 24, 1921, and *Boston Herald,* June 24, 1921.

142.   . . . two homers ruled foul after flying over the grandstand roof: July 2, 1921. Sources—*New York World,* July 3, 1921, and *Boston* Globe, July 3, 1921.

143.   . . . a foul home run to right field: July 10, 1921. Sources—*New York American,* July 11, 1921, and *New York Tribune,* July 11, 1921.

144.   . . . cleared the fifteen-foot wall at the corner of Trumbull Avenue and Cherry Street. . . . Of all Ruth's mighty home runs in 1921, this was probably his mightiest: July 18, 1921. Sources—*New York Daily News,* July 19, 1921, and *New York Morning Telegram,* July 19, 1921, and *New York Evening Journal,* July 19, 1921, and *New York American,* July 19, 1921, and *New York Herald,* July 19, 1921, and *New York Evening Telegram,* July 19, 1921, and *New York Tribune,* July 19, 1921, and *New York World,* July 19, 1921, and *New York Sun,* July 19, 1921, and *New York Times,* July 19, 1921, and *Detroit Free Press,* July 19, 1921, and *Detroit News,* July 19, 1921, and *Grand Rapids Herald,* July 19, 1921, and *Windsor Border Cities Star,* July 19, 1921, and *Toronto Globe and Mail,* July 19, 1921, and *Cleveland Plain Dealer,* August 23, 1921, and *Philadelphia Inquirer,* September 10, 1921.

144.   . . . one lengthy triple over Tris Speaker's head in distant center field . . . another one near the same spot: July 24, 1921. Sources—*New York American,* July 25, 1921, and *New York Herald,* July 25, 1921.

145.   . . . well over 500 feet: July 31, 1921. Sources—*New York Times,* August 1, 1921, and *New York Tribune,* August 1, 1921.

147.   . . . 550 feet: August 17, 1921. Sources—As above, *New York World, Chicago Daily Tribune, New York Tribune, New York Sun,* August 18, 1921.

147.   . . . another ball about the same distance that flew over the right field pavilion at Sportsman's Park. . . . ruled foul according to the rules of that time: August 21, 1921. Sources—*St. Louis Globe* Democrat ("Pitching to Ruth"), August 22, 1921, and *New York Times,* August 22, 1921.

148.   . . . 500 feet from home plate: September 9, 1921. Sources—*Philadelphia North American,* September 10, 1921, and *Philadelphia Bulletin,* September 10, 1921.

150.   . . . then cleared the right field roof in the fifth inning . . . a 450-foot opposite field double: September 26, 1921. Sources—*New York Times,* September 27, 1921, and *New York World,* September 27, 1921.

150.   . . . fly out to Chicago's Amos Strunk on September 14 came down near the Eddie Grant Memorial in deepest center field. Ruth then slammed a triple the next day that short-hopped the center field screen. . . . next triple, on the 18th, landed between the Grant Memorial and that screen. . . . All four drives flew a minimum of 450 feet, but none resulted in home runs: Stretch Run, 1921. Sources—*New York American,* September 15, 1921, and *New York Times,* September 16, 1921, and *New York Herald,* September 19, 1921, and *New York Tribune,* September 27, 1921.

151.   . . . into the center field bleachers. . . . longest drive that anyone had ever seen at the Polo Grounds: October 6, 1921. Sources—*New York Times,* October 7, 1921, and *New York American,* October 7, 1921.

SOURCES FOR 1921 SEASON

Two Primary Sources for Each Projected 1921 Home Run:

(N.B. Newspaper accounts are from the following day)

April 13, NY: 2B-*Philadelphia North American* and *New York World*

April 16, NY: Fly Out-*Philadelphia North American* and *New York Times*

April 16, NY: Fly Out-*New York Tribune* and *New York Herald*

April 21, Phil: 2B-*Philadelphia North American* and *New York Tribune*

April 26, NY: Fly Out-*New York Times* and *New York Tribune*

May 12, Det: 2B-*New York Times* and *New York Herald*

May 13, Det: 3B-*New York Herald* and *New York World*

May 16, Clev: 3B-*New York Times* and *New York Tribune*

May 20, Chic: 3B-*Chicago Tribune* and *New York Tribune*

May 25, StL: Fly Out-*New York American* and *New York Herald*

June 2, NY: 3B-*New York World* and *St. Louis Globe-Democrat*

June 3, NY: 3B-*New York Times* and *New York World*

June 4, NY: Fly Out-*New York Times* and *New York Herald*

June 5, NY: 3B-*New York American* and *New York Times*

June 9, NY: Fly Out-*NY Times* ("Curves and Bingles") and *New York Herald*

June 20, Bos: 2B-*New York Tribune* and *Boston Globe* (see sketch included in paper)

July 10, Chic: Fly Out-*New York American* and *New York Tribune*

July 11, Chic: Fly Out-*Chicago Tribune (Sox Notes)* and *New York American*

July 16, Det: Fly Out-*New York World* and *New York American*

July 24, Clev: 3B-*New York Times* and *New York Herald*

July 27, NY: Fly Out-*New York World* and *New York Times*

July 28, NY: Fly Out-*New York World* and *New York American*

July 31, NY: 3B-*New York Times* ("Curves and Bingles"*)* and *New York World*

Aug 4, NY: 2B-*New York World* and *New York American*

Aug 11, Phil: 2B-*Philadelphia Public Ledger* and *New York Tribune*

Aug 13, Phil: Fly Out-*Philadelphia North American* and *New York American*

Aug 19, Chic: 3B-*New York World* and *New York Tribune*

Aug 20, StL: 3B-*New York Times* and *St. Louis Globe-Democrat*

Aug 25, Clev: 2B-*New York World* and *New York Herald*

Aug 26, Det: Fly Out-*New York World* and *New York Tribune*

Aug 30, Wash: 2B-*New York Times* and *New York Herald*

Sept 1, NY: 2B-*Washington Post* and *New York Times*

Sept 5, Bos: 3B-*Boston Globe* and *New York Times*

Sept 5, Bos: Fly Out-*New York Times* and *New York Herald*

Sept 7, Bos: 3B-*New York Times* and *New York World*

Sept 14, NY: Fly Out-*New York Times* ("Curves and Bingles") and *New York American*

Sept 15, NY: 3B-*New York Times* and *New York World*

Sept 18, NY: 3B-*New York Herald* and *New York American*

Sept 26, NY: 2B-*New York Tribune* and *New York Herald*

Oct 2, NY: Fly Out-*Boston Globe* and *New York Tribune*

Acknowledgments

ANYONE WHO WRITES A book, especially a book of nonfiction, finishes the project with a considerable amount of indebtedness. So, acknowledgments and thank-yous are always in order.

First, I want to thank my wife, Marie, who has helped every step of the way. She provided constant encouragement, love, support, and assistance. Marie was both my research assistant and consultant, and read and critiqued everything I wrote. Essentially, she is the co-author of this book.

Second, I need to acknowledge my parents, Nadine and Bill. My mom typed all the early first drafts, and my dad saw Babe Ruth play many times at Shibe Park. He was a devout Philadelphia Athletics fan, but managed to love the Babe nonetheless. From the expressions of his feelings, I grew up knowing that Ruth must have been special.

Next, I want to thank my four wonderful children. Thanks to my eldest son Bill and his wife Amanda. Bill is the best T-ball player I ever saw, and he made the continuity of baseball from father to son very easy. My daughter Denise and her husband Stephen Stewart have been terrific. Denise, despite being a beautiful lady, was a female Babe Ruth in her days as a player. Wow, could she hit the ball! And Stephen is the family's computer guru, whose help has been invaluable. My son David has always shown a keen interest in baseball history, and he will inherit all my data on Ruth. I know that my work will be in good hands. My youngest son Michael has already shown an ability to write, and has offered many helpful suggestions. David and Michael are also good ballplayers, and, even as adults, still hook up with their buddies to play Wiffle ball in the backyard. That creates an atmosphere that is pleasingly conducive to writing about baseball. All my children have been generous in giving support and assistance.

I wish to say thank you to my sister, Jean Calhoun, who raised her children while working two jobs as a school teacher and librarian. She still found time to help me, and, with those two backgrounds, you can imagine just how helpful she was. My brother Joe is the family math wiz, there every time I needed guidance on any issue relating to probability, measurements, or statistical analysis.

Basically, I need to thank my entire family and all my friends. But a few specific friends need to be identified. My best friend Jonathan Herbst and cousin Tom Stock have always supported me in everything I do. Bob McConnell freely gave me the use of his home and his time while I was researching the history of Major League home runs. Ernestine Miller explained the realities of the publishing process to me. And Bruce Orser has been a stalwart in helping me research all aspects of this treatise. He is a first-rate historian with high standards of integrity.

All the folks at The Babe Ruth Museum are like family to me. But I owe special thank-yous to Greg Schwalenberg and, especially, Executive Director Mike Gibbons.

The authors of the books that I have read are listed in the bibliography, and I thank them one and all. More important, I must give boundless thanks to the hundreds of sportswriters who filed the thousands of eyewitness newspaper reports upon which this book is primarily based. There is insufficient space to identify every newspaper that I have reviewed while doing the research for this book. There are hundreds and hundreds of them, and we would not understand the true historical significance of Babe Ruth without them.

As a corollary, I want to thank the hundreds of libraries (and librarians) that have also contributed to the final product. I estimate that I spent more than 10,000 hours inside various libraries over the last quarter century working on this project. That's a lot of time, and there were a corresponding number of requests for assistance. Almost invariably, those requests were met with kind and efficient responses. There are four institutions that must be specifically identified: The Philadelphia Public Library, the Firestone Library at Princeton University, The Library of Congress, and my hometown library in Willow Grove, Pennsylvania. It is called the Upper Moreland Free Public Library, and everyone there has been helpful. Enjoy your retirement, Joan Greenberg.

Admittedly, I'm no Internet expert, but two Web sites did assist in tracking down some valuable data. They are BabeRuth.com and BabeRuthCentral.com.

As a member of the Society for American Baseball Research (SABR), I have the privilege of interacting with hundreds of dedicated researchers. Many of them have made contributions. I want to individually recognize Phil Lowry, Jim Charlton, David Stephan, Bob Bluthardt, David Vincent, Mike Dugan, and Nicole DiCicco.

I should also say a word or two about the help that I have received from different Major League Baseball teams in setting up interviews. Special thanks to the Baltimore Orioles and, most of all, to Larry Shenk and the entire Media Relations staff at the Philadelphia Phillies.

Thanks to everyone at Carroll & Graf, who made this happen by publishing my book. Ivelisse Robles Marrero did a fantastic job designing the book interior. Cole Wheeler was both creative and patient in designing the home run spray charts. And my editor, Keith Wallman, was great at every turn. He is a real baseball guy who, fortunately for me, is also a very bright fellow. I could not have done better. Further thanks to Verne O'Hara and Grace Morgan for their professional guidance and particular thanks to my agent Jim Fitzgerald.

I will always be grateful to all my teachers and coaches at Bishop McDevitt High School, who made a big impact on me at an important time in my life. But Joe Sanquilli, Walt Posadowski, Father Sidney

Burgoyne, Father Edward Cahill, Monsignor Michael Long, and Monsignor Richard Skelley rank among the best educators that anyone will ever have.

Finally, Babe Ruth's family has been very supportive. I specifically want to thank daughter Julia Ruth Stevens, grandson Tom Stevens, granddaughter Linda Tosetti, and great-grandson Brent Stevens.

And to all those who I can not thank individually (and there are many), I extend my heartfelt gratitude.

Hopefully, all these expressions of appreciation do not come across as pretentious. I know that this is just "a baseball book" and not a twenty-first-century version of *Moby-Dick*. But it did take a lot of work, and I really am indebted to many people.

And, of course, thanks to the Babe for living a life so full of joy and wonder that I just had to write about it.

Index

About the Author

BILL JENKINSON has served as consultant for The Baseball Hall of Fame, Major League Baseball, The Society for American Baseball Research, The Babe Ruth Museum, and ESPN. He is the acknowledged expert on the history of long-distance home runs and the country's top Ruthian scholar. Jenkinson lives in Willow Grove, PA.